# Vital Ecumenical Concerns

Ans J. Van der Bent

## Sixteen documentary surveys

World Council of Churches, Geneva

Cover design: Michael Dominguez

ISBN 2-8254-0873-5

© 1986 World Council of Churches, 150 route de Ferney,
1211 Geneva 20, Switzerland

Printed in The Netherlands

# Table of Contents

# Introduction

Brought together here is a selection of official statements
made at the six assemblies of the World Council of Churches, at
the meetings of its Central Committee, and at major ecumenical
conferences and consultations since 1948. The collection includes important statements of the Christian Conference of Asia,
formerly the East Asia Christian Conference, and of the All
Africa Conference of Churches. In several of the historical,
analytical and bibliographical surveys reference is also made to
the pronouncements of the Second Vatican Council.

The statements and declarations on vital concerns in the
ecumenical movement brought together here are obviously only a
small selection of the voluminous official literature. A more
comprehensive reproduction of it would take up several volumes.
Our hope is that the present volume will provide the reader
with an overall understanding of the historical development of
a given ecumenical theme or concern and the state of the present
debate. The bibliography of the sources at the end of each
survey may be consulted for additional information on a particular statement or subject. Particularly at assemblies and
major conferences of the sub-units of the World Council of
Churches far more has been stated than is gathered together in
the chapters of this book.

Each survey ends with a few observations and comments. They
are necessarily subjective, and frequently critical; they are
meant not to prejudge an issue but to help the readers as they
make their own independent evaluation. Not only are my own
evaluations tentative and provisional; there are, and there
should be, other interpretations, depending on personal depart-
mental perspectives. In the survey on the ecumenical concern
for world development, for instance, I have argued that it was
treated inadequately from 1948 to 1965, then tackled with per-
tinent insight and great commitment, and has become during the
current decade a highly complicated and controversial subject.
Some readers may want to stress that the history of the development concern moved in other directions.

The purpose of this book is to look at institutional pronouncements from a distance and to study them outside their
immediate contexts and constraints. The study of this volume
will also serve the unravelling of the complexity of the programme structures of the World Council of Churches and the
relating of all its reflections and activities to one meaningful whole. It is hoped that many staff persons in ecumenical
organizations, church leaders, professors and students of
ecumenics and adult lay Christians will use this reference work
to sharpen their ecumenical memory, to identify the ecumenical
trends of our present time and to anticipate intelligently the

future issues of the ecumenical movement. This volume may also be of help to those who are engaged in the writing on ecumenical history. It is, finally, a source book of general information and orientation.

# I.
## Christianity and Culture

At the beginning of this survey the classic book of H. Richard Niebuhr Christ and Culture[1] needs to be mentioned. Niebuhr
developed five conceptual types or molds which have shaped our
approach to Christ and culture: 1) Christ Against Culture;
2) The Christ of Culture; 3) Christ Above Culture; 4) Christ
and Culture in Paradox; 5) Christ the Transformer of Culture.
In his "Concluding Unscientific Postcript" he said, with almost
an audible sigh: "Our examination of the typical answers Christians have given to their enduring problem (of Christ and culture) is unconcluded and inconclusive." He did not develop a
sixth type, his own type, to deal with the enduring problem.
Was he unable to extricate himself from the limits of his own
brilliant theology ?

## I.

At the first meeting of the East Asia Christian Conference
at Bangkok in 1949 it was stressed "that the Christian message
may be made more challenging if it is presented in close relation
to the special needs of the human situation in any given time,
and also if it adopts and utilizes certain values in the traditional culture of each people." Churches were encouraged to
"engage in a much more thorough study of the language, literature, music, art and social structure of their peoples, so that
they may know more clearly where these are to be used, adapted
or rejected for the service of the gospel..."[2] At the Inaugural
Assembly of the East Asia Christian Conference at Kuala Lumpur
in 1959 it was repeated that "serious consideration should be
given to indigenisation understood as relating the Gospel to
local cultures, religious ideas, and rapidly changing social
situations..." Studies of "the sociological factors which tend
to make a local congregation a self-centred and inward looking
communal group" and of "the indigenisation of worship" should
be undertaken.[3]

At its Assembly in Bangkok in 1964 the East Asia Christian
Conference expressed itself as follows: "The Christians of Asia
must live more actually within the cultures of their own peoples.
This may involve the abandoning of much that is familiar - a kind
of self-emptying which will be both painful and dangerous. But
it is only so that the Spirit will show how the faith may be
restated in the idiom of the indigenous cultures, in forms of
community life where the faith becomes luminous, and in actions
relevant to the needs of contemporary society." It added that
churches are often afraid of achieving self-hood since they
have been so long dependent on missionary societies and missionaries and on "uncritical adherence to forms of organisation and
ways of behaviour devised during the period of dependence."[4]

1

The All Africa Church Conference meeting at Ibadan in 1958 paid attention to the question of Africanizing the church. Participants noted that "while the church cannot give a Christian content to every African custom, we believe that the church throughout Africa has a very rich contribution to make to the life of the world Church. Under God's guidance she will be enriched by the wealth which African culture can bring into her life."[5] During its first Assembly at Kampala in 1963, the All Africa Conference of Churches expressed itself rather carefully on the problem of culture in the following words: "The Church should study traditional African beliefs. Traditional African culture was not all bad; neither was everything good. As in all cultures, there were positive factors which held the culture together; there were negative factors which degraded human personality. The churches should become involved in a serious dialogue between the traditional world-view and the continuing revelation of Jesus Christ through the Scriptures."[6]

## II.

In the Report of the Committee on the Department on Church and Society to the Assembly of the WCC at New Delhi, 1961, the changing combinations of religion, nationalism and secular ideologies were discussed. "In many countries the problem of development is related to the varying combinations of traditional religion, historic culture, nationalism, and some form of socialism. The churches are often bewildered and they are in danger of retreating into isolation. The response of traditional religions and indigenous cultures to social change needs special study in this context." In the Report of the Section on Service the conflict of cultures was examined. Some conflicts are inevitable and necessary, other conflicts unnecessary. The cost of cultural conflict can be very high. The question was raised as to whether "the Christian church can be the nucleus around which the culture of tomorrow will crystallize ?" It was noted that "the ecumenical movement could render immense and vital service as an arena for the crossfertilization of concepts from different cultures within one fellowship."[7]

In the Report on Worship, adopted by the WCC Assembly at Uppsala, the recommendation was made that "Christian worship should be related to the cultures of the world. It should help a person to be truly Christian and truly a man of his own culture. It should take the risk of indigenization."[8]

At the meeting of the Central Committee in Addis Ababa in 1971, an Interim Policy Statement and Guide-Lines of the WCC and Dialogue with Men of Other Faiths and Ideologies was adopted. The following paragraph dealt with dialogue to be understood and practiced in the context of indigenization. "Wherever the Church expresses its life in concrete forms it has to express the Gospel through certain cultural and intellectual forms.

2

In the interplay between the elements of revelation and the aspects of a given culture there is the danger that the revelation may be submerged and compromised by these cultural elements. Nothing is gained by seeking to avoid this danger. New criteria have to be developed for judging what are the responsible ways of expressing the Christian faith in different cultures. Enquiries should be made whether any light is to be thrown on this question by cultural anthropology, social psychology and the history of religion. Dialogue is necessary to enable Christians to find out both what are the authentic changes which the Gospel demands and the authentic embodiment which the Gospel offers. In the context of living in dialogue with men of other faiths, Christians have the urgent task of expressing their faith in cultural forms that are transformed, redeemed and judged in the light of the Gospel."9

In a letter to the Churches, with the theme "Committed to Fellowship", the Central Committee at its next meeting at Utrecht noted that in the ecumenical combat of racism "many of us are bound to particular traditions and particular cultures which stand in the way of genuine open-ness to our neighbour."10

The WCC Humanum Studies, which were carried out under the leadership of Canon David E. Jenkins between 1969 and 1975, referred several times to the problem of culture. Facing the question of "how man is dehumanized and prevented from achieving true humanity", the Report of the First Meeting of the Humanum Consultative Committee stressed that "being human, and this includes being Christian, means being free and encouraged to express one's self in one's own national, racial, and local family and individual way." Otherwise there is "cultural oppression with its attendant cultural deprivation and distortion." In his final report Canon Jenkins wrote that "in the ecumenical movement we have only just begun to glimpse the implications and possibilities of cultural diversity taken absolutely seriously in the context of the ecumenical activity of God." The report ended with the following recommendations: "Ways must be sought at the (Nairobi) Assembly and beyond to develop methods of study and mutual search which will enable different cultural areas and localities to make their full and authentic contribution to our understanding of and participation in the human struggle, its possibilities, as well as its anguish. We believe that there are many urgent and existing opportunities for a deeper adventure and a more positive inquiry, rooted in a variety of cultural settings, towards a new grasp of what we mean and can mean by the human... The creative indigenous resources for furthering both the human search and the progress and understanding of the Gospel are to be found, not in any centre, but throughout the whole world."11

In a document entitled "Inquiry into Indigenous Cultural Energies", Kiyoko Takeda Cho distinguished three sources of indigenous energy: the energy of despair, the energy of traditional moral or religious ethos or philosphical ideas or value concepts which interprete the meaning of life, and the energy of women. Speaking about the Western imperialistic

cultural domination and the laziness or lack of dignity and
effort on the side of receivers in the Third World, she stresses
universalistic and particularistic elements in Asian traditional
culture. "Indigenous culture is a mixture or interwoven totality of the hidding blessing, the immanent potentiality towards
universalism and unique forms of particularism bearing the roots
of the unclean spirit, the root of the mystery of evil, in the
depth of its cultural soil. This is the concrete human reality
in Asia."[12]

## III.

In the section discussions of the Commission on Faith and
Order meeting at Louvain in 1971, Section V dealt with "The
Unity of the Church and Differences in Culture". The theme was
understood to be the church dialectical relation to its cultural
situation. Beginning with the different cultural environments,
the discussion quickly focussed upon the church's relation to
the new "unified, interdependent, technological" culture, and
opinions varied as to the viability of traditional Christian
cultural forms, the need of new synthesis, and the project of
overcoming "civil religion".

Eight summary points, which emerged as a framework for discussion, indicated the principal points touched: 1) cultural
differences and contradictions; 2) the gospel calls human beings
out of their cultural ties; 3) the gospel sends believers into
their culture; 4) various degrees of Christian transformation
and penetration of culture; 5) the endangering of the church
by Christian culture; 6) the endangering of the unity of the
church by the Christian penetration of different cultures;
7) the unity of the church in recognizing the fundamental break-
through of the apostolic witness to Christ into Jewish and
Hellenistic culture; 8) the necessary visible manifestation
of the unity of the church before the world.[13]

In his address on "How Can the Unity of the Church be achieved", delivered at the meeting of the Commission on Faith and
Order at Accra in 1974, V.C. Samuel from Ethiopia examined the
influence of Greek and Latin cultures on Christianity. The three
divisions - Orthodoxy, Roman Catholicism and Protestantism -
"constitute three different general ways in which the Christian
faith came to be adopted by people within their various cultural
and intellectual conditions. Regarding each of them, the question
to be asked is not whether it is an authentic form of Christianity,
but whether it has in fact failed to conserve any of the distinctive truths of the Christian faith and life. This question should
be a subject of serious study by the churches. This does not
justify any one of them to assume that it constitutes exclusively
the Church. Each of them should try to understand the others
objectively, taking them as comprising the Church's unity."[14]

4

The Report of a Conference on "Technology, Faith and the Future of Man", sponsored by the Department on Church and Society at Geneva in 1970, questioned Western assumptions about technology, civilization, Christianity and "the good life". The logic which equates Christianization with modernization was criticized as short-circuited. The Conference noted that several "cultural revolutions" are under way. "The children of Western technology are repudiating their parentage, in more ways than one, and this is a phenomenon which carries profound implications for the churches." It was agreed, that, whatever the strengths and weaknesses of particular cultural heritages, a more adequate framework should be found "within which to understand the man/machine/nature relationship."[15]

IV.

At the Consultation on "Human Rights and Christian Responsibility" at St. Pölten, Austria, in 1974, sponsored by the Commission on the Churches in International Affairs, Working Group A concentrated on: "The Right to Life and Work: the Basic Social, Economic and Cultural Rights." Discussing the rights of people to cultural development, the group was aware of the fact "that there is hardly any possibility of either developing of promoting a common culture for the whole world. The vast majorities of people who experienced cultural invasions during the period of colonialism and imperialism view any efforts to promote ideological unities internationally not only as return to colonialism but downright destruction of their possibilities of a meaningful cultural and social life in the context of their own authentic experience." It was stressed therefore by the group "that cultural, religious, ideological and ethnic pluralities must not only be recognized but respected in the interest of full enjoyment and development of cultural rights under the conditions of peace... Peace in the context of justice provides opportunities and possibilities for full human and cultural development."[16]

The following paragraph of a report of a Consultation on "Faith and Ideologies", held at Cartigny in 1975, should also be quoted. "As Christians live and work with their neighbours in different countries, they should recognize that the criteria derived from one cultural situation cannot be applied to others. Christians in different parts of the world need to share their experience and reflections with each other. New insights in the understanding of the Gospel, biblical exegesis and in Christian life can be discovered in action and discussions shared with people who ignore, question or contest the Christian faith on the basis of their own religious or ideological positions. In working together with their neighbours one community of faith should not simply assert its own values over against the others but may rediscover or transform values which both they and their neighbours share."[17]

At the meeting of the Commission on World Mission and Evangelism at Bangkok in 1973, Section I was devoted to "Culture and Identity". The discussion centred on  a) racial identity;  b) identity of women;  c) identity in the context of conversion and cultural change;  d) identity in the context of dialogue with people of living faiths.  With regard to racial identity and identity of women the following was stated: "Culture shapes the human voice that answers the voice of Christ.  Many Christians who have received the Gospel through Western agents ask the question: Is it really I who answers Christ ? Is it not another person instead of me ?"  Races and women need to be liberated from the evil of cultural power, domination and manipulation.  Conversion must be always related to the place and the circumstances where it occurs.  The group recommended "that a detailed study be made of the form and consequences of conversion in different situations."  With regard to dialogue with people of other faiths it was said: "... we meet persons who are formed by specific religious and cultural traditions and claim an authentic relationship with the Ultimate, which they acknowledge.  We must recognize our partners as they perceive and experience their existence and the world as religious persons committed to a definite faith.  They share in dialogue from this starting point as we are called from our commitment to Christ, grateful for what he has done for us and for others, for his love for the world and his desire that all men shall be saved and come to know the truth (I. Tim. 2:4)."18

V.

The Nairobi Assembly developed the concerns of cultural identity of the Bangkok Assembly.  Section I: "Confessing Christ Today" stated: "In our sharing with one another we have discovered that the Christ who meets us in our own cultural contexts is revealed to us in a new way as we confess him...  We affirm the necessity of confessing Christ as specifically as possible with regard to our own cultural settings...  We can say that Jesus Christ does not make copies; he makes originals. We have found this confession of Christ out of our various cultural contexts to be not only mutually inspiring, but also a mutually corrective change.  Without this sharing our individual affirmations would gradually become poorer and narrower...  Sharing in this way we are all changed and our cultures are transformed ... Although our reading and interpretation of the Scriptures is to a certain extent itself culturally conditioned, we believe that it is part of the mystery of Christ that even as we confess him in different ways it is he who draws us together." Participants in Section I also examined "Power structures and socioeconomic factors that obscure the confession of Christ."

A sub-section of Section III "Seeking Community: The Common Search of People of Various Faiths, Cultures and Ideologies" dealt with "Cultures and the Search for Community". It examined the diversity of cultures as they include various world-views and ways of life of a people.  It emphasized that, "though tech-

nological culture is international, it is not the final answer
to the quest for wider community... Christians are themselves
caught up in the world-wide confrontation between technological
and traditional cultures. The question of whether there is a
specific Christian culture is overshadowed by cultural superiority and self-sufficiency. The Church manifests itself in
scattered communities in varying cultures where, too often,
egoism and arrogance, even between Christians, threaten the
wider community. Christ unites us in a community which transcends any particular culture."

Section IV "Education for Liberation and Community" also
dealt with culture in the context of "alienation from and
assimilation into our culture and history." "We cannot be
liberated if we are divorced from the culture which bred us
and which continues to shape and condition us. Many are taught
to despise their culture, many are not participants - except
by omission - in the shaping of it. Some educational programmes
play a large part in creating false images: prejudice, fear,
hatred are instilled into persons through selective and biased
curricula and teaching... We are not romanticizing indigenous
culture: it too can have elements which enslave and degrade,
but we advocate that people be brought to a critical awareness
of the strength and weaknesses of their own culture for the
development they desire for themselves, rather than being
disruptively separated from it to serve the purpose of others...
As we search for and stress indigenous values, we must also
affirm that there is a universality in Christianity and a
growing awareness of the global nature of problems which calls
for an education which both informs and transcends the local...
The dynamic nature of society means both assimilation into a
culture and alienation from it."[19]

VI.

The Consultation at Chiang Mai, Thailand, in 1977, organized by the sub-unit on Dialogue with People of Living Faiths
and Ideologies, was much concerned with various aspects of
culture, the conflict of cultures and cultures of traditional
religions, especially African religions. On the relationship
between faith and culture the following insight was expressed:
"The Gospel of Jesus Christ is the judgment upon, as well as
the fulfilment of, every religion and culture. It is judgment
in as far as man in his traditional religion and culture is in
need of being reconciled with God in Christ. But, where the
new Being in Christ and His Church reach people, their history
and culture can become resources for a necessary and full
expression of what Christ in His presence might be. This is
not just a question of contextualizing the Gospel in a
particular culture, but can be a way of enriching the life
of other churches."

Illustrations from Africa for Christian reflection on faith
and culture were given in the context of: a) Humanity as created
beings; b) Humanity and time; c) The human being in community;

d) Humanity's relation to nature;  e) "Religious" symbolism;
f) Sickness and healing.  A "study of the theological importance
of the beliefs and cultic practices of traditional peoples and
cultures"[20] was recommended.

Discussing racism and ethnocentrism in education, the World
Council of Christian Education meeting at Lima in 1971, adopted
a very strong and critical statement, called the "Barbados Declaration", by a group of Latin American "indigenists". In this
document the churches are called to: "
-  assume a position of true respect for Indian culture, ending
   the long and shameful history of despotism and intolerance
   characteristic of missionary work...
-  halt the theft of Indian property by religious missionaries
   who appropriate labour, lands and natural resources as their
   own...
-  extinguish the sumptuous and lavish spirit of the mission
   themselves
-  stop the competition among religious groups and confessions
   for Indian souls...
-  break with the pseudo-moralist isolation which imposes a
   false puritanical ethic...
-  abandon those blackmail procedures implicit in the offering
   of goods and services to Indian society in return for total
   submission
-  suspend immediately all practices of population displacement
   or concentration in order to evangelise and assimilate more
-  effectively..."[21]


                              VII.


     During the Vancouver Assembly in 1983, participants in a sub-
section on "Culture: the Context for Our Witnessing" of Issue I
"Witnesssing in a Divided World", noted that "the question of the
nature of the relationship between the Gospel and culture has
been with us for some time..."  It defined culture as follows:
"Culture is what holds a community together, giving a common
framework of meaning.  It is preserved in language, thought
patterns,ways of life, attitudes, symbols and presuppositions,
and celebrated in art, music, drama, literature and the like.
It constitutes the collective memory of the people and the
collective heritage which will be handed down to generations
still to come."

     It was re-affirmed that cultures express the plural wonder
of God's creation, that each culture has life-affirming and
life-denying aspects, and that Christ judges and transcends all
cultural settings.  It was recommended that a search for a
theological understanding of culture should be initiated, and
that the role which secular and religious ideologies play in
the formation of culture should be reassessed.  The last sentence of the report reads: "We need to look again at the whole
matter of witnessing to the Gospel across cultural boundaries,
realizing that listening to and learning from the receptor
culture is an essential part of the proclamation of the Christian
message."[22]

## Observations and Comments

1. As the definition of the Vancouver Assembly outlined,
and as the CWME Riano Consultation (May-June 1984) affirmed,
culture is, first of all and above all, a culture of people.
All theology which deals more with concepts than with people
is not equipped to grasp the relations between gospel and culture. Faith ossified in rigid doctrines does injustice to cultures. Mission and evangelism as Christian monologues, instead
of dialogues with people of living faiths and no faith, are
depriving cultures of their promise and meaning. Concerns in
the realm of church and society and of Christian service to the
world are by-passing the technological and traditional predica-
ments of cultures if they are not related to the struggles, the
sufferings and the achievements of people. Ecclesiology, proclamation and soteriology, and the theology of culture belong
together and condition one another.

The pluralism of cultures is the pluralism of peoples. The
incarnated Christ is neither above cultures, nor in paradox
with cultures, nor simply transforming cultures, as he is ceaselessly a part of the suffering and the well-being of people and
manifests his redemptive love. His passion for people is their
salvation. His salvation takes place in and through culture.

The themes of "Religion and Culture", "Christianity and
Culture", "Gospel and Culture", "Christ and Culture" are related
to each other in a dynamic and dialectical tension. We will
never be able to deal with one or the other theme totally
satisfactorily. As human beings we cannot exclusively concentrate on Christ and culture, e.g., without taking gospel, Christianity and religion, that is concepts, ideas, structures,
traditions into account. The Niebuhr exercise shows that Jesus
Christ is the sovereign, unfathomable and uncontrollable Lord
of all cultures. Only he separates the sheep from the goats
and decides who will enter the kingdom.

2. The Riano working statement makes amply clear that we
should be more careful in distinguishing the problem of culture
and the problem of ideology, yet not losing sight of their inner
relations. An analysis of democracy and socialism, of global
forces (technocratic-militaristic, neo-conservative, consumerist),
of justice, of issues related to community and participation -
enumerated in the Riano statement - is primarily related to the
problem of ideology, and only then to the question of culture.

A Forum on Gospel and Culture has met several times in the
Council from 1984 ownards. It has repeatedly stressed that the
WCC should not attempt to develop a theoretical study on the
subject. Many others, theologians, sociologists and cultural
anthropologists, have done professional work in the field, which
can serve as background material for ecumenical reflection without trying to replicate it. The most important task is "to help
member churches in developing an understanding of the relationship between evangelism and culture in respect of both the con-

textual proclamation of the gospel in all cultures and the transforming power of the gospel in any culture." A working towards "a new ecumenical agenda in which various cultural expressions of the Christian faith may be in conversation with each other" has an become urgent matter.

In this context of conscientization, sharing and action a number of case studies have been suggested, e.g. on the caste system in India, deculturation and uprootedness in urban slums, the plight of exploited Asian women, the emergence of a new technological universal culture, popular religiosity in Brazil, ancestor worship in various parts of the world, relation of culture and church in the Soviet Union, right wing movements in the USA, Pacific cultures, nomadic peoples in Africa. The Forum has also suggested that the Communication Department finds ways of communicating to some extent at least with symbols and images instead of only written texts. The question remains as to whether these tasks can be accomplished in the rather élite setting of the WCC.

3. The survey of Christianity and culture in the ecumenical movement has shown, that although CWME had the main stake in the discussion of the theme and the concern of culture, practically all other WCC sub-units have been involved in some reflection and study at some earlier or later stage. More inter-unit work is needed.

A. <u>Faith and Order</u>. An attempt was made in the fifties to analyze and to evaluate the "non-theological factors" of the unity of the church. From 1971 onwards the theme of "The Unity of the Church in Relation to the Renewal of Human Community" was lodged in Faith and Order. Article 20 of the chapter on the eucharist in <u>Baptism, Eucharist and Ministry</u> stresses that the eucharist embraces all aspects of life. It demands reconciliation and sharing of the brothers and sisters in the one family of God, the search for appropriate relationships in social, economic and political life, challenges all kinds of injustice, racism, separation, lack of freedom, restores human pride, material interest, power politics, and above all unjustifiable confessional oppositions within the body of Christ. If there is ecumenical agreement on this description of the nature and function of the eucharist, then Faith and Order has to share in the overall concern for Gospel and culture. The eucharist protects against superficial notions of the unity of humankind (and the unity in the plurality of cultures) and against triumphalist claims about the church as a "sign" which is culturally coloured.

No answers have been given sofar to the questions raised at the East Asia Christian Conference in Bangkok, 1964, as to whether world confessional organizations rest on a theological principle or whether they simply gather together churches because of a common cultural history; and as to whether the historical basis of these confessional organizations are living cultural realities among the people in these confessional families. Answers can only be given if an ecumenical study in depth of the cultural roots of Orthodoxy, Roman Catholicism and Protestantism (Anglicanism, Methodism, etc.) will be undertaken.

B. <u>Church and Society</u> (including Racism, Development, International Affairs). Past assemblies and conferences have shown that the cultural differences which enrich human life easily have become and still become barriers which divide the human community, foster injustice, racism, underdevelopment and lead to war. The conflicts of cultures, the threat of technocratic-militaristic and multinational industrial cultures, and the plurality of cultures relate to issues of peace, justice and the integrity of creation. Studies of the relationship between culture and the biblical and theological basis of social ethics are needed. The earlier study programme on God, Humanity and nature relates directly to the theme of Gospel and Culture.

C. <u>Education</u> (including Programme on Theological Education, Renewal and Congregational Life, Women in Church and Society). Unit III proposes to concentrate on "an <u>inclusive</u> community enabling participation of all the different sections of its membership in its total life, a community where discrimination based on age, sex, race, disability, class and <u>culture</u> is elim- inated." The sub-units, it seems, approach the various problems of culture rather timidly and uncommittedly. Learning in a world of many faiths, ideologies and <u>cultures</u> amounts to more than to collect and analyze existing materials and examples of Christian responses and to provide a platform for discussions. The various cultural components of Christian and theological education, and general education in various continents and regions need to be examined and compared in historical and present contexts. RCL concentrates too exclusively, I believe, on spirituality and worship in and for themselves. The search for spiritualities for our time (not <u>a</u> spirituality for our time) and the sharing of spiritualities are undoubtedly vital for the life of con- gregations. But still more important is to raise the conscious- ness of the people of God at the grass roots as to why and how their ways of spirituality and modes of worship are influenced by and correspond to various cultures and religions. A feminist critique of "patriarchal culture" in church and society is essential. But the direct and indirect contributions of women to past and present cultures influencing religion need also careful scrutiny.

D. <u>The Dialogue with People of Other Living Faiths</u>. It is surprising that DF hardly mentions culture in its outline of future activities. In the realm of traditional religions it does state that it "has a specific interest in the relationship between religion and culture." But in its proposal of studying the theological significance of the people of other faiths the cultural dimensions of other faiths are not mentioned. It is also surprising that in the overall concern of the unity of the church in relation to the unity of humankind F and O, CCIA, PCR, CCPD, C and S and Women are interested to share, but DF is left out. Both the unity of the church from the angle of cultures and the unity of humankind in the plurality of cultures needs to be approached simultaneously by F and O and DF, as both are intimately linked to one another. Otherwise the evaluation of the theological significance of the people of other faiths leads nowhere. Has DF grown weary of the monopoly of CWME on gospel and culture during the last twelve years ?

E.  **Mission and Evangelism**.  This ecumenical concern is
purposely put at the end because the question which was raised
is answered by the Riano statement.  Half of this statement on
gospel and culture spells out contemporary implications for
mission.  This reflects ecumenical orientation, preference and
strategy during the last two decades.  Without minimizing the
urgency of missionary activities and the search for contemporary
cultural context of these activities, I venture to say that, as
we now increasingly agree that culture is a culture of people,
and that Jesus Christ is the Lord of both his people and their
culture, F+O, DF and RCL have a primary stake in the overall
concern of gospel and culture, enriched by the complementary
experiences and insights of several WCC sub-units.

Perhaps the Humanum Studies have provided us with a model
of approach and this past methodology could be applied anew to
the problem of gospel and culture.  I repeat what David Jenkins
wrote in his final report: "In the ecumenical movement we have
only just begun to glimpse that implications and possibilities
of cultural diversity taken absolutely seriously in the context
of the ecumenical activity of God."  The being and the doing of
the church in a multi-religious, multi-ideological and multi-
cultural world needs still to be spelled out in a more embracing
and more coherent WCC programme.

---

1.  Niebuhr, H. Richard.  Christ and Culture.
    New York: Harper, 1951.

2.  The Christian Prospect in Eastern Asia. Papers and Minutes
    of the Eastern Asia Christian Conference, Bangkok, December
    3-11, 1949.  New York: Friendship Press, 1950. pp. 118-119.

3.  Witnesses Together. The Official Report of the Inaugural
    Assembly of the East Asia Christian Conference, held at
    Kuala Lumpur, May 14-24, 1959.  Rangoon, 1959.  pp.109-110.

4.  The Christian Community within the Human Community. State-
    ments from the Bangkok Assembly of the EACC, Febr.-March,
    1964.  Bangalore: Christian Literature Society, 1964.
    pp. 15 and 52.

5.  The Church in Changing Africa. Report of the All Africa
    Church Conference Held at Ibadan, Nigeria, Jan. 10-19, 1958.
    New York: International Missionary Council, 1958. p. 72.

6.  Drumbeats from Kampala. Report of the First Assembly of the
    All Africa Conference of Churches held at Kampala, April
    20-30, 1963.  London: Lutterworth Press, 1963.  p. 48.

7.  The New Delhi Report.
    London: SCM Press, 1962.  p. 177, 98, 99, 111.

8.  The Uppsala Report.  Ed. by Norman Goodall.
    Geneva: WCC, 1968.  p. 80.

9. Central Committee of the World Council of Churches. Minutes and Reports of the Twenty-Fourth Meeting. Addis Ababa, Jan. 10-21, 1971. Geneva: WCC, 1971. p. 133.

10. Central Committee of the World Council of Churches. Minutes and Reports of the Twenty-Fifth Meeting. Utrecht, August 13-23, 1972. Geneva: WCC, 1972. p. 142.

11. The Humanum Studies, 1969-1975. A Collection of Documents. Geneva: WCC, 1975. pp. 76, 82, 88.

12. Ibid., pp. 97-103.

13. Faith and Order, Louvain 1971. Study Reports and Documents. Geneva: WCC, 1971 (Faith and Order Paper, No. 59). p. 193.

14. Uniting in Hope. Reports and Documents from the Meeting of the Faith and Order Commission, Accra, 23 July - 5 August, 1974. Geneva: WCC, 1975 (Faith and Order Paper, No. 72). p. 105.

15. From Here to Where ? Technology, Faith and the Future of Man. Report of an Exploratory Conference. Geneva June 28 - July 4, 1970. Ed. by David M. Gill. Geneva: WCC, 1970. pp. 17-22.

16. Human Rights and Christian Responsibility. Report of the Consultation at St. Pölten, Austria, 21-26 October, 1974. Geneva: WCC, CCIA, 1975. pp. 36-37.

17. Faith and Ideologies. An Ecumenical Discussion. Cartigny, May 1975. Geneva: WCC, 1975. p. 11.

18. Minutes and Reports of the Assembly of the Commission of World Mission and Evangelism, Bangkok, Dec. 31, 1972 and January 9-12, 1973. Geneva: WCC, 1973. pp. 70-79.

19. Breaking Barriers. Nairobi 1975. Ed. by David M. Paton. London: SPCK; Grand Rapids: Eerdmans, 1976. pp. 45-47, 78-80, 87-90.

20. Faith in the Midst of Faiths. Reflections on Dialogue in Community. Ed. by S.J. Samartha. Geneva: WCC, 1977, pp. 160-165.

21. Encuentro. New Perspectives for Christian Education. In: World Christian Education, vol. 26, 1971, nos. 3-4, p. 256.

22. Gathered for Life. Official Report of the VI Assembly of the World Council of Churches, Vancouver, Canada, 24 July-10 August, 1983. Ed. by David Gill. Geneva: WCC, 1983. pp. 32-34.

23. Churches among Ideologies. Report of a Consultation and Recommendations to Fellow Christians. Grand Saconnex, December 15-22, 1981. Geneva: WCC, DFI, 1982. p. 3.

# II.
## Mission and Evangelism

Mission and evangelism have been a primary concern of the
20th century ecumenical movement. This movement is generally
reckoned to have begun at the World Missionary Conference at
Edinburgh in 1910. Two of the principal architects of this
conference, John R. Mott (1865-1955) and J.H. Oldham (1874-1969),
together with one of the ushers, William Temple (1881-1944),
later Archbishop of Canterbury, were destined to play at a
later stage a leading role in the formation of the World Council of Churches. John R. Mott remains known chiefly for his
zealous propaganda on behalf of missions, based upon the
watchword "The Evangelization of the World in Our Generation".

The Edinburgh Conference led to the International Missionary Council (IMC) in 1921, created "to help coordinate the
activities of the national missionary organizations of the
different countries and to unite Christian forces of the world
in seeking justice in international and inter-racial relations."
To achieve this lofty goal a whole series of world missionary
conferences followed. From 1939 onwards the IMC worked closely
with the WCC (while the latter was 'in process of formation').
Then in 1961, after the Third Assembly at New Delhi, the IMC
became the Division of World Mission and Evangelism of the WCC.
It had taken several decades to realize that the unity of the
church and the mission of the church are but two sides of the
same coin. The International Review of Mission, the major
organ of the ecumenical missionary movement since 1912, is still
published today.

From 1954 to 1961 the Department on Evangelism and the
Department of Missionary Studies in the WCC Division of Studies
supplemented the work of the IMC Research Department. Their
activities continued afterwards. In 1967, the Department on
Evangelism and the Department of Missionary Studies were integrated into the Department on Studies in Mission and Evangelism.

Little or no reference is made in this survey on mission
and evangelism to missionary societies and institutions, missionary personnel and finance, missionary training, and urban and
industrial mission.

## I.

Section II, "The Church's Witness to God's Design", of the
Amsterdam Assembly in 1948 was divided into the following parts:
I. The Purpose of God; II. The Present Situation; III. The
Church's Task in the Present Day (A. Worship and Witness;
B. A People of God in the World; C. The Ecumenical Sense);

IV. Missionary and Evangelical Strategy (A. Lay Work and Witness; B. Co-operation in Evangelism; C. The Problem of Our Divisions); V. "Now is the Accepted Time".

Discussing the Present Situation and the Church's Task some sobering notes were struck: "... A formidable obstacle to Christian faith is the conviction that it belongs definitely to a historical phase now past. More thoughtful men, who hold that it enshrines some spiritual and cultural values, regard it as no longer honestly tenable as a system of belief. And yet there is an earnest desire for clearly formulated truth... the Church has largely lost touch with the dominant realities of modern life, and still tries to meet the modern world with a language and technique that may have been appropriate two hundred years ago... by its failure to speak effectively on the subject of war, it has appeared impotent to deal with the realities of the human situation... it is a Church under suspicion in many quarters of having used its missionary enterprise to further the foreign policies of states and the imperialistic designs of the powers of the West...

"The Church must find its way to the places where men really live. It must penetrate the alienated world from within, and make the minds of men familiar with the elementary realities of God, of sin and of purpose in life. This can be done partly through new ventures of self-identification by Christians with the life of that world, partly through Christians making the word of the Gospel heard in the places where decisions are made that affect the lives of men. It can be done fully only if, by the inspiration of the Holy Spirit, the Church recovers the spirit of prophecy to discern the signs of the times, to see the purpose of God working in the immense movements and revolutions of the present age, and again to speak to the nations the word of God with authority." On Evangelism it was stated: "As we have studied evangelism in its ecumenical setting we have been burdened by a sense of urgency. We have recaptured something of the spirit of the apostolic age, when the believers 'went everywhere preaching the word'. If the Gospel really is a matter of life and death, it seems intolerable that any human being now in the world should live out his life without ever having the chance to hear and receive it."[1]

II.

Section II, "Evangelism: The Mission of the Church to Those Outside Her Life" of the Evanston Assembly in 1954 had the following headings: I. The Evangelizing Church; II. The Evangelistic Dimension; III. Communicating the Gospel; IV. Exploring Frontiers (A. Renewal of the Inner Life; B. The Witnessing Laity; C. Christian Education; D. Chaplaincies; E. Parish Experiments; F. Media of Mass-Communication; G. A Trained Ministry); V. Non-Christian Faiths; VI. Come, Lord Jesus.

"... The people of God are in this world as the Church, and they are never alone with their Lord in isolation from the world. It is the world which He came to save. Without the gospel the world is without sense, but without the world the gospel is without reality. Evangelism is no specialized or separable or periodic activity, but it is rather a dimension of the total activity of the Church. Everything the Church does is of evangelizing significance. Through all the aspects of its life the Church participates in Christ's mission to the world, both partaking of the gospel and seeking to communicate it. Evangelism is the place where the Church discovers itself in its true depth and outreach."

Concerning the Witnessing Laity, Section II stated: "The laity stand at the very outposts of the Kingdom of God. They are the missionaries of Christ in every secular sphere. Theirs is the task to carry the message of the Church into every area of life, to be informed and courageous witnesses to the will of our Lord in the world. To this end they will need training and guidance." With regard to Non-Christian Faiths it was asserted that "in our task of evangelism among the adherents of non-Christian religions we must claim the whole truth of the Christian gospel. But we must always bear in mind that there are human elements in our witness to it which stand under the judgment of God. The gospel is greater than any particular human testimony to it. It is also the ultimate standard of God's judgment on every aspect of our response to His light and truth. There is always the danger, in the case of both the Christian and the non-Christian, of limiting the gospel to his own understanding. In our missionary effort we must always measure our conformity to the gracious will of God by the gospel, assured that, as we pray, the Holy Spirit will lead us into all truth..."[2]

One of the main themes of the Central Committee meeting at Rolle, Switzerland, in 1951 was: "The Calling of the Church to Mission and Unity". The headings in the Report were: I. The Purpose of this Enquiry; II. Terminology; III. The Biblical Basis for the Church's Unity and Apostolicity; IV. Implications for the Life of the Church; V. Implications for the World Missionary Task; VI. Implications for the Future Structure and Relationship of the IMC and the WCC. With regard to the Terminology the Central Committee said: "... We would especially draw attention to the recent confusion in the use of the word 'ecumenical'. It is important to insist that this word, which comes from the Greek word for the whole inhabited earth, is properly used to describe everything that relates to the whole task of the whole Church to bring the Gospel to the whole world."[3]

The Report of the International Missionary Council, meeting at Willingen, Germany, in 1952, contained several appendices: A. A Statement on the Missionary Calling of the Church; A Statement on the Calling of the Church to Mission and Unity; The Indigenous Church - The Universal Church in Its Local Setting; The Role of the Missionary Society; Missionary Vocation and Training; Reshaping the Pattern of Missionary Activity.

B. The Missionary Obligation of the Church;  C. Report of the
Committee on Interpretation and Action;  D. Report of the Com-
mittee on the Christian Approach to the Jews;  E. International
Missionary Council and World Council of Churches;  F. Some
Comments on IMC Research.[4]

The Report of Committee IV, "New Forms of Mission" of the
IMC Assembly in Ghana in 1958 contained recommendations on:
1) Exchange of Personnel;  2) Evangelistic Teams;  3) Christian
Laymen as Non-Professional Missionaries;  4) New Study Centres;
5) Christian Literature.  In a Statement "The Christian Mission
at This Hour", received by the Assembly and commended to the
member organizations of the IMC, it was repeatedly emphasized
that "the Christian world mission is Christ's, not ours. Prior
to all our efforts and activities, prior to all our gifts of
service and devotion, God sent His Son into the world."

With regard to the urgency of mission it was stated: "...
We are convinced of the centrality and the urgency of the continuing missionary task.  For some, it is focused in the fact
that there are more non-Christians in the world today than
when the modern missionary movement began.  For others the
spectacle of a technological age which is in danger of deserving
the judgement that it has 'exchanged the truth of God for a lie
and worshipped and served the creature rather than the Creator,
who is blessed for ever' arouses the sense of the desperate
need to point men to the already present Lord of all life. Still
others find the renascence of the ancient religions and the
encounter with the Christian faith at a new depth and with a
new directness the point at which the need for Christian proclamation throughout the world becomes most insistent.  But we
are all agreed that this is an hour in which Christians must
go out into the world in the name of Christus Victor."[5]


                              III.

In the Report to the Churches of the Third World Conference
on Faith and Order at Lund in 1952, the following was stated on
The Unity of the Church: "... In the New Testament the mission
of the Church and the unity of the Church are deeply related.
Christ called His apostles that they might be one and that He
might send them forth to his Mission in the world.  He prayed
for their unity that the world might believe.  It was in obedience to this missionary task, including the willingness to
suffer for Christ, that the Church experienced the dynamic
power of its unity."

In the section "Where Do We Stand ?" the following was
outlined: "... Members of the younger Churches have contributed
to the understanding of our common task a distinctive emphasis
which has greatly enriched our discussion.  Under the constraint
of the missionary imperative, they have discovered that the need
of unity is fully understood only when related to the great task
of evangelism.  Their strong awareness of our fundamental one-

ness in Christ is due not merely to their relative immunity to the influences which produced and still maintain divisions among the older Churches, but also to their response to the demand for full obedience to the requirements of faithfull witness and service.  In their experience we can surely see the leading of the Holy Spirit.  The miracle of this unity has disclosed to the older Churches the tragic extent to which their own witness has been impaired by their separation..."[6]


IV.

In Section III, "The Proclamation of the Gospel in Eastern Asia", of the Eastern Asia Christian Conference in 1949, the following was stated: "... The occasion calls for a bold declaration  of the message of the gospel, preaching the Word with pointed reference to the saving power of God in Jesus Christ. But the occasion also demands of us and the churches of the lands of East Asia that we show forth in our own lives the fruits of God's forgiveness, and demonstrate through service of our fellow men that in renewed consecration of our powers to the will of Almighty God there is hope of man's natural gifts and talents being sanctified and transfigured.

"Since the gospel has to be preached in all the languages of East Asia, and the Christian life lived in all its various cultural and social situations, it is essential that the churches should engage in a much more thorough study of the language, literature, music, art, and social structure of their peoples, so that they may know more clearly where these are to be used, adapted or rejected for the service of the gospel and the Church.  It is our conviction that the life and witness of our churches is at present seriously weakened by failure to discharge this duty."[7]

In a Message to its Member Churches and Councils the First Assembly of the East Asia Christian Conference in 1959 said: "... There is much evidence of the work of the Holy Spirit in our Churches.  In areas of extreme difficulty and danger the Church is growing.  New ways of evangelism are being pioneered. Most of the Churches in Asia are now sending out missionaries to other lands as well as receiving them, and helping one another with many kinds of service, as well as receiving manifold help from Churches in other parts of the world.  The Gospel is being carried out not only by organised missions, but also by the spontaneous witness of Christians going to other places as workers or traders, or even as refugees.  We are beginning to see a new pattern of missionary work... every Church has gifts which others need, and every one needs what others can give..."

In the Commission Report on "The Missionary Obligation of Asian Churches" various recommendations were spelt out concerning functions primarily in the realm of mission and service, the exchange of workers, ecumenical scholarships, ecumenical

loan fund and cooperation with the WCC Division of Inter-Church
Aid and Service to Refugees.[8]

In the Report of Group V on "Church and Mission Relationship" of the All-Africa Church Conference in 1958 the following
was stated: "... It was found that in many areas the mission
has already been integrated or is being integrated into the
local church, and we rejoice that in fulfilling its purpose
of planting the church the mission organization is beginning
to disappear. However, the formal granting of independent
status does not mean that missionaries from the mother churches
are no longer needed. Fellow workers are welcome, but they
should be careful not to exercise disproportionate influence,
particularly in the disposition of funds from outside... It is
expected that the on-going work of the church will become self-
supporting as quickly as possible. Money from outside should
be used chiefly for pioneer projects... The independence of
the church places on it a new responsibility for the calling
and stationing of those who used to be called missionaries,
and may now be called fraternal workers (or some other suitable
term). The mere statement by the church of its needs, such
as theological tutors, doctors, secondary school teachers, or
young people's leaders, is not enough."[9]

## V.

The following consultations were held during the period
1948-1961. "Evangelism" was the theme of a consultation at
Bossey, March 2-8, 1949. Besides the introductory report by
H. Kraemer, papers were presented by J.-P. Benoit (The City -
the Object of Evangelism); E.R. Wickham (The Problem of Evangelism in the Mass Society of the Industrial World); W.Becker
(Evangelistic Possibilities in Different Spheres of Life and
the Role of Laymen in the Church). There were furthermore
three commission reports, and two short statements by J.Groser
and J.-P. Benoit.[10]

Organized by DICARWS, a consultation at Les Rasses, Switzerland, May 28 - June 2, 1956, discussed the subject "The
Church's Mission and the Role of Inter-Church Aid". The programme was divided into three sections: committees on needs,
commissions which discussed specific problems, and plenary
sessions which heard major addresses and received the reports.
Individual contributions were made by H. Alivisatos, M. Barot,
C. Berg, A. Carleton, W.A. Visser 't Hooft, J. Peterson,
J. Karefa-Smart, E. Rees, S.A. Morrison.[11]

At a consultation at Bossey, May 20-24, 1957 on "Evangelism
and the Structure of the Church in City and Industry" papers
were presented by E. van Cleeff, H.M. de Lange, P. Smits,
H. Symanowski, Ch. West. The consultation was chaired by
E. de Vries and concluding remarks were made by D.T. Niles.
The main questions were: With what kind of a city are we confronted ? What is evangelism in the urban situation ? How are
the theological directions to be put into practice ?[12]

"The Role of the Laity in the Missionary Outreach of the Church" was the theme of discussion of a consultation at New Haven, Conn. July 21-23, 1957. Papers were given by G.H. Williams (The Role of the Laymen in the Ancient Church); C.W. Nortier (The Role of the Laity in the Missionary Outreach of the Church in East Java); R.D. Hyslop (The Role of the Laity in the Mission of the Church); Th.O. Wedel (The Interrelation between 'Koinonia', 'Diakonia' and 'Kerygma').[13]

At a consultation at Bossey, March 19-25, 1958, on "A Theology for Evangelism" papers were presented by M. Barth, A.Greiner, J.C. Hoekendijk, D.T. Niles and R. Obermüller. G.W.Webber, C. Williams and J. Hamel introduced a preparatory paper on various questions. The documents: "The Lordship of Christ over the World and the Church", and "The Word of God and the Living Faith of Men" formed a part of the debate.[14]

The IMC together with the Commission on Theology of Mission of the WCC Department of Missionary Studies sponsored a consultation on "The Christian World Mission in the Ecumenical Age" at Greenwich, Conn., October 30 - November 1, 1959. Contributions were made by: M.S. Bates, D.M. Stove, J.H. Nichols, D.T. Niles, Ch. Forman, C. Michalson, J.K. Mathews, J.C. Smith, R.P. Barnes, A. Carleton. The consultation had a confidential and exploratory nature.[15]


VI.

Section I, "Unity", of the New Delhi Assembly in 1961 stated on the relation between mission and unity: "Mission and service belong to the whole Church. God calls the Church to go out into the world to witness and serve in word and deed to the one Lord Jesus Christ, who loved the world and gave himself for the world. In the fulfillment of our missionary obedience the call to unity is seen to be imperative, the vision of one Church proclaiming one Gospel to the whole world becomes more vivid and the experience and expression of our given unity more real. There is an inescapable relation between the fulfillment of the Church's missionary obligation and the recovery of her visible unity."

The New Delhi Report contained a Report of the Committee on the Department on Studies in Evangelism, a Report of the Committee on the Department of Missionary Studies and a Report of the Committee of the Assembly on the Commission and Division of World Mission and Evangelism which dealt with: Policy regarding the structure of the Division; Joint action for mission; Helping the churches in evangelism; Relationships with the Division of Inter-Church Aid and Service to Refugees, with the Division of Studies, with the Division of Ecumenical Action, and with National Christian Councils; Programme matters, such as: The role of the Christian laymen abroad in the mission of the Church; Bible weeks; Broadcasting, Christian literature; Study centres; Publications; The training of the professional missionary; The renumeration of missionaries; 'The pattern of the ministry in a missionary church'.[16]

The meeting of the Commission on World Mission and Evangelism at Mexico City in 1963 devoted its attention to four sections: I. The Witness of Christians to Men of Other Faiths; II. The Witness of Christians to Men in the Secular World; III. The Witness of the Congregation in its Neighbourhood; IV. The Witness of the Christian Church across National and Confessional Boundaries. There were also five committees: 1. Reference and Finance; 2. Education for Mission and Evangelism; 3. Laymen in World Mission; 4. Joint Action for Mission; 5. Structure and Relationships.

In Section I it was stated: "... The Christian attitude towards men of other faiths is basically one of love for all men, respect for sincerity wherever found, and patience to search for ways to bear effective witness. Christian witness to men of other faiths involves more than a simple declaration of Christian truth, to be accepted or rejected by them. It is important to recognize that a follower of another religion has his reasons for believing in it. These reasons may be part of the preparation for his understanding of the Gospel. It is important, also, to recognize that many followers of other faiths today find satisfaction and inspiration in the ways their faiths are being re-interpreted to lend added meaning to individual, social and national life. The vitality, or lack of it, that any man finds in his faith, and the sincerity of his search for God, may in the providence of God become opportunities for Christian witness...

"The Christian witness to men of other faiths also calls today for vigilance against religious relativism and syncretism. These may take various forms, such as the mixing of beliefs and practices, slow absorption into other religious systems, the loss of conviction as to the finality of Christ, and the sophistication that likes to feel itself at home in every variety of belief. Behind all these forms lies the presumption that it is the wisdom of man that establishes the truth."

In Section II the following was expressed on the process of secularization: "... We are neither optimistic nor pessimistic about the process of secularization as such. It should not be judged simply by the criterion of what it does to the Church. We mean it when we say that secularization opens up possibilities of new freedom and new enslavement for men. We have no doubt that it is easy to forget God, to give up all traditional religious practices, and at the same time lose all sense of meaning and purpose in life. Yet we are overwhelmingly convinced that it is not the mission of the Church to look for the dark side and to offer the Gospel as an antidote to disillusionment. We believe that at this moment our churches need encouragement to get into the struggle far more than they need to be primed with warnings. It simply does not do for us to talk about the problems of affluence, of too much leisure, and so on, to whose whose backs are breaking under loads we have never had to bear. We therefore want our words to be urgent, even at the risk of appearing to be one-sided."

Concerning neighbourhood Section III outlined the following: " 'Neighbourhood' - those near us, who therefore have a claim upon us - must be defined today not simply in terms of residence. In our mobile world, lives impinge upon each other in an increasing variety of 'worlds'. Thus, for example, in modern cities and suburbs our lives often are intertwined less with those who reside near us than with those who are 'given' to us in other communities such as work, or recreation or politics. The variety and mobility of these increasingly important non-residential neighbourhoods, gives new dimensions to the task of Christian witness. It suggests the need for new forms of congregation. It underlines the need to discover the essential unity of the mission of the church in relation to the mobile variety of modern communities. It daily makes more absurd our denominational divisions which cut across the unity men are given in these natural communities."

With regard to crossing national and confessional boundaries Section IV stated: "The missionary frontier runs around the world. It is the line that separates belief from unbelief, the unseen frontier which cuts across all other frontiers and presents the universal church with its primary missionary challenge. Other frontiers exist. The most important of these today are between nations and races, between ideological and cultural groups. Many of these nations are newly independent and are struggling for selfhood and a better way of life than they have known. They are caught between old forces dying and new forces struggling to be born. The gospel must be preached to men where they actually live. This variety of nations and groupings must be welcomed as a part of God's creation but, because of sin, these frontiers become formidable barriers which must be crossed if the witness of the Church is to be truly universal. When we cross such natural frontiers to witness to the gospel, we find that the divisions of Christians into their several traditions and confessions build up other barriers which must somehow be crossed if the world is to heed or even to hear the proclamation of the good news in Jesus Christ..."[17]

In Section I, "The Church in the Purpose of God", of the Fourth World Conference on Faith and Order in 1963 the following was expressed on the ecumenical dimension of mission: "In the fulfilment of their missionary task most churches claim not merely to be reproducing themselves, but in some sense to be planting the una sancta ecclesia. Surely this fact has implications which are scarcely yet realized, let alone worked out, both for the life of the mother-churches, and also for all that is involved in the establishing of any new church in an ecumenical age. It demands the liberty of newly-founded churches be recognized, so that both mother- and daughter-churches may receive together the one gift of God's grace. This demands faithfulness to the whole koinonia of Christ's Church, even when we are engaged with particular problems. In this connection we recognize a vital need for the study of the history of the Church's life and mission, written from an ecumenical perspective. All must labour together in seeking to receive and manifest the fullness of Christ's truth."

Section V, "All in Each Place: The Process of Growing Together" contained a sub-section on The Mission of the People of God in Each Place with the following heads: As Christians forming a local congregation; As Christians in relation to neighbouring congregations; As Christians in the world. Several recommendations were made with regard to joint action for mission.[18]

<br>

## VII.

A part of the work of the Assembly of the East Asia Christian Conference in 1964 was devoted to Asian Missions. The statement forwarded to member churches and councils in Asia contained the following headings: I. The Missionary Task; II. Sending and Receiving Missionaries; III. New Patterns; IV. Renumeration of Missionaries; V. The Preparation of Missionaries; VI. Mission in Unity. Regarding the last concern it was stated: "When we speak of mission we are speaking of a church - world relation. Because it is the whole Church that has to perform a task in the world, the structures and procedures which are devised for the performance of this task must reflect this unity of the Church's mission. It is in this perspective that we talk about inter-church aid for mission. In other words, inter-church aid by itself is not mission: rather, it is our common involvement in mission which is the reason for inter-church aid."[19]

In the Section, "Freedom and Unity in the Church", the First Assembly of the All Africa Conference of Churches expressed itself as follows on the relation between Christianity and Islam: "The rapid expansion of Islam in Africa (an annual increase of about 3 million persons) ought to be taken extremely seriously by the churches. But they should not see it primarily as a menace, and they should not react with a minority-complex. Far from this, the churches in large parts of Africa should see and use with thankfulness the great God-given opportunities for witness. Constituting 20 per cent of the African population (Muslims outnumbering the Christians two to one), the Christians are in a position to bring into being, on this continent and in this time, a new and, maybe in many respects, a decisive phase in the age-long encounter between Islam and Christianity." Strong emphasis was placed on the necessity that "every missionary effort from abroad should be channelled through the African Churches."[20]

## VIII

Both the Decree on the Missionary Activity of the Church
(Ad Gentes) and the Dogmatic Constitution on the Church (Lumen
Gentium) of the Second Vatican Council illustrate the rediscovery of the true biblical nature of the Church and its mission
to unbelievers.  The mission of the Church to 'those without',
as belonging to the essential nature of the People of God, receives major stress in the Constitution on the Church; the
Church has been sent to unbelievers to be the "sacrament of
unity of the whole human race".  The decree on the missions
continues this theme, not merely by way of repeating it, but
by locating this mission within the history and geography of
the globe and in specifying its yet unaccomplished task in the
context of the modern world.  It is quite evident throughout
the text that the focus of missionary activity is less on
territorial expansion, which has been virtually achieved, than
on making the Church an active presence within and native to
the diverse and developing non-Christian cultures in which it
exists.  Hence the emphasis on dialogue with other believers
and non-believers, adaptation to local conditions, and participation in community and national life.

Ad Gentes contains the following chapters:  I. Doctrinal
Principles;  II. Mission Work Itself (1. Christian Witness;
2. Preaching the Gospel and Gathering God's People Together;
3.  Forming the Christian Community);  III. Particular Churches;
IV. Missionaries;  V. Planning Missionary Activity;  VI. Missionary Cooperation;  VII. Conclusion.  In Article 29 it is stated:
"... In coordination with the Secretariat for Promoting Christian Unity, it (the Office of the Propagation of the Faith)
should search out ways and means for bringing about and directing fraternal cooperation as well as harmonious living with
the missionary undertakings of other Christian communities.
Thus, as far as possible, the scandal of division can be
removed."[21]


IX.

The following ecumenical consultations were held in the
period 1961-1968.  A consultation on "The Mission of the Church
in Urban Africa" at Nairobi, March 1961, was sponsored by AACC
and IMC-DWME.  Single contributions were made by D.G.S.M'Timkulu,
P.D. Fueter, A.A.G. Hake, H.F. Makulu.  The working groups of
the consultation concentrated on: A. The Pattern of Church Life
in the Urban Church;  B. The Church's Mission in Urban-Indus-
trial Power Structure;  C. Urban Community;  D. The Biblical
Basis of the Church's Mission in Urban/Industrial Africa.[22]

The purpose of a consultation at Bossey, July 1-10, 1961,
on "The Missionary Task of the Church" had the double purpose
of considering a draft on the theology of mission by D.T. Niles,

and of making a report to the New Delhi Assembly on points of
theological agreement. The Report, in six parts, dealt with
theological reflections on the missionary task of the church
and the hermeneutical problems.[23]

"The Missionary Structure of the Congregation" was the
theme of five consecutive consultations at Bossey, June 6-8,
1962, Villemetrie, France, October 3-4, 1963, Esslingen, FRG,
September 21-25, 1964, Driebergen, Holland, March 15-18, 1965,
and Berlin, FRG, September 13-17, 1965. Each time the Western
European Working Group of the WCC Department on Studies on Evangelism met to discuss different aspects and dimensions of the
theme. The final report was submitted to the Working Committee
of the Department on Evangelism, which met at Boldern, Männedorf,
August 22-26, 1966. It was resolved that the report be adopted
and that the WCC be asked to publish it in its WCC Series. The
sections of the report were: I. Secular Society; II. World
and History; III. God and World; IV. A Church for the World;
V. Reasonable Service; VI. Christian Presence; VII. Reform
and Renewal; VIII. Recommendations. Also included is a report
of the North American Working Group.[24]

Sixty youth leaders from churches in 16 European countries
met at Bièvres, France, October 1962, to concentrate on "The
Missionary Structure of the Congregation", initiated by the WCC
Department on Evangelism, and to join local groups already
established under auspices of a special study on the topic.
National Roman Catholic youth organizations in Austria, the
Netherlands and Switzerland were represented by their general
secretaries.[25]

A consultation on "The Preparation of Missionaries" at
Toronto, Canada, August 10-16, 1963, was organized by DWME.
Among the sixty persons present were twenty leaders of churches
in Asia, Africa and Latin America. The discussions were based
on the assumptions: 1) That the universality of the Gospel and
the nature of the Church demand that men and women "cross
frontiers" in the mission of the Church; 2) That every church
is potentially both a sending and receiving church; 3) That
God in His mission to the world will continue to use many
types of 'missionaries'. The findings of the consultation
were presented to the Commission on World Mission and Evangelism, meeting at Mexico City in December 1963.[26]

A regional consultation was held at New Haven, Conn.,
September 9-12, 1963 on "The Missionary Structure of the Con-
gregation". Thomas Wieser wrote the report. Contributions were
made by H.J. Margull, C. Williams, P. Berger, B. Johnson,
M. Niemöller. There were panel discussions in which G. Winter,
R. Cornelsen, R. Raines, R. Spike, J. Morikawa, W. Hollister,
J. Lee, B. Weaver, A. Young participated.[27]

Youth delegates from six continents participated in the
first meeting of CWME at Mexico City, December 8-20, 1963,
discussed the theme "Divided Witness" and issued a statement.[28]
The National Christian Council of India, the EACC and the DWME

sponsored a consultation on "Industrial Evangelism" at Pach-
marhi, India, March 10-15, 1964. The report includes, besides
the findings, papers by A.E.D. Frederick, T.S. Wilkinson,
S.L. Parmar, K.E. Wright, H. Daniel.[29]

"Missionary Presence in God's World" was the theme of a
consultation at Bossey, April 9-16, 1964. The aim of the meeting was the writing of a memorandum on issues and questions
arising out of the first phase of the study on the "Missionary
Structure of the Congregation". The document was outlined as
follows: I. The First Fruits of the New Humanity: (1) The
Church; 2) The World in Constant Change; 3) The Presence of
Christians in the World; 4) The Problem of the Local Congregation; 5) The open Congregation) II. Parables of Missionary
Forms: (1) The Church in Racial Revolution; 2) House Churches;
3) Brotherhoods) III. Next Steps (Urgent Exploration);
IV. The Hour of Renewal.[30]

The LWF and the DWME sponsored a consultation on "The Healing Ministry in the Mission of the Church" at Tübingen, FRG,
May 1964. The Report of the consultation includes the preparatory papers by L. Newbigin (The Healing Ministry of the
Church), E. Kayser (Medicine and Modern Philosphy), M. Scheel
(Some Comments on Pre-scientific Forms of Healing), J. Wilkinson (Christian Healing and the Congregation), and the findings
and proposed next steps.[31]

Thirty East German theologians and pastors participated in
a consultation at Cottbus, GDR, November 1964, on the theme
"Renewal of Congregational Life for Mission".[32]

A consultation on "The Communication and Interpretation of
the World Mission of the Church" at New York, September 15-24,
1965 was sponsored by the Division of Overseas Ministries of
the National Council of Churches of Christ in the USA, the
Department of Information of the Division of Inter-Church Aid,
Refugee and World Service, and the Division of World Mission
and Evangelism. Lectures were given by J.C. Smith, H.-J.Schultz,
L. Cassels, J. Sellers, C. Williams, Z.K. Matthews, Ph. Maury,
J. Lacey, L. Cooke. Seminars were directed by J. Abbott,
H. Haines, A. Brash, L. Cooke, B. Thompson, B. Latham, A. Carle-
ton, C.I. Itty.[33]

"Confessional Movements and Mission and Unity" was the
theme of the annual meeting of the officers of World Confessional Bodies at Geneva, October 12-13, 1965. Together with
representatives of mission agencies the gathering discussed the
significance of the confessional movements for the task of the
churches in mission and unity. A statement was issued.[34]

A consultation at Bossey, February 21-26, 1966 took place
on "The Mission of the Church and the Communications Revolution".
Contributions were made by Ch.S. McCoy, Z.K. Matthews, D.W.
Smythe, E.C. Parker, P. Eberhard, G. Heidtmann, E.J. Lynch,
T.B. Douglas, N.A. Nissiotis, J.-M. Chappuis. The paper by
E.C. Parker on "Christian Communication and Secular Man" was

published in the Ecumenical Review, vol. 18, 1966, pp. 331-344. The consultation made a proposal on a study on "The Church and Mass Communications".[35]

Another consultation took place on "The Missionary Structure of the Congregation" at Birmingham, April 25-28, 1966. The report, including contributions by J.G. Davies, H. Frankham, C.T. Day, M. Symons, T.T. Rowe, R.F. Taylor, E. Jones, C.C.Harris, D. Martin, P. Webb and W. Hollenweger, was edited by Trevor Beeson.[36]

Continuing the discussion, started in a previous consultation in May 1964, a second consultation at Tübingen, September 1-8, 1967, concentrated on "Health and Salvation" and examined the nature of the Church's ministry through medicine, particularly as it was exemplified in 'missionary' medicine in the developing nations. Contributions were made by H. Hellberg, M.H. Scharlemann, D.C. Moir, I.T. Ramsey, L. Jansen Schoonhoven, G. Hoffmann, D.C. Luke, D.E. Jenkins, G.C. Harding, H. Florin, R.A. Lambourne, S. Hiltner, A.D. John, T.F. Davey, F. Norstad, A.H. van Soest.[37]


X.


Section II, "Renewal in Mission", of the Uppsala Assembly in 1968 included the following headings: I. Mandate for Mission; II. Opportunities for Mission; III. Freedom for Mission. In the opening paragraphs the following statement was made on mission: "... Mission bears fruit as people find their true life in the Body of Christ, in the Church's life of Word and Sacrament, fellowship in the Spirit and existence for others. There the signs of the new humanity are experienced and the People of God reach out in solidarity with the whole of mankind in service and witness. The growth of the Church, therefore, both inward and outward, is of urgent importance. Yet our ultimate hope is not set upon this progress, but on the mystery of the final event which remains in the hand of God."

Concerning the church in the local situation it was said: "Though some believe that the basic structures of church life are given and therefore unchangeable, others are convinced that all institutional forms of church life are provisional and open to change. In a given locality the ministry of the church may be exercised in many forms, including congregations, chaplaincies, health and welfare services, youth projects, political and economic pressure groups, functional and professional groups and others. These have often inherited a pattern of life which was the response of a past generation to a situation which is now fast changing. In all the contemporary localities of mission, we must find new and effective ways in which the Gospel can be proclaimed today and understood in all these areas of life..."

Appendix XI, "The Church and the Media of Mass Communication" included a section Media and Mission. The following was expressed: "... The media can be seen as potential tools of mission. They must be used properly, stressing the need for good quality performance, a language understood by all, and respect for people of other or no faith. Unless these criteria are heeded, the use of the media works against the mission of God. The Gospel is by nature a 'scandalous' story, a stumbling-block and an offence. We cannot change that; but the true scandal does not need to be confused with a scandalous presentation. The preaching of the good news in Christ should not be confused with poor techniques, cheap advertising methods, and presentations designed as propaganda for our own groups. The presentation of the Gospel requires respect for the freedom of the audience and the integrity of the media."38

The Report of the World Conference on Salvation Today at Bangkok in 1973 contained three Sections:  I. Culture and Identity (A. On Racial Identity;  B. On Women;  C. On Conversion and Cultural Change;  D. On Dialogue with People of Living Faiths); II. Salvation and Social Justice (A. Introduction; B. Salvation and Social Justice in a Divided Humanity : Economic Exploitation, Salvation in Relation to National Planning, Local Struggles). III. Churches Renewed in Mission (A. The Local Mission of Each Church;  B. Growing Churches and Renewal;  C. Churches in Relationship).  All three sections included a number of recommendations.

The following was stated on personal identity.  "The problem of personal identity is closely related to the problem of cultural identity.  Culture shapes the human voice that answers the voice of Christ.  Many Christians who have received the Gospel through Western agents ask the question: 'Is it really I who answers Christ ?  Is it not another person instead of me?' This points to the problem of so-called missionary alienation. Too often, in the history of Western missions, the culture of those who received the Gospel was either ignored or condemned. At best, it was studied as a subject of missiology.  However, the problem is: how can we ourselves be fully responsible when receiving Salvation from Christ ?  How can we responsibly answer the voice of Christ instead of copying foreign models of conversion - imposed, not truly accepted ?  We refuse merely to be raw materials used by other people to achieve their own salvation.  The one faith must be made to be at home in every context and yet it can never be completely identical with it. Therefore there will be a rich diversity."

On the relation of salvation and social justice it was said: "... Without the salvation of the churches from captivity in the interests of dominating classes, races and nations, there can be no saving church.  Without liberation of the churches and Christians from their complicity with structural injustice and violence, there can be no liberating Church for mankind. Every church, all Christians face the question whether they serve Christ and His saving work alone, or at the same time also the powers of inhumanity.  'No man can serve two masters, God and Mammon'(Matt. 6:24).  We must confess our misuse of

the name of Christ by the accomodation of the churches to
oppressive powers, by our self-interested apathy, lovelessness
and fear. We are seeking the true community of Christ which
works and suffers for his Kingdom...

"Within the comprehensive notion of salvation, we see the
saving work in four social dimensions:
a) Salvation works in the struggle for economic justice
against the exploitation of people by people.
b) Salvation works in the struggle for human dignity against
political oppresssion of human beings by their fellow men.
c) Salvation works in the struggle for solidarity against
the alienation of person from person.
d) Salvation works in the struggle of hope against despair
in personal life."

In the context of church renewal the following was expressed: "... A local congregation that lives to itself sab-
otages the saving action of God in the neighbourhood; one that
exposes itself to share the needs and aspirations of its neighbourhood and to join with others in relevant action is an instrument of God's salvation, enabling men and women to find in
Jesus Christ ultimate meaning and sacredness for their lives.
Such a missionary congregation will have to include in its
programme a continual renewal of its own life, proclamation,
dialogue, service of the needy, projects to improve the re-
lational life of the community, and action for social justice."

The Bankok Assembly also had a word on moratorium. "We have
examined more radical solutions, such as the recent proposal
for a moratorium in the sending of funds and personnel for a
set period of time. The whole debate on the moratorium springs
from our failure to relate to one another in a way which does
not dehumanize. The moratorium would enable the receiving
church to find its identity, set its own priorities and discover
within its own fellowship the resources to carry out its authentic mission. It would also enable the sending church to re-
discover its identity in the context of the contemporary situation. It is not proposed that the moratorium be applied in
every country. Missionary policy should be adapted to the
particular situation in each area. In some parts of the world
other alternatives to bilateralism should be considered. In
devising new strategies for mission it is essential that all
partners look together at the total challenge to mission..." 39


XI.

The Report of the meeting of the Commission on Faith and
Order at Louvain 1971 contained several references to mission.
Speaking of The Church as a Missionary Fellowship it noted:
"... Whatever may have been the advantages or disadvantages
of the 'Christian' society of previous generations, today the
Churches have to learn again to be a minority missionary fel-
lowship. More than ever before, such a fellowship calls for

Christians who are aware of their fellowship with Christ and recognize the commission this implies. Does this not also mean a shift in the understanding and practice of baptism ? Does it not call for a greater emphasis on the note of commission ? It is significant that in the Churches which especially associate confirmation with the gift of the Spirit this rite is being given an increasingly missionary perspective."

Concerning The Eucharist, Mission to the World, the report said: "... Mission is not simply a consequence of the Eucharist. Whenever the Church is the Church, mission must be part of its life. At the Eucharist the Church is supremely itself and is united with Christ in his mission... Reconciled in the Eucharist, the members of the body of Christ are servants of reconciliation amongst men and witnesses of the joy of resurrection. Their very presence in the world implies full solidarity with the sufferings and hopes of all men, to whom they can be signs of the love of Christ who sacrificed himself on the cross and gives himself in the Eucharist. The Eucharist is also the feast of the continuing apostolic harvest, where the Church rejoices for the gifts received in the world and welcomes every man of good will."

In connection with Apostoliticity the report stated: "... Sent by the Father, Jesus Christ gave to men the mystery of the Kingdom (Mk. 4:11), He called them to conversion, He pardoned sinners, He healed the sick and the possessed, He preached the Gospel to the poor, He participated in the death of men by His passion in order to make them participate in His life in His resurrection. He called men to His Church and charged them to continue His mission. To His Church He gave authority (exousia) in the Holy Spirit to accomplish this mission and entrusted to certain men the exercise of this authority within the community. It is therefore in virtue of its participation in the mission of Christ in the mission of disciples that the Church is apostolic. For the Holy Spirit manifests this mission, realizes it and communicates it in a community 'consecrated and sent' like Christ (cf. Jn. 17:18 f.)."

On Christian and Relations between the Churches the following was spelt out. "Missionary action should be carried out in an ecumenical spirit which takes into consideration the priority of the announcement of the Gospel to non-Christians. The missionary effort of one Church in an area or milieu where another Church is already at work depends on an honest answer to the question: What is the quality of the Christian message proclaimed by the Church already at work, and in what spirit is it being proclaimed and lived ? Here frank discussion between the Churches concerned would be highly desirable, in order to have a clear understanding of each other's missionary and ecumenical convictions, and with the hope that it would help to determine the possibilities of cooperation, of common witness, of fraternal assistance, or of complete withdrawal. In the same manner and spirit the relations between minority and majority Churches should be considered."40

Addressing the Commission on Faith and Order at Accra in 1974, V.C. Samuel stated on the mission of the Church: "... The mission of the Church is an ongoing service rendered as much to its own membership as a historical community, as to those who do not constitute its membership. Therefore, to the end that salvation may be made real in every situation, the Church, on the one hand, should adopt changes and adjustments in its own life without being unduly inhibited by existing structures and established traditions; and on the other hand, it should develop new ways of meeting man's existential needs. The authority of the Church should be exercised rather in these areas than for the maintenance of a conservative attitude.

"The Church, in other words, should be understood, not as something already completed, but as a dynamic movement within the historical realm, through which God is unceasingly at work for the transformation of the world in every generation and every place. Its fulness is ever awaited in the eschaton. The historical Church can never claim to be infallible or inerrant in regard to any of its decisions or traditions, for all of them are relative to historical conditions. Even the relative authority which can be claimed for a decision or tradition will depend upon its adherence to the mandate: "As the Father has sent me, even so I send you."[41]


XII.

An exploratory consultation was called by the Department on Studies in Mission and Evangelism on "Missionary Participation in Human Institutions" at Bethesda, Maryland, February 13-15, 1969. Comments on the scope and method of the study were made by St. Mackie, J. Morikawa, and J.C. Hoekendijk.[42]

"Education for Mission - Slogans and Realities" was the theme of a consultation at Hothorpe Hall, Rugby, England, Nov. 17-21, 1972. It was sponsored by CWME and the Department of Church Cooperation of the LWF. It was felt that many of the slogans in use at that time, such as 'partnership in mission', 'mission in six continents', 'the home-base for mission is everywhere', or 'internationalization of mission' were still just and usable words. Education for mission must take these slogans into honest, living and sometimes costly realities. The consultation stressed the oneness of mission.[43]

At a consultation on "Evangelism" at Geneva, September 26-27, 1973, contributions were made by W. Arnold, M. Cassidy, O.E. Costas, M.V. George, Yap Kim Hao, E.C. Makunike, H. Bortnowska, G. Linn, W.A. Visser 't Hooft, E. Castro. A report of the discussions and findings was published.[44]

A document on "Common Witness and Proselytism" was prepared by a Joint Theological Commission which met in Arnoldshain,
Germany in 1968, and in Zagorsk, USSR, in 1968.  This document
was received by the Joint Working Group between the Roman Catholic Church and the World Council of Churches at its meeting
in May 1970 which recommended it to its parent bodies that it
be offered to the churches as a study document for their consideration.

The document consists of the following parts: Introduction;
Meaning of the Terms: Christian Witness, Common Witness,
Religious Freedom, Proselytism;  I. Common Witness;  II. Proselytism and Relations Between Churches (1. Required Qualities
for Christian Witness; 2. Christian Witness and Relations
between Churches);  III. Conclusion.

It was stated in the Introduction: "... Today, moved by the
Holy Spirit, the various Christian Communities are seeking to
restore the unity they have lost, in the hope that one day,
when they are fully renewed and united in faith and charity,
they may be better able to glorify God by bringing home to the
whole world the hope of the coming kingdom.  They are striving
to overcome whatever indifference, isolation and rivalry has
marked their relations to each other and thus has distorted
Christian witness even to that unity with which God has already
blessed them."[45]

The Joint Working Group elaborated a study document on
"Common Witness" and published it, after several years of
labour in 1981.  The document consists of the following parts:
I. The Fact of Common Witness;  II. Christian Witness - Common
Witness;  III. Realizations of Common Witness;  IV. Struggle
and Hope;  V. Appendix: Common Witness in Practice (Common
Witness in Diaconia/Koinonia; Common Witness in the Promotion
of Human Rights; Common Witness through Bible Work; Common
Witness through Theological Dialogue; Common Witness in
Religious Education).

Reference was made in the introduction to "striking and
clear convergencies on evangelization in the reports of the
Bangkok Assembly on 'Salvation Today' (1973); the International Evangelical Congress on World Evangelization at
Lausanne (1974); and the papal document, issued after the
1974 Synod in Rome on Evangelization in the Modern World,
Evangelii Nuntiandi.  The latter called for a greater common
witness to Christ before the world in the work of evangelization."[46]

Section I, "Confessing Christ Today" of the Nairobi
Assembly in 1975 was divided into the following parts: Confessing Christ as an Act of Conversion; Many Cultures, One
Christ; The Confessing Community; Confessing Christ in Worship
and Life; A Call to Confess and Proclaim; Recommendations. The
report stressed under the heading Confessing Christ and Being
Converted to his Discipleship Belong Inseparably Together:
"... We deplore cheap conversions, without consequences. We
deplore a superficial gospel-preaching, an empty gospel without a call into personal and communal discipleship... We
deplore conversions without witness to Christ.

"We regret all divisions in thinking and practice between
the personal and the corporate dimensions. 'The whole gospel
for the whole person and the whole world' means that we cannot
leave any area of human life and suffering without the witness
to hope. We regret that some reduce liberation from sin and
evil to social and political dimensions, just as we regret that
others limit liberation to the private and eternal dimensions.
In the witness of our whole life and our confessing community
we work with passionate love for the total liberation of the
people and anticipate God's Kingdom to come. We pray in the
freedom of the Spirit and groan with our suffering fellow
human beings and the whole groaning creation until the glory
of the Triune God is revealed and will be all in all..."[47]

In the Statement adopted by the Theological Consultation
on Dialogue in Community, held at Chiang Mai, Thailand, April
18-27, 1977, it was said in the Introduction: "... It will be
noted that the words 'mission' and 'evangelism' are not often
used in our statements. This is not because we seek to escape the Christian responsiblility, re-emphasized in the
Nairobi Assembly, to confess Christ today, but in order to
explore other ways of making plain the intentions of Christian
witness and service, so as to avoid misunderstanding. This was
a Christian conference and Christian integrity includes an
integrity of response to the call of the risen Christ to be
witnesses to Him in all the world.

On Community it was stated: "... We understand our calling
as Christians to be that of participating fully in the mission
of God (missio Dei) with the courage of conviction to enable
us to be adventurous and take risks. To this end we would
humbly share with all our fellow human beings in a compelling
pilgrimage. We are specifically disciples of Christ, but we
refuse to limit Him to the dimensions of our human understanding. In our relationships within the many human communities
we believe that we come to know Christ more fully through faith
as Son of God and Saviour of the world; we grow in His service
within the world; and we rejoice in the hope which He gives."[48]

In _Jewish-Christian Dialogue - Six Years of Christian-Jewish Consultations_ Krister Stendahl expressed the following: "... The universalism of the Christian Church is real, the church is a new community with universal participation, not limited to the Jewish people. As such, this community with disciples from all nations (Matt. 28:19) is a new outburst of the witness to God's will, and it is grounded in the faith in Jesus Christ. But its function remains that of a witnessing community, leaving the results to God. It remains a minority, now drawn together from many people. It does not envisage the Christianization of the world.

"It is striking how Paul, the most eager of missionaries, comes to criticize the feeling of superiority over against the Jews that he detects among his converts (Rom. 11:20) and how he reaches the to many astonishing conclusion that God may have other plans for the salvation of Israel than he, Paul, had envisaged earlier in his missionary zeal. For God's plan is a mystery and cannot be secularized into the potential success of Christian missions. 'Lest you be wise in your own conceits, I want you to understand this mystery...' (11:25)."[49]

Besides several plenary presentations, section plenary presentations and appendices, the Report on the World Conference on Mission and Evangelism at Melbourne in 1980, concentrating on the theme "Your Kingdom Come", contains four Section reports: I. Good News to the Poor; II. The Kingdom of God and Human Struggles; III. The Church Witnesses to the Kingdom; IV. Christ - Crucified and Risen - Challenges Human Power. Section I outlined "... God identified with the poor and oppressed by sending his Son Jesus to live and serve as a Galilean speaking directly to the common people; promising to bless those who met the needs of the hungry, the thirsty, the stranger, the naked, the sick and the prisoner; and finally meeting death on a cross as a political offender. The good news handed on to the Church is that God's grace was in Jesus Christ, who 'though he was rich, yet for your sake he became poor, so that by his poverty you might become rich' (II Cor. 8:9)." Section I recommended to the churches "to become churches in solidarity with the struggles of the poor, to join the struggle against the powers of exploitation and impoverishment, to establish a new relationship with the poor inside the churches."

Section II said: "... When the churches and individual members of the churches get involved in the struggles for human rights they do so because they have seen in Jesus Christ as the Lord of the Kingdom of God a radical challenge of all attempts at depriving women and men of their human rights. Churches and Christians are called to participate in such struggles as those who witness in their obedience to the unique character of the Gospel's demand for love towards the enemy, forgiveness and reconciliation. Evangelism is part of the local mission of the church in the social, economic and political life of human societies. Thus such participation in the struggle for human rights is in itself a central element in the total mission of the church to proclaim by word and act the crucified and risen Christ."

The first paragraph of Section III on "The Church Witnesses to the Kingdom" stated: "This title is a frightening claim, but a wonderful reality. It is frightening because it causes everyone of us to examine our personal experience of the empirical church, and to confess how often our church life has hidden rather than revealed the sovereignty of God the Father whom Jesus Christ made known. Yet there is reality here. The whole church of God, in every place and time, is a sacrament of the kingdom which came in the person of Jesus Christ and will come in its fulness when he returns in glory."

On the relation between the challenging of destructive human powers and evangelism Section IV stated: "... In a world of large-scale robbery and genocide, Christian evangelism can be honest and authentic only if it stands clearly against the injustices which are diametrically opposed to the kingdom of God and looks for response in an act of faith which issues in commitment. Christian life cannot be generated, or communicated, by a compromising silence and inaction concerning the continuing exploitation of the majority of the human race by a privileged few. 'You cannot love the God whom you do not see, if you do not love the neighbour whom you see' (I John 4:20). The neighbour today also is fallen among robbers as in the Gospel parable. Woe unto the evangelizer who proclaims the word but passes by his neighbour like the priest and the levite in Jesus' parable."[50]

The Central Committee meeting in 1980 encouraged "CWME to enter into an intensive dialogue with churches, Christian communities and missionary organizations around questions like:
   a) How does our evangelistic proclamation incorporate the promises and demands of the justice of the Kingdom ? How does our involvement for the Kingdom in the struggles of the world incorporate a dimension of witness ?
   b) How do the 'churches of the poor' or Christian communities of the poor, both in rich and in poor countries, fulfil their evangelistic vocation ? What do we learn, for our missionary obedience, of the amazing reality of the gifts of the Spirit in the churches of the poor ?
   c) How do churches in communities without material poverty fulfil their evangelistic calling ?
   d) The majority of those who do not know the story of Jesus are poor. How do we relate our Lord's missionary sending - Matt. 28:20 - to the injustice done to the poor of the earth by our lack of missionary commitment ? And how does our Christian life-style add, or substract, credibility to the proclamation of the Gospel in the world ?"[51]

XV.

From 1976 onwards the following consultations took place. Overseas workers gathered in Geneva, March 1976, under the auspices of CWME to discuss their experiences of "Missionaries to Europe". Participants in the consultation were serving churches in Sweden, Holland, Great Britain, the FRG, France and Switzerland. Specific recommendations of the consultation included: 1) receiving congregations should be adequately prepared in advance and vote to invite an overseas worker; 2) overseas workers should be given an opportunity to participate fully in policy-making committees and boards; 3) churches in countries having laws prohibiting Asians and Africans from serving as pastors should see how this situation could be changed.[52]

"Christian Witness Today" was the theme of a consultation at Prague, March 26-30, 1979, in which representatives of WCC member churches in Eastern Europe participated. E. Castro and I. Bria were co-moderators. The group reports were on: I. Proclamation and Worship; II. Evangelism in Big Cities and New Towns; III. Witness from Person to Person; IV. Evangelism in the Secularized Socialist Society.[53]

Two consultations on the theme "A New Process for Mission and Service" took place at New Windsor, Maryland, April 24-28, 1979, and at Wuppertal, FRG, May 14-22, 1979. Donald O. Newby, a WCC consultant compiled the report of the two meetings of CICARWS and CWME.[54] Some 90 people attended a consultation on "Heads of Mission Agencies" at Glion, Switzerland, May 23-27, 1979. The four foci of the consultation were: Mission Today; The Western Mission Agency - Its Identity, Role and Relevance; Our Captivities; Other Models in Mission - New and Old.[55]

CWME and the Ecumenical Institute organized at Bossey, June 4-15, 1979 a consultation on "Evangelism Today". Individual contributions were made by M. Arias, R. Fung, A. Krass, Ma Mpolo Masamba, J. Maury, W. Pannell, J. Poulton. A statement on evangelism in Latin America was elaborated.[56]

Five small consultations on "The Sharing of People in Mission" were organized by CWME at Caracas, Venezuela, September 1-4, 1981; Singapore, November 23-27, 1981; Savu, Fiji, December 3-9, 1981; San Fernando, Trinidad, December 15-18, 1981; Lomo, Togo, May 1-7, 1982. These consultations spelled out the future directions of ecumenical sharing of personnel in the various continents and regions.[57]

From 1974 to 1981 six Orthodox consultations, organized by the Desk for Orthodox Studies and Relations of CWME, were held at Cernica, Romania, June 4-8, 1974 ("Confessing Christ Today"); Etchmiadzine, Armenia, September 16-21, 1975 ("Confessing Christ Through the Liturgical Life of the Church Today"); Prague, September 12-18, 1977 ("The Role and Place of the Bible in the Liturgical and Spiritual Life of the Orthodox Church"); Paris, September 25-28, 1978 (Contribution to the theme "Your Kingdom Come"); Amba Bishoy Monastery, Egypt, April 30 - May 5, 1979 ("The Place of the Monastic Life Within the Witness of the Church Today"); Monastery of Zica, Yugoslavia, September 20-25, 1980 ("Preaching and Teaching the Christian Faith Today"). The reports of these six consultations were published in the International Review of Mission.[58]

A consultation on "The Ecumenical Nature of the Orthodox Witness", arranged by the WCC Orthodox Task Force, was held at the New Valamo Monastery, September 24-30, 1977, at the invitation of the Orthodox Church of Finland. The consultation dealt with three specific items on today's ecumenical agenda: The Local Church, The Proclamation and Articulation of Our Faith, and The Churches' Responsibilities in the World Today. The report contains also papers by Metropolitan John of Helsinki, J. Meyendorff, C. Yannaras, N.A. Zabolotsky and various comments on the New Valamo Report.[59]

XVI.

The Central Committee meeting in 1982 received the document "Mission and Evangelism: an Ecumenical Affirmation" and recommended it to the churches for their study and implementation. The document, elaborated by CWME, outlines the theological discussions concerning the shape and content of Christian mission today, and facilitates the conversations, collaboration and support of Orthodox, Protestant churches and the Roman Catholic Church as they endeavour to go into all the world to make disciples of the nations. A consultation on "Mission in a New Age", organized by the Vatican Secretariat for Promoting Christian Unity, which studied the CWME Affirmation on Mission and Evangelism, issued in May 1982 a Memorandum.[60]

Issue I, "Witnessing in a Divided World" of the Vancouver Assembly in 1983 contained the following parts: Introduction; Culture: The Context for Our Witnessing; Worship: The Perspective and the Power with which We Witness; Witnessing among Children; Witnessing among the Poor; Witnessing among People of Living Faiths.

In the Report of the Assembly's Programme Guidelines Committee the following was outlined on Evangelism: "Evangelism should undergird the work in all WCC programmes, based on the 'Ecumenical Affirmation on Mission and Evangelism', adopted by the Central Committee in 1982. The Council should assist member churches in their mission to proclaim Christ, the life of the world, and in their calling of men and women to faith and discipleship. The implementation of this priority should have three dimensions. The WCC should:
a) help member churches in developing an understanding of the relationship between evangelism and culture in respect of both the contextual proclamation of the Gospel in all cultures and the transforming power of the Gospel in any cultures;
b) seek to develop dialogue with evangelicals not related to the WCC on the meaning and methods of evangelism, particularly with concern for the relation between evangelism and the wholeness of salvation and the criteria for authentic church growth;
c) help to clarify the distinction between evangelism, carried out in the spiritual freedom and power of the Gospel, and proselytism in all its forms, particularly in view of activities, some of which evidence an arrogant disregard for

people's cultural integrity and which are sometimes - consciously or unconsciously - at the service of foreign political
interests."61

## Observations and Comments

1.  The questions which were most strenuously discussed
during the period of 1948-1968 concerned the form and structure
of missions.  The shift from the 'three-continent' to the 'six-
continent' perspective was mainly a matter of structure.  The
problems posed for missions by the rise of younger and independent churches, the end of colonialism, and the development of
inter-Church aid on a massive scale were questions about the
forms and patterns of missionary action.  Although these problems have not been entirely solved, sufficient structures have
been created within which missions can operate in a truly ecumenical context.  It has been shown that it is not necessary to
abandon missionary calling, the calling to take the gospel across
the frontier to those who do not have it, in order to be part of
the modern ecumenical reality.

2.  The questions which the ecumenical movement has faced
during the last two decades are increasingly questions about
the substance of the gospel itself.  What is the relation of
the proclamation of the good news to the action of God in the
secular and unjust world, to the validity of service rendered
by Christians to their fellow human beings, and to the authentic
life of the Church ?  The course of the world-wide mission of
the Church depends ever more upon the recovery by the Church of
the dialogical dimension of the gospel which it has to spread.

The danger, however, persists that churches and their
experts are deplorably unaware that the drafting of documents
in missionary conferences and the careful work given to getting
terms right, all tends to become an end in itself and thus a
monologue.  The continuous exercise of many Christians who put
their missionary obligation on paper can be a surrogate for
actual witness in concrete human situations.  The grandiose
imagination and the mutual encouragement to be faithful ambassa-
dors of Christ are in fact burdens and obstacles in the meeting
of neighbours of other faiths and little or no faith.  The more
Christians are indoctrinated into the writing and reading of
ever more books and reports on the sacred vocation of mission,
the more they become preposterous individuals unable to tell
the marvellous story of Jesus.  It is only in person-to-person
dialogue that the words 'mission' and 'evangelism' have any
meaning.  The integrity of response to the witness to the risen
Christ depends solely on the unlimited power of the Holy Spirit
and never on the correctness of the biblical testimony by
influential individuals or impressive Christian establishments
blocking only profound person-to-person encounter beyond the
church space.

3.  It is surprising that there are so few published records
of personal stories of Christians meeting fellow human beings in
their daily life and their own environment and experiencing the

joy of their gradual or sudden conversion. There are equally
few recorded life stories of persons who have been touched by
the healing power and reconciling love of Jesus Christ. It is
in the concrete testimonies of agonizing, burdened and searching
people that the relation between the confrontation with enslaving human powers and liberating evangelism, the solitude and
abandonment in society and the koinonia of the church, the deliverance from corporate sin and evil and private and eternal
salvation, now often theoretically discussed in ecumenical
missionary documents, shapes the witness to God's continuous
action in history.

Evangelicals and charismatics preach the message of Jesus:
"Repent because the kingdom of God is at hand". But their
emphasis is too often on individual repentance rather than on
God's transformation of his creation. Ecumenical Christians
dwell on a new Christian life in society, but 'political conversion' tends to become more important for them than God's
re-creation of a new humanity. The deepest salvific meaning
of the resurrection is that all world history, the life and
death of mortals, the finest and most broken human relationships,
the rise and decline of cultures, the achievements and tragedies
of people are all an intimate part of God's eternal design of
deliverance.

The wrestling of the Bangkok Conference with the plan of
God's salvation needs to continue in the analysis of human
stories of how in the upheavals in history faith in Jesus Christ
is born and strengthened. Households of God on China's Soil[62]
is a good example and a step in the right direction. The description of the accounts of how Chinese Christians have clung
to their faith in times of trial are not only disarmingly un-
complicated but an inspiration to Christians everywhere. Through
services of worship and sessions of Bible study, through caring
for people and participating in the nation's life, believers in
China witness to their salvation.

4. When this survey on Mission and Evangelism is read in
conjunction with the survey on The Dialogue with People of
Living Faiths it becomes clear that mission and dialogue are
intimately related in structure, method and content. After a
long history of separate and parallel developments the time has
come for the combination of the Sub-unit on World Mission and
Evangelism and the Sub-unit on Dialogue into one Sub-unit on
Mission and Dialogue. True dialogue is never opposed to witness. Lynn de Silva underlined this fact when he wrote: "Fears
have been expressed that dialogue blunts proclamation. (But) how
can we proclaim the love of God if we do not love our neighbours?
If we are not prepared to listen to what people of other faiths
have to say, how can we expect them to listen to what we have
to say to them ?"[63]

Dialogue is both a dynamic contact of life with life which
transforms the partners and makes them grow together, and a
mutual life exercise in converting each other. Mission has
its place in encounter because its absence would diminish the

credibility of dialogue both within the church and among its partners. At the same time witness is pointless in the absence of dialogue. The ecumenical movement still needs a clear declaration on mission in dialogue and dialogical mission. Such a convincing statement can only be made when ecumenical endeavours in the realms of mission and dialogue are combined.

5. When this survey on Mission and Evangelism is read in conjunction with the survey on Christianity and Culture it becomes clear that the ecumenical watchword of this century, "the evangelization of the world in our generation", still needs to be replaced by another watchword. It is not enough to state that the problem of the absence of the context of witness has been caused by the ignoring or denigrating of receptor cultures during the Western missionary era, which often went hand in hand with Western colonial expansion. The words "world mission and evangelism" continue to point to the danger that churches and Christians still today inhibit the gospel from taking root in whatever cultural soil of humanity. The obedience to "Go, teach, baptize" (Matt. 28:18-20) needs to be supplemented by the prayer for the coming of the kingdom of God. Mission is not primarily the winning of souls or the expansion of the church in whatever circumstances but the extension of the invitation to peoples of different cultures and religions to the great banquet (Luke 14:16ff).

Through many parables Jesus revealed and concealed the mystery of the kingdom to his disciples. God's kingdom is concerned not just with Christianity and Christians but with all neighbours of other faiths and of no faith, with their hopes and aspirations. A watchword like "the proclamation of the kingdom in the plural world" would make the preaching of the Sermon of the Mount mandatory. God's plan of salvation surpasses the potential success of the church's mission. All religions and cultures find their destiny in his unfathomable universalism. Only the Holy Spirit is wholly engaged in world mission and evangelism.

---

1. The First Assembly of the World Council of Churches held at Amsterdam, August 22 to September 4, 1948. Ed. by W.A. Visser 't Hooft. New York: Harper, 1949. pp. 64-70.

2. The Evanston Report. The Second Assembly of the World Council of Churches 1954. London: SCM, 1955. pp. 98-108.

3. Minutes and Reports of the Fourth Meeting of the Central Committee at Rolle (Switzerland), August 4-11, 1951. Geneva: WCC, 1951. pp. 63-68.

4. Minutes of the Enlarged Meeting of the Committee of the International Missionary Council, Willingen, Germany, July 5-21, 1952. London: IMC, 1952. pp. 53-101.

5.  Minutes of the Assembly of the International Missionary Council, Ghana, December 28, 1957 to January 8, 1958. London: IMC, 1958.  pp. 58-62, 89-92.

6.  The Third World Conference on Faith and Order held at Lund, August 15-28, 1952.  Ed. by Oliver S. Tomkins. London: SCM, 1953.  pp. 24, 63-64.

7.  The Christian Prospect in Eastern Asia. Papers and Minutes of the Eastern Asia Christian Conference, Bangkok, December 3-11, 1949.  New York: Friendship Press, 1950. pp. 118-120.

8.  "Witnesses Together", Being the Official Report of the Inaugural Assembly of the East Asia Christian Conference, held Kuala Lumpur, Malaya, May 14-24, 1959.  Ed. by U Kyaw Than. Rangoon, 1959.  pp. III, 88-103.

9.  The Church in Changing Africa. Report of the All-Africa Church Conference, held at Ibadan, Nigeria, January 10-19, 1958.  New York: IMC, 1958.  p. 92.

10. Study Conference on Evangelism.  Bossey, 1949 (mimeographed).

11. Addresses and Reports to the Annual Consultation, Les Rasses, Switzerland, 1956.  DICARWS (mimeographed).

12. Consultation on Evangelism and the Structure of the Church in City and Industry.  Bossey, 1957 (mimeographed).

13. WCC Laity Archives.

14. Consultation on a Theology for Evangelism. Bossey, 1958 (mimeographed).

15. The Christian World Mission in an Ecumenical Age, 1960 (mimeographed).

16. The New Delhi Report. The Third Assembly of the World Council of Churches 1961.  London: SCM, 1962. pp. 121, 188-195, 249-257.

17. Minutes of the Second Meeting of the Commission on World Mission and Evangelism, Mexico City, December 8-19, 1963. Geneva: WCC, 1964.  pp. 116-127.

18. The Fourth World Conference on Faith and Order, Montreal 1963. Ed. by P.C. Rodger and L. Vischer.  London: SCM, 1964. (Faith and Order Paper, No. 42).  pp. 59, 87-90.

19. The Christian Community within the Human Community, Containing Statements from the Bangkok Assembly of the EACC, February-March 1964. Minutes - Part 2. Bangalore: CLS, 1964.  pp. 59-70.

20. Drumbeats from Kampala. Report of the First Assembly of the All Africa Conference of Churches held at Kampala, April 20-30, 1963.  London: Lutterworth Press, 1963.  pp. 41-44.

21. The Documents of Vatican II. New York: Guild Press, America Press, Association Press, 1966. pp. 584-630.

22. The Mission of the Church in Urban Africa. The Report of a Consultation. New York: Commission on World Mission and Evangelism, 1962.

23. Bulletin. WCC Division of Studies. Vol. VII, Autumn 1961, pp. 3-23.

24. The Church for Others and the Church for the World. A Quest for Structures for Missionary Congregations. Geneva: WCC, 1967.

25. Ecumenical Youth News, Issue no. 7, October 1962.

26. Statement from a Consultation on the Preparation of Missionaries. Geneva: DWME, 1963.

27. Concept, January 1964. See also: Concept, Special Issue, no. 4, July 1963.

28. Ecumenical Youth News, Issue no. 1, January 1964.

29. Report of the International Mobile Team and Findings of Consultation on Industrial Evangelism. Kottayam: C.M.S. Press, 1964.

30. Concept VII, May 1964, pp. 1-45.

31. The Healing Church. The Tübingen Consultation. Geneva: WCC, 1965. (World Council Studies, no. 3).

32. Ecumenical Press Service, no. 42, 12 November, 1964.

33. Report on the Conference on the Communication and Interpretation of the World Mission of the Church. New York: NCCCUSA, 1966.

34. Ecumenical Review, vol. XVIII, no. 1, January 1966.

35. Consultation on the Mission of the Church and the Communications Revolution. Bossey, 1966 (mimeographed).

36. Concept, September 1966.

37. Health. Medical - Theological Perspectives. Geneva: WCC, LWF, 1967.

38. The Uppsala Report 1968. Official Report of the Fourth Assembly of the World Council of Churches, July 4-20, 1968. Ed. by Norman Goodall. Geneva: WCC, 1968. pp.27-36,396-397.

39. Minutes and Report of the Assembly of the Commission on World Mission and Evangelism, December 31, 1972 and January 9-12, 1973. Geneva: WCC, 1973. pp. 73, 89,100, 106.

40. Faith and Order, Louvain 1971. Study Reports and Documents. Geneva: WCC, 1971. (Faith and Order Paper, No. 59). pp. 41, 76, 139, 166.

41. Uniting in Hope. Reports and Documents from the Meeting of the Faith and Order Commission, 23 July - 5 August, 1974, University of Ghana, Legon. Geneva: WCC, 1975. (Faith and Order Paper, No. 72). p. 108.

42. Concept. Special Issue, no. 23, July 1969.

43. Ecumenical Review, vol. XXV, no. 2, April 1973.

44. International Review of Mission, vol. LXIII, no. 249, January 1974.

45. Ecumenical Review, vol. XXIII, no. 1, January 1971.

46. Common Witness. A Study Document of the Joint Working Group of the Roman Catholic Church and the World Council of Churches. Geneva: CWME, 1981. (CWME Series, 1). See also: One in Christ, vol XVII, no. 2, 1981.

47. Breaking Barriers. Nairobi 1975. Ed. by David M. Paton. London: SPCK; Grand Rapids: Wm. B. Eerdmans, 1976. pp. 43-57.

48. Faith in the Midst of Faiths. Reflections on Dialogue in Community. Ed. by S.J. Samartha. Geneva: WCC, 1977. pp. 136 and 143.

49. Jewish-Christian Dialogue - Six Years of Christian-Jewish Consultations. The Quest for World Community: Jewish and Christian Perspectives. Geneva: WCC, 1975. p. 61.

50. Your Kingdom Come. Mission Perspectives. Report of the World Conference on Mission and Evangelism, Melbourne, Australia, 12-25 May 1980. Geneva: WCC, 1980. pp. 171, 177-178, 186, 193, 218.

51. Central Committee of the World Council of Churches. Minutes of the Thirty-Second Meeting, Geneva, 14-22 August, 1980. Geneva: WCC, 1981. pp. 43-44.

52. Ecumenical Press Service, no. 10, 1 April, 1976.

53. CWME Archives, 1979.

54. Toward a New Process for Mission and Service. Geneva: WCC, 1979 (mimeographed).

55. Heads of Mission Agencies Consultation, Glion. Geneva: CWME, 1979.

56. Consultation on Evangelism Today. Bossey, 1979 (mimeogr.).

57. CWME and CICARWS Archives, 1981-1982.

58. Martyria/Mission. The Witness of the Orthodox Churches Today. Ed. by Ion Bria. Geneva: WCC, 1980.
    See also: Go Forth in Peace. A Pastoral and Missionary Guidebook - Reports and Documents from the Orthodox Missionary Consultations, 1974-1980. Compiled and edited by Ion Bria. Geneva: WCC, 1982.

59. The New Valamo Consultation. The Ecumenical Nature of Orthodox Witness. New Valamo, Finland, September 24-30, 1977. Geneva: WCC, 1981.

60. International Review of Mission, vol. LXXI, no. 284, October 1982.

61. Gathered for Life. Official Report of the VI Assembly of the World Council of Churches, Vancouver, Canada, 24 July - 10 August, 1983. Ed. by David Gill.
    Geneva: WCC; Grand Rapids: Wm. B. Eerdmans, 1983.
    pp. 31-42, 254.

62. Households of God on China's Soil. Compiled and translated by Raymond Fung. Geneva: WCC, 1982. (WCC Mission Series, 2).

63. De Silva, Lynn. The Understanding and Goal of Dialogue. In: Dialogue, vol. IV, nos. 1 and 2, 1977. p. 6.

# III.
# The Dialogue with People of Living Faiths

Christianity and non-Christian religions from the thirties to the fifties, the Word of God and the living faiths from the seventies onwards have been a concern in the ecumenical movement. The Assembly of the International Missionary Council at Madras, in 1938, was pre-occupied with the study of the Christian message in a non-Christian world. At its Assembly in Whitby, Ontario, in 1947, the IMC set itself to discover the relevance of the gospel to the world recovering from war. The IMC Assembly in Ghana, in 1958, which decided in favour of the integration of the IMC with the WCC, ratified the study on "The Word of God and the Living Faiths of Men."

This analytical and bibliographical survey starts with 1971, the year the Sub-unit on Dialogue with People of Living Faiths was created and started its work with the WCC. For the period 1955-1970 "The Word of God and the Living Faiths of Men: Chronology and Bibliography of a Study-Process", by Gérard Vallée, which is the last chapter of the book Living Faiths and the Ecumenical Movement,1 should be consulted. It lists various consultations, conferences and meetings of the WCC Executive and Central Committee in chronological order. A few important ecumenical gatherings before 1971, however, are included in this survey, because they have a significant bearing on futher developments in the seventies. A useful source of information also are the Minutes of the Sixth Meeting of the Working Group on Dialogue with People of Living Faiths and Ideologies in 1985. They provide a list of major meetings since 1969 and a list of major WCC publications.2 Only a few statements of bi-lateral consultations (Christian-Muslim dialogue, etc.) are included in this survey.


## I.

A consultation on "Christian Dialogue with Men of Other Faiths" at Kandy, Ceylon, 27 February - 6 March, 1967, was organized by the WCC Department of Missionary Studies, in which Orthodox, Roman Catholics and Protestants participated. Papers were presented by K. Gragg, L. de Silva, J. Blauw. The consultation produced a Statement, including the following paragraphs. Concerning the "Basis of Dialogue" it was stated that "The Christian needs to be more joyfully and responsibly aware than he often is of his human solidarity with all his fellow-men, no matter what their colour, culture, faith or unbelief. There is an essential identity of the human species to which full significance should be accorded, God having 'made of every nation of men'. All mankind is furthermore being caught up into one universal history, and made increasingly aware of common tasks and common hopes. This provides a basis for dialogue which all can share. For the Christian, a deep sense of community is given by his belief that all men are created in the image of God, by his realization that Christ died for every man, and by the expectation of His coming Kingdom. Here is the foundation of the Christian's approach to any human being. And since he must take seriously the personalities of his neighbours, he must of course respect their particular religious faith as an integral aspect of their culture and humanity. As our dialogue with men of other faiths develops, we may gain light regarding the place held by other religious traditions in God's purposes for them and for us; this is a question which cannot be answered <u>a priori</u> or academically, but must continue to engage our earnest study and reflection."

With regard to the "<u>Nature of Dialogue</u>" it was asserted that "love always seeks to communicate. Our experience of God's communion with us constrains us to communion with men of other beliefs. Only so can the Christian live the 'with-ness' which was shown him in the Incarnation. His intercourse takes the form of dialogue, since he respects the differences between him and others, and because he wishes to hear as well as to speak. The fundamental nature of dialogue is the genuine readiness to listen to the man with whom we desire to communicate. Our concern should not be to win arguments... Good dialogue develops when one partner speaks in such a way that the other feels drawn to listen, and likewise when one listens so that the other is drawn to speak. The outcome of the dialogue is the work of the Spirit."

On the concern of "<u>Living in Dialogue</u>" it was noted that "true dialogue is a progressive and cumulative process, which takes place not only through verbal communication, but through the dynamic contact of life with life. Christians today meet men of other faiths anywhere in the world. Nothing less than living in dialogue is the responsibility and privilege to which we are called." Finally on "<u>Dialogue and Proclamation</u>": "Dialogue and proclamation are not identical but related. At any time or place within the course of our living in dialogue, moments for proclamation of the Gospel may be given. For Christians, proclamation is the sharing of the Good News about God's action in history through Jesus Christ. Proclamation is made in other ways besides dialogue, but should always be made in the spirit of dialogue. On the other hand, dialogue may include proclamation, since it must always be undertaken in the spirit of those who have good news to share."[3]

The consultation heard, moreover, papers by K. Klostermaier, C.M. Rogers, S. Prakash, L. de Silva, M. Doc, J.B. Taylor. Section II, "<u>Renewal in Mission</u>", of the Fourth WCC Assembly at Uppsala in 1968 observed on dialogue that: "The meeting with men of other faiths or of no faith must lead to dialogue. A Christian's dialogue with another implies neither a denial of the uniqueness of Christ, nor any loss of his own commitment to Christ, but rather that a genuinely Christian approach to others must be human, personal, relevant and humble. In dialogue we share our common humanity, its dignity and fallenness, and express our common concern for that humanity. It opens the possibility of sharing in new forms of community and common services. Each meets and challenges the other; witnessing from the depths of his existence to the ultimate concerns that come to expression in word and action. As Christians we believe that Christ speaks in this dialogue, revealing himself to those who do not know him and connecting the limited and distorted knowledge of those who know. Dialogue and proclamation are not the same. The one complements the other in a total witness. But sometimes Christians are not able to engage either in open dialogue or proclamation. Witness is then a silent one of living the Christian life and suffering for Christ."[4]


II.


A consultation on "<u>Dialogue between Men of Living Faiths</u>" at Ajaltoun, Lebanon, 16-25 March, 1970, under the auspices of the WCC, brought together members of four living faiths: Buddhists, Christians, Hindus and Muslims. The emphasis of the conversations was primarily on the experience of dialogue itself rather than on academic discussion about its nature and purpose. Questions of inter-religious dialogue of human beings and their temporal and ultimate destiny in the context of the struggle for world community and increasing inter-religious contacts were explored. Recognizing that a formal statement would be inadequate to express an experience that was so new, varied, and tentative, the consultation requested four of its members - to write their personal reflections, which are included in the Memorandum.

A Hindu stated: "Dialogue is for the sake of man, to help recover his religious sense in the modern world <u>vis-à-vis</u> its anti-religious forces. To recover one's religious meaning is, among other things to detect in oneself sources of irreligion, precisely in one's feeling of complacency and self-sufficiency about one's religious beliefs. Dialogue can be effective, as perhaps nothing else, in helping one recover from being lost, religiously speaking to the sense of self-assurance or adequacy or completeness."

A Buddhist said: "... We found that the semantic problem of terminology peculiar to each faith, was a major factor that hindered a more fruitful dialogue. We also keenly felt that in the consultation, particularly in specialized group sessions, it was structured in a manner of one-way traffic in that, our Christian brethren had the opportunity of knowing and sharing more about Buddhism and the opportunity afforded to Buddhists to know about Christianity was not as much as we desired. We would have preferred had it been a two-way traffic."

A Muslim asserted: "We have thought of what we should look for beyond these days. For my part our onward duties, mutual and separate, mean that we shall see faiths-in-relation as the deep test of faith itself. Whether we take it as paradox, or transcendental unity, or merely culture, the fact of our contrasts is the arena of our integrity. That test is set in the singleness and urgency of our contemporary humanity. We have to refuse the temptation to immunize faith from the tensions of the actual world..."

A Christian finally made the following observations: "By the very fact that we lived together, over these nine days, shared our common religious concern, and also prayed together, we were made to feel something new, something which cannot be put into words except that we were all too small before God, too small to dispute Him among ourselves, and that we had just to surrender, kneel down, and pray. This was the internal sign of the dialogue what it did to us in our deep inside, and its consequence, many of us were led to feel that we are talking too much about God. This feeling tended to blunt the sharpness of our theological differences, and helped us to enter into a realm of ambiguity, as one participant remarked, which was creative on both the occasions when we prayed together, when we talked.

"Out of this creative ambiguity arose, as it were, an existential ambiguity linking us all in some deep sense of fellowship intensifying on one side our respective identities as related to different religious backgrounds and on the other bringing them into a relation that was not experienced before. To most of us the 'other' faith was, before we actually met, an abstraction or just a different faith about which we knew less or more. But as we met, we became aware of a new situation, a kind of personal encounter, unfolding between us and within our common humanity which was, to translate it into religious terms, our common need of God..."5

III.

A consultation, held at Zürich, 20-23 May, 1970, on "Christians in Dialogue with Men of Other Faiths", in which Orthodox, Protestant and Roman Catholic Christians participated, wished to give a theological evaluation of the Ajaltoun consultation. It heard papers by S.J. Samartha on "More than an Encounter of Commitments" and David E. Jenkins on "Commitment and Openness". It also produced an Aide-mémoire from which the following paragraphs are quoted: "... Like proclamation, dialogue is a means of communication. Both are open to abuse and ineffectiveness. Dialogue may degenerate into sophistic intellectualism or the dilution of all conviction for the sake of a false harmony. It may result in the enrichment of all, in the discovery of new dimensions of truth, or merely lead to sterile confusions and unresolved conflicts. At any rate the objective of dialogue is not a superficial consensus or the finding of the greatest common factor. It aims at the expression of love which alone makes truth creative. Love is always vulnerable. But in love there is no room for fear. Genuine love is mutually transforming. Dialogue thus involves the risk of one partner being changed by the other. The desire for false security in ghetto communities or for continuing in one-way patterns of mission betrays both fear and arrogance and therefore the absence of love... True dialogue is a progressive and cumulative process, in which communities shed their fear and distrust of each other, enter into a living together in dialogue. It is thus a dynamic contact of life with life, transforming each other and growing together.

"... There are those Christians who fear that dialogue with men of other faiths is a betrayal of mission. Conversely, there are men of other faiths who suspect that dialogue is simply a new tool for mission. If the fears of such Christians are to be allayed it would seem that the suspicions of men of other faiths are to be justified. We suggest, however, that there is an understanding of mission which neither betrays the commitment of the Christian nor exploits the confidence and the reality of men of other faiths.

"Clearly we are only at the beginning of exploring a new dimension and possibility in the Church's life and mission in the world. We must seek to be as realistic about the dangers as about the promises. Nothing in the Christian faith suggests that there is creativity without risk or newness without suffering. Our hope lies in the continuing work of the Holy Spirit in judgement, mercy and new creation. Christians must surely show great boldness in exploring ways forward to community, communication and communion between men at both the local and the world level. All the circumstances of human life on the globe at this present stage force upon us the search for a world community in which men can share and act together..."6

The Central Committee meeting at Addis Ababa in 1971 issued "An Interim Policy Statement and Guidelines" on the World Council of Churches and Dialogue with Men of Other Faiths and Ideologies. This statement includes a preamble, points to be noted, issues to be studied, and recommendations. The following major questions were raised: What are the fundamental theological implications of dialogue? What is the relation between dialogue, mission, and witness ? How is dialogue to be understood and practiced in the context of indigenization ? The recommendations included actions the member churches should undertake in educational areas, the holding of courses at the Ecumenical Institute in Bossey, the organization and sponsoring of various consultations on different subjects and selective participation in world religious meetings.7

Two papers were presented to the Central Committee at Addis Ababa, "Christianity in a Pluralistic World - the Economy of the Holy Spirit" by Metropolitan George Khodr, and "Dialogue as a Continuing Christian Concern" by Stanley J. Samartha.8 The sentence in G. Khodr's address: "Christ is everywhere hidden in the mystery of his lowliness... It is Christ alone who is received as light when grace visits a Brahman, a Buddhist or a Moslem reading their own Scriptures", received much criticism.

S.J. Samartha responded to the misgivings on common worship shared by people of all faiths at the Ajaltoun consultation. "The question of worship in dialogue must not be misunderstood. Christian worship is a corporate act of the Church adoring God through Jesus Christ and cannot be confused with the prayers and meditations of other religions... The aim of being present during the worship of particular religions was to go beyond the theological ideas and to open ourselves and others to the deeper dimensions of religious symbolism."

He expressed himself in the following words on the problem of dialogue in the Bible: "It is sometimes said that the word 'dialogue' is not found in the Bible and that, therefore, it lacks biblical authority. However, there are quite a few words in the contemporary ecumenical vocabulary which also are not found in the Bible. It has already been said that by dialogue we do not mean just detached, intellectual discourse. While the noun 'dialogue' itself is not found in the Bible, the warm relationships and the intense personal encounters suggested by the active verb are very much in evidence throughout the Bible. God's dealing with his people and the nations, the very relationship and obligations implied in the covenant both with Noah and with Abraham, the work of kings and judges, of prophets and priests, the book of Job, the writings of the prophets and some of the Psalms where people talk back and forth to God - surely these do not suggest a one way traffic of monologues from on high.

"In the New Testament too, where we see different ways in which our Lord deals with people, the way of dialogue is not contrary to the spirit in which he dealt with Nicodemus, the Samaritan woman, the Centurion, and his own disciples throughout his ministry. There are occasions, of course, when he refuses to be drawn into discussions and when his presence divides people and, therefore, one should not overdo this and claim that everything in the Bible is dialogue. But the Bible gives considerable support to those who do not wish to be theological bull-dozers trying to push through the jungle of religions, and seeking to flatten mountains of ideologies."9

Father Paul Verghese, who took an active part in the reflections and discussions at the Addis Ababa meeting in 1971, asserted in "Christ and All Men - A Personal Statement on the Relationship between Christians and Adherents of Other Religions" "I believe that God's saving power is operative outside the limits of the (Christian) community also, though it is more difficult to pinpoint or locate the working of that saving power. I am convinced that in the final denouement, when the results of God's saving action in Christ are fully manifested, many people of other religions will be seen to benefit more from the redemption in Christ than even the vast majority of baptized members of the Christian churches."10

In a Report of the Discussions by John Deschner, included in the Study Reports and Documents of the Faith and Order Commission meeting at Louvain in 1971, the following was stated: "In a crucial shift of accent, Section II (The Unity of the Church and the Encounter with Living Faiths - English-speaking section) took 'dialogue', not 'encounter' as its focal concept. Contexts and motives for dialogue were appraised: to Christianize, to find common ground, to express Christian love (here a discussion of the distinction between a crusading and a crucified mind). Theological issues were raised: Is encounter with other faiths an encounter 'in Christ'? Does God reveal himself outside the specific stream of Christian history ? Must Christians believe other faiths contain authentic revelation before true dialogue can begin (sharp divisions here)? Can there be a positive and creative Christian meaning for 'syncretism', or does that word indicate the decisive threat in dialogue ? How can the particularity of Christian faith be claimed as the basis for mankind's unity amidst other religious and ideological claims of a similar kind ?

"The striking thing about this section's work was its readiness to let new ground be broken for Faith and Order thinking. As a discussion of the problem of Christianity and other religions it may offer little that is original. But in its insistence that Faith and Order thinking about <u>Christian</u> unity must embrace <u>this</u> problematic; in its acknowledgment that the problem is not merely man's disunities and the unity of the Church, but church unity amidst a number of religious claims to unity; in its openness to the question whether 'dialogue' is not a different but important and valid aspect of Christian witness and 'proclamation', with the obvious implications for how we understand mission - in these ways, at least, this section contributed to the enrichment of our study of church unity."[11]

At the next meeting of the Commission on Faith and Order at Accra in 1974 the following questions were raised by John Deschner in "<u>The Unity of the Church and the Unity of Mankind.An Appraisal of the Study</u>": "... Has our work on the authority of the Old Testament yet begun to probe the implications of the fact - immediately apparent in our work on <u>inter-religious dialogue</u> - that these writings are also authoritative scripture for Jews and Muslims ? For that matter, have we yet really faced the question which our commitment to dialogue poses for our traditional concepts of preaching, proclamation, confession ? And does not our work on cultural <u>divisions</u> offer guidance for our "Giving account' study when it emphasizes the dialectical vitality of the Church's sign-character: how its sign for humankind must penetrate and then distinguish itself from the organic unities in which we live ?"[12]


IV.


A Christian-Muslim dialogue took place at Broumana, Lebanon, in 1972. Papers were presented by H.A. Mukti Ali, Paul Löffler, Mushir-ul-Haq, Imam Musa al-Sadre, Willem A. Bijlefeld, Ali Merad, Peter D. Latuihamallo, Zafar Ishaq Ansari, John B. Taylor, Ali E. Hillal Dessouki, and S.J. Samartha. In a Memorandum, "In

Search of Understanding and Cooperation", the following was
expressed on religious freedom: "We should be scrupulous about
our protection of religious liberty. This involves not only the
rights of any religious minority, but also the rights of each
individual. While we accept that both religious traditions have
a missionary vocation, proselytism should be avoided, whether by
a majority intent upon pressing a minority to conform, or whether
by a minority using economic or cultural inducements to swell
its ranks. It is especially unworthy to exploit the vulner-
ability of the uneducated, the sick and the young."

On revelation: "Some of us felt that in further exploration
of the experience of revelation in history and of God's guidance
in our own lives we should be more open to the inexhaustible
nature of the grace of God. We should also be more ready to bear
a feeling of estrangement from our fellowmen, even in our own
tradition, as we strive, perhaps indeed on their behalf, to
achieve a more critical self-awareness." On religion and society:
"Our involvement in society is part of our duty towards God.
Some Muslims and Christians can speak of being co-workers with
God in making history and in transforming society. We are aware
of how we are confronted in new ways with the issue of religion
in society. How far have our traditions failed our fellow men ?
How far do they hold new promise ? We work together for self-
critical re-evaluation of our roles and of our mutual relationships."13

V.

"Primal World-Views. Christian Involvement in Dialogue with
Traditional Thought Forms" was the subject of a consultation at
Ibadan, Nigeria, in September 1973. It was organized by the
Sub-unit on Dialogue with People of Living Faiths and Ideologies,
the All Africa Conference of Churches and the Theological Education Fund. The word 'primal' was preferred to the term 'tribal'.
The hope was expressed that follow-ups will take place in those
parts of Asia and Oceania where Christians are influenced by
primal world-views. There were three Group Reports: A. Man
(1. Man-in-relation; 2. Man in relation to tradition; 3. Man,
myth and symbols; 4. Man in relation to nature; 5. Man and
divine presence; 6. Man's freedom). B. Community (Solidarity
and alienation; 2. Christ and community; 3. Church and community). C. Healing (1. Sickness and healing; 2. Biblical insights; 3. Suggestions for continuing discussion on healing).14

A second multilateral dialogue took place at Colombo, Sri
Lanka, 17-26 April, 1974, bringing together people of five
different faiths, on the theme, "Towards World Community: Resources and Responsibilities for Living Together". Papers were
presented by K. Sivaraman, Shemaryahu Talmon, Anastasios Yannou-
latos, Mushir-ul-Haq, Serajul Haque, H.A. Mukti Ali, L.G.Hewage,
John Francis. Critical reflections were made by: K.R. Sundara-
rajan, D.C. Mulder, Mohamed Talbi, Hans-Jochen Margull, Aloysius
Pieris, S.J. Samartha. "World community" was not regarded as a

"super-organization", but rather as a matter of interdependence,
the quality of mutual relationships and working together for
immediate goals.

The Memorandum of the Colombo consultation includes the
following headings:  I. "Towards World Community" (Multilateral
Dialogue; Provisional Approach to World Community; Structures
towards World Community).  II. "Resources  for Living Together"
(Obstacles to our Search for World Community; Possibilities of
Finding Common Resources; The Sharing of Distinctive Resources;
Dialogue as One of the Resources for World Community; Yardsticks
for Religious and Ideological Resources).  III. "Responsibilities
for Living Together" (Responsibility to Overcome Barriers; Common
Commitment to Reconstruct Community; Ways of Working Together);
Recommendations.

"In facing the crisis of the future, there are five aspects
that need to be examined more carefully:
1) the re-ordering of the relationship between the developed
and the developing countries (radical and effective redistri-
bution of power and resources including the reallocation of
access to science and technology) while striving towards a new
form of society;
2) the crisis of development within both developed and
developing nations;
3) the phenomenon of violence in the struggle for liberation
and social change;
4) the internal crisis in newly formed states - where people
are grappling with the problems of nationalism, regionalism,
linguistic exclusiveness and communalism;
5) the emergence of new models of society and their impact
upon the fate and the role of religion.

"We feel that enough resources exist in each religious
tradition to strengthen the intuitive longing for world community.
While respecting the peculiar sources that are valid for only one
group or the other and which need to be spelled out in greater
detail, we note with gratitude common elements in our religions
that promote life-in-community."[15]

"The Conference on World Cooperation for Development", at
Beirut, in 1968, sponsored by the Exploratory Committee on Society, Development and Peace, urged Christians to undertake a
wider inter-religious collaboration in the matter of world
development: "We recognize that in many of the developing countries, the Christian effort, to be effective, requires a joint
action  with men of other faiths.  Christians are urged to
undertake this wider inter-religious collaboration.  It points
the way to an extension of the spirit of collaboration, drawing
together all the world's religions in common policies for the
betterment of mankind.  We aim at this wider cooperation while
attempting to establish full ecumenical understanding between
Christians."[16]

## VI

"Jewish-Christian Dialogue: Six Years of Christian-Jewish Consultations" includes an account of various meetings, essays by Uriel Tal, Shemaryahu Talmon, Norman Lamm, Krister Stendahl, and a summary of five contributions (Aaron Tolen, Rudolf Weth, Krister Stendahl, Robert Martin-Achard, André Dumas) by Ellen Flesseman-van Leer. In addition to previous consultations in 1962, 1965, 1968, 1969, a consultation of Jews and Christians was held at Lugano, 27-30 October, 1970, which discussed the theme "The Quest for World Community: Jewish and Christian Perspectives". Another consultation on the theme, "Biblical Interpretation and its Bearing on Christian Attitudes Regarding the Middle East", was held at Cartigny, Switzerland, 21-25 January 1974.

In "The Christian-Jewish Dialogue: An Account by the World Council of Churches" the following was stated: "... One expression of the ongoing WCC interest in questions related to Jewish-Christian relations was the study on "The Church and the Jewish People", jointly undertaken by the Faith and Order Commission and the WCC Committee on the Church and the Jewish People (1964-1967). This study emphasizes that "Christian and Jewish faiths share also a common hope" (the world and its history are being led by God to full realization and manifestation of his Kingdom), that "an ongoing encounter with Jews can mean a real enrichment of our faith."

"Christians should therefore be alert to every such possibility, both in the field of social cooperation and especially on the deeper level of theological discussion." At this point for the first time in the ecumenical discussion the term 'dialogue' with Jews is used and defined: "... such conversation... should be held in a spirit of mutual respect and openness, searching together and questioning one another, trusting that we together with the Jews will grow into a deeper understanding of the revelation of the God of Abraham, Isaac and Jacob. What form this understanding may take we must be willing to leave in His hand, confident that He will lead both Jews and Christians into the fullness of His truth."[17]

Six other consultations of Jews and Christians were held at London, 13-16 January, 1975, on "The Concept of Power in Jewish and Christian Traditions"; at Sigtuna, Sweden, June 1975, on "Jewish and Christian Worship"; at Zürich, 20-23 February, 1977 on "Jewish and Christian Traditions Concerning Nature, Science and Technology"; at Jerusalem, 16-26 June, 1977 on "Christian-Jewish Relations in Ecumenical Perspectives"; at Toronto, September 1980 on "Religion and the Crisis of Modernity"; at Boston, November 1984 on "Religious Pluralism".

"Christians Meeting Muslims" includes papers on ten years of Christian-Muslim dialogue from 1966-1976.[18] From 1974 onwards consultations took place at Legon, Ghana, 17-21 July, 1974 on

"The Unity of God and the Community of Mankind. Cooperation between African Muslims and African Christians in Work and Witness";
Hong Kong, 4-10 January, 1975 on "Mulims and Christians in Society. Towards Goodwill, Consultation and Working Together in
South-East Asia"; Chambesy, Switzerland, 26-30 June, 1976 on
"Christian Mission and Islamic Da'wah"; at Beirut, November 1977
on "Faith, Science and Technology and the Future of Humanity";
at Colombo, 20 March - 5 April, 1982 on "Christians and Muslims
Living and Working Together: Ethics and Practices of Humanitarian
and Development Programmes".


VII.


    At the Fifth WCC Assembly in Nairobi in 1975, Section III
was devoted to the theme, "Seeking Community: The Common Search
of People of Various Faiths, Cultures and Ideologies". As several objections were voiced - particular that the text would be
understood as a spiritual compromise or as opposition to the
mission of the Church - the Report was referred back to the
Section for reconsideration. A preamble to the document was
then added in which agreement was expressed that "the skandalon
(stumbling block) of the gospel will always be with us...", that
"the Great Commission of Jesus Christ which asks us to go out
into all the world and make disciples of all nations, and to
baptize them in the Triune Name, should not be abandoned or
betrayed, disobeyed or compromised...", and that "we are all
opposed to any form of syncretism, incipient, nascent or developed, if we mean by syncretism conscious or unconscious human
attempts to create a new religion composed of elements taken
from different religions.

    When the Report was re-introduced into the plenary of the
Assembly, Lynn A. de Silva, Director of a Study Centre in Colombo,
spoke out of his own experience of actual dialogue during many
years:
    "1. Dialogue does not in any way diminish full and loyal
commitment to one's own faith, but rather enriches and strength-
ens it...
    "2. Dialogue, far from being a temptation to syncretism, is
a safeguard against it, because in dialogue we get to know one
another's faith in depth. One's own faith is tested and refined
and sharpened thereby...
    "3. Dialogue is a creative interaction which liberates a
person from a closed or cloistered system to which he happens
to belong by an accident of birth, and elevates him to spiritual
freedom...
    "4. Dialogue is urgent and essential for us in Asia in order
to repudiate the arrogance, aggression, and negativism of our
evangelistic crusades which have obscured the gospel and cari-
catured Christianity as an aggressive and militant religion...
Jesus Christ was not a Christian - he belongs to all - but we
have made him appear as a Western Christian of an affluent society, somewhat like a Julius Caesar.

"5. Dialogue is essential to dispel the negative attitude
we have to people of other faiths, which makes proclamation ineffective and irrelevant. A negative attitude invites a negative
response; if we are not prepared to accept the others in love
they will not accept us... Above all, dialogue is essential for
us to discover the Asian face of Jesus Christ, as the Suffering
Servant, so that the Church itself may be set free from its
institutional self-interest and play the role of a servant in
building community - the community of love or the kingdom of God."

The recommendations to the churches of Section III are on:
Preparations within the churches; The search for community; Involvement in Dialogue; Sharing in Spirituality; Ecumenical Reflections about Faiths, Cultures and Ideologies; Requisite church
structures. It was noted that "living-in-dialogue may often be
more important than organized dialogue. Organized or occasional
dialogue may lead to a situation of living-in-dialogue, where
religious communities may seek to resolve conflicts arising between them in an atmosphere of mutual trust and peaceful negotiations."19

VIII.

"Dialogue in Community" was the overall theme of a large
consultation at Chiang Mai, Thailand, 18-27 April, 1977, in which
85 people from 36 countries participated. The notion of the
unity of humankind, of a world community as a community of communities was clarified, as well as the relation between dialogue
and witness and the issue of syncretism. The Report contains
contributions by P. Löffler, R. Friedli, J. Deschner, E. Mveng,
W. Ariarajah, N. Zabolotsky, Y. Raguin, M. Brown, H. Ott, P. Sud-
hakar, P. Nontawasee, L.O. Sanneh, R. Zander; Bible studies by
C. Barth, B.J. Nicholls, K. Stendahl, K. Opoku; Concluding reflections by P. Rossano, G. Cashmore, T.K. Thomas, S.J. Samartha.

The Statement adopted by the consultation has the following
parts: I. On Community (A. Communities and the community of
humankind; B. The Christian Community. The Churches and the
Church); II. On Dialogue (C. Reasons for dialogue; D. The
theological significance of peoples of other faiths and ideologies; E. Syncretism); III. Group Report A: Christian-Jewish-
Muslim Relations; Group Report B: Christian-Buddhist-Hindu
Relations; Group Report C: Christian Concern in Traditional
Religions and Cultures; Group Report D: Ideologies.

In the introduction to the Statement it was asked: "Why the
theme 'Dialogue in Community'? As the work of the sub-unit on
Dialogue with People of Living Faiths and Ideologies has developed, emphasis has come to be placed not so much on dialogue itself
as on dialogue in community. The Christian community within the
human community has a common heritage and a distinctive message
to share; it needs therefore to reflect on the nature of the
community that we as Christians seek and on the relation of dialogue to the life of the churches, as they ask themselves how
they can be communities of service and witness without diluting

their faith or compromising their commitment to Christ. Such an enquiry needs to be informed both by a knowlegde of different religions and societies and by insights gained through actual dialogues with neighbours..."20

IX.

Parts I and II of "Guidelines on Dialogue with People of Living Faiths and Ideologies" were received by the Central Committee at its meeting in Geneva, August 1977. Part III was adopted at its meeting in Kingston, Jamaica, January 1979. The content of the document is: I. On Community (A. Communities and the community of humankind; B. The Christian community: The churches and the Church). II. On Dialogue (C. Reasons for Dialogue; D. The theological significance of people of other faiths and ideologies; E. Syncretism). III. Guidelines recommended to the churches for study and action.

The document ends with the following bold statement: "To enter into dialogue requires an opening of the mind and heart to others. It is an undertaking which requires risk as well as a deep sense of vocation. It is impossible without sensitivity to the richly varied life of humankind. This opening, this risk, this vocation, this sensitivity are at the heart of the ecumenical movement and in the deepest currents of the life of the churches. It is therefore with a commitment to the importance of dialogue for the member churches of the WCC that the Central Committee offers this Statement and these Guidelines to the churches."21

In 1983 "Ecumenical Considerations on Jewish-Christian Dialogue" was published by the WCC. It deals with: Towards a Christian Understanding of Jews and Judaism, Hatred and Persecution of Jews - A Continuing Concern, Authentic Christian Witness. At the end of this document it was stated: "As Christians of different traditions enter into dialogue with Jews in local, national, and international situations, they will come to express their understanding of Judaism in other language, style, and ways than has been done in these Ecumenical Considerations. Such understandings are to be shared among the churches for enrichment of all."22

The Report of the WCC Conference on Faith, Science and the Future, at Cambridge, Mass., 1979, contains a section report on "The Christian Understanding of God, Humanity and Nature in Relation to Neighbours of Other Faiths." "... The encounter with other religions sharpens our awareness that the dominant occidental view of the relationships of humanity, nature and God is not the only viable one. Some of the views of other religions may prove both closer to the Bible and more appropriate to the intellectual and social needs of our time. This means that learning from neighbours of other faiths can lead to a valuable enrichment of our understanding of the Bible and to a fruitful reformulation of our theology.

"Among the achievements of some of our neighbours of other faiths to which we should attend are the following: a deep piety and obedience to a merciful God who is close to the faithful; the awareness of the interconnectedness of all things, the emphasis on the transient character of all existence, stressing continuities instead of discontinuities and eventuating in serenity, calmness and acceptance of suffering as part of life; the spirit of non-attachment, the ability to find oneself by letting go of material possessions; acting according to the principle of causing least harm and disturbance to all creation.

"Though all these may be found in our Christian tradition, we do not gain credibility by asserting in a triumphalistic manner that we ourselves already possess everything. We can only be credible witnesses to our faith if we are on the 'way' (Acts 18: 24 ff) towards God's future. If we listen, other religions remind us of our blind spots and insights we may have lost on our journey. We need this help in our efforts properly to understand humanity, nature and God in our shared struggle for a just, participatory and sustainable society..."[23]


X.


In March 1972 at Geneva, Christians, Buddhists, and Cao Daists discussed the theme "Christian and Buddhist Contributions for the Renewal of Society in Vietnam". At Colombo, Sri Lanka, February 1978, a group of Buddhists and Christians discussed the question of the religious dimensions in humanity's relation to nature at a time when science and technology dominate human life. The general theme was "Man in Nature: Guest or Engineer ?" Papers were read by L. de Silva, H. Crusz, M. Palihawadana, S. Patumtevapibal, D.L. Gosling, A.D.P. Kalansuriya, T. Ling, P. de Silva, W. Strolz. The consultation also published an aide-mémoire.[24]

"Religious Resources for a Just Society" was the theme of a consultation at Rajpur, North India, 30 May - 6 June, 1981, which brought together for the first time Christians and Hindus from areas of the world where people of these two religious traditions live together in great numbers. Participants included theologians, philosophers, spiritual leaders, pastors and social workers, who brought different dimensions to the quest for social justice.[25]

"The Role of the Study Centres" was the subject of discussion of three consultations that took place at Kandy, Sri Lanka (March 1967); Hong Kong (1971); and Singapore (December 1980). The first consultation explored issues in dialogue with neighbours of living faiths.[26] The second consultation discussed and elaborated further the role of the study centres in dialogue. The Report of the Singapore consultation includes: I. Our Basic Convictions Concerning the Mission of the Church; II. The Vocation of Study Centres; III. The Actual Tasks of Study Centres; IV. Instruments for Research and their Inter-Relationships; V. Issues and Problems of Financial Support; VI. Fellowship of Christian Study Centres.

At the Sixth Assembly of the Christian Conference of Asia at Penang, Malaysia, 31 May - 9 June, 1977, the following was expressed on the nature of dialogue. "Dialogue is a form of communication between two persons or different groups who adhere to different religious beliefs or ideological systems. Dialogue takes place at all levels. When a Christian lives in a Hindu society, for instance, he or she carries a 'dialogue' within himself of herself. Two persons or more can have dialogue on the personal level. There can be dialogue between groups and communities. It can take place on an intellectual and also at a political level. In dialogue there are present dimensions of encounter, mutual transformation, and even of critical relationships. We want to understand dialogue in this broad sense and as taking place at all levels."[27]

Section II, "Living in Christ with People: A Call to Community", of the Seventh Assembly of the Christian Conference of Asia at Bangalore, 18-28 May, 1981, stated: "... It is in obedience to the call of Jesus Christ that we enter into dialogue with people of living faiths and ideologies. Any enterprise to enter that dialogue is justified, if we base it upon Jesus Christ, the Incarnate God, who through His life, death and resurrection, makes people and community more human. In this light, dialogue is a recognition of our common humanity. The call to dialogue is a call to discover and appropriate our rich mutuality. It is by thus realizing our togetherness that we further it and grow in community. As a matter of fact, we are not quite satisfied with the term 'dialogue', as it gives the impression of mutual interchange of ideas and beliefs more on the intellectual level. We need a more suitable word which can convey the sense of mutual cooperation between people of living faiths and ideologies in coping with social evils in concrete measures for building truly human communities."[28]

A multifaith consultation in preparation for the Sixth WCC Assembly was held in Mauritius, 25 January - 3 February, 1983. Its theme was "The Meaning of Life". The four sub-themes and eight issues of the Vancouver Assembly were also discussed. The consultation issues a Message to Assembly Delegates.[29]

Issue I. "Witnessing in a Divided World" of the Sixth Assembly at Vancouver in 1983 contained a sub-section on "Special Areas of Concern: Witnessing among People of Living Faiths." The whole Issue was criticized by several speakers as lacking imput from recent WCC work on mission and evangelism, as too negative in speaking of the work of missionaries, as lacking a more scriptural approach. The report was sent back to the Issue Group for reworking. A revised version reached the plenary on the last day of the Assembly, but the pressure of time made this one of several pieces of unfinished business that were referred to the new Central Committee, which approved the substance of the revised report.

Perhaps the debate would have taken a better turn if an introduction had been added to the original document stating that "the starting point for our thinking is Jesus Christ" and that "Christians are called to witness to Christ in all ages; in each generation we are called to examine the nature of our witness." This litany must be heard over and over again if the concern for dialogue is to find an appropriate place in the debate on the missionary obligation of the Church.

In the sentence, "While affirming the uniqueness of the birth, life, death and resurrection of Jesus, to which we bear witness, we recognize God's creative work in the religious experience of people of other faiths", the words 'religious experience' were replaced by 'the seeking for religious truth'. This small change in wording is a clear indication that the period of fifteen years of ecumenical dialogue with people of living faiths has been moving forwards and backwards, because all 'non-Christians' in the judgment of many Christians are only searching for the truth, but never experience a glimpse of it, unless they are converted to the Christian faith.

The solemn admonishment to Christians that they are prone "to attribute to their own religious and cultural identity an absolute authority and to exclude others from their community"[30] is deceiving and hollow. The irrelevance of this exhortation is even more embarrassing in view of the fact that three times as many distinguished guests of other faiths were invited to the Vancouver Assembly than to the Nairobi Assembly. They played at the most a token role of strange but tolerated participants. Their official speeches in one plenary session were limited to three minutes. In the Visitors' and Public programmes, they spoke frequently to large audiences.


## Observations and Comments

1. The real break-through in the dialogue with various people in our pluralistic and multi-religious world took place in the late sixties and the early seventies. The statements issued and the convictions and concerns expressed during this period witness to the deep sensitivity and the daring insight of theologians and lay people, and have laid the basis for ongoing ecumenical reflection and activity in the realm of interfaith dialogue. As the Christian Conference of Asia stated, the word 'dialogue' does actually not cover the means of a common search for a new humanity and an ultimate salvation.

2. A more concerted ecumenical effort must be made to win many (conservative) evangelical Christians over to the 'dialogical Jesus' of the gospels. This is a tedious process. In his teachings and healing Jesus is the unique man of person-to-person dialogue. His dialogical approach to people is without parallel in Judaism of his time. In all encounters with Jesus his interlocuters are there in their justice, the publicans and sinners with their guilt, the scribes with their burden of doctrine, the sick, the poor and those possessed of a devil with the origins and consequences of their misery. Jesus compels

them to come simply out of themselves without any fear or reserve and experience his healing and forgiveness. In evangelistic campaigns people are called to come forward and commit their lives to Christ. Jesus, however, does not require a spectacular and convulsive conversion. His people experience great joy and freedom. "Neither do I condemn you; go, and do not sin again" (John 8:11). "Daughter, your faith has made you well; go in peace"(Luke 8:48). The emphasis is on the 'go', not on the 'come'.

3. The educational process of mission in dialogue and dialogue in mission must be propelled at all levels in order that a section on Christian witness and human dialogue at a next assembly of the WCC does not bog down again and many churches and their faithful 'in mission' remain adolescent and in disarray. Dialogue is as much a continuous practice of human solidarity and love as a faithful exercise in converting the other to Jesus Christ. It is only in dialogue that we can share the suffering, the aimlessness, and the hopelessness of our fellow human beings.

The problem of syncretism must be shelved at last because many interreligious dialogues have amply proved that humanity is not on its way to produce a syncretistic world religion, a new normative faith for all members of the world community. Such a combined faith is not only a poor alternative to religious search for truth and an impoverishment of the human race, but it is strongly resisted by any religion defending its own spiritual integrity.

4. Reference has been made to the function and role of study centres. Their tasks are numerous and vital. But the dialogue between people of various faiths can no longer be limited to a few institutes for dialogue and some religious experts. The curricula of many theological faculties and seminaries need to be thoroughly updated. Still the comparative study of world religions and Religionsgeschichte is taught. Students remain ignorant of issues and trends in the dialogue with people of living faiths. They have little knowledge of the contemporary ecumenical literature. The reading and the interpretation of the Qu'ran and other holy scriptures of world religions should be part of several required courses in order to gain a more intimate knowledge of living faiths by which millions of people live and die.

Most new Christian catechisms and religious instruction books have no section, not even a page, on the basic beliefs of neighbours. A vast majority of Christians do not gain insight in the spirituality and ethics of others. Unless Christians, young and old, can contrive intelligently and spiritually to be faithful not merely in a Christian society or a secular society, but in the world, in which there are other intelligent, sensitive and educated believers, it makes little sense to be a Christian at all. The concern for dialogue with people of living faiths needs to be translated, introduced, popularized on the level of local congregations, in order that they attain true Christian maturity. This is a particularly urgent task of education and conscientization.

"For all God's People - Ecumenical Prayer Cycle" contains week 43, which outlines prayers of intercession for those who profess other faiths or no faith at all. "They too are our brothers and sisters. For them, too, we intercede in the name of him whose compassion embraces all." We have to repent and to acknowledge "that we Christians bear part responsibility for the misunderstandings of years gone by."[31] How many local Christian congregations do pray for other believers in their own city, nation, and in the world ? How can pastors and priests communicate to their parish that Christianity is not the only true religion while all other religions are false and pointless, that there is much in all religions - including Christianity - that is impersonal, static, and absolute, and that true experiences of salvation can only be expressed in personal and dynamic religion that has living - and dying - quality ? The people of God in adoration and intercession need not only to plead _for_ the world, but _in_ the world and _with_ the world for the overcoming of its fatal divisions, biases and rancours.

5.  In regions, such as the Middle East, the advocacy of religious liberty is ever more of crucial importance. Judaism, Christianity, and Islam - all three monotheistic religions are guilty of violating the conscience of people of other faiths. All citizens, and not just a privileged majority or minority, are to enjoy personal rights and religious freedom and to be immune from coercion on the part of individuals or of social groups or of any state power. War, terrorism, and murder are the utter perversion of any religion. Lasting peace will only be attained when all world religions openly declare that religious liberty is a most basic human right. No true democracy can be established when the manifestation of any religion in teaching, practice, worship, and observance is denied. The denial leads in fact to inhuman superiority, ugly oppression, blatant racism, and horrible homicide. All fanaticism in religion is worse and more destructive than fanaticism in politics or ideology. After several centuries of Christian domination over many parts of the world, churches cannot but give the example of practizing religious liberty and encourage other religious communities to acknowledge that same God-given freedom.

6.  For almost fifteen years the WCC has been unable to explore the relationships of "Unity of the Church" to the "Unity of Humankind" and to the "Renewal of Human Community" in depth. Programmatic cooperation of the sub-unit on Dialogue with the Commission on Faith and Order is indispensable, but the "Nairobi to Vancouver Report" on the DFI activities stated that"unfortunately no programmatic cooperation has yet been planned..."[32] The reason for this is the belief that the growing unity of the Church will automatically radiate and magically influence the renewal of other religious and secular communities. There is, however, no promise of unity of the Church in its confession of faith, in its sacramental life, and in its pastoral care, if agonizing and yearning peoples are not already part of

that unity. If the oneness of the Church is not unconditionally linked to the quality of a new human community in Christ, the Church only continues to manifest a pseudo-unity.

The ecumenical movement will only be able to admit that the divisions and conflicts in the churches mirror to a great extent the divisions and conflicts in the multireligious and secular world, when the dialogue with people of living faiths and secular convictions is intensively practised at all levels. It is in this dialogue that Christians can proclaim that the potential unity of the world, in the midst of its enmities and brokenness, and the urgent renewal of the Church, are parts of the same goal of God's universal salvation.

It is in this dialogue that Christians can stress that the sacramental Church is but a function of human community until the kingdom of God arrives. Baptism, eucharist, and ministry are only meaningful in the very conflicts of racism, classism and sexism. It is in this dialogue that the Church lives from the hopefulness of solidarity in sin and the praise of God's forgiveness. In this dialogue its strength is marvellously initiating and its love unexpectedly enabling. The systematic and concentrated preoccupation with the dialogue with people of living faiths and ideologies, the unity of the Church and the renewal of human community will inaugurate another ecumenical era, in which joy and hope will triumph over introspection, fear and exasperation.

7. Various plans are made in the WCC and elsewhere to explore and to spell out the theological significance of other contemporary faiths. It is of great importance that this enterprise does not begin and end, as in the past, with the analysis, comparison and evaluation of different systems of belief and doctrine. Any faith is only living and meaningful when it is a faith of a people, that is a community of human beings who live their daily life in suffering and joy; who tell their stories of defeat and hope in music, dance, poetry and drama; who practice kindness, patience and humility towards their neighbours; who manifest the richness and the shortcomings of their own language, attitudes and symbols.

The WCC Sub-unit on Dialogue needs to be deeply drawn into the crucial concern of Christianity and culture. This ecumenical concern has been too exclusively discussed in the realms of World Mission and Evangelism, and has hardly been a subject of debate in Faith and Order. The document on "Baptism, Eucharist and Ministry" is deeply marked by Western cultural memory. It is in the actual dialogue with people of other living faiths that a deeper understanding of the meaning and function of culture and of its plurality, and a better understanding of the ways in which the gospel has interacted and still interacts with various cultures will be attained. The exploration of the theological significance of other faiths of living and dying quality is only possible when it is realized that listening to and the learning from cultures of people are an essential part of the sharing of the Christian message.

1) Living Faiths and the Ecumenical Movement, ed. by S.J. Samartha.  Geneva: WCC, 1971.  pp. 165-182.

2) Dialogue with People of Living Faiths and Ideologies. Minutes of the Fifth Meeting of the Working Group. Bali, Indonesia, Dec.-Jan. 1981/82.  pp. 72-78.

3) Study Encounter, vol III, No. 2, 1967.  pp. 53-55.

4) The Uppsala Report 1968, ed. by Norman Goodall. Geneva: WCC, 1968.  p. 29.

5) Dialogue between Men of Living Faiths. Papers presented at a consultation held at Ajaltoun, Lebanon, March 1970. Ed. by S.J. Samartha.  Geneva: WCC, 1971.  pp. 109-113.

6) Living Faiths and the Ecumenical Movement.  Ed. by S.J. Samartha.  Geneva: WCC, 1971.  pp. 34-43.

7) Central Committee of the World Council of Churches. Minutes and Reports of the Twenty-Fourth Meeting, Addis Ababa, Ethiopia, Jan. 10-21, 1971. Geneva: WCC, 1971.  pp. 130-135, 18-22.

8) The Ecumenical Review, Vol. XXIII, No. 2, April 1971. pp. 118-142.

9) Ibid, p. 139.

10) Living Faiths and the Ecumenical Movement. Ed. by S.J. Samartha.  Geneva: WCC, 1971.  p. 163.

11) Faith and Order, Louvain 1971. Study Reports and Documents. Geneva: WCC, 1971 (Faith and Order Paper, No. 59). pp. 191-192.

12) Uniting in Hope. Reports and Documents from the Meeting of the Faith and Order Commission, 23 July - 5 August, 1974, University of Ghana, Legon.  Geneva: WCC, 1975 (Faith and Order Paper, No. 72).  pp. 86-87.

13) Christian-Muslim Dialogue. Papers presented at the Broumana Consultation, 12-18 July, 1972. Ed. by S.J. Samartha and J.B. Taylor.  Geneva: WCC, 1973.  pp. 151-161.

14) Primal World-Views. Christian Involvement in Dialogue with Traditional Thought Forms. Ed. by J.B. Taylor. Ibadan: Daystar Press, 1976.

15) Towards World Community. The Colombo Papers. Ed. by S.J. Samartha.  Geneva: WCC, 1975.  pp. 117-118, 121-122.

16) World Development - The Challenge to the Churches. The Conference on World Cooperation for Development, Beirut, Lebanon, 21-27 April, 1968. Geneva: SODEPAX, 1968.  p. 42.

17) Jewish-Christian Dialogue. Six Years of Christian-Jewish Consultations. The Quest for World Community: Jewish and Christian Perspectives. Published by the International Jewish Committee on Interreligious Consultations and the Sub-unit on Dialogue with People of Living Faiths and Ideologies. Geneva: WCC, 1975. p. 9.

18) Christians Meeting Muslims. WCC Papers on Ten Years of Christian-Muslim Dialogue. Geneva: WCC, 1977.

19) Breaking Barriers. Nairobi 1975. Ed. by David M. Paton. London: SPCK; Grand Rapids: Wm. B. Eerdmans, 1976. pp. 72, 73-85.

20) Faith in the Midst of Faiths. Reflections on Dialogue in Community. Ed. by S.J. Samartha. Geneva: WCC, 1977.

21) Guidelines on Dialogue with People of Living Faiths and Ideologies. Geneva: WCC, 1979.

22) Ecumenical Considerations on Jewish-Christian Dialogue. Geneva: WCC, 1983.

23) Faith and Science in an Unjust World. Report of the WCC Conference on Faith, Science and the Future, Massachusetts Institute of Technology, Cambridge, USA, 12-24 July 1979. Vol. 2: Reports and Recommendations. Ed. by Paul Abrecht. Geneva: WCC, 1980. pp. 35-36.

24) Man in Nature: Guest or Engineer ? Ed. by S.J. Samartha and L. de Silva. Published by the Ecumenical Institute for Study and Dialogue, Colombo, in cooperation with the WCC, 1979.

25) Religious Resources for a Just Society. A Hindu-Christian Dialogue. Geneva: WCC, 1981.

26) Study Encounter, vol. III, No. 2, 1967.

27) Christian Conference of Asia, Sixth Assembly, at Penang, Malaysia, 31 May - 9 June, 1977. Singapore: CCA, 1977. p. 95.

28) Christian Conference of Asia, Seventh Assembly, at Bangalore, India, 18-28 May, 1981. Singapore: CCA, 1981. p. 92.

29) The Meaning of Life - A Multifaith Consultation in preparation for the Sixth WCC Assembly, 25 January - 3 February, 1983 in Mauritius. Ed. by Allan R. Brockway. Geneva: WCC, 1983.

30) Gathered for Life. Official Report of the Sixth WCC Assembly, Vancouver, Canada, 24 July - 10 August, 1983. Ed. by David Gill. Geneva: WCC; Grand Rapids: Wm. B. Eerdmans, 1983. pp. 31, 40.

31) For all God's People - Ecumenical Prayer Cycle.
    Geneva: WCC, 1978.  p. 183.

32) Nairobi to Vancouver, 1975-1983. Report of the Central
    Committee to the Sixth Assembly of the World Council
    of Churches.  Geneva: WCC, 1983.  p. 114.

# IV.
# Church Unity


This survey includes excerpts of statements and of reports of major conferences and of a few consultations on church unity, unity experienced in the ecumenical movement, unity as God's gift, visible unity, non-theological factors of unity, uniformity and diversity in unity, the unity we seek, what unity implies, what unity requires. It does not include references to themes and concerns such as church union negotiations, bilateral dialogues, the week of prayer for Christian unity, the unity of the church and the renewal of human community, the unity of the church and the community of women and men in the church.


## I.


In the Message of the Amsterdam Assembly in 1948 it was stated: "... Here at Amsterdam we have committed ourselves afresh to Him, and have covenanted with one another in constituting this World Council of Churches. We intend to stay together. We call upon Christian congregations everywhere to endorse and fulfil this covenant in their relations one with another. In thankfulness to God we commit the future to Him."

Section I, "The Universal Church in God's Design", was divided into the following parts: I. Our Given Unity; II. Our Deepest Difference; III. Common Beliefs and Common Problems; IV. The Unity in Our Difference; V. The Glory of the Church and the Shame of the Churches; VI. The World Council of Churches. In the last part it was stated: "We thank God for the ecumenical movement because we believe it is a movement in the direction which He wills. It has helped us to recognize our unity in Christ. We acknowledge that He is powerfully at work amongst us to lead us further to goals which we but dimly discern. We do not fully understand some of the things He has already done amongst us or their implications for our familiar ways..."

With regard to our deepest difference the following was expressed: "It is in the light of that unity that we can face our deepest difference, still loving one another in Christ and walking by faith in Him alone. It has many forms and deep roots. It exists among many other differences of emphasis within Christendom. Some are Catholic or Orthodox in clearly-understood senses; some are Protestant after the great Reformation confessions; others stress the local congregation, the 'gathered community' and the idea of the 'free church'. Some are deeply convinced that Catholic and Protestant (or Evangelical) can be held together within a single church. Yet, from among these shades of meaning, we would draw special attention to a difference to which, by many paths, we are constantly brought back. Historically it has been loosely described as the difference between 'Catholic' and 'Protestant', though we have learned to mistrust any over-simple formula to describe it. The essence of our situation is that, from each side of the division, we see the Christian faith and life as a self-consistent whole, but our two conceptions of the whole are inconsistent with each other."

Concerning the shame of the churches the Section said clearly: "Within our divided churches, there is much which we confess with penitence before the Lord of the Church, for it is in our estrangement from Him that all our sin has its origin. It is because of this that the evils of the world have so deeply penetrated our churches, so that amongst us too there are worldly standards of success, class division, economic rivalry, a secular mind. Even where there are no differences of theology, language or liturgy, there exist churches segregated by race and colour, a scandal within the Body of Christ. We are in danger of being salt that has lost its savour and is fit for nothing..."[1]

Meeting at Toronto in 1950, the Central Committee issued a document on "The Church, the Churches and the World Council of Churches - The Ecclesiological Significance of the World Council of Churches". The document contained the following theses with regard to what the WCC is not:

1) The World Council of Churches is not and must never become a Super-Church.
2) The purpose of the World Council of Churches is not to negotiate unions between Churches, which can only be done by the Churches themselves acting on their own initiative, but to bring the Churches into living contact with each other and to promote the study and discussion of the issues of Church unity.
3) The World Council cannot and should not be based on any one particular conception of the Church. It does not prejudge the ecclesiological problem.
4) Membership in the World Council does not imply the acceptance of a specific doctrine concerning the nature of Church unity."

Concerning assumptions underlying the WCC the statement outlined the following theses:

1) The member Churches of the Council believe that conversation, cooperation and common witness of the Churches must be based on the common recognition that Christ is the Divine Head of the Body.
2) The member Churches of the World Council believe on the basis of the New Testament that the Church of Christ is one.
3) The member Churches recognize that the membership of the Church of Christ is more inclusive than the membership of their own Church-body. They seek, therefore, to enter into living contact with those outside their own ranks who confess the Lordship of Christ.

4) The member Churches of the World Council consider the relationship of other Churches to the Holy Catholic Church which the Creeds profess as a subject for mutual consideration. Nevertheless, membership does not imply that each Church must regard the other member Churches as Churches in the true and full sense of the word.

5. The member Churches of the World Council recognize in other Churches elements of the true Church. They consider that this mutual recognition obliges them to enter into a serious conversation with each other in the hope that these elements of truth will lead to the recognition of the full truth and to unity based on the full truth.

6) The member Churches of the Council are willing to consult together in seeking to learn of the Lord Jesus Christ what witness He would have them to bear to the world in His Name.

7) A further practical implication of common membership in the World Council is that member Churches should recognize their solidarity with each other, render assistance to each other in case of need, and refrain from such actions as are incompatible with brotherly relationships.

8) The member Churches enter into spiritual relationships through which they seek to learn from each other and to give help to each other in order that the Body of Christ may be built up and that the life of the Churches may be renewed."[2]


## II.

"Non-Theological Factors that May Hinder or Accelerate the Church's Unity" was the theme of a consultation at Bossey, November 6-12, 1951. A Report was issued on behalf of the Commission on Faith and Order to all churches participating in the Lund Conference in 1952. It is in four parts: I. The Urgency of Facing These Factors; II. Non-Theological Factors Causing and Perpetuating Divisions; III. Non-Theological Factors which Accentuate the Need for Unity; IV. What Can Be Done? Papers were presented by P. de Jong, J. Ellul, E.G. Léonard, G. Every, O. Weber.[3]

In a Word to the Churches the Third World Conference on Faith and Order at Lund in 1952 stated: "... We have seen clearly that we can make no real advance towards unity if we only compare our several conceptions of the nature of the Church and the traditions in which they are embodied. But once again it has been proved true that as we seek to draw closer to Christ we come closer to one another. We need, therefore, to penetrate behind our divisions to a deeper and richer understanding of the mystery of the God-given union of Christ with His Church. We need increasingly to realize that the separate histories of our Churches find their full meaning only if seen in the perspective of God's dealings with His whole people."

Chapter III, "Continuity and Unity", of the Lund Report was divided into the following parts:  I. The Unity of the Church as indicated in the New Testament;  II. Unity, Continuity and Discontinuity (1) The Unity of Christ and His Church; 2) The Nature of Continuity; 3) Discontinuity: a) Schism; b) Apostasy; c) Heresy);  III. Unity and Diversity (a) Personal faith in Jesus Christ; b) Consensus in doctrine; c) Forms of worship and the sacraments; d) Evangelism; 4) The Christian life; f) Cultural factors; g) Varying degrees of recognition);  IV. The Unity we have and the Unity we seek;  V. Illustrations of United Advance;  VI. Summary and Prospects.

Regarding the concern for the Unity we have and the Unity we seek, chapter III stated: "... We differ in our understanding of the relation of our unity in Christ to the visible holy, Catholic and Apostolic Church.  We are agreed that there are not two Churches, one visible and the other invisible, but one Church which must find visible expression on earth, but we differ in our belief as to whether certain doctrinal, sacramental and ministerial forms are of the essence of the Church itself. In consequence, we differ in our understanding of the character of the unity of the Church on earth for which we hope, though none of us looks forward to an institution with a rigid uniformity of governmental structure and all of us look forward to a time, when all Christians can have unrestricted communion in Sacrament and fellowship with each other.

"Yet our differences in the doctrinal and sacramental content of our faith and of our hope do not prevent us from being one in the act of believing and of hoping.  For our faith and our hope are in the crucified and risen Christ, who is already working in us the purpose of His perfect will, and is already gathering up every fragment of obedient endeavour into the consummation of that purpose."

In chapter IV, "Ways of Worship", non-theological factors promoting and hindering unity were outlined, in particular social and psychological factors.  In chapter VI, "Where Do We Stand", the following was stated on the divisions within the churches: "The Gospel is always received by men living within certain particular circumstances - cultural, social, political and economic.  Within these circumstances Christians are called to embody and maintain their allegiance to God.  The Church, constantly renewed and sustained by God's saving activity, lives in history and fulfils its mission under the manifold pressures of man's finite and sinful life.  It stands on the frontier between the Word and the world, constantly tempted by the motives of a society that seeks to organise and preserve itself apart from God.  Many of our pre-suppositions and prejudices, usually unconscious and unavowed, are the outcome of worldly pride and self-assertion.  Cultural conditions are sometimes treated as essential to the Gospel.  National aims are on occasion identified with God's will.  We have all received patterns of thought not only from the Gospel but also from the structure of society (e.g. we are influenced by conflicting conceptions of freedom and justice, equality and

democracy). These conceptions sometimes colour our understanding of the Gospel and tend to divide us.

"The importance of such influences upon our Churches cannot
be denied. They have played a part in creating our divisions
... Unless they are seriously tested as in the sight of God,
they may involve us unawares in a dangerous complacency. The
Churches must therefore examine those areas in which these
influences are most productive of suspicion and even hostility
among Christians. We meet such problems, for example, in the
tension between Roman and non-Roman expressions of Catholicity,
and where Churches are living and working in areas dominated by
political systems which are sharply divided from one another."[4]

Meeting at Willingen in 1952, the International Missionary
Council issued A Statement on the Calling of the Church to
Mission and Unity. "... The love of God in Christ calls for
the threefold response of worship, unity and mission. These
three aspects of the Church's response are interdependent; they
become corrupted when isolated from each other. Division in
the Church distorts its witness, frustrates its mission, and
contradicts its own nature. If the Church is to demonstrate
the Gospel in its life as well as in its preaching, it must
manifest to the world the power of God to break down all barriers and to establish the Church's unity in Christ. Christ
is not divided."

In the Report on "Reshaping the Pattern of Missionary
Activity it was recommended that "Christian Councils should
consider afresh their responsibility in relation to the cause
of Christian unity within their own areas. It is not the
purpose of the ecumenical movement to set up an ecclesiastical
superstructure, and action in matters of faith and order must
remain the responsibility of the churches. Nevertheless within
the co-operative activity of the Christian Councils the disunity
of the churches continues to hinder the fulfilment of the
Church's mission."[5]


                              III.


Section I of the Evanston Assembly in 1954 was devoted to
"Faith and Order: Our Oneness in Christ and Our Disunity as
Churches" and asserted: "From the beginning the Church has been
given an indissoluble unity in Christ, by reason of His self-
identification with His people. But the Church has never
realized the fulness of that unity. From the beginning discord
has marred the manifested unity of Christ's people (Lk 22:24ff;
Mk 10:35ff.). Thus we may speak of the oneness of the Church
in its earthly pilgrimage as a growth from its unity, as given,
to its unity, as fully manifested (Eph. 4:3,13).

"In this way we may think of the Church as we are able to
think of the individual believer, who may be said at one and
the same time to be both a justified man and a sinner (simul
justus et peccator). In each Christian there is both the 'new

man' who has been created and yet must be put on daily (2 Cor.5:17) and also the 'old man' who has been crucified with Christ and yet must daily be mortified (Col. 3:1-5). So the Church is already one in Christ, by virtue of His identification of Himself with it (Jn 14:20; 15:1-5) and must become one in Christ, so as to manifest its true unity (Eph. 4:11-16) in the mortification of its divisions.

"... When churches, in their actual historical situations, reach a point of readiness and a time of decision, then their witnessing may require obedience unto death. They may then have to be prepared to offer up some of their accustomed, inherited forms of life in uniting with other churches without complete certainty as to all that will emerge from the step of faith. Otherwise, acts of apparent re-union might be merely acts of calculated self-aggrandizement and a betrayal of the true calling of the Church. But when churches have been ready in this sense 'to die with Christ', they have found that He who raised Jesus from the dead is faithful and powerful still.

"... We have discovered that the old confessional divisions are being criss-crossed by new lines of agreement and disagreement... We must consider frankly the influence of social and cultural differences upon the matters of faith and order which cause divisions, and also perceive how the events and developments of current history make disunity a most urgent question.

"... The measure of our concern for unity is the degree to which we pray for it. We cannot expect God to give us unity unless we prepare ourselves to receive His gift by costly and purifying prayer. To pray together is to be drawn together. We urge, wherever possible, the observance of the Week of Prayer for Christian Unity, January 18-25 (or some other period suited to local conditions) as a public testimony to prayer as the road to unity."6

The second main theme of the Central Committee meeting in 1955 was: "The Various Meanings of Unity and the Unity which the World Council of Churches Seeks to Promote". The Toronto Statement tried to explicate the ecclesiological nature of the World Council and the assumptions underlying membership in it. The paper by W.A. Visser 't Hooft on the Central Committee's second theme attempted to clarify the way in which the World Council can promote Christian unity positively without being partisan to any one concept of unity not held by all member churches.7

In the Report on the Future of Faith and Order, presented to the Central Committee in 1960, it was stated: "... The Commission on Faith and Order understands that the unity which is both God's will and His gift to His Church is one which brings all in each place who confess Christ Jesus as Lord into a fully committed fellowship with one another through one baptism into Him, holding the one apostolic faith, preaching the one Gospel and breaking the one bread, and having a corporate life reaching out in witness and service to all; and which at the same time unites them with the whole Christian fellowship in all places and all ages in such wise that ministry and members are acknowledged by all, and that all can act and speak together as occasion requires for the tasks to which God calls the Church.

"It is for such unity that we believe we must pray and work. Such a vision has indeed been the inspiration of the Faith and Order movement in the past, and we re-affirm that this is still our goal. We recognize that the brief definition of our objective which we have given above leaves many questions unanswered. In particular we would state emphatically that the unity we seek is not one of uniformity, nor a monolitic power structure, and that on the interpretation and the means of achieving certain of the matters specified in the preceding paragraph we are not yet of a common mind. The achievement of unity will involve nothing less than a death and rebirth for many forms of church life as we have known them. We believe that nothing less costly can finally suffice."[8]

A North American Study Conference took place at Oberlin, Ohio, September 3-10, 1957, on the theme "The Nature of the Unity We Seek". The conference was designed with three main aims in mind: 1) to bring together the results of earlier significant developments in the movement towards unity in the churches; 2) to extend knowledge of the North American situation; 3) to project lines of ecumenical study which might become most fruitful in the years ahead.[9]

"Church Unity in Europe" was the theme of a consultation at Le Chambon, France, September 1958. Among the 150 participants were 80 officially-appointed delegates from Protestant churches in six Latin countries of Europe. There was an agreement that "unity between our churches and evangelical groups must be made a reality everywhere and as fully as possible." The conference was supported by DICARWS. It adopted resolutions arising out of the statement, expressing dissatisfaction with the 'ecclesiastical status quo' in Latin countries, and calling for the working out of methods of closer united action.[10]

IV.

The Message of the New Delhi Assembly to the churches in 1961 contained the following paragraph: "... We must together seek the fullness of Christian unity. We need for this purpose every member of the Christian family, of Eastern and Western tradition, ancient churches and younger churches, men and women, young and old, of every race and every nation. Our brethren in Christ are given to us, not chosen by us. In some things our convictions do not yet permit us to act together, but we have made progress in giving content to the unity we seek. Let us therefore find out the things which in each place we can do together now; and faithfully do them, praying and working always for that fuller unity which Christ wills for his Church."

The Report of the Section on "Unity" was divided into the
following parts: I. The Church's Unity (A Commentary upon this
Picture of Unity; In him alone... the Church has its true unity;
All in each place; Who are baptized into Christ; By the Holy
Spirit; Fully committed fellowship; The one apostolic faith;
Preaching the one Gospel; Breaking the one bread; Joining in
Common Prayer; A corporate life reaching out; Ministry and
members accepted by all; In all places and all ages); II. Some
Implications to Consider (A. Implications for Local Church Life;
B. Implications for the Life of our Confessions (1.Doctrinal
agreement; 2. Baptism and unity; 3. Eucharistic unity and division; 4. Common action); III. Implications for the Ecumenical
Movement (1. What are the proper functions and limits of the
WCC in regard to unity among its member churches? 2. How does
current thinking on unity affect our understanding of the nature
of the WCC itself? 3. How may world confessional bodies contribute to the ecumenical movement and the unity of the churches?
4. Is the World Council now able to find new light on the problem
of intercommunion?).

With regard to Implications for Local Church Life it was
stated: "The place where the development of the common life in
Christ is most clearly tested is the local situation, where
believers live and work. There the achievements and the frustrations are most deeply felt: but there too the challenge is
most often avoided. It is where we live and work together daily
that our Lord's own test is most clearly imposed, 'by this shall
all men know that ye are my disciples, if ye have love one to
another'... But all of us must confess that, in the life of our
churches at the local level, we are still far from being
together in all those ways in which, with a good conscience,
we might be. It will be through daily obedience in the paths
that are already open to us than our eyes will ben enlightened
to the fuller vision of our life together..."

On doctrinal agreement the following was expressed: "In our
consideration of next steps towards an agreed doctrinal basis
for the unity we seek, two useful distinctions may be made -
that intellectual formulations of faith are not to be identified
with faith itself, and the koinonia in Christ is more nearly the
precondition of 'sound doctrine' than vice versa. The primary
basis of this koinonia is the apostolic testimony in the Holy
Scriptures and 'the hearing of faith'. Yet this primary biblical revelation was given to and through the apostolic church
and has continued to be witnessed to by our common historic
Creeds, specifically the Apostles' Creed and the Nicaeo-Constantinopolitan Creed. There is, as it were, an 'ecumenicity
in time' which may be realized by serious attention both to the
ancient witnesses and also to the gifts of light and truth given
by the Spirit in various ages and traditions in the history of
the people of God..."

Concerning the role of world confessional bodies the New
Delhi report said: "... The critical question is whether or not
the leaders of confessional bodies agree with the emphasis we
have already made upon the centrality of unity of all Christians
in each place, which must, of course, always seek to be a 'unity

in the truth'. If they agree, they will not consider the union of one of their churches as a loss, but as a gain for the whole Church. And a service can be rendered to such churches if the confessional bodies assist them in the responsible study of all issues which are involved in a proposed union."[11]

Section I, "The Church in the Purpose of God" of the Fourth World Conference on Faith and Order at Montreal in 1963 was made up of the following parts: Introduction; Christ, New Creation, Creation; The Church: Act and Institution; Christ, the Church and the Churches; The Church and the World Council of Churches. Regarding The Church: Act and Institution it was stated: "The reality that God has given in Jesus Christ through the Holy Spirit is confessed by the Church in terms of its unity, holiness, catholicity and apostolicity. Such is the nature of God's giving and our believing that what is given once and for all is given ever anew and must be received ever anew in the action of God's gracious self-giving and the response of a living faith. So, for example, the Church which is one in Jesus Christ becomes one in him as it receives in faith the good news of its oneness and seeks to pattern its existence in accordance with its reality. Thus these gifts (unity, holiness, catholicity and apostolicity) are also tasks. In considering the relationship between gift and task, what has been said above concerning event and institution is most relevant."

In the sub-section on Christ, the Church and the Churches the following was outlined: "We agree that the criteria for distinguishing a Christian community from a church (in the full sense of the word) are not to be found simply in formal adherence to a creed or confession, submission to a particular hierarchical authority, or possession of a particular ministerial order, but in the nature of its faith and worship and its resultant witness. Therefore it is most important that the aim of all conversation about Faith and Order should be mutual understanding not only in the sphere of doctrine, but also in that of devotion and spirituality, for it is in these fields that there probably lie unrecognized areas both of disagreement and of profound agreement. Such an understanding cannot be reached by any merely superficial comparision of externals, but rather by focusing attention upon the way in which spirituality of each tradition is related to our common christological and soteriological affirmations."

In Section V, "All in Each Place: The Process of Growing Together" the following was noted: "... In the course of Christian history, division and separation have taken place. Now, however, we live in an era when the churches are seeking to overcome their separations. The proving ground of unity is the local church. Here the process of growing together exhibits the fruits of the Spirit, the tensions of our divisions, and the strains and conflicts arising from the contemporary revolutionary situation. Here the divisive factors of racial enmity, class conflict and national and ideological loyalties, are acutely manifest in their relationship to Christian unity and mission... It is in the local community that the scandal of Christian disunity is particularly conspicuous and injurious. Therefore it is in each place where people live, work and worship, that our partnership in the body of Christ has to be made manifest and lived out...[12]

## V

In the report of Committee 4, <u>Joint Action for Mission</u> of the Second Meeting of CWME at Mexico City in 1963 it was stated: "... While church union removes many difficulties, it cannot guarantee that Joint Action for Mission will be easily achieved. On the other hand, the subordination of particular vested interests, and spiritual readiness for the risks and commitments involved in joint action are possible without church union, although as they are developed they take us a long step toward that full unity which must always be recognized as our goal."

Section IV of the meeting at Mexico City was devoted to <u>"The Witness of the Christian Church Across National and Confessional Boundaries"</u>. It noted the following: "... Ecumenical experience has revealed that co-operation in action can take place at almost every point. The most intractable frontier is that of structure, ecclesiastical and missionary. The growing recognition of the missionary nature of the Church sometimes tends to strengthen confessional frontiers in the world mission. World-wide confessional bodies, denominational churches and missionary societies have, in some places, helped the achievement of organic union; in some other places their influence has blocked locally desired unions. We would therefore urge churches and missionary societies to perform their work in relation to the total missionary task and in awareness of the problems of mission in unity."[13]

The Central Committee discussed at its meeting in 1966 the theme <u>"On the Ecumenical Way"</u>. The following was noted: "Our Lord Jesus Christ has opened for all mankind the way to the Father and to one another. He himself is the Way. Therefore faith in him can simply be called 'the way' (Acts 9:2). This way remains the same for all generations but there are many manners of following the living Christ. The way therefore takes different forms in different circumstances, according to the guidance of the Holy Spirit. In our time, more than ever before, he is leading us as churches on the way of closer co-operation and towards full unity. The conditions of the world in which we now live do not merely make this possible - they make it imperative. By walking on this ecumenical way we express our faith in him who is the Way, who reconciles us with God and with one another and who wants the whole inhabited earth, the <u>oikumene</u>, to be gathered under him as its Head. The ecumenical way is thus an expression of the very essence of the Gospel.

"... The present stage of the ecumenical way is not one with which the churches can rest content. There is a real danger that they will regard fraternal relationships and co-operation as sufficient or the continued existence of differences as intractable. Such a conclusion would tempt us to be satisfied with a consolidation of the achievements of recent decades rather than to renew our commitment for the common journey. The ecumenical movement would then cease to be a movement of renewal leading toward the goal of unity embracing faith and order, worship and sacraments, mission and service. The obstacles on the ecumenical way should test our obedience, not stop our progress."[14]

VI.

A Statement on "Confessional Families and the Churches in Asia" was received by the EACC Assembly in 1964 and forwarded to member churches and councils for their study and appropriate action. The following was expressed: "... The fact must be faced that, while in the West, the churches drew up their historic confessions and adopted their various forms of Church order in the light of controversies that took place within the Church and within Christendom, the confessional need of the churches in Asia is primarily in relation to their mission to the world. The issues for them do not so much concern those things in which the churches differ from one another as those things which Christians together must confess before the world. Indeed, even in the lands where the historic confessions and confessional positions had their origin, the present missionary situation of the churches call for a radical questioning of the adequacy of these confessions.

"... There is an increasing conviction in the Churches of Asia, that those churches which are in the same country or region should find one another, and, in that place, live together a common life. In this search for unity, the controlling impulse has to be the fact that the churches in the same place share a common mission. It is not a question of seeking Church Union for the sake of being more effective in mission; it is a matter of being true to the mission itself, for the mission presupposes a common life. This being said it is equally important to say that a Church is not a national or geographical entity. Nation and country give the context within which the Church must ful- fill its mission and, therefore, live its life; but every local Church must maintain its organic place in the Church Universal. World confessional groupings of churches would appear to be one way of providing this universality, though the problem is that, if this is the way it is done, then universality is being pro- vided by giving form and strength to that which does not belong to the Church, namely, its divisions. A true way of providing this universality is to strengthen the missionary movement of the churches, so that, in every church in every country, there are Christians from other churches and other countries... the best thing for United Churches is not to join any world con- fessional organisation."

In a Statement "On Relations with Roman Catholics" the following conclusion was reached: "... The growth of the ecu- menical dialogue may lead to the point where we can join with Roman Catholic brethren in common acts of service and witness to our non-Christian neighbours. At this point it is, however, necessary to insist that this does not mean the attempt to create a common 'front' behind which Christians can protect

their minority rights and privileges against the majority of
the nation.  We recall here the word spoken by the late Pope
to the effect that there can be no true encounter among Christians without openness to the world."[15]

In the section on "Freedom and Unity in the Church" of the
Report of the AACC, meeting at Kampala in 1963, it was stated:
"... It seems to us that the unity we seek according to the will
of Christ can be attained in stages.  The step which we have
already taken by forming the Federation of Churches in the All
Africa Conference of Churches is the first, and if we are faithful to the commitments we have made in joining AACC, this will
lead us to closer co-operation and mutual understanding, a grow-
ing-together in love.  However, we must beware of using our
co-operation and fellowship within the AACC in such a way that
this becomes a cloak or an umbrella covering the continuing sin,
in which we all share, of the underlying disunity among the
different parts of the Church.  Therefore, we must continue to
be faithful and submissive to the guidance and encouragement of
the Holy Spirit, who will be leading us forward towards a totally
'incarnate' union, the visible expression of the fullness of the
Body of Christ, to which Christ calls us.

"... The question of independent Churches is very closely
related to Church unity in Africa.  At this stage we are unable
to recommend a line of conduct either in one direction or
another... Yet we would like to recommend to the Churches that
they take an attitude of understanding and Christian love that
avoids a spirit of judgment and censoriousness toward the
followers of these groups to whom we should regard ourselves
as having a very special missionary responsibility since they
were people groping for that fullness of life which only Christ
can give.  We should receive such persons in a spirit of Christian brotherhood, and, wherever prayer and Bible study groups
are constituted, they should be open to these people."[16]


VII.

The Decree on Ecumenism (Unitatis Redintegratio) of the
Second Vatican Council was made up of the following chapters:
Introduction;  I. Catholic Principles on Ecumenism;  II. The
Practice of Ecumenism;  III. Churches and Ecclesial Communities
Separated from the Roman Apostolic See (The Special Position of
the Eastern Churches; The Separated Churches and Ecclesial
Communities in the West).

In the last chapter the following was stated: "... A love,
veneration, and near cult of the sacred Scriptures lead our
brethren to a constant and expert study of the sacred text...
But when Christians separated from us affirm the divine authority
of the sacred Books, they think differently from us - different
ones in different ways - about the relationship between the
Scriptures and the Church.  In the Church, according to Catholic

belief, an authentic teaching office plays a special role in the explanation and proclamation of the written word of God. Nevertheless, in dialogue itself, the sacred utterances are precious instruments in the mighty hand of God for attaining that unity which the Savior holds out to all men.

"... The ecclesial Communities separated from us lack that fullness of unity with us which should flow from baptism, and we believe that especially because of the lack of the sacrament of orders they have not preserved the genuine and total reality of the Eucharistic mystery. Nevertheless, when they commemorate the Lord's death and resurrection in the Holy Supper, they profess that it signifies life in communion with Christ and they await His coming in glory. For these reasons, dialogue should be undertaken concerning the true meaning of the Lord's Supper, the other sacraments, and the Church's worship and ministry... This most sacred Synod urgently desires that the initiatives of the sons of the Catholic Church, joined with those of the separated brethren, go forward without obstructing the ways of divine Providence and without prejudging the future inspiration of the Holy Spirit..."[17]

In the Second Report of the Joint Working Group between the Roman Catholic Church and the World Council of Churches, presented to the Central Committee in 1967 the following was stated on unity and mission: "Division is an obstacle to the effective proclamation of the Gospel. For is the message of reconciliation not denied if Christians live side by side without themselves being reconciled to each other ? All churches feel the contradiction of this situation. It is one of the reasons why they are seeking today to re-establish their communion. A common witness will proclaim the Gospel more effectively. The member churches of the World Council of Churches express this intention by their common life and action in the Council... The Roman Catholic Church has affirmed the same intention in the Decree on Ecumenism (para. 12) and on the Missionary Activity in the Church.

"Common witness presupposes ecclesial communion. Therefore it can become full reality only when the churches will have reached unity in doctrine and life sufficient to live in communion. Such communion will be the perfect form of common witness. This does not mean that the churches cannot already in many respects bear witness together to the name of Christ. As common witness raises questions with regard to the central content of the Gospel, it can happen that ecumenical activities avoid anything which goes beyond practical collaboration. This tendency must be resisted. All ecumenical work must serve the purpose of glorifying the name of Christ."[18]

## VIII

Section I, "The Holy Spirit and the Catholicity of the Church", of the Uppsala Assembly in 1968 was composed of the following parts: The Quest for Diversity; The Quest for Continuity; The Quest for the Unity of the Whole Church; The Quest for the Unity of Mankind. Concerning The Quest for the Unity of the Whole Church it was stated: "The New Delhi Assembly emphasized with good effect the need to manifest the unity of 'all Christians in each place'... To the emphasis of 'all in each place' we would now add a fresh understanding of the unity of all Christians in all places. This calls the churches in all places to realize that they belong together and are called to act together. In a time when human interdependence is so evident, it is the more imperative to make visible the bonds which unite Christians in universal fellowship.

"... But the clearest obstacle to manifestation of the churches' universality is their inability to understand the measure in which they already belong together in one body. Some real experience of universality is provided by establishing regional and international confessional fellowships. But such experiences of universality are inevitably partial. The ecumenical movement helps to enlarge this experience of universality, and its regional councils and its World Council may be regarded as a transitional opportunity for eventually actualizing a truly universal, ecumenical, conciliar form of common life and witness. The members of the World Council of Churches, committed to each other, should work for the time when a genuinely universal council may once more speak for all Christians, and lead the way into the future.

"The Church is bold in speaking of itself as the sign of the coming unity of mankind. However well founded the claim, the world hears it sceptically, and points to 'secular catholicities' of its own. For secular society has produced instruments of conciliation and unification which often seem more effective than the Church itself. To the outsider, the churches often seem remote and irrelevant, and busy to the point of tediousness with their own concerns. The churches need a new openness to the world in its aspirations, its achievements, its restlessness and its despair."

In his paper "The Mandate of the Ecumenical Movement", contained in Appendix V of the Uppsala Report, W.A. Visser 't Hooft stated the following: "... I believe that we must hold on to the original conviction of the ecumenical movement, that it belongs to the very nature of the people of God to live as one reconciled and therefore united family, and that it belongs to its witness to present to the world the image of a new humanity which knows no walls of separation within its own life. Even the best cooperation and the most intensive dialogue are no substitutes for full fellowship in Christ.

"But I wonder at the same time whether it is not largely our own fault that so many conceive of unity in terms of uniformity and centralization and are therefore afraid of it. Should we not have learned after these decades of common life in the ecumenical movement that the Holy Spirit has used very many different forms of church order for his work of inspiration, conversion and prophecy ? And have we given sufficient attention to the indisputable fact that the earliest Church knew quite distinct types of church order ? My point is simply that there seems to be no really urgent reason to identify unity with acceptance of one and the same church order. Do we not discover in our increasingly pluralistic cultural situation that what is good for one continent or region is not necessarily good for another ? And must we not draw the conclusion that there can be real fellowship in faith and in sacrament even when structures differ ?"[19]

The Report of the Conference of the Faith and Order Commission at Louvain in 1971 contained a study document on "Catholicity and Apostolicity" which had been prepared by a Joint Theological Commission on the initiative of the Joint Working Group. Appendix VI of this study document was devoted to the problem of Unity and Plurality.

Concentrating on the question of Conciliarity and the Future of the Ecumenical Movement Committee IV of the Louvain Conference stated the following: "... The New Delhi statement on the nature of the unity we seek spoke of a 'fully committed fellowship' both 'in each place' and also universally embracing the Church in all ages and places. To accept conciliarity as the direction in which we must move means deepening our mutual commitment at all levels. This does not mean movement in the direction of uniformity. On the contrary, our discussions here at Louvain have emphasized the fact, that, if the unity of the Church is to serve the unity of mankind, it must provide room both for wide variety of forms, and for differences and even conflicts. The conciliarity of the Church requires the involvement of the entire lay membership, including as it should every segment of mankind. There must be opportunity within the life of the Church for each community of mankind to develop and express its own authentic selfhood; for the oppressed and exploited to fight for justice; and for the 'marginal' people in society - the handicapped in mind and body - to make their own distinctive contribution. This becomes all the more necessary because modern technology has forced all mankind into a tight inter-dependence which constantly threatens freedom and individuality. The Church's unity must be of such a kind that there is ample space for diversity and for the open mutual confrontation of differing interests and convictions.

"True conciliarity, moreover, has a temporal dimension; it links the past, the present and the future in a single life. This is part of the meaning of what New Delhi said about the unity of one committed fellowship 'in all ages and all places'. Through the work of the Spirit in the life of the Church we are enabled to discern his teaching through the words of the Councils of the past. Within the living fellowship of the one Church we are enabled to enter into a conversation with the past, to put questions and to receive illumination on our own problems. We are not called upon simply to reproduce the words of the ancient Councils, which spoke to different situations and in languages other than ours. But it is an essential part of our growth into full conciliarity that we should be continually engaged in a process of 're-reception' of the Councils of the past, through whose witness - received in living dialogue - the same Holy Spirit who spoke to the Fathers in the past can lead us into His future."[20]

In the Report of the Secretariat to the meeting of the Commission on Faith and Order at Accra in 1974 Lukas Vischer stated under the heading Common Vision of Unity ?: "Far more important than any of the detailed reflections about unity in which we may engage during this conference is the question whether we are in a position to provide once more an agreed description of the unity we are seeking to achieve in the ecumenical movement. What can we say together today ? It is not to be taken for granted that we can agree on a description of the goal we are seeking. The ecclesiological positions from which we start are so different that the possibility of agreed statements is very limited. But for that very reason, an agreed description of 'the unity we seek' would perhaps be the most significant help the Commission could offer the churches in their search for unity. Earlier attempts have been made to provide such a description. At both the Third and Fourth Assemblies, the Commission submitted short texts on the theme of unity. A year from now, the Fifth Assembly will be held. Will a similar contribution be possible there ?"

In the chapter on The Unity of the Church: the Goal and the Way a section was devoted to Moving into the Fullness of Conciliar Fellowship and divided into the following parts:
1. Unity in the truth of the Gospel. The churches must be able to recognize one another as holding and confessing the apostolic faith...; 2. Unity around the table of the Lord. Baptized into the same Body of the one Lord, the members of local churches must be able to share in the celebration of the eucharist...; 3. Fellowship in the Church is for the sake of the quality of human life in the world. Our current discussions on the relation of church unity to the unity of mankind have clarified many points here...; 4. Unity in each place is basic...; 5. Conciliar fellowship requires the mutual acceptance of the appropriate representatives of each expression of the Church... ; 6. The fullness of fellowship will thus be an interlocking scale of corporate relationships, in which each grouping will have its proper autonomy (in missionary responsibility to the surrounding world) and its proper dependence on the Church as a whole... ; 7. This conciliar fellowship must also lead us into exploration of the proper forms of fellowship at the universal level... ; 8. The counterpart of mutual pastoral responsibility in interdependence is that councils of the Church at every level are invested with an appropriate authority. Who says 'authority' says 'power', and power in the Church always must be exercised in transparent ways, as a service and not a

domination...; 9. The whole structure of conciliar fellowship depends essentially upon <u>the active presence of the Holy Spirit</u> and on the Church's active acknowledgment of his leading...21

IX.

In the final report of the Humanum Consultative Committee, presented to the Central Committee in 1974, David E. Jenkins stated in view of the preparations for the Fifth Assembly in 1975: "... We shall have to be very careful about how we understand the unity which Jesus Christ offers. We must be free to ask how, in our specific churches, actual traditions and concrete historical situations, Jesus Christ sets us free to be agents of human unity in a world where we Christians are a minority and in relation to cultures many of which have suffered greatly from the 'Christian West'. We may well discover that Jesus Christ unites us in the confession of his name and so in the praise of God, Father, Son and Holy Spirit and in the freedom to repent, but on that basis we are liberated into all sorts of conflict, confrontation and anguish. In our humble and hopeful exploration here it will be necessary also to do our best to ensure that the very structures of the Assembly are not more dehumanizing than they need be..."22

Considering the relationship between faith and ideology and the manner in which ideologies affect Christian thought, action and fellowship in the ecumenical movement, a consultation at Cartigny, near Geneva, May 19-24, 1975 stated the following on <u>Different Approaches to Unity</u> and on <u>What Constitutes Visible Fellowship and What Are Its Limits</u>: "There have been several different approaches to these questions. 1) Unity has sometimes been expressed so vaguely that it lacks ethical content, an invisible 'spiritual' unity without evident anchor in history. 2) It has also been expressed as an ideal which is primarily transhistorical, even though imagined in social forms, because the form of its realization is utopian. In this case a few Christians might seek to realize it for themselves, attempting the vocation of perfectionism, serving as a witness to the rest who are left to cope with the real world. 3) Still another way to view Christian unity has been to see it as a real social bond superseding all differences and commanding mutual love, assistance, and sharing, while yet recognizing that in a sinful world these bonds will be repeatedly tested and even temporarily broken by human divisions like wars, nationalism and revolution. 4) And finally, Christian unity has been narrowly defined to include only those who share a particular assessment of the Christian role in the world - or more or less sectarian approach.

"If we are to define what belonging to the Christian community means today, we might begin in classic fashion with a verbal formulation, such as 'those who have been baptized and who have accepted Jesus Christ as Lord and Saviour, and who have not explicitly renounced this allegiance'. Many others

would prefer a definiton which, while including as essential
some form of explicit verbal adherence to the tradition, would
concentrate on doing rather than saying - those who attempt in
some way to make the agape of God real in life, who participate
in a community of other Christians and are recognized as fellow
participants by them. Both of these definitions have an empirical character, but there is a third level of belonging which
does not. We may disagree on the empirical marks of a Christian community, but the final judgment who belongs is not ours:
it is God's and cannot be submitted to historical verification.
Whatever may be our criteria, we remember the parable of the
wheat and the tares, and leave the ultimate word to God.

"Our problem is to describe the community of Christians
with whom we have visible fellowship, and particularly to note
the effects of ideology on the description. We find that the
differences among us centre on the role of deeds, of active
engagement for others. We all regard commitment in action as
a Christian obligation. But whether the absence of that commitment, in whatever form, should be the occasion for a rupture
of fellowship is quite another matter...

"Perhaps, given our differences of approach, it is unwise
to try to define the Christian community as a neutral, storm-
free place, transcending the world's battles, rescuing for the
peace of God both those who war and those who are warred upon.
Perhaps it would be better to acknowledge that the Church is
engaged in the world, and that it is therefore necessarily
varied, a fellowship of many forms rather than one, open to
new insights and ready to bear conflict. It would be, then,
as one member of our group put it, a 'space for confrontation
in Christ'..."23

X.

"Concepts of Unity and Models of Union" was the theme of
a consultation at Salamanca, Spain, September 1973. The Report
was in two parts. Part A: I. The context; II. The unity of
the Church in God's purpose for the world; III. The vision of
a united Church as a conciliar fellowship; IV. Conciliar
fellowship and organic union; V. Different levels of unity -
complementarity and interaction; VI. Identity, change and unity.
Part B: I. How can consensus (agreed statement on doctrine)
contribute to unity among the churches; II. The role of world
confessional families in the ecumenical movement. Papers were
presented by L. Vischer, R. Beaupère, J. Miguez-Bonino, I. Bria,
P.A. Crow, G.F. Moede, N. Ehrenström.24

"Church Union in Africa" was the subject of discussion of
a consultation at Accra, July 17-20, 1974. Representatives of
united churches and church union committees from various countries in Africa considered the ways and means by which the unity
of the church could be more fully manifested on the continent.
The Report included: A. The Call to Organic Union in Africa;
B. Unity - In Self-Hood and Self-Reliance; C. African Theology
- A Means to Promote the Organic Union of the Churches;

D. Unity at Different Levels;  E. Reflections on the Process of
Church Union;  F. Relationships Between Historic and Independent
Churches.[25]

Some 35 theologians from both the Eastern Orthodox and
Oriental Orthodox traditions participated in a consultation on
"Unity and Liberation" at Gonia, Crete, March 8-14, 1975, called
by the WCC.  The report, which was sent to the various Orthodox
churches, called attention to several aspects in Section II
(What Unity Requires) and Section V (Structures of Injustice and
Struggles for Liberation) of the Nairobi Assembly.  The participants asked the WCC to call a follow-up consultation for Orthodox
churches a year after the assembly.[26]

A consultation on "Unity and Common Witness" at Rome, June
16-20, 1975, sponsored by the Joint Working Group of the RCC
and the WCC, made comments on the Annotated Agendas for Section
I and II of the Nairoby Assembly.  Section I: "Confessing Christ
Today";  Section II: "What Unity Requires".[27]


XI.

Section II, "What Unity Requires", of the Nairobi Assembly
in 1975 was constituted of the following parts:  I. Foreword;
II. Unity Requires a Commonly Accepted Goal;  III. Unity Requires a Fuller Understanding of the Context (The Handicapped
and the Wholeness of the Family of God; The Community of Women
and Men and the Wholeness of the Body of Christ; Organization
and Personal Community in the Unity of the Church; Political
Struggle and the Unity of the Church; The Search for Cultural
Identity and the Oneness of the Church Universal);  IV. Unity
Requires Companionship in Struggle and Hope;  V. Implications
and Recommendations.

With regard to the concept of conciliarity the following
was noted: "... Conciliarity expresses the interior unity of
the churches separated by space, culture, or time, but living
intensely the unity in Christ and seeking from time to time,
by councils of representatives of all the local churches at
various geographical levels to express their unity visibly in
a common meeting.  Our present interconfessional assemblies are
not councils in this full sense, because they are not yet united
by a common understanding of the apostolic faith, by a common
ministry, and a common Eucharist.  They nevertheless express
the sincere desire of the participating churches to herald and
move forwards towards full conciliar fellowship, and are themselves a true foretaste of such fellowship."

Concerning companionship in struggle and hope, the Section
stated: "... Many, especially (but not only) in the younger
churches of Asia, Africa, and Latin America, find that the
language which earlier generations used to confess the one
faith does not help them to confess the same faith in the language of their own peoples.  They find that the truth they confess in common as they witness to their neighbours is more

important than the separate formulations of an earlier time and another culture. In many places united churches have been formed by the action of separated churches in surrendering their separate identities in order to become one. Thus surrender has been costly, but those who have experienced it testify that it has been the way to new life... These two ways of approaching unity must be complementary and not competitive. Local or national unions of churches could fall into confusion and error by not taking seriously enough the issues of the continuity with the past which are involved in the dialogue between the confessional families..."[28]

In a theological consultation on "<u>Dialogue in Community</u>" at Chiang Mai, Thailand, April 1977, sponsored by the Sub-unit on Dialogue with People of Living Faiths and Ideologies, the following was noted in a adopted statement: "... We must acknowledge the close relation between our concern for dialogue and our work for visible Church unity. It is not only that the different confessional traditions have been an influence on the different approaches to dialogue and that questions concerning dialogue are seriously discussed within and between churches, but also that the Christian contribution to dialogue is weakened by division among Christians."[29]

The Reports of the Committees on <u>Growing Together in Unity</u> of the Faith and Order Commission, meeting at Bangalore in 1978, were on the following themes: Reflections on the Common Goal; The Common Expression of the Apostolic Faith; Towards an Ecumenical Consensus on Baptism, the Eucharist and the Ministry; Towards Common Ways of Teaching and Decision-making; Mutual Intercession; The Unity of the Church and the Community of Women and Men in the Church; The Unity of the Church: Two Examples of Interdisciplinary Work; New Ecumenical Experiences and Existing Ecumenical Structures.

In a <u>Re-affirmation of the Goal of Visible Unity</u> the following was stated: "... We are fully aware of the sad and scandalous fact that the goal of visible unity is still far away. But we wish to affirm that the vision of unity in a 'conciliar fellowship', sharing the one apostolic faith as well as the gifts of baptism and the eucharist, is alive in us. Although it may seem to be only a distant possibility, the vision provides inspiration and guidance already in the present age as we envisage the way ahead. Christ himself summons us to pursue the goal. He is the centre of our lives, the realization of the unity for which He prayed is a central task for us...

"Why repeat what has been stated many times? Simply because the striving for visible unity is slackening in many quarters. Some who have set out on this road have become victims of frustration. Others declare themselves content with the measure of good will and cooperation which has developed among the churches over the last decades, and cease to reach out to new stages of unity.

"... The search for unity must proceed at many levels and
involve more and more Christians. There is no uniform strategy
in moving towards unity. According to different situations and
conditions, different methods must be employed. The multiplicity of efforts is not without problems, however. We are
concerned that instead of being complementary, they might
counteract and neutralize each other. There is need to work
in concert. The vision of full visible unity in conciliar
fellowship provides the frame for working in concert. The agreements which have emerged or are emerging from multilateral and
bilateral dialogues must be taken seriously by all churches and,
as far as they are acceptable to each church, translated into
practical decisions which affect the relations with other churches. The far-reaching results of dialogues present the churches with the challenge to give new expression to the oneness
in Christ for the sake of the Gospel and to the glory of God...
Churches which consider the one, holy, catholic and apostolic
Church to be a reality far greater than the historical reality
of any church tradition need to reflect on the ways in which is
the presupposition of true conciliar life."[30]

In the Working Group Report on "Unity" of the Faith and
Order Commission, meeting at Lima, Peru in 1982, it was stated:
"... All purpose in human life is grounded in a vision of what
may be, of what ought to be. Any such vision of a renewed
world has a central criterion. Christians are inspired by the
teaching, the example and above all the suffering and resurrection of Jesus, to set their hope on a new oikoumene of peace
and justice growing out of vulnerable love, reflecting here on
earth the fullness of life that God has shown us in Christ and
has by his Spirit laid up for his people in his kingdom.

"Yet this vision, this hope, is mere vain dreaming if there
is no community to show, however fragmentarily, that it can be
achieved in this frustrating and sinful world. The achievement
of each new unity in the Church, however ambiguous and limited,
even if it must always lead us beyond further repentance and
forgiveness to yet other unities, is nothing less than a witness
to the actuality of God's promise of reconciliation. To spurn
the possibilities that the Spirit is holding out in our time,
whether because of laziness or of over-attention to detail, is
in practice to suggest that God wants us as we are - which in
a fragmented Church and a world of oppression is nothing short
of blasphemy. The biblical vision is of a promise grounded in
the life, death and rising of one who gathered his followers
into a single body and who prayed that they might be one 'as you
Father are in me and I in you, that the world may believe'."[31]

The document on Baptism, Eucharist and Ministry[32], the
result of a long process of study and consultation, was discussed at Accra (1974), Bangalore (1978) and Lima (1982). At
the last meeting it was recommended to transmit this agreed
statement - the Lima text - for the common study and official
response of the churches.

## XII

Issue 2 of the Vancouver Assembly in 1983, "Taking Steps
Towards Unity", was made up of the following parts: I.The goal:
Church unity as a credible sign and witness;  II. Marks of such
a witnessing unity;  III.Steps we can take now towards this goal.
A. We can engage the process of reception of "Baptism, Eucharist
and Ministry" by the churches.  B. We can clarify the meaning of
"a common understanding of the apostolic faith".  C. We can help
our churches to explore and express more clearly the relation
between the unity of the Church, the eucharistic fellowship of
believers, and the transformation of human community.  D.We can
further the churches' common quest for agreement on common ways
of decision-making and teaching authoritatively.  IV. Towards a
Fifth World Conference on Faith and Order;  V. The World Council
of Churches within the one ecumenical movement.

In the last paragraph of Issue 2 it was stated: "... At this
Assembly we have been especially blessed as our theology has
climaxed in doxology, our doctrinal convergences in our praise
and adoration of the triune God.  Celebrating the Lima eucharistic liturgy together could become a most powerful step in the
spiritual process of receiving the teachings of the ecumenical
text which lies at its base.  What we believe truly governs how
we pray and work, even as prayer and action help deepen our
understanding of faith.  May our growing doctrinal agreements
within the fellowship of the World Council of Churches enable
both more profound united worship and more effective common
witness..."33

"Conciliar Unity" was the theme of a consultation at Banga-
lore, India, January 31 - February 4, 1978, sponsored by the
Commission on Faith and Order and the Ecumenical Christian Centre
in Whitefield, Bangalore.  Representatives of the Church of North
India, the Church of South India, the Mar Thoma Syrian Church of
Malabar, the Roman Catholic Church, the Orthodox Syrian Church
of the East, the Malankara Jacobite Syrian Orthodox Church, the
Methodist Church in Southern Asia, the Salvation Army, the
United Evangelical Lutheran Churches in India and the Baptist
Union in India participated in the consultation.  Contributions
were made by J. Pathrapankal, V.C. Samuel, M.A. Thomas, Bp. P.
Mar Chrysostom, L. Vischer, Metr. P. Gregorios, A.M. Mundadan,
A.C. Dharmaraj, S. Doraiswamy, A.A. Pylee, E.C. John, Bp. K.
Kunnacherry. 34

In 1976 the Joint Working Group decided to begin a reflection
on "The Unity of the Church: the Goal and the Way", with a view
to making further progress in the search for visible unity in
one and the same faith and one and the same eucharistic community.  From June 12 to 16, 1978 a colloquium was held at
Venice on the theme "Unity in Faith".  The Report includes:
1) Unity in Faith;  2) The Apostolic Faith;  3) The Content of
the Apostolic Faith;  4) The Form of a Profession of Faith Today;
5) Unity of Faith and Communion of Churches.35

"Elements of Unity, Obstacles to Unity" was the theme of
a consultation at Bossey, June 23 - July 4, 1981. The meeting
was organized by the Sub-unit on Faith and Order (W. Lazareth
and M. Kinnamon). It dealt with contemporary conception of
Christian unity. A paper was read by D. Popescu.[36]

"Growing Towards Consensus and Commitment" was the theme of
a consultation at Colombo, Sri Lanka, November 18-25, 1981.
For the fourth time since 1967, representatives of united churches and church union negotiating committees met to exchange
information, seek solutions for common problems, and lift up
their vision of Christian unity. The first three consultations
were held at Bossey (1967), Limuru (1970), and Toronto (1975).
The report of the fourth consultation includes: Growing Towards
a Deeper Understanding of the Church; Particular Issues Facing
United and Uniting Churches; Summary of Recommendations;
Message to the Churches.[37]

## XIII.

The Sixth Assembly of the Christian Conference of Asia,
meeting at Penang in 1977, stated the following on Directions
for Realizing Unity: "The aim of Christian unity is not simply
to bring churches to share in a common life and the resources
for mission, it is to actualize its calling to be a sign of
the unity of all peoples in the purpose of God. The realization of this fact is particularly important for us in Asia
where there are great religious and cultural diversities.
Therefore, there is the need to search for community and unity
at all levels.

"Although we have spoken of diversities in Asia, we have
not studied at depth these diversities as true resources for
understanding the nature of the unity we seek. If therefore
we are to broaden our ecumenical experience, we should analyse
carefully the factors that actually divide and unite us as
Asian peoples. For until we understand this, our search will
be narrow, i.e. purely ecclesiastical, and without significance
for our peoples as the sign of unity of all peoples in the
purpose of God. In broadening our understanding of unity, we
already have certain resources.
    a) There are the resources from Asian religious traditions
and secular ideologies which speak to the issue of community
and unity.
    b) There are also experiences of groups of people - women,
youth, and people's movements - which have realized a unity
which holds together cultural and religious diversities in
the struggle for liberation."[38]

Meeting at Seoul in 1985, the Eighth Assembly of the Christian Conference of Asia stated in Section II, "Realising the
Freedom and the Unity of the Church", the following on Towards
a New Vision of Unity and Mission: "... It is a historical fact
that the Church came to Asia in obedience to our Lord's command
to make disciples of all nations, but it did so in bits and

pieces that issued from the theological and political quarrels of our older brothers in the West. And the Church came to Asia in its diverse forms, which later related to each other in various nuances of indifference and antagonism... Though the original impuls towards unity which had its auspicious beginnings in the West... still draws Christians from various communions into unity, a lot of their ecumenical efforts has been held back by serious differences in their interpretation of Christian symbols, as well as by institutional and financial interests. And these latter considerations have sucked the Church's vested interests into the worldly drive for power and glory - that same drive that has condemned Asia's teeming millions to dire poverty and its curses for the sake of a greedy and powerful few.

"... It is the transformation of the whole society through the exercise of the freedom that we have in Christ, that opens up a new vision of the unity and mission of the Church. It is an endeavour where the Church should engage in an act of metanoia for having concentrated far too much on the spiritual dimensions of mission and evangelism and far too little on their implications on the legitimate claims of man's earthly existence. Asia, caught in between the pressures of an economics of greed and a politics of death, can only rear up her vast millions in sub-human conditions in an atmosphere of fear, terror, and certain death. In such a context, the Church ought to break out of its captivities to heed God's call of renewal and trans-formation of our societies. Jesus Christ ought to be declared in cosmic dimensions akin to the spirit of the letter to the Colossians and such a declaration be matched by a selflessness, courage and love that were in Jesus Christ himself as he went about doing his ministry"[39]

## Observations and Comments

1. In contrast to all other sub-units in the WCC, the Sub-unit on Faith and Order has engaged in few consultations, particularly on church unity and unity in the ecumenical move-ment. From 1948 onwards the major work has been undertaken in and between the Faith and Order Commission meetings and in the six assemblies of the WCC. Even the meetings of the Central Committee - only its sessions in 1950, 1955 and 1966 are an exception - have not concentrated on the crucial concern of unity. Consultations which Faith and Order has sponsored were on a variety of other subjects such as baptism, worship, ministry, the ordination of women, patristic studies, the week of prayer for Christian unity, the authority of the Bible, a fixed date for Easter, the Council of Chalcedon, the authority of the Bible, church union negotiations, bilateral dialogues, the Filioque controversy, eucharist with children, etc. Also various study programmes of Faith and Order on the Finality of Jesus Christ in the Age of Universal History, Tradition and Traditions, Institutionalism, Ways of Worship, God in Nature and History, Man in Nature and History, Giving Account of the

Hope That Is In Us, How Does the Church Teach Authoritatively Today, etc. were undertaken over a period of time in commission meetings and were only indirectly related to the theme of unity. The Faith and Order Commission is largely composed of professional theologians and ordained ministers. Broader participation by the membership of all churches, in particular lay people, has so far not been achieved.

2. The question of church unity has been largely absent in the churches of the Third World. Only from the middle of the sixties onwards do reports of assemblies of regional conferences of churches occasionally contain a few references to the problem of unity. But the emphasis in this context has been far more on church cooperation, living together a common life for the sake of a united witness, universality to strengthen the missionary movement, not creating a common front for the protection of minority rights, the breaking out of the church's captivity to power and security, the church as an instrument of transformation of the whole society, the identification with the millions of poor and oppressed than on confessional ecclesiology, internal ecclesiastical matters, and the important role of the WCC in the ecumenical movement.

3. During the first fifteen years a strong emphasis was placed on the shame of the churches for not recognizing each other as part of the one, holy, catholic and apostolic Church and on the non-theological factors of unity and disunity. No real advance towards unity can be made if cultural, social, political and psychological components of the life of the churches are not painstakingly analyzed and evaluated. Many unconscious and unavowed pre-judices and false pre-suppositions are too often treated as essentially in harmony with the gospel and not as the conditioning by a particular culture and society. The history of church divisions is to a large extent reflected in the history of political systems and concepts. The church experiences, as did its incarnate and sinless Lord, the consequences of the broken relationship between the Creator and his creatures. Division is a universal reality.

Although it has also later been stressed that in a sinful world the bonds of mutual love, understanding and sharing in the churches are repeatedly challenged by human divisions, and that the pluralism of cultures and societies is the pluralism of churches and their peoples, more recent documents and statements on ecclesiology have not sufficiently grasped the possibilities and implications of historical diversity taken absolutely seriously in the context of the ecumenical activities of God. An example is the recent document on Baptism, Eucharist and Ministry (BEM). This text, to be sure, is a milestone in the ecumenical movement. Consensus and concerted action of the churches which are based on the three basic ecclesial conditions that sum up church life and give it coherence and continuity are be lauded.

But the real crux is that BEM is still a typical Western document, rooted in the old cultural traditions of Roman Catholicism, Orthodoxy and Protestantism of the European continent.

It is in fact a rather stale, anachronistic, lopsided and intro-
verted theological charter of unity of the Western hemisphere.
Its language, its style of reasoning and its conclusions are
based on traditional theological argumentation, hardly understandable to many nonwhite Christians with minimal catechetical
instruction. Not accidentally African and Asian theologians
had little part in it and not surprisingly cannot identify with
its reasoning. Christianity in the First World has still to
show that it is open to and can learn much from missionary and
independent churches which differently interpret the being and
the nature of the Church according to their cultural heritage
and experience.

The BEM document lacks reflection on the necessary fluidity
and adaptability of all Christian ministries, already distinctly
recognized and practized during the New Testament times and the
early countries. Not surprisingly also even in the West BEM
carries in itself newly divisive elements. Old and well-estab-
lished churches claim the text as truly catholic and apostolic,
while a number of Reformation and free churches lament the
absence of the gospel as the origin of all church life.

4. When this survey on church unity is studied in connection
with the survey on mission and evangelism, it becomes clear that
the long debate on the relation of unity and mission, and mission
and unity, has remained inconclusive. Faith and Order and World
Mission and Evangelism, to be sure, have penetrated into each
other's 'territory' and stressed at many occasions that when the
response of the Church to unity and mission is not interdependent,
both become corrupted as they are isolated from each other.
Division in the Church distorts its witness, frustrates its
mission, and contradicts its own nature. On the other hand, the
Church's unity in its Lord spills necessarily over into mission
and evangelism. Also the Joint Working Group has emphasized
that there can be no true dialogue between the churches without
a wide openness to the world.

Yet the teachings of Melbourne 1980 on the Church's witness
to the kingdom and its identification with the poor and the
statements of Lima 1982 on the growth towards visible unity are
so different that an even greater fragmentation of the churches
in the ecumenical movement is taking place. The sole reason for
this is that the ecumenical camps of the 20th century continue
to put far more thought and energy into their own specific
concerns instead of feeding each other's insights and hopes.
The vision of unity and the vision of obedience in mission can
only be jointly dreamed and lived. The mortification of the
Church's divisions and the witness to Jesus Christ who was raised
from the dead are the two sides of the same coin. The unity of
the Church which is God's will and gift is spoiled when it is
not shared with humanity.

The true catholicity of the Church is as much constituted
in its apostolicity across all national and confessional boundaries as genuine common witness presupposes fully ecclesial
communion. As long as Faith and Order and Mission and Evangelism
fall apart into two independent endeavours (the unity and the

mission of the Church were considered separately at all six WCC assemblies), the unity of the Church as an inter- and trans-confessional matter and the unity in mission to and solidarity with the world are one-sidedly, and therefore peril-ously, pursued. The gap between the old and rich churches in the North, struggling for a sophisticated and prestigious theological unity in itself, and the young and poor churches in the South, struggling for an instrumental unity of God's people for the sake of all others, can only be closed in the ecumenical movement through mutual sharing and learning.

5. During the last few years of his life W.A. Visser 't Hooft has repeatedly stressed that the Toronto Statement of 1950 needs to be newly analyzed and up-dated. The question is how this can be done in a convincing manner. What is today the ecclesiological significance of the World Council of Churches ? Although the Faith and Order Commission has increasingly drawn attention to the unity experienced in the ecumenical movement, to the unity we seek, what unity implies, and what unity requires, it has not been able to spell out what exactly the nature and purpose of that unity is. At its meeting at Sta-vanger in 1985 it engaged in a difficult debate on the Church as mystery and prophetic sign, a theme which was already dis-cussed at a consultation at Chantilly, France, January 3-10, 1985.

As before different opinions were expressed on the character of the Church as the body and bride of Christ and a historic human reality. The ontological and functional/instrumental elements of the Church, its sacramental character and the place of the saving activity of God are still broken up by divergent conceptions of divine community. Also the Synod of Bishops in Rome, evaluating the results of the Second Vatican Council, spoke at length of the Church as a mystery. This concept will not be conducive to the unity the churches experience and live already if either the sacramental character of the Church, or its ministerial structure, or its renewal through mission and service are over-emphasized at the expense of the other truths.

It is not accidental that the key notion of the Church as the people of God of the Second Vatican Council has not been fully re-introduced into the recent debate of the Synod, as the World Council of Churches has not made this same notion a backbone of the ecumenical movement. The Church as a mystery and prophetic sign subsists in its calling to be an extraordi-nary people and sharing the extraordinary quality of that calling and being with the world. God's people is a peculiar people because it is constantly re-born, renewed and re-united in Christ. In him it is ever newly endowed with oneness, holi-ness, catholicity and apostolicity. The Decree on Ecumenism, however, one-sidedly emphasized "that because of the lack of the sacrament of orders" other churches "have not preserved the genuine and total reality of the Eucharistic mystery." And in stating that "the Church is bold in speaking of itself as the sign of the coming unity of mankind", the Uppsala Assembly did not deem it necessary to circumscribe 'the Church'.

It is the mysterious existence of a people of God, and not the institutional Church, that points to the kingdom, often in remote and irrelevant ways. The real fellowship in faith and in sacrament can face ever new confrontation, conflict and anguish, including the inextricable problem of different church structures. As the gospel, the sacraments and orders of ministry will be superfluous in God's kingdom, so the humanizing and also the dehumanizing ways of God's people will be done away with. There will be no more tragic confessional divisions or any ugly form of racism, classism and sexism. This faith constitutes the unity of the Church experienced and lived in the ecumenical movement and communicates it to the whole inhabited earth.

---

1.  The First Assembly of the World Council of Churches held at Amsterdam, August 22 to September 4, 1948. Ed. by W.A. Visser 't Hooft. London: SCM Press; New York: Harper, 1949. pp. 9, 51-52, 56.

2.  Minutes and Reports of the Third Meeting of the Central Committee at Toronto (Canada), July 9-15, 1950. Geneva: WCC, 1950. pp. 84-90.

3.  Report on Non-Theological Factors that May Hinder or Accelerate the Church's Unity. Bossey, 1951 (mimeographed). See also: Faith and Order Paper, nos. 9 and 10, 1952.

4.  The Third World Conference on Faith and Order, held at Lund, August 15-28, 1952. Ed. by Oliver S. Tomkins. London: SCM Press, 1953. pp. 15, 33-34, 44-47, 62-63.

5.  Minutes of the Enlarged Meeting and the Committee of the International Missionary Council, Willingen, Germany, July 5-21, 1952. London: IMC, 1952. pp. 57 and 82.

6.  The Evanston Report. The Second Assembly of the World Council of Churches 1954. New York: Harper, 1955. pp.84-91.

7.  Minutes and Reports of the Eighth Meeting of the Central Committee of the World Council of Churches at Davos, Switzerland, August 2-8, 1955. Geneva: WCC, 1955. pp. 21-26, 92-93.

8.  Minutes and Reports of the Thirteenth Meeting of the Central Committee of the World Council of Churches at St. Andrews, Scotland, August 16-24, 1980. Geneva: WCC, 1980. p. 183.

9.  Minutes of the Working Committee on Faith and Order, Geneva, 1958. Geneva: WCC, 1985 (Faith and Order Papers, No. 26).

10. Ecumenical Press Service, no. 36, October 3, 1958.

11. The New Delhi Report. The Third Assembly of the World
    Council of Churches, 1961.  London: SCM Press, 1962.
    pp. 321-322, 122, 126, 133.

12. The Fourth World Conference on Faith and Order, Montreal
    1963.  Ed. by P.C. Rodger and L. Vischer.
    London: SCM Press, 1964.  pp. 45, 47, 80-81.

13. Minutes of the Second Meeting of the Commission on World
    Mission and Evangelism. Mexico City, December 8-19, 1963.
    Geneva: WCC, 1964.  pp. 60 and 127.

14. Central Committee of the World Council of Churches.
    Minutes and Reports of the Nineteenth Meeting. Geneva,
    February 8-17, 1966.  Geneva: WCC, 1966.  pp. 71 and 73.

15. The Christian Community within the Human Community.
    Containing Statements from the Bangkok Assembly of the
    EACC, February - March 1964.  Minutes - Part 2.
    Bangalore: CLS, 1964.  pp. 73, 75, 82-83.

16. Drumbeats from Kampala. Report of the First Assembly of
    the All Africa Conference of Churches held at Kampala,
    April 20 to 30, 1963.  London: Lutterworth Press, 1963.
    pp. 39-41.

17. The Documents of Vatican II.  New York: Guild Press,
    America Press, Association Press, 1966.  pp. 362-365.

18. Central Committee of the World Council of Churches.
    Minutes and Reports of the Twentieth Meeting. Heraklion,
    Crete, August 15-26, 1967.  Geneva: WCC, 1967.  p. 143.

19. The Uppsala Report 1968. Official Report of the Fourth
    Assembly of the World Council of Churches, Uppsala,
    July 4-20, 1968.  Ed. by Norman Goodall.
    Geneva: WCC, 1968.  pp. 17, 321-322.

20. Faith and Order. Louvain 1971. Study Reports and Documents.
    Geneva: WCC, 1971 (Faith and Order Paper, No. 59).
    pp. 133-158, 226-227.

21. Uniting in Hope. Reports and Documents from the Meeting
    of the Faith and Order Commission, 23 July - 5 August,
    1974. University of Ghana, Legon.
    Geneva: WCC, 1975 (Faith and Order Paper, No. 72)
    pp. 18-19, 116-120.

22. The Humanum Studies, 1969-1975. A Collection of Documents.
    Geneva: WCC, 1975.  pp. 87-88.

23. Faith and Ideologies. An Ecumenical Discussion. Cartigny,
    May 1975.  Geneva: WCC, 1975.  pp. 7-9.

24. What Kind of Unity ?  Geneva: WCC, 1974 (Faith and Order
    Paper, No. 69).
    See also: Ecumenical Review, vol XXVI, no. 2, 1974.

25. _Midstream_, vol XIV, no. 4, October 1975.

26. _Ecumenical Press Service_, no. 10, 20 March, 1975.

27. _Study Encounter_, vol. XI, no. 3, 1975.

28. Breaking Barriers. Nairobi 1975. Ed. by David M. Paton.
    London: SPCK; Grand Rapids: Wm. B. Eerdmans, 1976.
    pp. 59-69.

29. Faith in the Midst of Faith. Reflections on Dialogue in
    Community. Ed. by S.J. Samartha.  Geneva: WCC, 1977. p. 142.

30. Sharing in One Hope. Reports and Documents from the Meeting
    of the Faith and Order Commission, 15-30 August, 1978,
    Bangalore, India.  Geneva: WCC, 1982 (Faith and Order
    Paper, No. 92).  pp. 237-240.

31. Towards Visible Unity. Commission on Faith and Order
    Lima 1982. Volume II: Study Papers and Reports.  Ed. by
    Michael Kinnamon.  Geneva: WCC, 1982 (Faith and Order
    Paper, No. 113).  p. 228.

32. Baptism, Eucharist and Ministry.  Geneva: WCC, 1982
    (Faith and Order Paper, No. 111).

33. Gathered for Life. Official Report. VI Assembly of the
    World Council of Churches, Vancouver, Canada, 24 July -
    10 August, 1983.  Ed. by David Gill.
    Geneva: WCC, 1983.  pp. 43-52.

34. Conciliar Unity. A National Consultation.
    Geneva: WCC; Bangalore: Ecumenical Christian Centre, 1978.
    (mimeographed)

35. Towards a Confession of the Common Faith.
    Geneva: WCC, 1980 (Faith and Order Paper, No. 100).

36. Elements of Unity, Obstacles to Unity.
    Bossey, 1981 (mimeographed).

37. Growing Towards Consensus and Commitment. Report of the
    Fourth International Consultation of United and Uniting
    Churches.  Geneva: WCC, 1981 (Faith and Order Paper, No.110).

38. Christian Conference of Asia. Sixth Assembly, Penang,
    31 May - 9 June, 1977.  Singapore: CCA, 1977.  pp. 97-98.

39. Christian Conference of Asia. Eighth Assembly, Seoul,
    June 26 - July 2, 1985.  Singapore: CCA, 1985. pp.133-135.

# V.
## The Bible, the Church, Tradition, Confessions, Creeds and Unity

Questions about the place, the authority and the understanding of the Bible have always been central for the ecumenical movement. They have been often debated at assemblies of the WCC and at ecumenical consultations and conferences. Besides introducing the major statements of large ecumenical gatherings and describing the discussions of smaller specific consultations on the interpretation and the use of the Bible, this survey deals in particular with the whole question of the relation between Scripture, Tradition and Magisterium, a question which is at the heart of the unity of the Church.

A key person in promoting the study of the Bible in the ecumenical movement was Suzanne de Diétrich. She personified "the biblical renewal" about which she wrote and taught with great passion and clarity, and thereby formed generations of biblically literate students and leaders, in France, at the Ecumenical Institute Bossey and around the world. Two of her major works in English are Rediscovering the Bible[1] and God's Unfolding Purpose[2]. These and other books stimulated the biblical renewal in the Roman Catholic Church.

## I.

A first conference on the theme "Biblical Authority for the Church's Social and Political Message Today" was held in London, August 10-12, 1946. Papers were read by C.H. Dodd, R. Bring, H. Ehrenberg, W.M. Horton, S. van Veenen. A. Richardson. At the second meeting in Bossey, January 5-9, 1947, papers were presented on the same theme by K. Barth, A. Nygren, L. Aalen, N.H. Søe, C. van Niftrik, B. Nagy, W. Eichrodt, H. van Oyen.

The report of the London discussions included: 1) The Authorithy of the Bible; 2) The Interpretation of the Bible; 3) Old and New Testament; Law and Gospel; 4) The Bible and Political Questions. The report of the Bossey discussions included: 1) Bible, Church and Canon; 2) Old and New Testament; 3) The Bases of Christian Ethics; 4) Church and World: The Problem of the Sermon on the Mount; 5) Church and State: Theocracy vs. Luther's "Two Realms"; 6) The Social, Economic Message of the Bible; 7) Final Theses of the Bossey Study Conference on the Authority of the Bible.[3]

The Report of Section I, "The Universal Church in God's Design", of the first Assembly at Amsterdam in 1948 made a short reference to "a deeper understanding of our differences" by mentioning "the relation, in the saving acts of God in Christ, between objective redemption and personal salvation, between scripture and tradition, between the Church as once founded and

the Church as Christ's contemporary act." On the other hand it
asserted that fellow-Christians "discovered new life, found the
Bible as a living, contemporary book, made a good confession of
their faith and saw the Church come to life in the steadfastness
of thousands of humble Christians."4

Another consultation on "The Bible and the Church's Message
to the World" took place at Oxford, June 28 - July 6, 1969.
J. Marsh and W. Eichrodt presented papers on Guiding Principles
for the Interpretation of the Bible5. The words in this sentence became the title of the well-known Wadham College Statement. The guiding principles of this statement were reprinted
in The Bible - Its Authority and Interpretation in the Ecumenical
Movement, to which is later referred.


## II.


With regard to consensus in doctrine, the Third World Conference on Faith and Order at Lund, in 1952, expressed itself
as follows: "All accept the Holy Scriptures as either the sole
authority for doctrine or the primary and decisive part of those
authorities to which they would appeal. Most accept the Ecumenical Creeds as an interpretation of the truth of the Bible
or as marking a distinctive stage in the working-out of the
orthodox faith. Some assign a special importance to the credal
documents of the early Ecumenical Councils. Some would say that
to found unity on any creeds is to found it on something human,
namely, our understanding of the Gospel and our theological work
in formulating its meaning. Some judge in accordance with the
Inner Light and the leadings of the Spirit and are therefore
concerned to witness against the use of outward creeds when these
are held to be necessary or sufficient.

"Many denominations possess confessional documents in which
they express the Christian Faith as they read it in the Bible.
It would generally be admitted, however, that these last documents would not be regarded as irreformable and they do not in
fact occupy the same position in the Rule of Faith of all Churches which possess them."

Adressing itself on the question Where do we stand ?, the
World Conference at Lund stated the following: "By the final
revelation of God in Jesus Christ at a particular point in
history, the church lives, but it is within the continuous
movement of history that it bears witness to this Gospel and
applies it to human need. The thought forms and language
through which the Church proclaims the one Gospel are therefore
subject to the limitations and changes of history. But the
nature of any given historical period is such that in no one
age can the truth of God's revelation be given full expression.
This does not mean that the Church should subordinate its message to the relativities of history, for we believe that the
revelation of God in Jesus Christ and the scriptural witness
to it are unique and normative for all ages.

"The Church should seek to proclaim this truth in ever-new terms, but the language and thought forms coined in history must be constantly corrected by the content of the Gospel. This is also true of those means by which the Churches have confessed their faith in decisive moments of their history. We must always make sure in contending for our distinctive convictions that we distinguish between the confession of the Truth to which we are committed and those expressions of it that were in part products of a particular age. If all denominations are prepared to do this in obedience to the Gospel alone, we may well come nearer to one another.

"Furthermore, this work of interpretation of the Churches to each other and to the world takes place in an intellectual climate that has undergone far-reaching changes. Our understanding of the Scriptures to which the Reformers made their primary appeal has greatly advanced. Whereas this in itself has brought new problems it has given a new expression to the biblical revelation in its greatness and transcendence. As exemples we may cite developments in the study of biblical methods of interpreation. This biblical study cuts across denominational lines and often provides a fresh starting-point for re-thinking denominational relationships."[6]

In the Report of Section I, "Faith and Order: Our Oneness in Christ and Our Disunity as Churches" of the Second Assembly at Evanston, 1954, the following was stated: "We must all listen together in the midst of our disunity to our one Lord speaking to us through Holy Scripture. This is a hard thing to do. We still struggle to comprehend the meaning and authority of Holy Scripture. Yet whenever we are prepared to undertake together the study of the Word of God and are resolved to be obedient to what we are told, we are on the way toward realizing the oneness of the Church in Christ in the actual state of our dividedness on earth. In this connection we need also to study together the significance of Christian tradition and our various traditions, as reflected in liturgy, preaching and teaching."

In The Declaration of the Orthodox Delegates Concerning Faith and Order the following was expressed: "The whole of the Christian faith should be regarded as one indivisible unity. It is not enough to accept just certain particular doctrines, basic as they may be in themselves, e.g. that Christ is God and Saviour. It is compelling that all doctrines as formulated by the Ecumenical Councils, as well as the totality of the teaching of the early, undivided Church, should be accepted. One cannot be satisfied with formulas which are isolated from the life and experience of the Church. They must be assessed and understood within the context of the Church's life.

"From the Orthodox viewpoint, re-union of Christendom with which the World Council of Churches is concerned can be achieved solely on the basis of the total, dogmatic Faith of the early, undivided Church without either subtraction or alteration. We cannot accept a rigid distinction between essential and non-essential doctrines, and there is no room for comprehensiveness in the Faith. On the other hand, the Orthodox Church cannot

accept that the Holy Spirit speaks to us only through the Bible.
The Holy Spirit abides and witnesses through the totality of the
Church's life and experience. The Bible is given to us within
the context of Apostolic Tradition in which in turn we possess
the authentic interpretation and explication of the Word of God.
Loyalty to Apostolic Tradition safeguards the reality and contin-
nuity of church unity."

In the Report of Section II, "Evangelism: The Mission of the
Church to Those Outside Her Life" it was stated: "... in order
to possess the power to evangelize, the Church must nourish its
life on the Bible. To recover for current thought the great
biblical concepts is one of the pressing needs of evangelism.
In the communication of the gospel the Bible occupies a unique
and central place. The Bible speaks to all, provides a common
language for the Church, transcending our divisions. The translation and distribution of the Holy Scriptures is an inescapable
task of the evangelizing Church." 7

"Living with the Bible" was the theme of a consultation at
Bossey, June 15-27, 1959. Contributions were made by T.S.N.
Gqubule, Prof. Mayeda, H.-R. Weber, E.H. Robertson. The participants engaged in three ways of discussion: they were confronted with the living word of God by the Bible study as such;
they looked into possible methods of exegesis and the presuppositions for them; they considered how smaller and bigger groups
can be made to participate in a Bible study which they themselves
- mostly non-theologians - are to lead. 8

At the meeting of the Central Committee at St. Andrews in
1960 a proposal was made of a cooperative study on The Use of
the Bible in Evangelism. It was suggested that "a committee of
14 persons should be formed consisting of 7 representatives of
the United Bible Societies, 4 from the Department on Evangelism,
and 3 from the Division of Ecumenical Action. The following
general lines of inquiry were suggested: "The place of the Bible
in evangelism, both as a means of evangelism and a source of
inspiration and motivation for it; the effect of the use of the
Bible in the Christian encounter with those estranged from, or
on the fringe of the Church, and with non-Christians, including
adherents of other religions; and the way in which the Holy
Scriptures can best be utilized in present-day circumstances
as a means of furthering the evangelistic and missionary work
of the Church."9

III.

The Report of Section I, Unity, of the Third Assembly of the
WCC at New Delhi in 1961 said the following on the one apostolic
faith: "The Holy Scriptures of the Old and New Testaments witness to the apostolic faith. This is nothing else than those
events which constitute God's call of a people to be his people.
The heart of the Gospel (kerygma) is Jesus Christ himself, his
life and teaching, his death, resurrection, coming (parousia)

and the justification and sanctification which he brings and
offers to all men. The Creeds of the Church witness to this
apostolic faith.  There are important studies now being undertaken of the relationship between Scripture and Tradition (which
is Christian confession down the ages), and attention is drawn
to the work of Faith and Order's Theological Commission on
Tradition and Traditions."  The report of this Commission was
published in 1961 under the title The Old and the New in the
Church.[10]

Concerning doctrinal agreement the Report on Unity of the
New Delhi Assembly stated: "In our consideration of next steps
towards an agreed doctrinal basis for the unity we seek, two
useful distinctions may be made - that intellectual formulations
of faith are not to be identified with faith itself, and that
koinonia in Christ is more nearly the precondition of 'sound
doctrine' than vice versa.  The primary basis of this koinonia
is the apostolic testimony in the Holy Scriptures and 'the hearing of the faith'.  Yet this primary biblical revelation was
given to and through the apostolic church and has continued to
be witnessed to by our common historic Creeds, specifically the
Apostles' Creed and the Nicaeo-Constantinopolitan Creed.

"There is, as it were, 'an ecumenicity in time', which may
be realized by serious attention both to the ancient witnesses
and also to the gifts of light and truth given by the Spirit
in various ages and traditions in the history of the people of
God.  'The one apostolic faith', referred to in Part One of this
report, is, first and last, faith in Christ as Lord and Saviour
to the glory of God the Father.  An obvious practical corollary
of this understanding is the recommendation that a next step
towards unity, at the denominational level, would be a fresh
consideration of our various doctrinal bases, in the light of
the primacy of Scripture and its safeguarding in the church by
the Holy Spirit."[11]

It is important to remember that the "Basis" of the WCC was
amended and expanded at the New Delhi Assembly.  From Amsterdam
1948 onwards it read: "The World Council of Churches is a fellowship of churches which accept Jesus Christ as God and Saviour".
From 1961 onwards it reads: "The World Council of Churches is a
fellowship of Churches which confess the Lord Jesus Christ as
God and Saviour according to the Scriptures and therefore seek
to fulfill together their common calling to the glory of the
one God, Father, Son and Holy Spirit."

Section II of the Fourth World Conference on Faith and Order
at Montreal in 1963 dealt extensively with Scripture, Tradition
and Traditions.  "We speak of the Tradition (with a capital T),
tradition (with a small t) and traditions.  By the Tradition is
meant the Gospel itself, transmitted from generation to generation in and by the Church, Christ himself present in the life
of the Church.  By tradition is meant the traditionary process.
The term traditions is used in two senses, to indicate both the
diversity of forms of expression and also what we call confessional traditions, for instance the Lutheran tradition or

the Reformed tradition. In the latter part of our report the word appears in a further sense, when we speak of cultural traditions."

"... The Bible poses the problem of Tradition and Scripture in a more or less implicit manner; the history of Christian theology points to it explicitly. While in the Early Church the relation was not understood as problematical, ever since the Reformation 'Scripture and Tradition' has been a matter of controversy in the dialogue between Roman Catholic and Protestant theology. On the Roman Catholic side, tradition has generally been understood as divine truth not expressed in Holy Scripture alone, but orally transmitted. The Protestant position has been an appeal to Holy Scripture alone, as the infallible and sufficient authority in all matters pertaining to salvation, to which all human traditions should be subjected. The voice of the Orthodox Church has hardly been heard in these Western discussions until quite recently.

"For a variety of reasons, it has now become necessary to reconsider these positions. We are more aware of our living in various confessional traditions, e.g. that stated paradoxically in the saying 'It has been the tradition of my church not to attribute any weight to tradition'. Historical study and not least the encounter of the churches in the ecumenical movement have led us to realize that the proclamation of the Gospel is always inevitable historically conditioned. We are also aware that in Roman Catholic theology the concept of tradition is undergoing serious reconsideration..."

The Section outlined further the difficulty of evaluating the various traditions, the search of a criterion, the fact that loyalty to confessional understandings of Holy Scripture produces both convergence and divergence in the interpretation of Scripture, that at least two distinctive types of understanding the Tradition exist and therefore two distinctive positions on the relation between Tradition and traditions.

It continued to state: "The content of the Tradition cannot be exactly defined, for the reality it transmits can never be fully contained in propositional forms. In the Orthodox view, Tradition includes an understanding of the events recorded in the New Testament, of the writings of the Fathers, of the ecumenical creeds and Councils, and of the life of the Church throughout the centuries. All member churches of the World Council of Churches are united in confessing the Lord Jesus Christ 'as God and Saviour, according to the Scriptures, and in seeking together to fulfil their common calling to the glory of the one God, Father, Son and Holy Spirit'.

"This basis of membership safeguards a position from which we may seek constantly to grow in understanding of the fullness of God's revelation, and to correct partial apprehensions of the truth. In the task of seeking to understand the relation between the Tradition and the traditions, problems are raised as difficult to solve as they are crucial in importance. Such questions often cannot be answered apart from the specific situations which pose them. There are no ready-made solutions..."12

As the World Conference at Montreal had called for a clarification of the problems of biblical exegesis and interpretation, a study process was initiated on The Significance of the Hermeneutical Problem for the Ecumenical Movement. Several regional groups were formed and consultations took place. A concluding meeting at Heidelberg drew up a final report which was presented to the Faith and Order Commission at its meeting in Bristol in 1967 and afterwards published.13 This document is important because it reveals a strong impact of Western Roman Catholic and Protestant biblical scholarship on ecumenical thinking, especially in its paragraph on "Unity and Diversity".

IV.

In the Dogmatic Constitution on Divine Revelation of the Second Vatican Council the following was expressed on Sacred Scripture: "It is clear that sacred tradition, sacred Scripture, and the teaching authority of the Church, in accord with God's most wise design, are so linked and joined together that one cannot stand without the others, and that all together and each in its own way under the action of the one Holy Spirit contribute effectively to the salvation of souls.

"The Church has always venerated the divine Scriptures just as she venerates the body of the Lord, since from the table of both the word of God and of the body of Christ she unceasingly receives and offers to the faithful the bread of life, expecially in the sacred liturgy. She has always regarded the Scriptures together with sacred traditions as the supreme rule of faith, and will ever do so. For, inspired by God and committed once and for all to writing, they impart the word of God Himself without change, and make the voice of the Holy Spirit resound in the words of the prophets and apostles. Therefore, like the Christian religion itself, all the preaching of the Church must be nourished and ruled by sacred Scripture. For in the sacred books, the Father who is in heaven meets His children with great love and speaks with them; and the force and power in the word of God is so great that it remains the support and energy of the Church, the strength of faith for her sons, the food of the soul, the pure and perennial source of spiritual life..."

On the interpretation of Sacred Scripture the following was stated: "... Since God speaks in sacred Scripture through men in human fashion, the interpreter of sacred Scripture, in order to see clearly what God wanted to communicate to us, should carefully investigate what meaning the sacred writers really intended, and what God wanted to manifest by means of their words...

"Since holy Scripture must be read and interpreted according to the same Spirit by whom it was written, no less serious attention must be given to the content and unity of the whole of Scripture, if the meaning of the sacred texts is to be correctly brought to light. The living tradition of the whole Church must be taken into account along with the harmony which exists between elements of the faith. It is the task of exegetes to work according to these rules toward a better understanding and explanation of the meaning of sacred Scripture, so that through preparatory study the judgment of the Church may mature. For all of what has been said about the way of interpreting Scripture is subject finally to the judgment of the Church, which carries out the divine commission and ministry of guarding and interpreting the word of God.[14]

## V.

The Report of Policy Reference Committee II to the Uppsala Assembly in 1968 contained a Statement on the Bible in the Ecumenical Movement, prepared at the request of the Joint Committee of the WCC and the United Bible Societies. The Assembly recommended "that the Central Committee develop means by which the World Council could more effectively help the member churches to encourage the distribution, reading and study of the Bible by their members."

The Portfolio for Biblical Studies was established in 1971. Both in the initial period and later, the major work of the Director of this Portfolio was concentrated on three tasks: a) collaborating with ongoing studies and projects of WCC unity; b) stimulating the training of Bible study enablers in different member churches; and c) carrying out a research project on the role of cultural factors in biblical interpretation. In 1976 the Portfolio on Biblical Studies was transferred from the General Secretariat to the Sub-unit on Education. The Desk has responded to requests for seminars from regional and national councils of churches, WCC member churches, theological colleges, and Christian organizations like the YMCA and YWCA.

In the Report of the Assembly Committee on Faith and Order to the Uppsala Assembly the following reference was made to the quest for unity: "... The Roman Catholic Church, through the Second Vatican Council, has become an ecumenical partner in a new sense. Contemporary exegetical studies have posed the question whether this justifies a multiplicity of denominations. The renewal of interest in patristic studies and the renewed discussion of Tradition and traditions have given a new historical depth to our discussion of unity."[15]

In 1969 a Research Pamphlet by Richard C. Rowe on Bible Study in the World Council of Churches was published by the WCC. It is in four parts: I. The Context of Bible Study in the WCC; II. A History of Bible Study in the WCC; III. A Survey of Bible Studies in the WCC; IV. Basic Attitudes Toward the Bible in the WCC.[16]

A consultation on Bible Reading Notes and Biblical Theology
was organized at Bossey, March 25-30, 1963 by the Youth Department and the Ecumenical Institute. Chairmen were R. French and
H.-R. Weber. Speakers were: G. Amsler, G. Galitis, W. Harrelson,
P. Jones, C. Maurer, E.H. Robertson, A.G. Smith, W.A. Visser 't
Hooft, C.M. de Vries, C.W. Welsh. Five steps of cooperation
were envisaged: a) the establishment of channels of mutual consultations;  b) common Bible reading lists;  c) cooperation in
the preparation of the notes;  d) common series of notes; e) the
Bible reading societies and the churches.[17]

A third conference with conservative evangelicals took place
at Bossey, July 22-26, 1968, on the theme "What Do the Holy
Scriptures Say About Christian Responsibility in and for the
World ?" J.C. Weber chaired the meeting. Addresses were given
by E.G. Hinson and J. Rothermundt. Three sub-themes guided the
discussion: 1) Justification; 2) Christ's Lordship over the
World; 3) The Sermon on the Mount.[18]

After a consultation at Zürich, Oct. 21-26, 1968 on The
Authority of the Bible, James Barr provided the summary of the
conclusions which were reached at the consultation.[19]  In this
summary six major question areas were outlined: 1) The question
of priorities within the Bible itself and its relation to the
community which produced it;  2) The question of diversity in
the Bible;  3) The question raised by the changes of world-out-
look since biblical times and by our temporal distance from the
biblical situation;  4) The question of relations between past
and future in respect of the authority of the Bible;  5) The
question of the relation between biblical authority and other
kinds of authority;  6) Questions of the use, function and
application of biblical material.

The summary of the Zürich consultation served as a stimulus
for the formation of a number of study groups in different
countries. Representatives of the groups (in most cases the
moderators) met in the spring of 1971 to review and evaluate
the results of the diversified study-process. The result was
a Report on The Authority of the Bible with the following contents: I. The Problem (a. Confessional Difference; b. The Influence of Historical Criticism; c. Historical Remoteness);
II. The Concept of Authority;  III. Revelation and the Diversity of Interpretations;  IV. Holy Spirit, Church and Inspiration;  V. The Use of the Bible.[20]

A consultation on "Freedom and Social Structure in the Light
of the Gospel" took place at Bossey, August 31 - September 3,
1969. It was a continuation of a consultation on "Generations'
Involvement in Power Structures", June 1968. The meeting was
organized jointly by the Ecumenical Institute, the WSCF and the
WCC Youth Department. N.A. Nissiotis and M. Opocensky were
co-chairmen. There were 5 groups reports.[21]

Mention should be made here of two Graduate Schools at Bossey
which dealt during the four months course with the Bible. In 1970/
71 the overall theme was: "The Bible Contested and Contesting".
In 1980/81: "The Bible in the Life of the Church".

The Report on The Authority of the Bible was presented to the Faith and Order Commission meeting at Louvain in 1971. It was noted that "the Report makes clear that differing historical situations not only permit various interpretations of the biblical witnesses, but in fact demand them. But then the question arises how the continuing identity of the Gospel is still maintained in the various traditions." This gathering also discussed matters of tradition and change within the realm of the ordained ministry and noted that "there is today a greater awareness of the historical character of the patterns of ministry within the New Testament. Biblical scholarship has come to the conclusion that it is not possible to ground one conception of church order in the New Testament to the exclusion of others. It appears that in New Testament times differing forms co-existed and differing forms developed simultaneously in various geographical areas...

"In many respects the ministry in its present form does not seem to be fully adequate to its purpose anymore. In Western society, traditional and sacred in character, religious ministry conferred its holder a central position in the community with almost unequalled status, prestige and power... But modern society tends more to split into innumerable associations and organizations which function according to more rationalistic principles, both scientific and technical. This development has shifted the place of religion to a limited sector of human activity. Thus the professional minister whose duties and activities are dedicated exclusively to this limited religious sector finds himself removed from many functions he was fulfilling in a more "sacred" society. Such deprivation can lead to a serious crisis in "identity" of the ordained minister...

"The experience of different cultural settings and their needs as well as ecumenical contacts have helped relativise claims of permanence which once were attached to certain patterns of ministry... All are of the conviction that the Church is apostolic, i.e. that at all times it is and has to be in communion with the apostolic community and ministry. Though it changes in the course of history it must not lose the identity which it has been given by Christ. But in what way does the ministry assure this identity ? Or can identity be assured only through certain obligatory patterns ?"

With regard to the question of the starting point for renewal of worship the Louvain gathering expressed itself as follows: "... The existing situation cannot be postulated on the authority of biblical or even church-historical considerations, but should be grasped as it presents itself. To start from the biblical witness and church tradition, in particular, from liturgical tradition, could lead to "dogmatism, loss of touch with the present world" and, above all, to an "antiquarian" and ultimately, fruitless refurbishing of supposedly original forms. Although most participants favoured the renewal of sacramental practice, individual voices urged that even baptism and eucharist need not be regarded _automatically_ as settled forms of Christian worship. The first and most important consideration should be the experience of the present generation. Where in our modern world do acts of worship take place ? Only when this has been considered can it be profitable to study Holy Scriptures afresh."

In the section on _Catholicity and Apostolicity_ the Louvain commission meeting said: "... Both in Scripture and in tradition different senses of the word 'apostle' can be found. We must willingly accept this diversity which imposes new perspectives on the theological consensus. It prevents theologians from putting too much reliance on ready made notions and attributing to verbal formulae an exclusive and definitive character. Much more than by asking the letter of Scripture to give us a stereotype portrait of the apostle, it is by faithfully assuming the tasks entrusted by the Lord to His apostles that apostolicity of the Church is made worthy of credence."

In the section on _Common Witness and Proselytism_ it was noted that "cooperation has extended to include the production, publication and distribution of joint translations of the Scriptures. Moreover, an exploration is being made of the possibility of common texts to be used for an initial catechesis on the central message of the Christian faith..."[22]

The committee which evaluated the report on the _Authority of the Bible_ at Louvain in 1971 recommended that "the relationship of Old and New Testaments and particularly the contemporary significance of the Old Testament should be given careful study. A group complied with the request and worked out a paper _The Relation Between Old Testament and New Testament_. The Faith and Order Commission meeting at Accra in 1974 recommended to continue the study by solliciting reactions to the paper by individual scholars and groups from as many different sides as possible. A small group drawn from the membership of the Faith and Order Standing Commission met in Loccum (West Germany) in 1977 and drew up a final report which was approved by the Standing Commission meeting in Bangalore in 1978. The report appears in _The Bible - Its Authority and Interpretation in the Ecumenical Movement_.

The Faith and Order Commission meeting at Accra in the section on "_Moving into the Fullness of Conciliar Fellowship_" expressed itself on _Unity in the Truth of the Gospel_ as follows: "The churches must be able to recognize one another as holding and confessing the apostolic faith. There must be a common reliance on the Word of God as Scripture. Wherever, for instance, there have been condemnations of one another, the issues involved must be worked at until the condemnations can be seen on all sides to apply no longer. Any new conflicts that arise in the sphere of doctrine and truth (for example, those referred to by "confessing" groups) must be held _within_ the fellowship and worked out _together_ until they lose their power to divide."[23]

A Common Statement of our Faith, produced by the Faith and
Order Commission meeting at Bangalore in 1978 contained the
following paragraph: "As we seek to confess our faith together,
we want to be faithful to the apostolic faith according to the
Scriptures, handed down to us through the centuries. At the same
time we want to face the new situation and the challenge for
mission today. Furthermore, we are aware that a common confession of faith should be the sign of our reconciliation."[24]

## VII.

The meeting of the Commission on World Mission and Evangelism
at Bangkok in 1973 stressed the need of "a renewed understanding
of the Bible from the viewpoint of the community of the oppressed."
It recommended that a study process be initiated "to analyze
critically and from a biblical point of view the liberating and
oppressive elements which are often deeply interwoven in the
fabric of culture."[25]

A Conference on Sexism in the 1970s at Berlin in 1974 stated:
"Whereas Bible translations in many languages incorrectly suggest
maleness where original texts are inclusive, or misrepresent
women's roles; new translations continue to appear; translation
committees usually are composed of male scholars only; we recommend a) that female as well as male scholars be appointed to
Bible translation committees; b) that such committees be instructed to correct sexist errors in future translations;
c) that the WCC transmit this recommendation to those responsible
for Bible translations in the various countries."[26]

Section I "Confessing Christ Today" of the WCC Assembly at
Nairobi in 1975 contained the following paragraph: "While we
rejoice hearing the gospel speak to our particular situation
and while we must try to communicate the gospel to particular
contexts, we must remain faithful to the historical apostolic
witness as we find it in the holy Scriptures and tradition as
it is centred in Jesus Christ - lest we accomodate them to our
own desires and interests."[27]

A consultation on "Dialogue in Community" at Chiang Mai in
1977 was "aware of problems concerning the authority of the
Bible remaining unsolved among us and of the need for a much
closer attention than we had time to give to the problem of
relating Christian worship and the meditative use (rather than
simply the intellectual study) of the holy books of other faiths.
In one of our acts of Christian worship we were invited by the
leader in the course of the service to use responsively a passage
of the Bhagavadgita: this immediately made plain the rejection
or deep hesitation by some towards any such experience while we
discovered in conversation afterwards how meaningful some others
find such meditative acts. We recognize the need for further
study of the issues thus raised."

Participants in the Chiang Mai gathering also wondered how we are "to find from the Bible criteria in our approach to people of other faiths and ideologies, recognizing as we must, both the authority accorded to the Bible by Christians of all centuries, particular questions concerning the authority of the Old Testament for the Christian Church, and the fact that our partners in dialogue have other starting points and resources, both in holy books and traditions of teaching ? What is the biblical view and experience of the operation of the Holy Spirit, and is it right and helpful to understand the work of God outside the Church in terms of the doctrine of the Holy Spirit?"[28]

"The Gospel and International Life" was the subject of a consultation at Bossey, July 11-24, 1977. Papers were presented by Th. van Boven (Human Rights and the Role of International Organizations); C.I. Itty (The Search for a New International Economic Order and Its Challenge to the Churches); J. de Santa Ana (Militarism and the Arms Race). Other contributors were: M. Gallis, P. Hansen, J. Lucal, W. Sternstein, P.N.Williams.[29]

During a seminar at Prague, September 12-18, 1977, "The Role and the Place of the Bible in the Liturgical and Spiritual Life of the Orthodox Churches" was discussed. This seminar was the third in a series of Orthodox missionary consultations, organized by the Orthodox Studies Desk of CWME. The first seminar was held at Cernica-Bucharest in 1974, and the second in Etchmiadzine, Armenia in 1975. The report includes two work group reports on: I. The Bible and Liturgical Life; II. Preaching and Teaching the Holy Scripture Today.[30]

"The Bible in Our Situations and Work" was the theme of a consultation at Naramata, Canada, October 1977. This was another consultation of the World Collaboration Committee for Christian Lay Centres, Academies and Movements of Social Concern, operating jointly with the WCC Sub-unit on Renewal and Congregational Life. The basic material of the report was prepared by R. Booth, the regional communications director for the United Church on Canada's West coast. H.-R. Weber directed five Bible studies. The consultation was nourished by the conviction that ordinary Christians need tools for doing theology in the now.[31]


VIII.


"The Authority of Scripture in Light of New Experiences of Women" was the subject of discussion of a consultation at Amsterdam, December 1980. The report includes: I. Introduction; II. Women Speak: The Interaction of Scripture and Experience; III. Biblical Authority Reconsidered; IV. Recommendations: A. Regarding the Search for a New Understanding of Biblical Authority; B. Regarding Worship and the Preparation of Liturgical Materials; C. Regarding Christian Education; D. Regarding Ministerial Formation and Theological Education; E. Regarding Biblical Translation; F. Regarding Ecclesiastical Structures. Recommendations to the Faith and Order Commission and the entire WCC.[32]

At the meeting of the Central Committee in Geneva in 1984, the Committee on Unit III "noted the four options suggested for future work in Biblical Studies: 1) training courses for Bible study enablers; 2) biblical consultative work within the WCC; 3) creating a network of those involved in Bible study work; 4) further work in the field of the Bible and the arts."

With a view to inter-unit collaboration it was recommended that at least for the next three years the first option be chosen. The Central Committee accepted this recommendation.[33]

The Bible - Its Authority and Interpretation in the Ecumenical Movement was published in 1980. It deals with: 1) Guiding Principles for the Interpretation of the Bible; 2) Scripture, Tradition and Traditions; 3) The Significance of the Hermeneutical Problem for the Ecumenical Movement; 4) The Authority of the Bible; 5) The Significance of the Old Testament in Its Relation to the New. The book also lists some major Faith and Order documents - partly reproduced in this survey - which were written during the ongoing discussions. It finally includes a selective bibliography of books and articles.[34]


## Observations and Comments

1. The crucial function of the Bible in the ecumenical movement and in the World Council of Churches is undisputed. The Bible is a uniting factor. As a result of the consultations from 1946-1949 Biblical Authority for Today was published in 1951 as a World Council of Churches Symposium on "The Biblical Authority for the Churches' Social and Political Message Today."[35] Ever since churches engaged in the ecumenical movement have appealed to the Bible as the authoritative basis of their faith, life and witness. The relevance to and the impact of the Bible on theology, mission, liturgy, worship, social ethics, the dialogue with people of living faiths and ideologies has often been discussed and outlined in various ways.

All churches regard the Bible as the unique source of knowledge about the revelation of God in Jesus Christ. As they seek to overcome their differences, churches have turned to the Scriptures. In the light of the biblical witnesses they have re-examined their positions and re-thought together the controversies which have caused separation in the past and still continue to keep them divided today. As they re-read the Bible together they will discover dimensions and aspects whose neglect has led to one-sided emphases, and they will help one another at arrive to a fuller understanding of the truth.

The explicit reference to the Bible which was added to the Basis of the WCC in 1961 is more than a formality. It indicates that God's Word is the true meeting ground of the ecumenical movement. Without a common biblical theology it would have no backbone. The deepest motive for the seeking of unity is the biblical conception of the gathering of the people of God by the Lord Jesus Christ. The creation of the Portfolio of Biblical Studies in 1971 was another sign that the Bible is the centre of the life of the Council and its constituency.

2. Also in the Roman Catholic Church there has been a remarkable revival of Bible scholarship, study and concern for the use of the Bible by the faithful. It arose naturally out of the Second Vatican Council that this Church sought relations with international Christian organizations, such as the United Bible Societies. The fresh emphasis on the importance of the Bible in the life of the church, and, above all, the decision to give more place to the vernacular in the liturgy, made it necessary to increase the production of biblical translations and the number of its editions. The Constitution on Revelation had, in this connection, expressly encouraged "co-operation with the separated brethren" in producing such translations.

In 1968 the Secretariat for Promoting Christian Unity published jointly with the United Bible Societies Guiding Principles for Interconfessional Cooperation in Translating the Bible. This statement contains the following headings: I. Technical Features: A. Textual; B. Exegetical; C. Linguistic. II. Procedures: A. Climate for Cooperation; B. Revision vs. New Translation; C. Organizational Structure; D. Appointment of Personnel; E. Formulation of Principles; F. Editorial Supervision; G. Types of Editions; H. Imprint and Imprimatur.[36] Joint editions of the Bible have been published in many countries and others are in preparation. The French Traduction Oecuménique de la Bible (TOB) has been hailed as a most successful ecumenical enterprise.

3. During the sixties and the early seventies the difficult problem of the relation between Scripture, Tradition and traditions came to the forefront. By no means has the problem been solved. Unfortunately there has been considerably less debate on the Bible and the teaching authority of the Church during the last fifteen years.

In spite of an increased recognition of the authority of the Bible within the Orthodox churches the position is maintained that the Holy Spirit speaks through the Bible and through the totality of the Church's life and experience through the centuries. In spite of the recognition of the Roman Catholic Church that Sacred Scriptures are the supreme rule of faith and that biblical scholarship is vital for the life of the church in the modern world, the position is maintained that only the Church itself carries out the "divine commission" of interpreting and applying authoritatively the Word of God. And in spite of the fact that many Protestant churches now admit that the Bible itself is already part of Tradition and that denominationalism is not free of traditions, the dogmatic principle of sola scriptura tends to predominate over the incarnate and living Word of God itself. Evangelical belief that God the Holy Spirit is not confined in his action to the visible structures of the established church has led to confessionalism, perpetuated in the Christian World Communions. Confessionalism is still prone to confuse and to obscure the one message of salvation in its breadth and its depth.

All three positions, Orthodox, Roman Catholic and Protestant, are questionable and inconclusive because they do not state explicitly that the communion with the dying and risen Lord is through and beyond Holy Scripture and Tradition. Although the Holy Spirit is speaking through the Bible and the Church, he cannot be bound by the one or by the other. As the communion with and in Christ is utter freedom, Christ alone exercises his critical function over all authoritative biblical insights and ecclesiastical powers.

4. There is a great ecumenical need that questions of the authority of the Bible, of Tradition and of the Church are discussed in Bible study groups and training courses for Bible study enablers. The reading of and the living with the Bible needs still to be freed from 'Protestant' predestination and prerogative. The Bible is not a patrimony from which Christians are free to select at will the primary source of their inspiration. The decisive importance of its message for all times is only rightly acknowledged when its testimony is read in anticipation of its disclosure to Christian believers of the ultimate sense of their world and their lives.

The Bible's contents need constantly to be unfolded afresh. Its inner unity must become clear. It is not to be turned into a norm for every human problem and a law for every social situation. To do so would to press it too far. This applies not only to fundamentalism and evangelicanism but also to the attempt to formulate the biblical view of every ecumenical problem which happens to come under discussion. The Bible is not a norm imposed on Christians from the outside. On the contrary it is meant to be read and heard within the witnessing community, in the Church.

The Bible is finally a critical book. It is impossible to fit it neatly into prevailing concerns, frustrations and hopes of the day. Nor is it identical with the doctrine and the traditions of the Church. It is a critical court of appeal to which the church must constantly defer and from whose judgment not even the developments taking place in the world are exempted. It is not surprising, therefore, that the question of the right approach to Scripture and of the precise application of its message has led and still leads to vigorous controversies in the churches. It has become obvious that the dividing lines in these controversies no longer coincide with the traditional confessional boundaries. Whenever the Church is asked, from inside or outside, in whose name and by what authority it speaks and acts, the problem of biblical authority and its solution takes form, and the question of the genuine unity in Christ is raised and needs to be answered.

1.  Dietrich, Suzanne de.  Rediscovering the Bible.
    Geneva: World Student Christian Federation, 1942.

2.  Dietrich, Suzanne de.  God's Unfolding Purpose.
    A Guide to the Study of the Bible.
    Philadelphia: Westminster Press, 1960.

3.  From the Bible to the Modern World. Report of Two Ecu-
    menical Study Conferences.
    Geneva: WCC Study Department, 1947.

4.  The First Assembly of the World Council of Churches
    held at Amsterdam, August 22 to September 4, 1948.
    Ed. by W.A. Visser 't Hooft.
    London: SCM Press, 1949.  pp. 53 and 55.

5.  Ecumenical Review, vol. II, no. 1, Autumn 1949.

6.  The Third World Conference on Faith and Order held at
    Lund, August 15-28, 1952  Ed. by Oliver S. Tomkins.
    London: SCM Press, 1953.  pp. 31, 61-62.

7.  The Evanston Report. The Second Assembly of the
    World Council of Churches 1954.
    New York: Harper, 1955.  pp. 90, 93, 103.

8.  Course on Bible Study. Bossey, 1959.  Mimeographed.

9.  Minutes and Reports of the Thirteenth Meeting of the
    Central Committee of the WCC, held at St. Andrews,
    Scotland, August 16-24, 1960.
    Geneva: WCC, 1960.  pp. 47-48.

10. The Old and the New in the Church. WCC Commission on
    Faith and Order Report on Tradition and Traditions,
    Report on Institutionalism and Unity, Presented to the
    Commission 1961.
    London: SCM Press, 1961 (Faith and Order Paper, no. 34).

11. The New Delhi Report. The Third Assembly of the WCC 1961.
    London: SCM Press, 1962.  pp. 120, 126-127.

12. The Fourth World Conference on Faith and Order, Montreal
    1963.  Ed. by P.C. Rodger and L. Vischer.
    London: SCM Press, 1964 (Faith and Order Paper, no. 42).
    pp. 50-61.

13. New Directions in Faith and Order, Bristol 1967.
    Geneva: WCC, 1968 (Faith and Order Paper, no. 50).
    pp. 32-41.

14. The Documents of Vatican II.
    New York: Guild Press, 1966.  pp. 118, 120-121, 125.

15. The Uppsala Report 1968.  Ed. by Norman Goodall.
    Geneva: WCC, 1968.  pp. 187,223.

16. Rowe, Richard C.  Bible Study in the World Council of Churches. With a preface by Olivier Béguin, General Secretary of the United Bible Societies.
    Geneva: WCC, 1969 (C.W.M.E. Research Pamphlets, no. 16).

17. Report of a Consultation on Bible Reading Notes and Biblical Theology. Bossey, 1963.  Mimeographed.

18. Conference With Conservative Evangelicals.
    Bossey, 1968.  Mimeographed.

19. The Ecumenical Review, vol. XXI, no. 2, April 1969.
    pp. 135-150.

20. Ibid., vol. XXIII, no. 4, October 1971.  pp. 419-437.

21. Consultation on Freedom and Social Structure in the Light of the Gospel. Bossey, 1969.  Mimeographed.

22. Faith and Order, Louvain 1971. Study Reports and Documents.
    Geneva: WCC, 1971 (Faith and Order Paper, no. 59).
    pp. 214-215, 84-85, 108, 138-139, 162.

23. Uniting in Hope. Reports and Documents from the Meeting of the Faith and Order Commission, 23 July - 5 August, 1974, at Accra.  Geneva: WCC, 1975.  p. 117.

24. Sharing in Hope. Reports and Documents from the Meeting of the Faith and Order Commission, 15-30 August, 1978 at Bangalore.  Geneva: WCC, 1978.  p. 245.

25. Minutes and Report of the Assembly of the Commission on World Mission and Evangelism of the WCC, at Bangkok, December 31, 1972 and January 9-12, 1973.
    Geneva: WCC, 1973.  pp. 22, 28.

26. Sexism in the 1970s. Discrimination Against Women.
    A Report of a World Council of Churches Consultation, West Berlin 1974.  Geneva: WCC, 1975.  pp. 102-103.

27. Breaking Barriers. Nairobi 1975.  Ed. by David M. Paton.
    London: SPCK; Grand Rapids: Eerdmans, 1976.  pp. 52-53.

28. Faith in the Midst of Faiths. Reflections on Dialogue in Community.  Ed. by S.J. Samartha.
    Geneva: WCC, 1977.  pp. 142 and 147.

29. The Gospel and International Life. Bossey, 1977.

30. The International Review of Mission, vol. LXVI, no. 264, October 1977.

31. The Bible in Our Situations and in Our Work.
    Report of the Naramata consultation, 1978.

32. The Authority of Scripture in Light of New Experiences
    of Women.  Geneva: WCC Community of Women and Men in the
    Church Study, 1981.  Mimeographed.

33. Central Committee of the WCC. Minutes of the
    Thirty-Sixth Meeting, Geneva, 9-18 July, 1984.
    Geneva: WCC, 1984.  p. 63.

34. The Bible - Its Authority and Interpretation in the
    Ecumenical Movement. Ed. by Ellen Flesseman-van Leer.
    Geneva: WCC, 1980 (Faith and Order Paper, no. 99).

35. Biblical Authority for Today. Ed. by Alan Richardson
    and W. Schweitzer.  London: SCM Press, 1951.

36. Guiding Principles for Interconfessional Cooperation
    in Translating the Bible.  London: United Bible Societies;
    Rome: Secretariat for Promoting Christian Unity, 1968.

# VI.
## Peace and Justice
## in the Ecumenical Movement

This survey deals with questions of peace, the prevention
and elimination of war, political, socio-economic and international aspects of justice, and the relation between peace and
justice in the ecumenical movement from 1948 onwards.  It does
not deal with questions of military strategy and technical problems of disarmament, whether nuclear or conventional arms.
Questions on violence, non-violence and the struggle for social
justice, however, in as far as they relate to issues of peace,
are included in this survey.  Since the WCC, almost all its
Sub-units, and other ecumenical bodies have been deeply involved
in dealing with the issues of peace and justice, the choice of
major statements is greatly selective.  The reader can consult
the bibliography of documents for many other references.


                              I.


The Report of Section IV, The Church and the International
Disorder, of the WCC Assembly at Amsterdam in 1948, contained
the following sub-sections:
   I.    War is Contrary to the Will of God.
   II.   Peace Requires an Attack on the Causes of
         Conflict Between the Powers.
   III.  The Nations of the World Must Acknowledge
         the Rule of Law.
   IV.   The Observance of Human Rights and Fundamental
         Freedoms Should Be Encouraged by Domestic and
         International Action.
   V.    The Churches and all Christian People Have
         Obligations in the Face of International Disorder.

"Can war now be an act of justice ?"  Different opinions
were expressed ranging from the conviction that military action
is still "the ultimate sanction of the rule of law" to the
refusal of "military service of all kinds".  On certain points
of principle, however, all were agreed.

"In the absence of any impartial agency for upholding justice,
nations have gone to war in the belief that they were doing so.
We hold that in international as in national life justice must
be upheld.  Nations must suppress their desire to save "face".
This derives from pride, as unworthy as it is dangerous.  The
churches, for their part, have the duty of declaring those moral
principles which obedience to God requires in war as in peace.
They must not allow their spiritual and moral resources to be
used by the state in war or in peace as a means of propagating
an ideology or supporting a cause in  which they cannot whole-

heartedly concur.  They must teach the duty of love and prayer
for the enemy in time of war and of reconciliation between victor
and vanquished after the war.

"The churches must also attack the causes of war by promoting
peaceful change and the pursuit of justice.  They must stand for
the maintenance of good faith and the honouring of the pledged
word, resist the pretensions of imperialist power, promote the
multilateral reduction of armaments and combat indifference and
despair in the face of the futility of war; they must point Christians to that spiritual resistance which grows from settled convictions widely held, themselves a powerful deterrent to war.
A moral vacuum inevitably invites an aggressor."

With regard to the causes of conflict between the powers the
Assembly at Amsterdam stated: "The greatest threat to peace today comes from the division of the world into mutually supicious
and antagonistic blocs.  This threat is all the greater because
national tensions are confused by the clash of economic and
political systems.  Christianity cannot be equated with any of
these... A positive attempt must be made to ensure that competing
economic systems such as Communism, Socialism, or free enterprise
may co-exist without leading to war.  No nation has the moral
right to determine its own economic policy without consideration
for the economic needs of other nations and without recourse to
international consultation...

"... It is the duty of the Christian to pray for all men,
especially for those in authority; to combat hatred and resignation in regard to war; to support negotiation rather than
primary reliance upon arms as an instrument of policy... He
should respond to the demand of the Christian vocation upon his
life as a citizen, make sacrifices for the hungry and homeless,
and, above all, win men for Christ, and thus enlarge the bounds
of the supra-national fellowship."[1]


II.


Section III, The Church in Social and Political Life, of the
Eastern Asia Christian Conference at Bangkok in 1949, stated:
"... In East Asia, the majority of  people both in the rural and
urban areas live in conditions of abject poverty and under
oppressive systems that cramp their personality; and it is the
will of God that the Church should witness to his redeeming love
through an active concern for human freedom and justice.

"... In considering communism, the Christian must distinguish
between the social revolution which seeks justice and the totalitarian ideology which interprets  and perverts it. The Christian Church must welcome the demand of the peoples for a fuller
participation in the life of society at the level where power
is exercised, since this is an expression of human dignity; and
the rise of communism is a judgment on the churches for their
failure to do so.  Nevertheless the struggle for justice frus-

trates itself if the evil forces inherent in any human situation
are not held in check.  Because communism lacks a conception of
the independence of moral reality over against power, it denies
the supremacy of the moral law over power-politics and hence in
the long run defeats the very purpose of the social revolution.."[2]


III.

In the Report of Section IV, <u>International Affairs: Christians in the Struggle for World Community</u> of the Evanston Assembly, it was stated: "... This troubled world, disfigured and
distorted as it is, is still God's world.  He rules and over-
rules its tangled history.  In praying, "Thy will be done on
earth as it is in heaven", we commit ourselves to seek earthly
justice, freedom and peace for all men.  Here as everywhere
Christ is our hope... Christians everywhere are committed to
world peace as a goal.  However, for them "peace" means far more
than mere "absence of war"; it is characterized positively by
freedom, justice, truth and love.  For such peace the Church
must labour and pray.

"Christians must also face the fact that such a peace will
not be easily or quickly attained.  We live in a world in which
from generation to generation ignorance of God and rebellion
against Him have resulted in greed and an insatiable lust for
power.  War and its evils are the consequences.  Basically the
problem is a spiritual one, and economic and political measures
alone will not solve it.  Mens's hearts must be changed. This
is always the supreme evangelistic challenge of the Church,
although we must confess that our response has been tragically
casual and feeble."

The Report of Section IV contained the following sub-sections:
I.   The Desire for Peace and the Fear of War.
II.  Living Together in a Divided World.
III. What Nations Owe to One Another.
IV.  The United Nations and the World Community.
V.   The Protection of Human Rights.
VI.  Towards an International Ethos.
VII. The Churches and Specific International Tensions.

Concerning minimum conditions that must be met on all sides
to assure a lasting peace, the Report enumerated:
"a) A conviction that it is possible for nations and peoples
to life together, at least for a considerable period of years.
b) A willingness not to use force as an instrument of policy
beyond existing frontiers.  This would not mean the recognition
and freezing of present injustices and the unnatural divisions
of nations, but it would mean renouncing coercion as a means of
securing or redressing them.
c) A vigourous effort to end social and other injustices
which might lead to civil, and hence, international war.
d) A scrupulous respect for the pledged word.
e) A continuing effort to reach agreement on outstanding

issues, such as the peace treaties and disarmament, which are essential to a broader stabilization and pacification of relations.

f) Readiness to submit all unresolved questions of conflict to an impartial international organization and to carry out its decisions."

With regard to the fate of developing nations the following was expressed in a Resolution on International Affairs: "To meet the demands of justice, whether in a particular nation, or in the assistance of peoples in underdeveloped countries, is our moral duty. We recognize that progress in raising the standards of living in underdeveloped countries is discouragingly slow; and that increasing sacrifice on the part of the richer nations is essential. ...Fear and suspicion cannot be replaced by respect and trust unless powerful nations remove the yoke which now prevents other nations and peoples from freely determining their own government and form of society. Freedom and justice in their turn depend upon the steady proclamation of truth. False propaganda, whether to defend a national policy or to criticize the practice of another government will increase international tension and may contribute to war."[3]

The Central Committee meeting at Davos in 1955 adopted a Statement on Disarmament and Peaceful Change. The introductory words of the statement read as follows: "The CCIA has consistently advanced the thesis that both moral and political factors must be taken into consideration, as well as the mathematical and mechanical approach to the reduction of armaments. These factors apply to two indispensable and complementary processes:

1) The process whereby all armaments will be progressively reduced under adequate international inspection and control; and

2) The process of developing and securing international acceptance of methods for peaceful settlement and change to rectify existing injustices, particularly in situations where military conflict has arisen."[4]

Meeting at Nyborg Strand, Denmark in 1958, the Central Committee adopted a Statement on Disarmament and Atomic Tests of the CCIA Executive Committee and issued a Statement on the same subject on its own.[5]

Discussing the right use of world resources in the Section on Christian Responsibility for Economic Development, participants in an International Ecumenical Study Conference at Thessalonica in 1959 noted the following: "Injustice in the unequal division of the world's wealth cannot be corrected merely by protest, nor by the work of a few men. It requires patient, continuous study of the complicated facts and actions at many different levels involving individuals, business, government, voluntary groups, inter-governmental organizations, and churches. In all these Christians have some part to play. Stewardship is not merely a matter of the use of our individual time and income; it also involves our actions as producers, consumers, voters and church members.

"Nor can we deal with the tensions that arise from the in-
equities and injustices in the distribution of material goods
among mankind merely by redistributing money incomes or the sur-
pluses of the rich.  There is a danger that Christians may be
satisfied with charitable type giving (whether by individuals
or governments) when justice demands coming to grips with the
root causes of the conditions which require such giving...
Those with the greater resources and abilities have the greater
obligations..."[6]


IV.


In a Commission Report on Witness of the Churches Amidst
Social Change, presented to the Inaugural Assembly of the East
Asia Christian Conference, held at Kuala Lumpur in 1959, the
following on international relations was stated: "The Commission
considered the specific problem of atomic tests and nuclear
weapons.  This problem cannot be isolated from the related problems of international tensions and the prevention of war, and we
recognize the technical and political complexities involved in
dealing with this question... We hope that the nations which
carry on atomic tests will pay heed to the voice of Asia which
alone has experienced the terrible effect of the atomic bomb
and has suffered acutely the baneful consequences of atomic tests.
The churches in the area are unanimous in their desire that in
the larger interests of humanity the testing of atomic weapons
should stop.  We hope that none of the power bloc countries will
bring in or stock atomic weapons in the East Asian states which
are involved in military pacts.  We welcome the growth of a new,
realistic and dynamic pacifism in the world..."

Concerning economic development in Asia the Commission expressed itself as follows: "What is the Christian evaluation of
the people's urge for higher standards of living and economic
welfare ?  Many in the Church tend to dismiss this urge as
materialistic.  It is true that man does not live by bread alone.
But it must be affirmed strongly by the Churches that economic
welfare is a necessary means of the good life.  It becomes
materialistic when it is conceived as the end of life... The
relation of economic development to human values and to the
Christian meaning of life needs to be clarified in the present
Asia situation.  This is possible only through Christian participation in the processes and plans of economic development.  Productivity and industrialization are certainly not means of spiritual salvation, nor are they a panacea for all the social ills
of life... The basic aim of the development programmes of the
Asian countries should be to bring about social justice, to
provide equal opportunity for free development of the individual
person, to raise the standard of living and to secure the general
welfare."[7]

## V

In Section III, <u>Service</u>, the Third Assembly at New Delhi in 1961 said the following: "... Christians must press most urgently upon their governments as a first step towards the elimination of nuclear weapons, never to get themselves into a position in which they contemplate the first use of nuclear weapons. Christians must also maintain that the use of nuclear weapons, or other forms of major violence, against centres of population is in no circumstances reconcilable with the demands of the Christian Gospel.

"Total disarmament is the goal, but it is a complex and long-term process in which the churches must not under-estimate the importance of first steps. There may be possibilities of experimenting with limited geographical areas of controlled and inspected disarmament, of neutralizing certain zones, of devising security against surprise attack which could reduce tension, of controlling the use of outer space. The approach to disarmament needs to be both global and localized. Experts must debate techniques, but the churches should constantly stimulate governments to make real advances."

In the Report of the Committee on the CCIA to the Assembly it was stated: "... Since war is an offence against God, the task of the Christian is to do all in his power to prevent, and even to eliminate, war. Nevertheless, the elimination of war, though especially in the context of nuclear power essential to the future survival of mankind, would not by itself solve all outstanding problems. There are many areas of the world where so-called 'limited' wars have been raging for years. But the evils which they have brought in their train - subversion, terrorism, counter-terrorism, corruption of police and public values, concentration camps, refugees, even genocide - have been no less horrible or evil... As no universally acceptable definition of general and comprehensive disarmament exists, it is suggested that the CCIA should take this matter under consideration and see if it is not possible for them to reach a definition of the goal towards which all should be striving."

Significant paragraphs in a telegram of greeting to the Acting Secretary General of the United Nations were: "... To build peace with justice, barriers of mutual distrust must be attacked at every level. Mutual confidence is the most precious resource in the world today: none should be wasted, more must be found... Barriers to communication must go, not least where they divide peoples, churches, even families. Freedom of human contact, information, and cultural exchange is essential for the building of peace.

"To enhance mutual trust, nations should be willing to run reasonable risks for peace. For example, an equitable basis for disarmament involves, on the one hand, an acceptance of risks in an inspection and control which cannot be fool-proof, and, on amongst us to put forth their strong conviction that we must boldly pronounce and array ourselves against the threat of nuclear retaliation in any circumstance. Others fear that such a renunciation would increase general instability."[11]

The Central Committee meeting in Enugu, Nigeria in 1965 adopted a Statement on Current International Issues of Peace, Justice and Freedom. "... It is of highest importance that defence arrangements as long as they are needed, whether national or regional, will be so fashioned as not to impede, but to facilitate progress towards disarmament. This holds true for conventional weapons but has special relevance in the nuclear field. It is in the interest of all nations, and not least of the nuclear powers themselves, to prevent the proliferation of nuclear armaments. In this connection, the arguments for and against the multi-lateral force as originally conceived were taken into consideration. The constructive possibility of diverting money now spent for the manufacture of destructive weapons to the assistance of the developing countries is an additional incentive."[12]

VII.

The World Conference on Church and Society at Geneva in 1966 debated extensively The Law in a Revolutionary Age. "... Confronted with so many dimensions of the radical problems of our time, we did not find it possible to reach an easy consensus and we do not here pretend one, but we have become aware that law has both a positive and negative relation to revolutionary change and that any romanticizing of revolution must be regarded as irresponsible. Moreover, we have become aware of the profound need to find and state the proper relation of theology to law, a most neglected area of our social ethic and practice.

"... Christians agree that they themselves do not know the content of real divine justice and that, therefore, they may not absolutize any of their insights. They do not presume to desire any specific Christian order of law for a pluralistic world society. At the same time, they affirm as part of their Christian freedom the use of reason and experiences in the law-making process alongside and in cooperation with others."

Report of Section III of the World Conference at Geneva was entitled: Structures of International Cooperation: Living Together in Peace in a Pluralistic World Society. It contained the following sub-headings: Nuclear Warfare; Relations between the two Great Nuclear Powers (including their Allies); The Relation of the Major Nuclear Powers to Other Nations; Towards a Responsible International Community; The United Nations; Regional Organizations; The Church's Involvement.

In the Report of Working Group B on Theological Issues in Social Ethics it was stated: "... The Christian knows by faith that no structure of society, no system of human power and security is perfectly just, and that every system falls under

the other, the danger that inspection may exceed its stated
duties.  Those who would break through the vicious circle of
suspicion must dare to pioneer."

The Committee on the Division of Studies recommended that
the Assembly authorize the Division of Studies to convene a consultation under the title The Christian's Witness to Peace which
should concentrate on the biblical and theological bases for
such witness.[8]

An international consultation on Peace and Disarmament held
under the auspices of the CCIA took place at Geneva, June 20-22,
1962, during a recess of the Eighteen-Nations Committee, and at
a time when no agreement either on the regulation of armaments
or on the cessation of nuclear testing had been attained. The
statement of the consultation offered a formula for the resumption of negotiations especially in suggesting a few possibilities
of a system of effective control on a scientific basis.  It advocated that the Non-Aligned Powers Memorandum "be used as a
rallying point for a resumption of negotiations and as a basis
for agreement" when the UN Committee reconvenes in July.[9]

The Report of the Central Committee meeting in Paris in 1962
contained, besides the Statement of Consultation on Peace and
Disarmament, Geneva, 20-22 June, 1962, a Statement by the Executive Committee of the CCIA which included the sentences: "...
Disarmament obviously involves certain risks.  Yet the continuation or acceleration of the armaments race carries with it a
risk far more dangerous and threatening.  A choice of risk is
inescapable and the obligation on mankind is to choose that risk
which best promises to break the present impasse."[10]


VI.


In a section on Peace, International Justice and World Community: Problems in a Nuclear Age, the EACC Assembly at Bangkok
in 1964 expressed itself as follows: "... We fully support our
Governments, as well as the World Council of Churches, in their
anxious efforts to find methods for contributing to world
security other than reliance on nuclear weapons and for achieving
a total and trustworthy system of control, reduction and abolition of the use and possession of these weapons.  It is our
conviction that world security requires total and general disarmament which depends in turn on mutual confidence expressed
in a system of collective security.

"In furtherance of this objective, it is open to the
Governments in Asia to join hands with all other non-nuclear
powers in a self-denying undertaking never to seek possession
of these weapons for any purpose.  The Christians have a clear
duty in this to urge the governments of their respective countries to take this stand.  Nor must we despair of the possibility
of the great powers eventually undertaking to dismantle their
nuclear armaments.  Our horror at the prospect of a nuclear war
and the renewed resort to nuclear testing has led a section

the judgement of God in so far as it is unable to reform itself
in response to the call for justice of those who are under its
power.  There is no divinely ordained social order, and not
every change, as such, nor every status quo, as such, is necessarily good.  There are only relative, secular structures subject
to constant revision in the light of new human needs.  There is
in history a dynamic of evil as well as a dynamic of good. God's
action is continually reshaping the order of human power,
humiliting the proud and the rich and lifting up the oppressed.
The crucifixion of Christ is the ultimate judgement on a self-
protecting status quo, and the calling of the Church to be a
pilgrim people of God is a continuing challenge to the securities
of this world."13

Reconciliation and International Justice was the theme of a
consultation at Bossey, June 26-30, 1967.  It was the fourth
gathering in a series of consultations on reconciliation. The
first three were essentially an East-West dialogue to promote
better understanding in the cultural, political and religious
spheres.  The fourth meeting concentrated on issues emerging
from the North-South tension, the problem of relations between
developed and developing nations.  Contributions were made by
M. Kohnstamm, S.L. Parmar, L. Urban.14

The Report of the Central Committee meeting at Heraklion,
Crete, in 1967 contained the Second Report of the Joint Working
Group of the RCC and the WCC.  With regard to Peace and International Affairs it was stated: "The struggle for peace and
justice calls for common action... The churches will speak
where peace is in immediate danger; they will seek to make their
voice heard where decisions are being taken.  Both the Roman
Catholic Church and the World Council of Churches recognise
the importance of this task.  Through statements and other
means they seek to remind those on whom the cause of peace most
depends of their responsibility.  They are both active though
in a different way within the United Nations, etc.  Collaboration
in this field is still rather restricted.  The task is somewhat
differently conceived on the two sides and structures need still
to be found for joint or parallel action of the churches on a
world level.  But the task is of such importance that common
witness in this respect cannot be postponed.  The Joint Working
Group is of the opinion that the possibilities in this field
should continue to be actively explored."15


VIII.


Section IV of the Fourth Assembly at Uppsala in 1968 was
entitled: Towards Justice and Peace in International Affairs.
There were 5 sub-headings:  I. The Problem of Peace and War;
II. Protection of Individuals and Groups in the Political World;
III. Economic Justice and World Order;  IV. International Struc-
tures;  V. Conclusion.

124

With regard to the problem of war and peace it was stated: "The concentration of nuclear weapons in the hands of a few nations presents the world with serious problems: a) how to guarantee the security of the non-nuclear nations; b) how to enable these nations to play their part in preventing war, and c) how to prevent the nuclear powers from freezing the existing order at the expense of changes needed for social and political justice.

Since smaller nations are expected to accept the discipline of nuclear abstinence, the nuclear powers should accept the discipline of phased disarmament in all categories of weapons. At the same time, the nuclear nations should accept the right and responsibility of the non-nuclear nations to their share in vital decisions regarding their own security and the peace of the world."

In the Conclusion of Section IV it was stated: "The growing dimensions of the ecumenical movement offer new possibilities for concerted contributions to international relations. There is an increasing demand for common action by all Christians in the international field, and new possibilities in many sectors of the international situation for joint or parallel action by Christians. Even if differences in historical ecclesiastical structures, cultural backgrounds, political systems and styles of action present substantial obstacles to cooperation, these possibilities must be fully explored. More serious efforts at dialogue with the adherents of other religions and all men of good-will provide a potential resource on a wider scale. At the same time, responsive Christian witness to the world of nations should be expressed at the parish level..."

In Section III, World Economic and Social Development, the task of the individual Christian was outlined as follows:
1) to know the facts about areas of poverty and Christian responsiblity for economic justice;
2) to pray for the needs of men everywhere and to seek wisdom and courage to meet them;
3) to engage in constant dialogue with others and to join with them in forming groups pledged to launch a constructive effort of education and commitment;
4) to urge educational authorities to include information about development in their curricula;
5) to become involved in projects of community development;
6) to make the issue of development a major factor in his electoral choice and in other political commitments;
7) in developed countries, to make available for development aid, by means of a voluntary self-tax procedure, a percentage of his income related to the difference between what his government spends in development aid and what it should spend for this purpose;
8) to consider the challenge of world development in deciding on one's vocation and career;
9) to make a personal commitment of his resources, personal and material, to the struggle for human dignity, freedom and justice."[16]

In the Report of the CCIA to the Central Committee meeting at Canterbury in 1969, new directions of the Commission regarding structural changes, peace and security, and social justice and world order were outlined.[17]

## IX.

In response to the Uppsala Assembly's Martin Luther King resolution (1968), and the controversy provoked by the WCC's humanitarian aid to groups combatting racism (1970), the Central Committee meeting at Addis Ababa in 1971 asked the Sub-unit on Church and Society to conduct a two-year study on the problems and potentialities of violence and nonviolence in the struggle for social justice.[18] A Report, of which the main part took the form of a statement, was presented to and accepted by the Central Committee meeting at Geneva in 1973.

The Statement outlined the dilemmas:
"a) Some believe that nonviolent action is the only possibility consistent with obedience to Jesus Christ...
b) Some are prepared to accept the necessity of violent resistance as a Christian duty in extreme circumstances, but they would apply to it criteria similar to those governing a just war...
c) Some find themselves already in situations of violence in which they cannot help but participate...

... We are convinced of three things:
a) There are some forms of violence in which Christians may not participate and which the churches must condemn...
b) We are convinced that far too little attention has been given by the Church and by resistance movements to the methods and techniques of nonviolence, in the struggle for a just society...
c) We reject... some facile assumptions about nonviolence which have been current in the recent debate. Nonviolent action is highly political. It may be extremely controversial...

... violence should not be equated with radicalism and revolution, or nonviolence with gradualism and reform, nor vice versa. Either or both forms of struggle may be used with a wide range of intention, from the revolutionary overthrow of a whole system to relatively minor alterations within a social system."[19]

The Central Committee meeting at Berlin (West) in 1974 dealt with the follow-up of the Statement on Violence, Nonviolence and the Struggle for Social Justice.[20]

In 1983, in view of the forthcoming Sixth Assembly, a consultation was convened at Ballycastle (Northern Ireland), hosted by the Corrymeela Community, to review and assess the continuing debate on violence and nonviolence in the light of new features of violence and force which had emerged since 1973. It dealt in a fresh way with the problem of moving beyound the violence/nonviolence dichotomy in various realms of social ethics.[21]

In the Report of the Conference on Society, Development, and Peace (SODEPAX), held at Beirut in 1968, the following was stated in the realm of universal concern and action: "... Our world is divided into haves and have-nots, and its political and economic structures often thwart the development of men in particular countries and regions, and often offend against the simple principles of justice. Love for men shows itself in justice, in justice toward our fellowmen, in just political and economic structures, and just sharing of our talents, our resources, and our riches. This applies as much between nations as within nations, and leads us to press with all men for the development of international structures that can serve fully the needs of all mankind..."[22]

A Consultation on Christian Concern for Peace, at Baden, Austria, 1970, sponsored by SODEPAX, discussed: I. Political Conflict and Dynamics of Peace; II. Christian Responsibility for World Peace; III. Education for Peace; IV. Human Rights and World Peace. In the conclusion it was stated: "... Christians through their personal involvement in the power structures of the world must give expression to the implications of their faith in relation to social, economic and political matters, both domestic and international. Through such witness Christians can contribute to the achieving of an order of greater justice in which - as an essential condition for peace - each individual can enjoy the respect due to his person as a human being and every man, without any discrimination, and in full equality with other men, might have access to all civil, political, economic, social and cultural rights."[23]

In the Debate about Development at a Consultation on Ecumentical Assistance to Development Projects in Montreux in 1970, the following was expressed on dilemmas and opportunities: "... As the powerful countries seek to assist weak nations, the result may be either corrupting or crushing or both. The churches' development programmes must take account of this crucial problem, be responsive to different approaches and seek creative solutions to it. The criteria are self-determination as to goals and structures and a dynamic conception of social justice which alone can promote a satisfactory rate of economic growth and ensure progress toward self-reliance."[24]

XI.

Section II, Salvation and Social Justice, of the Assembly of the Commission on World Mission and Evangelism at Bangkok in 1973, included four sub-sections: I. Salvation and Social Justice in a Divided Humanity; II. Salvation and Economic Exploitation; III. Salvation in Relation to National Planning; IV. Salvation in Relation to Local Struggles. Within the comprehensive notion of salvation, the assembly saw the saving work in four social dimensions:

"a) Salvation works in the struggle for economic justice against the exploitation of people by people.
b) Salvation works in the struggle for human dignity against political oppression of human beings by their fellow men.
c) Salvation works in the struggle for solidarity against alienation of person from person.
d) Salvation works in the struggle of hope against despair in personal life."

On the means and criteria of saving work the following was stated: "... The Christian tradition is ambiguous on the question of liberating violence against oppressive violence because it provides no justification of violence and no rejection of political power. Jesus' commandment to love one's enemy presupposes enmity. One should not become the enemy of one's enemy, but should liberate him from his enmity (Matt. 5:43-48). This commandment warns against the brutality of violence and reckless disregard of life. But in cases of institutionalized violence, structural injustice and legalized immorality, love also involves the right of resistance and the duty "to repress tyranny" (Scottish Confession) with responsible choice among the possibilities we have. One then may become guilty for love's sake, but can trust in the forgiveness of guilt. Realistic work for salvation proceeds through confrontation, but depends, everywhere and always, on reconciliation with God."[25]

In an Appraisal of the Study on The Unity of the Church and the Unity of Mankind by John Deschner, contained in the Report of the Faith and Order Commission meeting at Accra in 1974, the following was expressed: "... Our discussion of the struggle for human justice, although it re-opened familiar problems of law and Gospel, Church and state, history and eschaton, also raised sharply one issue that Faith and Order cannot avoid: the relation between eucharistic fellowship and the principle of social justice. For, as was pointedly said, the Christ of the eucharist is the Christ of the poor. Does our consensus statement on the eucharist yet face this challenge ?"[26]

Science and Technology for Human Development - The Ambiguous Future and the Christian Hope was the theme of a Conference at Bucharest in 1974. In the Introduction, A New Ecumenical Vision of the Future, it was stated: "Salvation in the Christian Scriptures is a promise to the whole of creation. But people in past centuries knew only a rather small part of the world. Now communication, shared dangers and shared hopes unite the world. Justice, more obviously than ever before, must be justice for all humanity. And justice, once again, includes nature as well as society.

"Justice means awareness of the authentic interdependence of people and of people with their natural environment. Independence, in the sense of liberation from oppression by others, is a requirement of justice. But independence, in the sense of isolation from the human community, is neither possible nor just. We - human communites - need each other within the community of humanity. We - humanity - need nature within the community of creation. We - the creation - need God, our Creator and re-Creator."

In part one of the Report, under Hope for Greater Justice, the Conference expressed itself as follows: "In a world of great injustice, it is those who suffer most who should have the greatest stake in planning and decision making. And they, better than anyone else, can present their point of view. Nevertheless, it must be recognized that these are the very people who have least to say when decisions regarding orientations of the economic and social process - decisions which affect them directly - are being taken. Considerable emphasis is now placed on people's participation in the development process...

"We cannot effect immediately all imaginable changes, but the urgency of bringing about those which are essential must be stressed. In this connection, it is important to underline the theological significance of hope, understood as that quality which enables those who do not conform to the present state of affairs to strive - sometimes painfully ("groaning like a women in travail", as St. Paul said) - towards a world of greater justice - a world in which the necessary changes have been accomplished. But any realistic struggle for such a just world requires not only a critique of the conditions which are to be surmounted, but also the planning, the programming, of the new...

Part Five of the Report dealt with World Social Justice in a Technological Age. The Bucharest Conference developed a long-term concept of a sustainable and just society which developed a few years later into the concept of a just, participatory and sustainable society.27 The focal point of this new ecumenical programme theme was justice. The two other elements, participation and sustainability, are necessary dimensions of the contemporary struggle for justice. From the point of view of the kingdom of God, justice is not a principle or an ideal value which will never be fully realized. Rather, as the historical embodiment of love, it indicates a quality of relationships in community and a criterion for evaluating and changing social structures.

In the Report of the Consultation on Human Rights and Christian Responsibility, at St. Pölten, Austria in 1974, organized by the CCIA, Working Group A dealt with The Right to Life and Work - The Basic Social, Economic and Cultural Rights. "The group strongly felt that all human rights, be they social, economic, religious or political are interrelated. Therefore they must be taken as a whole and the Churches should give each one of these rights the same importance and seek the application of all of them.28

XII.

The Report of a multireligious dialogue of representatives of five world religions (Judaism, Christianity, Islam, Hinduism and Buddhism), meeting at Colombo in 1974, contains the following statement: "Although no single concept of dogma or spirituality was fully acceptable to all five traditions we found areas of agreement between two or more traditions which need to be explored further in bilateral and multilateral dialogue. For example it would be useful to explore concepts like freedom, man, community, values, prayer, mediation, quality of life, essence and existence, and to see how different traditions accept or reject those concepts. One could also ask how far people from different traditions would agree to define spirituality in terms of disengagement from evil or unjust structures of society and of a search to create new forms of community embodying values such as selflessness, compassion, service to one's fellow men, simplicity and spontaneity, contentment and equanimity."[29]

A consultation on Dialogue in Community at Chiang Mai in 1977 issued a Statement in which the following was asserted: "Because of the divisive role to which all religions and ideologies are so easily prone, we believe that they are each called to look upon themselves anew, so as to contribute from their resources to the good of the community of humankind in its wholeness. Thinking of the challenge to our Christian faith we were reminded both of the danger of saying "peace, peace" where there is no peace and Jesus' words in the Sermon on the Mount: "Happy are those who work for peace: God will call them His children." (Matt. 5:9). As workers for peace, liberation and justice, the way to which often makes conflict necessary and reconciliation costly, we feel ourselves called to share with others in the community of humankind in search for new experiences in the evolution of our communities, where we may affirm our interdependence as much as respect for our distinctive identities..."[30]


XIII.


Between 1969 and 1975, three separate consultations on peace, and or, justice took place. Alternatives to Conflict in the Quest for Peace was the theme of a consultation at Bossey, June 26 - July 1, 1969. Addresses were given by A.M. Barkat, J. Toth, S.L. Parmar, U. Scheuner, J.W. Burton, A. Roberts, J. Laloy, H. Ranke, W. Huber.[31]

A conference on Liberation, Justice, Development, jointly sponsored by the EACC and SODEPAX, took place at Tokyo, July 14-22, 1970. Among the 180 participants were representatives of the major religions of Asia, consultants from the United Nations, the WCC, the Vatican, fraternal delegates from Africa, the Pacific, Europe and North America. The moderators were K. Asakai, Archbp. A. Fernandes and T.B. Simatupang. The main work centred around seven working groups. The last group dealt with Theological Perspectives. The Report concluded with a Statement on Organizational Follow-Up at National and Regional Levels.[32]

The Struggle of the Poor for Social Justice and Liberation was the theme of a consultation at Montreux, December 1-7, 1974, sponsored by CICARWS and CCPD. Among the speakers were K. Raiser, Oh Jae Shik, E. Ander-Egg, P. Drego, C. Bellecourt, L. Pérez, J. Pronk, G. Linnenbrink. Moderators were R. Nugent, H. Thimme, J. Miguez-Bonino. Support was given to the implementation of a new world economic order as outlined by the Sixth Special Session of the UN General Assembly.[33]

Section V of the Nairobi Assembly was entitled: <u>Structures of Injustice and Struggles for Liberation</u>. The sub-sections were: Human Rights, Sexism, Racism. In Section VI, <u>Human Development: Ambiguities of Power, Technology and Quality of Life</u>, reference was made to the "urgent need to define new goals for both national and international societies" and several reasons were given. "... The third reason is God's permanent demand for justice to restore all broken relations. Human relations are disturbed by sin and guilt not only at the individual level but also in specific economic and political developments. Justice is a way of relating both to God and to other people. Its consequences are seen first in the poor, the humiliated, the exploited, and the oppressed. The search for a more just world and more just relations between nations, peoples, and generations brings us together as a uniting force."

In a sub-section on <u>Power and Justice</u> Section VI stated: "... We fraternally appeal to all churches to examine their interest in and concern for:
1) social justice;
2) peaceful coexistence of nations;
3) participation in people's organizations;
4) participation in educational process which will develop critical awareness in order to begin to shape the features of a new society."

The Report of Policy Reference Committee II of the Nairobi Assembly on Public Affairs dealt with the World Armaments Situation.[34]

The Central Committee meeting at Geneva in 1977 endorsed the plan of Unit II Committee to plan for a consultation on militarism and its call "upon the member churches to give renewed support to the Programme on Militarism and Armaments Race..."[35]

The Unit II consultation on "<u>Militarism</u>" took place at Glion, Switzerland, 13-18 November, 1977. It dealt with: The Concept of Militarism, External Factors which Promote Militarism, Internal Factors which Promote Militarism, National Security System, Military-Industrial-Technological Complex, Religious Attitudes, Social Consequences of Militarism, Theological Issues, Proposals for Action, Ecumenical Action for Peace. Regarding <u>Religious Attitudes</u> it was stated: "... Although most of the major faiths stand for peace, religious justifications are put forward to justify the threat of militarism. Attempts are made to equate the defense of a particular economic and social system with that of "Western/Christian civilization". Certain repressive governments define themselves as "Christian" and profess be defending "Christian values". This poses both a serious threat and a serious challenge to the Christian Churches in many nations. Furthermore this and similar claims on behalf of other religious faiths or ideologies make it imperative for the churches to join in dialogue with men and women of other religions or ideological convictions and to cooperate with them in the struggle against militarism."[36]

A Conference on Disarmament was also held by Unit II at Glion, Switzerland, 13-18 November, 1978. It dealt with the following issues: 1) The Ecumenical Movement and Disarmament Issues; 2) Issues at and Expectations from the U.N. Special Session; 3)Dynamics of the Present Arms Race; 4) The Arms Race and the Third World; 5) International Arms Sale and Transfer; 6) Disarmament and Development; 7) Theological Issues and Responses by Churches. With regard to the Exposure of Idols it was stated: "It is the prophetic duty of Christians to unmask and challenge idols of military doctrine and technology in the light of the Christian vision of justice and peace. Such idols include: 1) The doctrine of "deterrence" which holds millions hostage to the threat of nuclear war terror but which has led to the development of still more terrifying weapons of mass destruction; 2) Any doctrine of national security that is used to justify militarism and the arms race; 3) The doctrine that "qualitative improvements" in military technology will result in a reduction in arms. In fact, the arms race has escalated as the risks of nuclear war have vastly increased."[37]

The Report on The Programme on Militarism and the Armaments Race, presented to the Central Committee at Kingston, Jamaica in 1979, stated: "In its "Report on the World Armaments Situation", the Fifth Assembly expressed its alarm at the qualitatively new developments in the arms race, which, coupled with spiralling arms production and sales, pose to a degree hitherto unimagined, the threat of global destruction. It issued a dramatic appeal to governments, but indicated too, as one participant in the Glion conference on disarmament said: "The churches can no longer urge the governments to place disarmament at the top of their agendas so long as they themselves give it such low priority on their own."[38] The reports of the two meetings can be found in several CCIA publications.[39]

The Unit II Committee of the Central Committee meeting at Geneva in 1980 dealt with Public Issues (A. Human Rights and Religious Liberty; B. Threats to Peace; C. Statement on Nuclear Disarmament; D. Guidelines for Action on Nuclear Disarmament). In the statement the Central Committee urged "all nuclear powers to
- freeze immediately all further testing, production and deployment of nuclear weapons and missiles and new aircraft designed primarily to deliver nuclear weapons;
- start immediately discussions with a view to making agreements not to enhance the existing nuclear potentials and progressively reducing the overall number of nuclear weapons and speedy conclusion of a comprehensive test ban treaty."[40]

The minutes of the Central Committee meeting at Geneva in 1982 contain The Programme for Disarmament and Against Militarism and the Arms Race. It was stated explicitly that "the work under the programme has underlined that the quest for disarmament is an integral part of the struggle for justice and dignity."[41]

For several other statements and reports on militarism and armaments race by the CCIA, its Executive Committee and the WCC General Secretary the reports of The Churches in International Affairs from 1974 onwards should be consulted.[42]


XV.


In the Document Baptism, Eucharist, Ministry the following paragraph on the eucharist deals with injustice and reconciliation: "The eucharist embraces all aspects of life. It is a representative act of thanksgiving and offering on behalf of the whole world. The eucharistic celebration demands reconciliation and sharing among all those regarded as brothers and sisters in the one family of God and is a constant challenge in the search for appropriate relationships in social, economic and political life (Matt. 5:23f; I Cor. 10:16f; I Cor. 11:20-22; Gal. 3:28). All kinds of injustice, racism, separation and lack of freedom are radically challenged when we share in the body and blood of Christ. Through the eucharist the all-renewing grace of God penetrates and restores human personality and dignity.

"The eucharist involves the believer in the central event of the world's history. As participants in the eucharist, therefore, we prove inconsistent if we are not actively participating in this ongoing restoration of the world's situation and the human condition. The eucharist shows us that our behaviour is inconsistent in face of the reconciling presence of God in human history: we are placed under continual judgment by the persistence of unjust relationships of all kinds in our society, the manifold divisions on account of human pride, material interest and power politics, and above all, the obstinacy of unjustifiable confessional oppositions within the body of Christ."[43]

Section II, The Kingdom of God and Human Struggles, of the world meeting of CWME at Melbourne in 1980 dealt with unjust economic structures, voiceless people, escalating militarism and doctrines of national security, gross infringement of the sovereign rights of other nations, situations where human rights are violated on the false pretensions of ensuring human rights.

Concerning unjust economic structures it was stated: "The kingdom of God brings in shalom - peace with justice. Any socio-economic system that denies the citizens of a society their basic needs is unjust and in opposition to the kingdom of God. The churches have to exercise the prophetic gift of assessing the effectiveness of the various socio-economic systems in the world and speak in favour of exploratory models of a new international economic order in the light of the thrust of the Gospel..."[44]

Racism: No Peace without Justice by Barbara Rogers contains a Statement of a world consultation, organized by the WCC Programme to Combat Racism in the Netherlands in 1980. The Statement outlines the prophetic nature of the Special Fund, the continuing racism in some church structures, the witness against apartheid, the economic basis of racism, the question of land rights, new doctrines of national security and growing militarism.[45]


XVI.


A consultation at Cyprus in 1981 issued a Report on Ecumenical Perspectives on Political Ethics which includes 5 major sub-headings:  I. Basic Assumptions;  II. Ecumenical Political Ethics;  III. The Issues of Justice and Power; IV. People's Participation in Politics;  V. Methodological Considerations.  In Perspectives on Political Ethics, which contains this report and various individual contributions to the consultation, is also included a Report of the Advisory Committee on The Search for a Just, Participatory and Sustainable Society.

This Report states the following on justice, a messianic category: "Justice... is a messianic category.  It embraces both God's righteousness and fidelity and his will for a right ordering of human community.  Jesus proclaims justification of the repentant sinner before God and justice in society.  Justice takes the form of punishment and prophetic judgment as well as compassion for the guilty and release of the prisoner, liberation of the oppressed.  Justice is  the historical, penultimate embodiment of love.  We cannot put one against the other. It is mockery of the biblical witness to appeal to love and at the same time to deny justice.  The eschatological reality of the kingdom of God is the coming of love in the form of justice and righteousness  and of justice with love.  The inseparable relation of justice and love finds its dramatic expression in the cross and resurrection of Jesus Christ.

"Justice is today at the centre of the aspirations of people in their struggles all over the world.  How does justice as a messianic category actually relate to the historical struggles of our time ?  Christians are far from being clear and united in their response..."[46]

Among the ten sections of the World Conference on Faith, Science and the Future, Section VIII was devoted to Economics of a Just, Participatory and Sustainable Society.  The collection of reports contains also: Science for Peace: A Resolution on Nuclear Disarmament which outlines the immediate embarkment on several tasks.  It presses "for the full implementation of SALT II, to work without delay for the reduction of nuclear weapons through SALT III, and to complete at long last a comprehensive test ban, all of which are urgent and necessary steps in making the Non-Proliferation Treaty effective..."[47]

## XVII

A Public Hearing on <u>Nuclear Weapons and Disarmament</u>, organized by the WCC, took place in Amsterdam in 1981. The Report of the Public Hearing is in four parts: I. Introduction;  II. Critical Problems;  III. Basic Theological and Ethical Issues; IV. Urgent Tasks for the Churches. Numerous addresses were also given at the public hearing. The following theological considerations were made: "... War, any war, is an undoubted evil. There is a stark contradiction between the way of love and suffering, which is Christ's way, and the deliberate infliction of suffering and death on others. Yet most Christians in most ages have believed that there are circumstances in which fighting can be the lesser of two evils. All the theologians who gave evidence to the Hearing were in their different ways, caught in this dilemma, and none presumed any hope that theology could provide easy answers. The questions posed by nuclear weapons are new. There has been little world discussion from a theological perspective of the issues involved and there is no consensus. Each spoke against a different political background, and illustrated the extent to which theological and ethical judgements have to be related to the circumstances in which they are formed, and to the practical details of the subject in hand.

"... Prof. Schillebeeckx, A Roman Catholic theologian from the Netherlands, warned that "the churches should not pretend any kind of ethical superiority; they share the uncertainties of our so-called 'culture'. In spite of this they will have no choice but to speak out in all humility but from within a fundamental prophetic ethical indignation."  ... There are major ethical differences between nuclear weapons and all those which have preceded them."[48]

The Report of a WCC Conference on <u>The Community of Women and Men in the Church</u> at Sheffield in 1981, contained a section report on <u>Justice and Freedom in New Community</u> which referred to Racism, Sexism, Classism - A Web of Oppression;  Economic Disorder;  The Struggle Against Arms and Violence. At the end of this section report it was stated: "... While we believe that the call for justice is crucial, as Christians we affirm that justice is only the beginning point toward life in community. Even as we seek an equal distribution of resources and rights we believe that Christ calls us to life in a community of love. While traditionally women have been the ones who nurture relationship and embody love, we envision a new community wherein women and men shall share all things in common and respond in love to one another's needs. Only as we live in a community of love will we move beyond relationships that are oppressive."[49]

XVIII.

The Report of the Seventh Assembly of the Christian Conference of Asia at Bangalore in 1981 contains the report of
Section I, Living in Christ with People: Confronting the Structures of Power. The following was expressed: "One major criterion for evaluating the political structures is to see whether
it enhances justice and human dignity in a given society.  Unfortunately, political structures in Asia in recent years have
moved in the direction of militarization and authoritarian type
of governments, denying such values to the majority.  The countries in Asia, under the banner of national security, national
stability and development suppress and oppress the majority of
the people and deny their rights.

"We believe that there is no dichotomy between national
security, development and human dignity.  What we question are
the concepts of national security and development propagated
in Asia which keep people in bondage.  We believe that true
national security should ensure security to all its people and
true development should mean development of all the people in
a given society in all aspects of their lives."  It was recommended that the report of a consultation on militarism, called
People against Domination should be studied and implemented,
that the existing movements for a nuclear free zone in the
Pacific and Indian Ocean areas be supported.[50]


XIX.

From 1976 to 1979, the following consultation took place at
Bossey. Self-Reliance, Solidarity and International Justice was
the theme of a consultation at the Ecumenical Institute, April
3-9, 1976.  Comparative case studies were presented on China,
Brazil, India, Yugoslavia, Cuba and Tanzania.  Three working
groups focused on: 1) The ideology of self-reliance and dependence; 2) The economics of self-reliance and dependence; 3)Ecu-
menical theology in the context of self-reliance and dependence.[51]

Peaceful Solutions of Conflicts was the theme of discussion
of a consultation at Bossey, May 4-10, 1979.  Ninan Koshy made
the opening presentation, reviewing the work of CCIA on militarism and disarmament.  Other contributions were made by H.
Borrat, C. McKeown, B. Wirmark.  The last phase of the consultation was to work on specific suggestions on the role the
churches can play in conflict resolution.[52]

At Chambésy, Switzerland, January 17-19, 1980, the subject
of discussion was Peaceful Resolution of Conflicts.  Papers were
presented on: Peaceful Settlement of Disputes;  Non-Violent
Action as Substitute for International War, Reflections on the
Basis of Some Empirical Studies;  Some Conceptual Considerations.
The consultation dealt with issues such as: relevance of UN
machinery; reduction of tension; "freezing" of disputes; package

deal; legal and political conflicts; third-party settlement;
fact-finding; regional organizations; the issue of justice;
perception of interests; human rights; public opion; non-violent
alternatives; peaceful resolution of conflicts and disarmament;
the role of the WCC.[53]

A consultation at Rajpur, North India, May 30 - June 6, 1981,
brought for the first time together Christians and Hindus from
most areas of the world where people of these two religious
traditions live together in great numbers. The theme was
Religious Resources for a Just Society. Participants attempted
to bring different dimensions to the quest for social justice.[54]

CCIA also held a series of regional consultations on "The
Role of the Ecumenical Movement in the Building of Confidence"
at Kiev, USSR, June 4-7, 1979, on "Political Trends in Africa"
at Nairobi, November 17-21, 1980, and on "Political Issues
Linking the Pacific and Asia" at Manila, September 28 - October
3, 1981.

XX.

The issues of peace and justice were high on the agenda of
the Sixth WCC Assembly at Vancouver in 1983. The Message said
the following: "... We renew our commitment to justice and peace.
Since Jesus Christ healed and challenged the whole of life, so
we are called to serve the life of all. We see God's good gift
battered by the powers of death. Injustice denies God's gifts
of unity, sharing and responsibility. When nations, groups and
systems hold the power of deciding other people's live, they
love that power. God's way is to share power, to give it to
every person. Injustice corrupts the powerful and disfigures
the powerless. Poverty, continual and hopeless, is the fate of
millions; stolen land is a cause of bitterness and war; the
diversity of race becomes the evil imprisonment of racism. We
urgently need a new international economic order in which power
is shared, not grasped...

"Injustice, flagrant, constant and oppressive, leads to
violence. Today life is threatened by war, the increase in
armaments of all sorts, and particularly the nuclear arms race.
Science and technology, which can do so much to feed, cloth and
house all people, can today be used to terminate the life of
the earth. The arms race everywhere consumes great resources
that are desperately needed to support human life. Those who
threaten with military might are dealing in the politics of
death. It is a time of crisis for us all. We stand in solidarity across the world to call persistently, in every forum,
for a halt to the arms race. The life which is God's good gift
must be guarded when national security becomes the excuse for
arrogant militarism. The tree of peace has justice for its
roots."

Almost every Issue of the Vancouver Assembly dealt with problems of peace, and or, justice. In Issue 5, Confronting Threats to Peace and Survival, the following was stated: "...We recognize that an unjust peace can be unbearable. Many of us have only recently been liberated from the unjust peace of colonialism. Others are in the thick of the struggle for emancipation from injustice which precludes peace, from systems buttressed by brute force, by torture and murder and even attempts at genocide. A peace based on racism, sexism, domination, greed and militarism cannot be what Christians seek... As we witness to our genuine desire for peace with specific actions, the Spirit of God can use our feeble efforts for bringing the kingdom of this world closer to the kingdom of God."

Issue 7, Learning in Community, was much concerned "to encourage congregations to be open to local groups struggling for peace and justice, to give them a place in the congregation, and to learn together with them by sharing their commitment and reflecting on it from a perspective of faith", and "to take initiatives to ensure that in both church-related and state-governed schools, the concern for peace, justice and ecological survival is featured in the curriculum."

Passion for peace and justice was expressed on August 6 during an all-night vigil of the Assembly marking the anniversary of the destruction of Hiroshima.55

A WCC Workshop on Justice, Peace and the Integrity of Creation was held in Geneva, May 20-22, 1984, with the purpose:
    a) to listen to the reflection on Vancouver statements related to peace and justice from the various movements;
    b) to consult with these movements especially those which proposed the Vancouver appeal on the development of a programme of justice and peace;
    c) to discuss the issues of justice and peace in their complementaries and contradictions, including biblical, theological and ecclesiological aspects;
    d) to provide an opportunity to comment on the proposed "covenanting" process of churches and movements and to discuss the proposal to the Central Committee for its session in July;
    4) to look for ways of future cooperation and mutual support between them and the WCC in order to take first steps towards the proposed international network-building and conciliar process of covenanting."56

At the meeting of the Central Committee in Geneva in 1984 a report on a Unit-Wide Programme on Linking the Struggles for Justice, Peace and the Integrity of Creation was presented. The general directions were endorsed, also the proposal to hold a world conference on the concern, possible in 1989. Under Public Issues The Public Role of the WCC in International Affairs was outlined. "The General Secretary pointed out that public statements were only one form of action in international affairs and should be seen in the context of the regular work of the Council, including pastoral visits to churches, support to churches and action groups, delegations which report on specific situations, and representations to governments and inter-governmental bodies...

The General Secretary said that the Rules of the WCC explained the nature and status of public statements and over the years the Council had developed some criteria regarding such statements. A judgment had to be made on the appropriateness of a statement as opposed to other forms of action in regard to each situation."[57]

## Observations and Comments

1. Hardly any other themes and concerns have been so constantly, widely and intensively discussed in the ecumenical movement and in the WCC since 1948 than justice and peace. The involvement of the various ecumenical constituencies and of many committed individuals has been progressive and staggering. The recognition of this fact leads to the following paradoxical statements. The incessant search of ecumenical Christianity for solutions to problems of peace and justice is encouraging and discouraging, impressive and depressive, comprehensive and eclectic, fearless and fearful, universal and parochial, selfless and selfish, heart-warming and heart-breaking. The more Christians become aware of the intricacies of peace and justice, the more they have great difficulty to find lasting answers in the realms of liberation and reconciliation.

The more the need is felt for a truly united and universal stand of the churches on the burning issues of justice and peace, the more Christians in local situations everywhere need to respond to the challenges of poverty, oppression and survival. The "universal" can become artificial and crushing when the "local" is not authentic and outspoken. The stronger and more convincing the voices of the churches become in all matters of injustice and of conventional and nuclear war, the more they must express modesty, humility and proportion. The wider the disastrous effects of racism, sexism and classism are recognized, the more they are to be related to the healing powers of baptism, eucharist and ministry. The ecumenical movement is still greatly split on this basic issue. It is extremely difficult to admit that all church divisions are an integral part of the world's divisions. The absence of justice and peace in the Church is an adumbration of the absence of justice and peace among nations.

2. There is neither a theology of peace nor a theology of justice. The worldwide absence of peace and the many forms of grave injustices are so real that biblical and theological approaches to justice and peace cannot but have a provisional character, even in the eschatological kingdom perspective. This survey contains, not surprisingly, very few theological statements.

In the early period of the ecumenical movement, until approximately 1966-1968, many rather general, diplomatic and consensus statements on peace and on justice were issued. The armaments race was acknowledged, yet it was rather superficially analyzed. An incredible escalation in arms production and distribution was not anticipated. The slogan that "the rich

become richer and the poor poorer" caught the ears from 1968
onwards. The economic havoc the First World caused in the Third
World, however, was underestimated. The problems of political
autonomy and economic self-reliance could not be solved by the
underdeveloped nations without an impartial and generous assistance of the developed nations. But that assistance has been
seriously hampered by the staggering amount of money spent on
arms production.

3. From the seventies onwards it was increasingly recognized
that the tensions and conflicts between East and West, and North
and South, are intimately related to one another and condition
one another. There can be no peace without justice, and there
will be no justice without peace. The powerful and the powerless nations are both caught in the web of annihilation and
exploitation. Destruction and domination are two sides of the
same coin. There is no peace where injustice prevails. The
Vancouver Assembly in 1983 can be considered as a climax in the
process of interlinking peace and justice. Tensions and conflicts between East and West on the one hand, and between North
and South on the other are indeed deeply dependent upon each
other. Society is a single reality.

The issues surrounding the ecumenical programme of the
"just, participatory and sustainable society" are still fundamental ones. Justice will be achieved only in a society where
people are regarded as subjects able to transform by their own
resources their political, social and natural environment and
to establish and maintain relationships of equality with one
another. A just society, however, that is unsustainable is
self-defeating. At the same time, a sustainable society which
is unjust is not worth sustaining. It is again a threat to peace.

4. The level of the current debate about violence and nonviolence in civil conflicts does not match the complexity of the
international situation today and the actual experience of people
regarding the use of violence for political ends. Awareness of
the kingdom will deliver the churches from the erroneous perception of over-identification with the victims and oppressed of
their own communities. They must retain a critical distance so
that they become not hypocritical and captive to factional interests. This requires a continuous reappraisal of the way
Christian communities can and should be involved in socio-
economic and political affairs.

The conditions of many countries in the Third World differ
vastly from the accelerated process of European and North American
civilization. National tragedy and despair are their lot, not
of nations in the West. Applying democratic principles and
biblical anthropology to Guatemala, El Salvador or the Philippines is base and facile. It is the poor and the exploited in
Central America and other parts of the world that are squeezed
in between leftist and rightist guerrillas and corrupt government forces. It is they who are manipulated, threatened and
destroyed. They receive all the blows of domination, greed and
hatred. They are the toy of the mighty foreign powers, whether
"democratic" or "socialist", disowned by comfortable churches,
because they do not fit into any neat Christian classification.

140

It is fortunate that neither perceptive Christian social ethics nor revised Marxist theory of the dictatorship of the proletariat really corresponds to their dire needs. They are the people of faith because their history of powerlessness is exactly the history of God's passion. Where there is no road, suppressed peasants and workers make a road, as they walk along and cry, "Truly, He is Lord". Spectator churches are not entitled to say that it is the right or the wrong road and that the right or the wrong Lord of history is confessed. Fortunately many Christians in Latin America and elsewhere are part of years of struggle, mistakes, suffering and victories and wrestle at great length with the strong and frightening contradictions of salvation. In many situations churches in the First World cannot but say continuous intercessory prayers for the exhausting ministry in church and society of their fellow Christians.

5. <u>The Churches as Peacemakers ? - An Analysis of Recent Church Statements on Peace, Disarmament and War</u>58 makes it quite clear that Roman Catholic Bishops' Synods and Protestant churches have a different awareness of the intensification of the struggle for peace. Their approaches vary significantly according to historical, political and cultural conditions. It is now suggested that the churches throughout the world covenant for <u>shalom</u>. This covenant should be deeply related to an integral concept of justice, peace and the integrity of creation. A world conference of the churches on peace is planned in the future. Meanwhile many kinds of regional and national ecumenical networks of movements and organizations in and outside the churches are to be established. The WCC should not seek to merge all existing movements into one uniform concept; rather its goal should be to enable mutual cooperation, network-building and support of groups and movements existing already.

Undoubtedly a constant structural framework for increased fellowship between churches and movements is greatly needed. But does the creation of such a worldwide structural framework not surpass the capacity of the WCC ? Should not various Sub-units of the Council be totally devoted to that task retiring from much other business for the time being ? To what extent can the WCC stimulate the life of the churches in relation to people's movements for justice, peace and ecology ? Is not behind this impressive ecumenical programme an unrealistic desire for developing an universal theology of peacemaking ?

"The Week of Prayer for Christian Unity" has been celebrated by many churches around the world for half a century. The question now is whether they can also engage together in "The Universal Week of Prayer for Peace", interceding faithfully in anguish, repentance and praise for the survival of God's precious creation. The Assembly at Vancouver was but a foretaste of such an event. The inauguration of such a week, or two weeks per year, is the stiff test of the relevance and the seriousness of the contemporary ecumenical movement. It needs to find its own truly spiritual and prophetic strength. Only the power of humble prayer does surpass and absorb the denomic

power of nuclear weapons. It is the beginning of the courage
and the confidence to engage in multilateral, even unilateral,
disarmament.

In the garden of Gethsemane the disciples slept when Jesus'
sweat turned into blood and he prayed in anguish to the Father:
"... all things are possible to thee; take this cup away from
me. Yet not what I will but what thou wilt." (Mark 14:36).
As his disciples today we pray with Jesus Christ for the survival of this world since he is the resurrected Lord over all
atomic missiles and rockets. One million dollars is spent each
minute on the production of armaments. Investing much of this
incredible sum of money in the healing of the nations mustbe seen
in the light of Jesus' dying on the cross and his resurrection.

The Orthodox churches stressing the mystery of the sacraments
and the life of the Church in the midst of continous malice and
injustice in the world, the Pope of the Roman Catholic Church
expressing an ardent desire to be the symbol of the universal
Church in pursuit of world peace and justice, and the Protestant
churches believing that the community of the faithful is ever
newly created to be in the forefront of struggling for a new
society - all three have much new opportunity to manifest
together that they are a feeble instrument in God's design of
shalom. If their whole existence does not radiate the quality
of shalom, their official positions and lofty statements are
not only of little importance and will be ignored, but reflect
the same self-defensive attitude of security as in secular
pronouncements.

---

1.  The First Assembly of the World Council of Churches held at
    Amsterdam, August 22 to September 4, 1948. Ed. by W.A.
    Visser 't Hooft. London: SCM Press, 1949. pp. 88-95.

2.  The Christian Prospect in Eastern Asia. Papers and Minutes
    of the Eastern Asia Christian Conference, Bangkok, December
    3-11, 1949. Published for the IMC and the WCC by Friendship
    Press, New York, 1950. pp. 114-116.

3.  The Evanston Report. The Second Assembly of the World Coun-
    cil of Churches 1954. New York: Harper, 1955.
    pp. 130-144, 147.

4.  Minutes and Reports of the Eighth Meeting of the Central
    Committee of the WCC at Davos, Switzerland, August 2-8,
    1955. Geneva: WCC, 1955. pp. 118-119.

5.  Minutes and Reports of the Eleventh Meeting of the Central
    Committee of the WCC at Nyborg Strand, Denmark, August
    21-29, 1958. Geneva: WCC, 1958. pp. 126-127.

6.  Dilemmas and Opportunities. Christian Action in Rapid Social
    Change. Report of an International Ecumenical Study Con-
    ference, Thessalonica, Greece, July 25 - August 2, 1959.
    Geneva: WCC, 1959. pp. 73-74.

7. Witnesses Together. Being the Official Report of the Inaugural Assembly of the East Asia Christian Conference, held
   at Kuala Lumpur, May 14-24, 1959. Ed. by U Kyaw Than.
   Rangoon: EACC, 1959. pp. 64-65.

8. The New Delhi Report. The Third Assembly of the World Council of Churches 1961.
   London: SCM Press, 1962. pp. 108, 170, 264-266, 281.

9. The Ecumenical Review, vol XV, no. 1, October 1962.
   See also: Ecumenical Press Service, no. 24, 29 June, 1962.

10. Minutes and Reports of the Sixteenth Meeting of the Central
    Committee of the WCC at Paris, August 7-16, 1962.
    Geneva: WCC, 1962. pp. 81-82, 93-95.

11. The Christian Community within the Human Community. Con-
    taining Statements from the Bangkok Assembly of the EACC,
    Feb.-March 1964. Bangalore: CLS, 1964. pp. 36-37.

12. Central Committee of the WCC. Minutes and Reports of the
    Eighteenth Meeting, Enugu, Eastern Nigeria, January 12-21,
    1965. Geneva: WCC, 1965. p. 42.

13. Christians in the Technical and Social Revolutions of Our
    Time. World Conference on Church and Society, Geneva, July
    12-26, 1966. The Official Report.
    Geneva: WCC, 1967. pp. 103-105, 122-152, 200.

14. Conference on Reconciliation and International Justice.
    Bossey, 1967. Mimeographed.

15. Central Committee of the WCC. Minutes and Reports of the
    Twentieth Meeting, Heraklion, Crete, August 15-26, 1967.
    Geneva: WCC, 1967. pp. 145-146.

16. The Uppsala Report 1968. Ed. by Norman Goodall.
    Geneva: WCC, 1968. pp. 62-63, 70-71, 54.

17. Central Committee of the WCC. Minutes and Reports of the
    Twenty-Third Meeting at Canterbury, August 12-22, 1969.
    Geneva: WCC, 1969. pp. 238-244.

18. Central Committee of the WCC. Minutes and Reports of the
    Twenty-Fourth Meeting at Addis Ababa, January 10-21, 1971.
    Geneva: WCC, 1971. pp. 245-247.

19. Violence, Nonviolence and Civil Conflict.
    Geneva: WCC, 1983. pp. 20-32.

20. Central Committee of the WCC. Minutes of the Twenty-Seventh
    Meeting at Berlin (West), 11-18 August, 1974.
    Geneva: WCC, 1974. pp. 32-35.

21. Violence, Nonviolence and Civil Conflict.
    Geneva: WCC, 1983. pp. 9-15.

22. World Development: Challenge to the Churches. The official
    report of the Conference on Society, Development, and Peace
    (SODEPAX) held at Beirut, Lebanon, April 21-27, 1968.
    Ed.by Deny Munby.  Washington: Corpus Books, 1969. p. 9-10.

23. Peace - The Desperate Imperative. The Consultation on Chris-
    tian Concern for Peace. Baden, Austria, April 3-9, 1970.
    Geneva: SODEPAX, 1970.

24. Fetters of Injustice. Report of an Ecumenical Consultation
    on Ecumenical Assistance to Development Projects, 26-31
    January, 1970, at Montreux, Switzerland.  Ed. by Pamela H.
    Gruber.  Geneva: WCC, 1970.  p. 103.

25. Minutes and Report of the Assembly of the Commission on
    World Mission and Evangelism, at Bangkok, Dec. 31, 1972 and
    January 9-12, 1973.  Geneva: WCC, 1973.  pp. 89-90.

26. Uniting in Hope. Reports and Documents from the Meeting of
    the Faith and Order Commission at Accra, 23 July - 5 August
    1974.  Geneva: WCC, 1975 (Faith and Order Paper, no. 72).
    p. 86.

27. Science and Technology for Human Development - The Ambiguous
    Future and the Christian Hope. Report of the 1974 World
    Conference in Bucharest, Romania.  In: Anticipation, no. 19,
    Nov. 1974.  pp. 5, 7, 24-32, 12.

28. Human Rights and Christian Responsibility. Report of the
    Consultation St. Pölten, Austria, 21-26 October 1974.
    Geneva: WCC, 1975.  pp. 35-38.

29. Towards World Community. The Colombo Papers.
    Ed. by S.J. Samartha.  Geneva: WCC, 1975.  pp. 122-123.

30. Faith in the Midst of Faiths. Reflections on Dialogue in
    Community. Ed. by S.J. Samartha.
    Geneva: WCC, 1977.  p. 140.

31. Conflict, Violence and Peace.  Ed. by Anwar M. Barkat.
    Geneva: WCC, 1970 (World Council Studies, no. 8).

32. Liberation, Justice, Development. Printed at the Diocesan
    Press, Madras, 1970.

33. Ecumenical Press Service, no. 34, 5 Dec. 1974;
    no. 35, 12 Dec. 1974.

34. Breaking Barriers. Nairobi 1975.  Ed. by David M. Paton.
    London: SPCK; Grand Rapids: Wm. B. Eerdmans, 1976.
    pp. 97-119, 121, 139, 180-182.

35. Central Committee of the WCC. Minutes of the Thirtieth
    Meeting at Geneva, 28 July - 6 August 1977.
    Geneva: WCC, 1977.  p. 31.

36. Report of the Consultation on Militarism. Glion, Switzerland, 13-18 November, 1977.  In: CCIA Background Information, 1977.

37. Report on the Conference on Disarmament. Glion, Switzerland, 9-15 April, 1978.  In: CCIA Background Information, 1978/4.

38. Central Committee of the WCC. Minutes of the Thirty-First Meeting at Kingston, Jamaica, 1-11 January 1979. Geneva: WCC, 1979.  p. 164.

39. CCIA Background Information 1978/2 and 1978/4.  Other relevant material is contained in CCIA Background Information 1978/1, "WCC Statements on Disarmament";  "Militarism and Disarmament: Summary Reports" presented to the UN Special Commission on Disarmament;  and CCIA Background Information 1978/6, "Ecumenical Presence at the UN Special Session on Disarmament."

40. Central Committee of the WCC. Minutes of the Thirty-Second Meeting at Geneva, 14-22 August, 1980. Geneva: WCC, 1981.  pp. 63-67.

41. Central Committee of the WCC. Minutes of the Thirty-Fourth Meeting at Geneva, 19-28 July 1982. Geneva: WCC, 1982.  pp. 67-68.

42. The Churches in International Affairs. Reports 1974-1978; Reports 1979-1982.   Geneva: WCC, 1974-

43. Baptism, Eucharist and Ministry.   Geneva: WCC, 1982 (Faith and Order Paper, no. 111).  p. 14

44. Your Kingdom Come. Report on the World Conference on Mission and Evangelism, Melbourne, Australia, 12-25 May 1980. Geneva: WCC, 1980.  pp. 184-186.

45. Rogers, Barbara.  Racism: No Peace Without Justice. Geneva: WCC, 1980.  pp. 95-98.

46. Perspectives on Political Ethics. An Ecumenical Inquiry. Ed. by Koson Srisang.  Geneva: WCC;  Washington: Georgetown University Press, 1983.  pp. 14-44, 179.

47. Faith and Science in an Unjust World. Report of the WCC's Conference on Faith, Science and the Future at Cambridge, USA, 12-24 July, 1979.  Volume 2: Reports and Recommendations, Ed. by Paul Abrecht.  Geneva: WCC, 1980.  pp. 125-134, 169, 170.

48. Before It's Too Late. The Challenge of Nuclear Disarmament. The Complete Record of the Public Hearing on Nuclear Weapons and Disarmament.  Ed. by Paul Abrecht and Ninan Koshy. Geneva: WCC, 1983.  pp. 3-36.

49. The Community of Women and Men in the Church. The Report of the WCC Conference, Sheffield, England, 1981.  Ed. by Constance F. Parvey.  Geneva: WCC, 1983.  pp. 145-154.

50. Living in Christ with People. CCA Seventh Assembly,
    Bangalore, May 18-28, 1981. Singapore: CCA, 1981.
    pp. 83-84.

51. Self-Reliance, Solidarity and International Justice.
    Bossey, 1976. Mimeographed.

52. Peaceful Solutions of Conflicts. Bossey, 1979.
    Mimeographed.

53. The Security Trap. Ed. by José-Antonio Viera Gallo.
    Rome: IDOC International, 1979. pp. 188-196.

54. Religious Resources for a Just Society. A Hindu-Christian
    Dialogue. Geneva: WCC, 1981.

55. Gathered for Life. Official Report of the VI Assembly of
    the WCC at Vancouver, Canada, 24 July - 10 August, 1983.
    Ed. by David Gill. Geneva: WCC; Grand Rapids: Wm. B.
    Eerdmans, 1983. pp. 3, 73, 100-101, 11.

56. WCC Workshop on Justice, Peace and the Integrity of Creation,
    May 20-22, 1984, at Centre John Knox, Geneva. Mimeographed.

57. Central Committee of the WCC. Minutes of the Thirty-Sixth
    Meeting at Geneva, 9-18 July, 1984. Geneva: WCC, 1984.
    pp. 48-49, 32-33.

58. The Churches as Peacemakers ? - An Analysis of Recent
    Church Statements on Peace, Disarmament and War.
    Rome: IDOC-International, 1985.

# VII.
## Ecumenical Perspectives on Power

The discussion of power, state power, political and economic power, technological power, military power, nuclear power, ideological power has been on the agenda of the ecumenical movement in its various stages of development. This bibliographical essay traces the debates on power within the World Council of Churches' constituency at assemblies, conferences and consultations from 1948 onwards until the present day in a more or less chronological order. The precise bibliographical references are given at the end of the essay. In the second part of this bibliographical article also other literature, which was frequently inspired by trends in the ecumenical movement, is shortly described. In view of the limit and scope of this bibliographical contribution, the documentation reviewed is necessarily short and selective.

### I.

The Report of Section III: "<u>The Church and the Disorder of Society</u>" of the Amsterdam Assembly in 1948 was greatly concerned with the fact that a "coherent and purposeful ordering of society has now become a major necessity." It stated that "the Church cannot resolve the debate between those who feel that the primary solution is to socialise the means of production, and those who fear that such a course will merely lead to new and inordinate combinations of political and economic power, culminating finally in a omnicompetent State." The Report added that neither the institution of property is the root of corruption of human nature nor is ownership an unconditional right. In the context of the concept of 'responsible society' the Report said: "It is required that the people have freedom to control, to criticise and to change their governments, that power be made responsible by law and tradition, and be distributed as widely as possible through the whole community." Therefore "any denial to man of an opportunity to participate in the shaping of society"[1] is condemned.

Quoting the Oxford Conference on Church, Community and State in 1937 that "there can be for the Christian no ultimate authority but very God", Section III: "<u>Social Questions: The Responsible Society in a World Perspective</u>" of the Evanston Assembly in 1954 stated that "justice requires the development of political institutions which are humane as they touch the lives of people, which provide protection by law against the arbitrary use of power, and which encourage responsible participation by all citizens." It emphasized that "channels of political action must be developed by which the people can without recourse to violence change their government... at all stages of political development and in the face of all the problems (noted here), a Christian community must act as a conscience for the nation and ceaselessly remind all who hold power of God's purpose for the nation and of God's judgment upon their use of power."[2]

The Report of an International Ecumenical Study Conference, organized by Church and Society at Thessalonica in 1959, quoted from a statement made by the East Asia Christian Conference in May, 1959: "... When parliamentary methods of control over the power of government are abandoned, the Christian, who knows the danger of the corruption of power, is bound to ask what other methods of checks and balances are available in alternative systems. Ultimately, a system of government will be tested by its capacity to develop a sense of community among its people, to achieve their deliverance of economic bondage and preserve the basic liberty of individuals. It is our conviction that this balance of objectives will be best preserved only by a democratic system. The challenge before the East Asian countries is to find an indigenous and dynamic form of democracy."[3]

II.

Section III of the New Delhi Assembly noted that the two previous assemblies "set forth a series of criteria by which Christians should judge political institutions" but that since Evanston "many newly independent nations face oppressive regimes." The Report stressed that "both because of the opportunities afforded by political action for the improvement of conditions and because of many forms of evil and suffering which result from the misuse of political power, the Church should encourage the individual Christian to be active in the public life of his country."[4]

In May 1962 a consultation took place at the Ecumenical Institute in Bossey on the theme "The Responsible Use of Power by Industrialists". In the Report, prepared by Hans-Ruedi Weber, the major issues were outlined as follows: 1) Responsible decision; 2) Profit: a means or an end?; 3) The uneasiness of industrialists; 4) Criticisms and suggestions. In Laity, no.14, November 1962 four contributions to the consultation were published: "The Power of Men over People and Things According to the Bible", by André Bieler; "Power in Industry and Society", by Pieter Kuin; "The Changing Patterns of Power in Asian Industry and Society", by Abraham K. Thampy; "Power Structures, Ethical Concern, and the Church in the World", by Walter G. Muelder.

Seven years later, in August 1969, Bossey organized a consultation on "Man, the Steward of Power" in the series of specialized study meetings between scientists, medical doctors, philosophers, sociologists and theologians. The consultation faced the problem of power from the various angles of all disciplines. Contributions were made by G. Altner, N. Birnbaum, R. Budde, P. Evdokimov, A.T. van Leeuwen, B. Levrat, R. Mouton, C.A. van Peursen, J. Toth, R. Troisfontaines, W. Weber, Ch. West and E. von Weizsäcker.

Another consultation on "Power and Property in the Use of World Resources", in which economists, ecologists and theologians participated, took place at Bossey in April 1974. It dealt in particular with problems of changing to new patterns of ownership, in a setting of power relations among nation-states, which are not needlessly destructive of natural environment and decrease rather than increase the gap between the rich and the poor countries.

III.

The World Conference on Church and Society at Geneva in 1966 concentrated on the question of power in Section II: "The Nature and the Function of the State in a Revolutionary Age", II. "Power and the State - Especially in Developed Countries." "The state should not aspire to exercise all power in the society, particularly in view of the technological age in which we live." The Report continued to say: "We see that 'direct democracy' - in the sense that complicated decisions may be made by a referendum of citizens - is increasingly obstructive of decision-making, even in the best educated societies. We wonder whether the roles even of parliaments are declining in the traditionally democratic countries. Yet we cannot indulge in an idolatry of experts. The necessity of delegation of power, so obvious in our world, makes it all the more important that the few who make decisions, should be held accountable to the people, who themselves retain the ultimate right of decision over their destinies." At the end of the section it was outlined that "one of the most important aspects of the control of state power is the relationship between state and law. As an institution law is an instrument of political order, but it is always more than an instrument. For the law must not be simply handed over to the state as its instrument, but must rather be seen in jurisprudence and in theology as an independent factor alongside the state, whose officials are bound to act in accordance with this law... Revolutionary action needs law to keep open the path to further change."[5]

The Uppsala Assembly dealt with the question of power in two sections: I. "Renewal in Mission" and VI. "Towards New Styles of Living". "A priority situation for mission today are the centres of power." These "control human life for good or evil. Increasingly men struggle over this control. For example, the mass media can be employed for either powerful communication or deceitful manipulation. All existing centres of power such as government, business, industry, military establishments, labour, and the churches, must be called to account for their uses of power, especially by those affected. Frustration grows in proportion to human powerlessness and lack of dignity. For the sake of the new humanity the powerless must exercise power."

Section VI contained 8 paragraphs on "the constructive use of power" and described the awareness "that the existing economic order is in fact continually exerting violence on many people, in open or in subtle forms. Violence is the destructive imposition of power. Racism and ethnic discrimination deprive human beings

of their rights." Therefore "no style of life is Christian if
it is indifferent to the suffering of people." Some indications
for action were given: "a) participate in organizations of
collective bargaining; b) stimulate those in authority, and the
disinherited; c) support international development and participate in nation building; d) churches which tolerate racism
should be rebuked."[6]

The Report of the Notting Hill Conference on Racism in 1969
contained a section on "The Cruciality of Economic Power". It
recommended that "the Church and church-related institutions
must enter into the struggle against racism in areas of power."[7]

"A major obstacle to development is the fact that the 'developed' countries find it so difficult to see and accept the implication for their own societies of the search for new international political and social structures." This was the conclusion of an Ecumenical Consultation on Ecumenical Assistance
to Development Projects at Montreux in January 1970. The Report
continued to say: "For this reason, and because of the fact that
the centres of power and decision-making which determine the
fate of many underdeveloped countries are located in the rich
countries, a proportion of the money available for development
should be spent in the 'developed' countries for the purpose of
bringing to light the facts about the ways and means by which
this power is exercised. The churches have an important role
to play in ensuring that this critical task is not neglected."[8]


IV.


The Committee on Society, Development and Peace (SODEPAX)
organized in Baden, Austria in April 1970 a Consultation on
Christian Concern for Peace. In the first part of the Report
on "Political Conflict and Dynamics of Peace" it was stated:
"Political and technological power is a gift to be used for
human liberation and peace, while at the same time it is limited,
relativized and corrected by the power of God in Christ. It is
neither divine nor demonic. It is a means by which men may
become effective servants of others and co-workers with God to
promote his peace and justice for the salvation and development
of all men and of the whole man. At the same time, we know,
as Christians, of God's promises to men in their weakness, of
his correction and forgiveness of the sin which men often express
in their power, and therefore of the hope which opens up for man
even when all the powers of the world seem to point to despair."
Speaking to the question as to what balance of power and what
forms of decision-making in international affairs might be called
creatively peaceful, the Report stated: "We recognize that peace
is not served by the centralization of power and the exclusion
of the great majority of human groups whose interests are affected from effective participation in the molding of their own and
the world's future. The menacing division of the world into two
spheres of influence, each under the umbrella of a major nuclear
power, is the prime illustration of this in our time."

The Report criticized the United Nations for not being "flexible enough to take account of the variety of particular cultural traditions and needs of societies which are not rooted in the Euro-American traditions and structures. Its universality has an added Euro-American flavour because execution of its policies depends so heavily on the great powers. We therefore point out that the proliferation of other international organizations, both regional and functional, is a healthy development."[9]

V.

Section VIII: "Who Sets What Course ? - Systems and Ideologies" of the Report of an Exploratory Conference, organized by Church and Society in Geneva in 1970 contained four pages on "Technology: Bearer of Power". "Technology is power and that power is never neutral. It serves as a carrier of those economic systems and ideologies within which it has been nurtured. For the poorer nations, too much of the present transfer of technology is a projection of the economic needs of the givers rather than a response to the needs of the receivers." The Conference noted "the old European-based struggle between the powerful and the powerless." The last sentence of the section reads: "Technology seems to make possible the projection of power in such a way that the powerful come together, despite their ideological differences, to wreck havoc upon the powerless."[10]

The Central Committee of the WCC, meeting in Addis Ababa in 1971, was concerned about the terminological unclearity of words such as 'power'. In Appendix VIII: "Proposed WCC Action on Non-Violent Methods of Achieving Social Change", it was noted that "one complicating factor is the semantic confusion which surrounds words like 'violence', 'non-violence', 'revolution', 'power' and 'liberation'. When the debate takes place across cultural and linguistic lines, the possibilities for misunderstanding are magnified even further. The substantive differences run deeper than mere semantics, but if the discussion in future is to generate more light and less heat, there must be clarification of the use of key terms such as these." Among the key issues in the pacifist/non-pacifist debate are: "a) the meaning of power in the light of human experience and Christian convictions about love and justice..."[11]

VI.

The Commission on Faith and Order, meeting at Louvain in 1971, mentioned four ways in which the Gospel can be betrayed in the life of Christians. "The first lies in succumbing to the arrogance of the false finality which the possession of power suggests, whether it be by adopting the ways which belong properly to political power, whether it be by conforming or submitting to the powers of this world in such a way that the Church keeps

the poor at a distance and Christian brotherhood is restricted
to members of the same race, nation, culture or class. The second
would wish to justify the formation of sects or parties within
the Church. The third makes people become proud of their own
confession and despise others. The fourth, on the other hand,
allowing itself to be seduced by temporal ideologies which assail
it, consists in misusing the term 'catholic' and boasting of a
tolerance which results finally in the disappearance of Christian
identity."[12]

Three years later, in its Report "Giving Account of the Hope
That is Within Us", the Commission on Faith and Order, meeting
at Accra, stated: "Everywhere, we see the unjust exercise of the
power which God has given us for the protection, governance, and
welfare of all people. More often than not, dominating power is
in the hands of the industrial nations - the nations of the so-
called First and Second Worlds - which also possess huge military
power. Much of this power is the consequence of the long history
of slavery during the colonization of the New World and the
economic exploitation of the people of Africa, Asia and South
America." Speaking in the context of racism, the gathering noted
that "because of the extraordinary power of white racism in Western societies, Black Theology has characterized the disjunction
between the oppressed and the oppressors, the powerless and the
powerful, the rich and the poor, by the symbolic dichotomy of
Blackness and Whiteness. Thus, Black Theology as a theology of
liberation lifts up from the earth Jesus as the Black Messiah,
the Oppressed One of Isaiah 53, whose rising from the dead is
the assurance of the liberation of the oppressed and the
oppressors together."[13]


VII.

Also the Commission on World Mission and Evangelism has been
concerned about the issue of power. At its meeting at Bangkok
in 1973 it stated in a sub-section: "The Meaning of Power" the
following: "We believe that CWME should encourage clarification
of the meaning of the various kinds of power in our world as
they bear on the Christian mission. We do not envisage a cen-
trally directed study originating in Geneva, but rather an
action-reflection experience whereby CWME will assist in the
stimulation and coordination of a variety of locally based
efforts to discern how the Christian mission is affected by
various forms of power and how the Gospel bears on new understandings of power and power relationships."

In Appendix C of the Report, the implications of the conference on Salvation Today for CWME are spelled out: "We know very
little about the proper use of power by the churches and by
groups of Christians and still less of the use by churches and
groups of political power. We sense that the political power
churches and groups of Christians are called upon to use in their
struggle for social and racial justice is rather that of David
than that of Goliath, and one could list instances where

much was achieved with little means.  While it is necessary to
repeat that God chose what is foolish in the world to shame the
strong (I Cor. 1:27), we have to find out what is means in terms
of power."14

The Church and Society Conference on "Science and Technology
for Human Development" at Bucharest in 1974 was concerned about
the "perspectives of technology, power and justice of the developing countries."  It expressed itself as follows: "A major
problem for nearly all the developing countries is the influence
and intervention in their domestic affairs of foreign economic
power, heightened by technology, expressed through multi-national
corporations or other instrumentalities.  A dominant and wealthy
minority in the developing countries usually allies itself with
this foreign influence, accentuating the division between rich
and poor in the country itself.  Decisions made by this power
élite may create growth in terms of GNP but they do not develop
the country. At best they import an inappropriate technology
which perpetuates dependence on foreign know-how and supplies.
At worst they serve their own and foreign profits and power.
In certain cases, as in South Africa and the Middle East, this
economic and technological power becomes involved in war iteself
... To cope with this foreign power planned and organized self-
reliance is a first requirement...  This implies strong government and broad forms of participation by the people in political
policy-making."15

Section VI of the Nairobi Assembly was entitled: "Human Development: Ambiguities of Power, Technology and Quality of Life."
The importance of power was underlined: "It has become increasingly clear that power is to be conceived as the capability to
orient and to implement decisions.  This capability can be of
economic, political, ideological, and/or military nature, being
all these components in a dynamic interrelation among themselves."
Churches themselves are not only "involved in financial powers"
and "influential elements of political power, either as active
agents or as media of the establishment", but "they are particularly influential at the ideological level in sharing and
reinforcing dominant ideologies through religious teaching,
shaping public opionion."  At the end of the sub-section the
Assembly called the churches "to a serious self-criticism of
their economic, political, and ideological role in their own
societies."  They should "examine their interest in and concern
for: 1. social justice; 2. peaceful coexistence of nations;
3.participation in people's organizations; 4. participation in
educational process which will develop critical awareness in
order to begin to shape the features of a new society."16


VIII.

At an international consultation in Chiang Mai, Thailand,
in 1977, the WCC sub-unit on Dialogue with People of Living
Faiths and Ideologies statet in Report D: "Ideologies": "A key
issue lies in the relationship of ideology and power.  In en-

countering ideologies the church must always be alert not simply to ideas but to the realities of power. Decisions will need to be made between partners in dialogue who are involved in actual confrontations of economic, political and even military power, and the church will have to examine issues of acceptable or unacceptable means (violence?) as well as of questionable ends and goals."17

The same sub-unit organized in 1981 a consultation on ideologies in which the issue of power - ideology as power, the right use of power and the power of many churches - was faced. With regard to ideology it was stated: "Ideology is related to power because ideology aims at changing the society or maintaining the status quo. The dominating ideologies may be tempted to suppress differing ideological or religious views. On the other hand, we Christians have to confess that in the course of history, Christianity when it understood itself as a leading force, was often exclusive and intolerant to other religions and philosophies." Regarding the right use of power it was emphasized that "it is the task of Christians to analyze the existing power structures and to contribute to using power responsibly, i.e. to diminish the processes of dehumanisation in exercising power. The abuse of power sometimes starts when those in power are afraid of losing their position of influence." With regard to the power of many churches, the consultation reiterated the Nairobi statement:"Power manifested through weakness requires of the churches a review of their social behaviour, of their sometimes hierarchical and non-participatory structures, of their styles of life and decision-making processes."18

Section IX: "Science/Technology, Political Power and a More Just World Order" of the WCC Conference on "Faith, Science and the Future", held at Cambridge, Massachusetts, USA in July 1979 discussed: 1. Science and Technology as Instruments of Political Power; 2. Transfer of Technology and Its Implications; 3. Military Technology: Issues of Power and Peace; 4. The Role of the Churches. This last section contains various recommendations to the churches regarding their stance on the power of science and technology, and their challenge to military technology. Reference is made to the WCC Programme on Disarmament and Militarism.19

IX.

An international consultation, organized by the WCC Programme to Combat Racism in the Netherlands in June 1980, concentrated on the economic basis of racism, the question of land rights as survival and liberation of racially and culturally oppressed people, new doctrines of national security which have resulted in an intensification of racial discrimination and oppression, and on strategic competition and conflict among great powers which is reflected in growing militarism, increasingly sophisticated security systems and comprehensive computer-assisted surveillance. In a short statement it was recommended that "the PCR should pay attention to certain trends which will intensify

in their impact on racism in the 1980s, such as: a) the scramble
for raw materials;  b) the oppression of minorities under the
pressure of tightening economic circumstances;  c) increased
secrecy on the part of power structures..."[20]

Also a world consultation on the WCC Study of The Community
of Women and Men in the Church, which took place at Sheffield in
1981, deliberated on the matter of power and authority in its
section on "Authority and Church Structures in New Community."
It expressed itself as follows: "Power has often been seen as
possessing control or command over others.  We believe, however,
that power is the ability to implement action, to bring about an
effect, sometimes a change.  It is always operative in relationship, whether intended consciously or expressed unconsciously,
for loving purposes or for the destructive ends.  Therefore, the
first thing is to be conscious of the dynamics of power which
operate in all relationships, particularly between men and women:
when there are opportunities for choosing options, people experience the power they have as individuals.

"The traditional male view of power is that it is something
very precious, to be defended at all costs, or to be fought for
- as if the quantity of power in the world were limited. On the
other hand, many women experience power, like love, as something
limitless: the more one's power is shared with others, the more
power there is.  When persons both contribute and receive power,
all are enriched."[21]


X.


An international consultation on political ethics, held at
Ayia Napa, Cyprus, in October 1981, and organized by the Commission on the Churches' Participation in Development, concentrated in particular on problems of people's power, legitimacy
and power, people's participation in politics, structures of
participation and modes of action.  "People's power becomes
decisive when it grows to the point of a consolidated people's
organization based on awareness of the unjust situation, clarity
of goals and commitment to structured corporate action.  In this
process unity among the people is very important... Through the
pooling of forces, powerlessness can become meaningful political
power.

"People's power is a necessary instrument for the achievement
of justice.  People who suffer injustice long for equity and respect for human rights.  It is the persistence of people's movements in this kind of struggle which has contributed to the change
in public feeling about apartheid, imbalances in the distribution
of wealth, the violation of human rights, etc.  The vision of a
just society has nurtured and sustained people in their persistent effort to change structures and institutions."

With regard to the question of legitimacy and power, the consultation stated: "Legitimacy is often taken for granted. But it
is often necessary to challenge the concept of legitimacy. The

source of legitimacy is the people, not the governments or the anonymous power which operates through transnational corporations, or even ideologies.  It is necessary to indicate that governments can lose legitimacy in the people's eyes, and that it is valid to have a concept of delegitimization of authority, so as to create alternative power."

Pursuing a theological articulation of people's participation in politics, it was recommended that the "following aspects should be emphasized: a) recognition of the over-riding importance of the total context;  b) dialogue in depth and action with people of other faiths and ideologies;  c) actual experiences of parties, movements and communities committed to the practice of people's participation;  d) participation within the churches or participatory ecclesiology."

Finally, concerning structures of participation it was noted in the Report of the Advisory Committee on the JPSS, 1979 - added to the Cyprus Report - that "the call for people's participation is rendered problematic by the fact that the major components of power in social life, especially technocratically organized economic and military power, are structured globally and thus are beyond the political control of people.  The people are divided into various political units, i.e. nations, states, etc. Even where there is a strong conviction about democratic participation, its effectiveness is severely limited by the global power reality... It seems clear that participatory structures need to be developed at all levels, rendering the exercise of power more accessible and accountable to the people, and building confidence between people of different faiths and ideologies.  At the same time, it is clear that only a global perspective and approach to the questions of world order and peace can mobilize the necessary power of control."[22]

## XI.

In the realm of individual contributions to the question of power, the following works should be mentioned.  In a chapter, entitled "History, Power and Hope" of his book "The Power to be Human", Charles West deals with the covenant form of power, the use of power, the renunciation of power, forgiveness and power and the issue of violence and nonviolence.  This last issue is wrongly posed, according to the author.  "The real issue is the effective, responsible use of power-black power, poor power, revolutionary power, strike power, boycott power, vote power, demonstration power, or any other kind - to achieve the justice and to bring about the peace which is now being denied."

Prof. West also published a recent article on "Christian Witness to Political Power and Authority" in Missiology, which he examines the role of the church to call government to justice and repentance as well as to be a sign of hope in the world. "Government also lives under the Cross.  No political institution has the right to eternal life.  Its security is never the ultimate value. There are times when the state must learn to renounce power without foreseeing all the consequences of such renunciation, and above all without having the resources to counter them. Afterwards such renunciation may turn out to have been good political tactics."[23]

In "Technology and Social Justice". An International Symposium on the Social and Economic Teaching of the World Council of Churches, two contributions by J. Robert Nelson on "Racism or Christian Faith - the Categorical Choice" and by Candido A. Mendes de Almeida on "The Structural Ambivalence of Latin America" deal with issues of power. The first points to the fact that the struggle for power will involve constant competition and conflicting interests and that the persistence in selfishness and the callous disregard for the poor and oppressed will heighten the likelihood or revolutionary action with concomitant acts of violence. The second refers to "the excess of 'technicism' which weakens or even annuls sensitivity to the historical or meta-economic conditions of the social structure" and to "a neutral technocratic élite capable of repeating endlessly with slight adjustments the same diagnosis and the same therapies."[24]

In several of his works, Jacques Ellul has been concerned with the greatest contemporary problem we have to face, namely "the citizen in the clutches of political power." He regards modern domination as having developed from the premise that "only an absolute, all-powerful state, itself using violence, could protect the individual against society's violence." Against what he takes to be the overpowering reality of present society, the French philospher, theologian and political scientist juxtaposes a vision of 'true politics' rooted in independent social, political, intellectual, or artistic bodies, associations and interest groups.[25]

In his book "The Transfiguration of Politics", Paul Lehmann sees revolution as the moment of truth which exposes the falsehoods in established structures and as an instance of the power of God giving human shape to human life. God upholds the world by changing it. Revolutionaries are bearers of a righteousness not their own. Options of transvaluation of power "are no longer as simply or as pragmatically determinable as a change from one kind of power to another, from one use of power to another, implies. There is an immediacy and decisiveness, as well as an inescapable concreteness about the experience of power: its application, its consequences and possibilities, which require a markedly altered perspective and purpose in the assessment and the use of power."[26]

David E. Jenkins, in his book "The Contradiction of Christianity", deals with aspects of power in the perspective of radical spirituality and radical politics and in a discussion on the contradiction of violence. "Radical repentance, radical change and radical distribution of power and privilege are overwhelmingly required by the realities of the kingdom of God and the possibilities of being human... If we are ever to get a state

157

of equilibrium in which we are all fulfilled in each other and each can enjoy all (a creative Kingdom of love) then there must be a power at work which will absorb powerful power rather than counter power with power. If Christians believe that there is such a power, the power of God as embodied in Jesus Christ, how does this affect their attitudes and responses to the 'powerful' sort of power (i.e. power as the world and its institutions including the churches, know and practise it) ?... To build any creative human society (and not one which is just a repetition of an old power-structure with the components arranged differently) it is literally necessary to love your enemy (in class struggle, the revolution, the schism)."[27]

An issue of Church and Society, March-April 1979 was devoted to "The Responsible Use of Power." Among the several contributions an article by Donald B. Shriver on "Theology of Power" should be mentioned. "In our relationship to power, our own and those of other people, the Christian orientation is repentance... Christians must seek to make power increasingly available to the weakest people of the earth."


## Observations and Comments

1. In the realm of biblical exegesis and theology of power - almost totally neglected in the ecumenical movement - the uniqueness of Old Testament critical historiography of royal power needs to be studied. Kings in the ancient Middle Eastern world were vested with divine power. But royal power without qualification was not applied to the kings of Israel and Judah. In Northern Israel kingship remained a vulnerable and changing institution. Kings were appointed and dethroned by the will of the people and the army, often on the basis of prophetic initiative. In the Southern kingdom of Judah the continuation of the Davidic dynasty was not based on the idea of sacred kingship but on God's promise to David.

2. Also the dialectical relationship in the New Testament between Romans 13 and Revelations 13 (and the Book of Daniel), between power ordained by God and demonic and destructive power at the end of the times needs to be re-examined. St Paul argued that Christians, who claimed to be exonerated from obeying political authority, because Jesus alone was their Lord and King, were wrong. They have to obey secular authorities and laws as all other citizens. In Revelations 13 the Roman state becomes the servant of the dragon (the devil) and takes on the appearance of a horrible beast. But its days are numbered because God will not permit his apostate servant to reign forever. Contrary to what many affirm, apocalyptic faith is not exclusively pessimistic, dualistic, deterministic or escapist. The tradition of the faith is realistic because it reveals that within and behind the human power struggles their are cosmic powers at work. Only God's future judgment and a new act of creation can change the state of this world. When human intervention in power struggle are in vain, spiritual resistance movements lead to an ultimate hope.

3.   The incontrollability, irrationality and inhumanness of concentrated political, economic, technological and military power conditioning one another in the contemporary world should be deeper analyzed and evaluated.  As the concept of national security depends increasingly on an ideology of keeping the power of the enemy in check and eventually destroying the enemy with all possible means, political systems thriving on hostility and defense and justifying the concentration of every kind of power in the hands of an oligarchy need to be critically examined.

4.   There is also the need to expose the mysterious powers of ecclesiastical institutions, so far only partly demythologized. The hierarchical structures of the churches, even amended and reformed at some juncture in history, are hardly conducive to what is now called participatory ecclesioloy.  No Christian community can claim to correspond to the Pauline image of the body of Christ in which each limb and organ has its own place and is indispensable (I Cor. 12:14-26).  Even highly egalitarian and participatory evangelical communities are often directed by a small group of people who feed the masses of believers on a gospel diet of their own choice.  How far can the WCC engage in a more thorough examination of ecclesiastical power structures and share its findings with the member churches ?  Ecumenical diplomacy and polite fellowship go hand in hand.  Ecumenical exhortation is resisted as interference in domestic matters.

5.   The Advisory Committee on the JPSS ill advised not to try "to elaborate and present a blueprint or a Christian programme of an ideal society which would be just, participatory and sustainable."  The elaboration of a model of an _ideal_ society would undoubtedly be preposterious and doomed to failure in advance. But the whole ecumenical debate on the various aspects of power and its misuse has been diffuse and inconclusive so far because a working model of society - perhaps one for the North and one for the South - spelling out more concretely the structures and mechanisms for the distribution, control and balance of power has become indispensable.  The discussion of the components of such a provisional blueprint  must take place, including the crucial problem of the legitimation of power, leading to a re-examination of traditional liberal-democratic, social-democratic and socialist-communist societies.

---

1.   The First Assembly of the World Council of Churches, held at Amsterdam 1948.  Ed. by W.A. Visser 't Hooft. London: SCM Press, 1949.  pp. 76-78.

2.   The Evanston Report. The Second Assembly of the World Council of Churches, 1954. London: SCM Press, 1955.  pp. 115-116.

3.   Dilemmas and Opportunities. Christian Action in Rapid Social Change. Report of an International Ecumenical Study Conference, Thessalonica, Greece, July 25 - August 2, 1959.  Geneva: WCC, Department on Church and Society, 1959.  pp. 53-54.

4. The New Delhi Report. The Third Assembly of the WCC, 1961.
London: SCM Press, 1962.  pp. 99-101.

5. World Conference on Church and Society. Geneva, July 12-26,
1966. The Official Report.
Geneva: WCC, 1967.  pp. 97-101.

6. The Uppsala Report 1968.  Ed. by Norman Goodall.
Geneva: WCC, 1968.  pp. 30-31, 89-92.

7. Vincent, John J.  The Race Race.
London: SCM Press, 1970.  p. 98.

8. Fetters of Injustice. Ed. by Pamela H. Gruber.
Geneva: WCC, 1970.  pp. 101-104.

9. Peace, the Desperate Imperative. The Consultation on Christian Concern for Peace. Baden, Austria, April 3-9, 1970.
Geneva: SODEPAX, 1970.  pp. 12-13, 22-27.

10. Gill, David M.  From Here to Where ? Technology, Faith
and the Future of Man.  Geneva: WCC, 1970.  pp. 71-75.

11. Minutes of the 24th meeting of the Cental Committee
held in Addis Ababa, 1971.
Geneva: WCC, 1971.  pp. 245-247.

12. Faith and Order, Louvain 1971. Study Reports and Documents.
Geneva: WCC, 1971 (Faith and Order Paper No.59), p. 138.

13. Uniting in Hope. Reports and Documents from the Meeting
of the Faith and Order Commission in Accra, 1974.
Geneva: WCC, 1975 (Faith and Order Paper No.72), p. 38.

14. Bangkok Assembly 1973. Minutes and Reports of the Assembly
of the Commission on World Mission and Evangelism.
Geneva: WCC, 1973.  pp. 37-38, 65-66.

15. Science and Technology for Human Development. The Ambiguous
Future and the Christian Hope. Report of the 1974 World
Conference in Bucharest, Romania.
In: Anticipation, no. 19, November 1974.  p. 25.

16. Breaking Barriers, Nairobi 1975. The Official Report of the
Fifth Assembly of the WCC. Ed. by David M. Paton.
London: SPCK; Grand Rapids: Eerdmans, 1976.  pp. 120-140.

17. Faiths in the Midst of Faiths. Reflections on Dialogue
in Community. Ed. by S.J. Samartha.
Geneva: WCC, 1977.  pp. 166-169.

18. Churches Among Ideologies. Report of a Consultation and
Recommendations to Fellow Christians. 15-22 December 1981,
Grand-Saconnex, Switzerland.
Geneva: WCC, 1982.  pp. 29-31.

19. Faith and Science in an Unjust World. Volume 2: Reports
    and Recommendations.  Ed. by Paul Abrecht.
    Geneva: WCC, 1980.  pp. 135-146.

20. Rogers, Barbara.  Racism: No Peace Without Justice.
    Geneva: WCC, 1980.  pp. 95-98.

21. The Community of Women and Men in the Church.
    The Sheffield Report. Ed. by Constance F. Parvey.
    Geneva: WCC, 1983.  p. 133.

22. Perspectives on Political Ethics. An Ecumenical Enquiry.
    Ed. by Koson Srisang.
    Geneva: WCC, 1983.  pp. 30, 32-33, 43-44, 184-185.

23. West, Charles.  The Power to be Human.
    New York: Macmillan, 1971.  pp. 212-237;
    "Christian Witness to Political Power and Authority",
    in: Missiology, vol. IX, no. 4, Oct. 1981, pp. 423-448.

24. Technology and Social Justice. An International Symposium
    on the Social and Economic Teaching of the World Council
    of Churches from Geneva 1966 to Uppsala 1968.
    Ed. by Ronald H. Preston.
    London: SCM Press, 1971.  pp. 289 ff, 371 ff.

25. Ellul, Jacques.  The Politics of God and the Politics of Man.
    Grand Rapids: Eerdmans, 1972;
    False Presence of the Kingdom.
    New York: Seabury Press, 1972;
    Hope in Time of Abandonment.
    New York: Seabury Press, 1973;
    The New Demons.
    New York: Seabury Press, 1975;
    Apocalypse. The Book of Revelation.
    New York: Seabury Press, 1977.

26. Lehmann, Paul.  The Transfiguration of Politics.
    London: SCM Press, 1974.  p. 74.

27. Jenkins, David E.  The Contradiction of Christianity.
    London: SCM Press, 1976.  pp. 119 and 131.

# VIII.
## Ideology and Ideologies

From the thirties to the sixties the term 'ideology' in the ecumenical movement was used in an exclusively pejorative sense. Ideologies, and particularly revolutionary ideologies of Marxist origin, were regarded as total systems of thought competing for the spiritual allegiance of mankind. As they are based on utter godlessness, the consequence of distorted social perspectives and surrender to utopian expectations, they must be unequivocally rejected. The Second World Conference on Church and Society at Edinburgh (1937) stated: "Every tendency to identify the Kingdom of God with a particular structure of society or economic mechanism must result in moral confusion for those who maintain the system and in disillusionment for those who suffer from its limitations."[1]

A year later the Tambaram Conference of the International Missionary Council expressed itself as follows: "Marxist communism in its orthodox philosophy stands clearly opposed to Christianity. It is atheistic in its conception of ultimate reality and materialistic in its view of man and his destiny. Its utopian philosophy of history lacks the essential Christian notes of divine judgement, divine governance and eternal victory. This revolutionary strategy involves the disregard of the sacredness of personality which is fundamental to Christianity. The challenge it presents should deepen our conviction that, whatever one's social philosophy, the Christian faith alone gives the vision and power that are essential for the basic solution of the problems of our troubled world."[2]

In his Encyclical Letter "Divini Redemptoris" Pope Pius XI condemned communism more strongly than any 20th century ecumenical gathering. Quoting Pope Leo XIII, who defined communism as "the fatal plague which insinuates itself into the very marrow of human society only to bring about its ruin", he warned all the faithful that "communism is intrinsically wrong, and (that) no one who would save Christian civilization may collaborate with it in any undertaking whatsoever."[3]

### I.

The contribution of the first two assemblies of the World Council of Churches to the ecumenical analysis of ideologies carried the argument in a new direction. At Amsterdam (1948) the churches were admonished "to reject the ideologies of both Communism and laissez-faire capitalism", seeking "to draw men away from the false assumption that these extremes are the only alternatives." The idea of the 'responsible society' was pro-

posed as an alternative to such ideological extremes and as
a way of seeking "creative solutions which never allow either
justice or freedom to destroy the other."[4]

The Evanston Assembly, reflecting cold war experiences,
reiterated the main points of the First Assembly on the conflict
between Christian faith, Marxist ideology and totalitarian practice.  It pointed, however, also for the first time to the unfortunate effects which sterile anti-communism was producing in
many Western societies.  Nevertheless, until 1966 it was repeated
several times that Christians must say a very clear 'No' to the
communist state before they can begin to recognize positive
aspects within the communist achievement.  The churches must
work to enlarge the area of freedom through 'gradual and slow'
reform.


## II.


At the World Conference on Church and Society in Geneva in
1966 ideologies like communism were for the first time approached
in a largely new non-Western world context.  The Conference suc-
ceeded in defining ideology in a non-pejorative sense: "By ideology we mean a process quite different from a total system of
ideas which is closed to correction and new insight.  Ideology
as we use it here is the theoretical and analytical structure
of thought which undergirds successful action to realize revolutionary change in society or to undergird and justify its status
quo. Its usefulness is proved in the success of its practice.
Its validity is that it expresses the self-understanding, the
hopes and values of the social group that holds it, and guides
the practice of that group."

This new, positive, understanding of ideology reflected the
concern for open Christian thought to new ideological development arising in the liberation struggles in Africa, Asia, Latin
America and the Middle East.  The gathering in Geneva admitted
that "theology reflects not only action but interaction between
God's revelation and man's ideological understanding of his own
condition and desires.  Christians, like all other human beings,
are affected by ideological perspectives."[5]  The Council's Department on Church and Society, organizing in 1970 an exploratory
conference on the subject "Technology and the Future of Man and
Society" went on to say that "the relation of faith to ideology
remains a question to be worked out in concrete situations."[6]

The Working Committee on Church and Society meeting in Nemi,
Italy, in 1971, to plan the next steps in the ecumenical enquiry
on the "Future of Man and Society in a World of Science-Based
Technology" compiled in its Third Report, entitled "Images of
the Future", a list of current ideologies describing very briefly:
(1) liberal ideology; (2) Marxist ideology; (3) social democratic
ideology; (4) technocratism; (5) nationalism; (6) reactive ideologies; and (7) cultural traditionalism, adding to each charac-
terization in a few sentences a critical evaluation and a healing

vision of their future.  Although the attempt to give an equal number of bad marks to each ideology and to suggest a few cures for every ideology's ills might seem to stem from a magnanimous (ecumenical) mind and even to follow an objective method of sociological enquiry, the whole descriptive catalogue of current ideologies was a useless instrument providing no challenge or inspiration for specific political actions in actual power conflicts and social struggles.

The Department on Church and Society was obviously not very interested in following up the valid suggestion of the 1970 exploratory conference that the relation between faith and ideology in concrete situations should be worked out and that there should be more exploration in depth of the degree to which theology should risk becoming clearly ideological in order to indicate to individuals and peoples ways of liberating themselves from oppressive political and socio-economic systems, and building a responsibly affluent, more equal, just and human society. Only one participant remarked that the Nemi report "was going up a blind alley" and that utopias are needed "projected by adventurous ideologies on the basis of convincing analysis of present trends and leading to actions that engage us fully in their realization.  We need pictures of how human community might be structured so as to be peaceful, hopeful and loving, pictures which convince us by realistic analysis that we could get from here to there."[7]

III.

As the concern for a deeper analysis and a better understanding of the problem of ideology had to be inserted somewhere and more officially into the World Council's programme, the Central Committee at Addis Ababa in 1971 decided to add the two words 'and ideologies', to  the phrase 'Dialogue with People of Other Faiths'.  By doing so it indicated that the outreach of dialogue should include the proponents of both religious and ideological world views.  No suggestions or recommendations, however, were made as to how to work out a combined dialogue between religions and ideologies or even a bilateral Christian -Marxist dialogue.  While it was right not to put ideologies in a totally different category, because religions in dialogue are apt to defend their common religious front against a threatening secular world, and because all religions tend to deny forcefully any ideological infiltration or bias within their own systems of faith, the followup of the 1971 mandate resulted in a twofold embarrassment.

On the one hand a small Christian-Marxist consultation, sponsored by the Department on Church and Society in 1968, remained a single and isolated event.  One repeatedly emphasized the impossibility of finding East-European Marxists and communists from Asia, Africa and Latin America, willing to participate in an ongoing and meaningful dialogue.  The old questions were also still raised as to what the purpose of such a dialogue is, what specific issues are to be discussed and what method of approach at the ecumenical level should be recommended. On the other hand, in spite of a more positive ecumenical view of ideology in theory and practice, one of the conclusions of the 1966 Church and Society Conference remained valid: "... there is no agreement among Christians themselves on the degree to which analysis and action in Christian ethics itself must wrestle with ideological bias."[8] Thus the World Council of Churches continued to wonder how to face the task of defining the term ideology more precisely for its own use and of undertaking some conclusive studies of ideological presuppositions and perspectives implict in the formulation and implementation of a number of its programmes and activities.

IV.

A few years later the World Council's Central Committee, meeting in Berlin, 1974 looked again into the following recomendations: (a) "to propose an alternative terminology" as 'ideology' ambiguously refers "to a constructive vision for social change or to an idolatrous system," (b) to ask "how far ideological presuppositions may be contributing to the unity or disunity of the Church" and (c) to find "appropriate ways to support Christians for whom ideologies represent a threat rather than positive challenge."[9]  This mandate was followed up by an "<u>Ecumenical Consultation on Faith and Ideologies</u>" held at Cartigny, near Geneva, in May 1975.  The memorandum issued by this exploratory conference was a general and defensive domestic document, in no way related to the actual ideological struggles and hard clashes in all parts of the world.  By adopting the neutral usage of the term 'ideology' as "an expression - systematic or not - of human views of social reality which reflect the basic conditions of the life of social groups," the process of dealing concretely with ideologies was reversed and pushed back into the period before the Geneva Church and Society Conference.

The main concern of the Cartigny meeting was "to see how Christians of different ideological commitments can live together in the 'space for confrontation in Christ' without turning diversity into hostility."  The participants were therefore quite satisfied with raising the questions of how the unity of the Church is affected by the diverse ideological commitments of Christians in different parts of the world and what are the limits beyond which diversity may break the fellowship of the Church.  Not the theoretical and analytical structure of ideological reflection undergirding successful action to realize social change but the integrity and continuity of the world-wide Christian community were the backbone of the discussion.  By repeating once more that "ideological expressions have religious implications... in so far as they make statements of ultimate significance about human nature, society and history and demand total commitment,"[10] the Consultation ignored the fact that, as an integral part of contemporary society, ideology can provide an opportunity for self-understanding and serve as a dynamic factor in social change.  Only a few were concerned that the common task is not to 'prove' that the ecumenical fellowship can comprehend various ideological encounters, but to emphasize that in many present situations the elaboration of an efficacious ideology, creating a new conscious and critical infra-structure of society, is a matter of Christian discipleship and obedience. From this it does not follow at all that a concrete ideological commitment must be interpreted as a total religious commitment.


## V.


The Nairobi Assembly was not able to carry the debate on ideology and on the seeking of community with ideological groups and parties a step further. Participants in the third sub-section of Section III on "Seeking Community: The Common Search of People of Various Faiths, Cultures and Ideologies" frankly admitted that they were not well prepared to discuss such an unusual and difficult topic. Much time was spent on a suitable working agenda, on the questions of whether socialism (in contrast to communism) is an ideology (and not rather a movement) and whether ideological co-existence is possible.[11] When a Bulgarian and a Russian delegate expounded the view that Christianity is not an ideology but that nevertheless the church and the state in their countries are in continual dialogue, an African participant asked whether the Christian faith has not ideological consequences, what the very daily subjects of the dialogue are and whether the church practises co-existence because of its faith or out of necessity for sheer survival. Another African Christian, impressed by the speeches of his East-European brethren on religious freedom in their countries and on the churches' manifestation of solidarity with their governments' social policies, posed the question whether the Russian model of communism, apparently so successfully corresponding to the aspirations and needs of all citizens, should not more widely be adopted by African nations.

Only one voice pointed out that the church is directly confronted with institutional ideology. As Christendom stood for a long time on the wrong side of society, ideology had to be embodied in concrete societal structures. For that very reason Christians today, the participant concluded, are still fearful of the word 'ideology' and do not know how to reply to the challenge of institutional Marxism. Section III was unable to make any specific proposals to search for possible forms of community between Christians and Marxists, just as Section V dealing with "Structures of Injustice and Struggles for Liberation" and Section VI discussing "Human Development, Ambiguities of Power, Technology and Quality of Life" ignored the necessity of dealing with ideological analysis of society, ideological commitment to the change of social structures, and of facing the achievements and victories of Marxist orientated governments.

Dealing with the theme "Giving Account of the Hope that is Within Us", the Faith and Order Commission, meeting at Accra, in 1974, faced the challenge of a hope with a special political commitment from a Latin American perspective. The following was stated. "In the present situation, two things are new in the relation of Christian hope to political understanding and commitment: (a) We are now acutely aware of the fact that our ideas, including our religious ideas, do not hang in the air, or mirror non-temporal realities, but emerge within and under the conditions of our historical existence including our economic and social life. (b) We are also aware that often our conceptions have an ideological function, in the sense of disguising, first of all from ourselves, but also from others, the real conditions of their origin and the relations, actions, and purposes to which they are connected.

The fact is that Christian hope - as it lives and is lived in our life - is no exception to these rules. For (a) Christianity has taken up the hopes and needs of mankind; it has reflected the conditions of mankind's existence, and has expressed its own hopes in, with, and under such hopes and needs (witness the 'mythological' expressions used at different times and the subjectivistic forms of Christian hopes in bourgeois culture, etc.). But (b) these expressions of Christian hope have often also played an ideological role in the sense mentioned above. In the contemporary debate, we find a particular illustration of this ideological function in the attempts to claim an a-political, non-ideological expression of Christian hope. The attempt to claim the separability of the two 'realms' seems clearly an expression of an idealized philosophy and a liberal ideology.

What is the Christian response to this situation ? Can Christians commit themselves to a particular form of politics ? At a time when a significant sector of mankind is developing a growing consciousness of the priority of political action, Christians participation in this situation claim the political dimension as a proper field for living and expressing the Christian hope. That is to say: (a) Christian hope becomes active and finds expression within the conditions of political life and thought. (b) This certainly means running the 'ideological risk' in the negative sense described above. The very fact, nevertheless, that a specific analytical and ideological articulation is consciously assumed, makes it possible to exercise a critical reflection which is absent when the ideology is unrecognized. (c) This also means that we must ask for the confession of hope as it becomes operative in the total life, presence, action, and witness of the churches and of Christians. The main question is not to establish what they say it means to hope in Christ, but what shape their hope really takes in the total existence and historical praxis of Christians. (d) In turn, this requires the examination of the socio-analytical framework

in which such hope finds expression.  Such a discussion of our
presuppositions is today indispensable for a true ecumenical
dialogue."12

Discussing the plans of Church and Society to hold a World
Conference on a Just, Participatory and Sustainable Society, the
Central Committee, meeting in Geneva in 1976, stated that "this
Conference will necessarily involve a substantial contribution
of many sub-units (especially those of Unit II) and a significant
contribution also from the sub-unit on Dialogue to interpret the
technological crisis in its relation to all ideologies and spiritualities.  And the planning and educational process before and
after the Conference must see that the Conference remains close
to the existential questions of its concerned publics, and especially to those of the rank and file church members."13


VII.


Meeting at Chiang Mai, Thailand, in 1977, the Sub-unit on
Dialogue with People of Living Faiths and Ideologies shared
contemporary experiences on ideologies.  The report of Group D
included a list of various societies in Western Europe, North
America, Africa, Asia and Latin America, conditioned by a
specific ideological outlook and practice.

A valuable individual contribution was made by Miss Ruth
Zander from the GDR.  She pointed out that antagonism, indifference, and a ghetto mentality constantly threaten the churches in
Eastern Europe.  Yet since the justification of the godless is
at the very heart of the Christian faith, the atheism and
critique of religion which accompany socialism cannot be obstacles to a realistic evaluation of its aims and practices.
Christians are obligated by their faith not to concentrate
exclusively on what does not yet exist or on what they must
reject in their context.  For Christians under socialist regimes
this is an immensely difficult task, because Christianity is
still dismissed as a vestige of class society.  To give the
church any independent power to shape society would be incompatible with the leadership of the working class and the role of
the Communist Party.

Still, there are opportunities for Christians under socialism
to be present at the bleeding points of their commonwealth without
identifying fully with the self-styled progress made towards the
classless society.  Christians can express the primacy of compassion, of love for the enemy, of reconciliation, and of an
eschatological view of history as aspects of their faith which
are as essential as participation in the building up of a new
and better society.  Opportunities also exist to help free their
fellow-citizens from socialist provincialism and obsession with
one particular model of society, thus aiding them to become more
open to different situations and struggles in the world.14

The Sub-unit on Dialogue with People of Living Faiths and Ideologies sponsored a specific consultation on ideology and ideologies at Geneva in 1981. The theme of the consultation was not Churches of Christians against ideologies, but among ideologies. Using the working definition of ideology of the Church and Society Conference in 1966 the consultation added: "The given definition needs one qualification. There are, on the one hand, comprehensive blueprints for the structure of society. On the other hand, there are to be found ideological elements or factors that might not be part of a well thought out system but are nevertheless of great influence on the behaviour of human beings, perhaps without their conscious knowledge."

Experiences from Christians and churches among ideologies in Asia, Africa, the Americas, and Europe were reported. The participants faced the issues of faith and ideologies, power, cultural identity and the ideological factors in interfaith dialogue. The last part of the report of the consultation includes a discussion on the WCC structures and ideologies, ideologies in the WCC as perceived by others, ideological convictions in the WCC as consciously expressed, the need for 'internal dialogue' within WCC structures, an encouragement to WCC member churches to similar patterns of self-examination, and an encouragement to member churches to positive encounter with people of other ideologies.

Concerning the role of DFI the following was stated: "In the WCC Guidelines on Dialogue with People of Living Faiths and Ideologies one may read in paragraph 5 of the Introduction: It will be noted that the statement and the guidelines touch religions more than ideologies. This is a conscious self-limitation because so far the sub-unit on Dialogue with People of Living Faiths and Ideologies (DFI) has more experience of actual dialogues with people of living faiths than of ideologies."[15]

Receiving the report "Churches among Ideologies", the Central Committee, meeting at Geneva in 1982, recommended "1. That additional dialogue programmes be developed by DFI which focus on: a) the so-called ideological captivity of the churches; b) the ideological elements in interfaith dialogue; and c) direct dialogue between and among Christians and persons for whom ideological convictions alone give meaning to their lives...
2. That in order to implement this programme on ideologies, the DFI sub-unit would require additional staff who possess competency in the field of ideologies and with sufficient financial resources to pursue the programme with vigour."[16]


VIII.

The Central Committee, meeting at Geneva in 1984, concentrated again on the necessity "that the churches themselves must study and analyze the influence of ideologies in their own life and witness. Concretely, this seems to require an approach with two foci: a) dialogue with people of ideologies, to be carried out at various points in the work of the WCC; b) analytical study of the roles and functions of ideologies, especially as they relate to the struggle for justice, peace and the integrity of creation."

The following areas that relate to several ideologies and merit analytical and critical study were singled out:
"a) militarism, which constitutes a threat to peace and justice throughout the world as well as to the integrity of creation itself;
b) modern technocratic culture which is altering not only the physical and social organization of the modern world but also the very notion of personhood and community itself;
c) economic imperialism which perpetuates the dominant position of the economically powerful at the expense of the poor;
d) racism which perpetuates the oppression of others on the basis of the colour of the skin or ethnic origins;
e) sexism which sanctifies patriarchy and subjugates women as objects."

The following recommendations were made:
"1. That the DFI be relieved of its responsibility of being the primary locus of programmatic expression to the Council's concern for ideologies;
2. That the sub-unit be renamed 'Sub-unit on Dialogue with People of Living Faiths' (Sub-unit on Dialogue);
3. That Unit II serve as the locus of responsibility for the WCC work on ideology during the next period, with the understanding that it will be administratively lodged in one of the sub-units within Unit II and carried out in collaboration with other concerned sub-units of the Council;
4. That a staff task force on ideologies, drawn from across the units coordinate the work on ideologies;
5. That the need to mobilize resources and staff with special competence to carry out the different programmatic aspects of the concern for ideologies be considered;
6. That the location of the programme be reviewed in 1986 and that the General Secretary be requested then to submit proposals for future work as well as for administrative and staffing arrangements."

In a progress report of the WCC Staff Task Force on Ideologies of July 1985 the problem of defining ideologies was raised again and elements of definition and evaluation were suggested. Perspectives for future work were outlined: 1. Working description of ideologies; 2. Identification of ideologies; 3. Ideology and Christian faith; 4. Christian-theological criteria for evaluating ideology.

With regard to sub-unit programmes, the CCPD Commission sees its role as regards the issues of ideology as being primarily:
- to concentrate on organizing a study on ideological factors in socio-economic domination and in the struggle for social transformation in one or more specific countries, including cultural and other dimensions with participatory approach,
- to also study the issue of ideology and faith(s) in the situations of struggles of the people and minorities and other oppressed communities in the local, regional levels.

Plans are also to be developed, in conjunction with the CCIA, Church and Society and PCR, on other areas in which several ideologies play a role and which merit analytical and critical study, like:

a) militarism, which constitutes a threat to peace and justice throughout the world as well as to the integrity of creation;

b) modern technocratic culture which is altering not only the physical and social organization of the modern world but also the very notion of personhood and community itself;

c) racism and apartheid as an ideology for racial superiority and domination, perpetuating oppression on the basis of the colour of the skin or ethnic origins.

The Sub-unit on Dialogue is engaged in compiling a survey of what has gone on in the Marxist-Christian experience and will seek to identify the present dialogue situations and persons who are involved and interested in it.

## Observations and Comments

1. It has taken several decades for churches and Christians to be aware of the fact that all religions (including Christianity) have ideological dimensions, and all ideologies (even those based on militant atheism) have religious dimensions. The educational process of learning and understanding that a human being is both a homo religiosus and a homo ideologicus is still in an initial stage. A majority of Christians is still inclined to separate faith from ideology and to view the ideological components of their social ethics as accidental, insignificant and 'harmless'. The dialogue with people of secular convictions requires both the awareness of one's own ideological position as well as a thorough understanding of the peculiar historical and existential position of the other. In spite of the Christian-Marxist dialogue, which flourished in the fifties and the sixties, not only people of strong ideological persuasions but also Christians in East and West Europe, and in other continents, are still today deeply divided by prejudices, misunderstandings and misrepresentations. Anti-communism and anti-imperialism still widely nourish strong human passions, uncontrolled emotions and attitudes of self-righteousness. They see the world only in black and white terms.

Clearly the primary interest of Christians in dialoguing with Marxists should not be the mere fact of talking to Marxists, but the higher goal of enhancing human dignity, freedom, creativity and wholeness. To the extent that the Christian-Marxist dialogue has missed the mark here, it must be modified or even discontinued. What is needed is the increasing humanization of both Marxism and Christianity. There are some countries, particularly in Latin America, where the theoretical exchange of views has attracted little interest. Instead, Christians and Communists have found themselves side by side in a common struggle against immediate and concrete cases of oppression and enforced dependency.

These are situations in which Christianity and Marxism cannot be set over against each other as neat alternatives.

The dialogue on ideological convictions in whatever situation, in whatever form, and between whatever partners needs very long and careful preparations, a thorough grasp of the other's outlook, and a deep sense of solidarity and purposefulness. It is a major and demanding ecumenical enterprise.

2. The history of the concepts of 'responsible society', of 'a just, participatory and sustainable society', and of the still more recent concept of 'people's participation in power politics'[17] has shown that so far no attempt has been made in the ecumenical movement to work out a consistent, practicable and coherent ideology - perhaps one for the developed world and another for the underdeveloped world.

Churches and Christians have been constantly reminded in the ecumenical movement that the 'principles' of the 'middle axioms' need always to be redefined so that they may live 'critically' and 'responsibly' in diverse societies. They must be on their guard not 'to take too much initiative' in defining a 'too definite shape' of a particular human society. All this can be characterized as 'Christian situation ethics' which helps Christian communities to orientate themselves in the confusing and complicated battles of this world. But this kind of social ethics neither faces the intensely ideological battles which have to be fought nor does it openly recognize the very existence of zealous secular societies committed to the practical implementation of a particular ideology.

Time is more than ripe to combine a proper awareness of our individual and collective helplessness and inadequacy with a properly resolute programme to attempt what needs to be done or, at least, what can be done. A consistent, practicable and coherent blueprint for society will always be provisional; it needs in fact to be revised as soon as it is drafted. But we need to move beyond our vague talking on changing life-styles which has continued at many ecumenical gatherings.

In spite of the fact that the search for more radical solutions is never free from hasty judgments, false denunciations, and errors of economic analysis and social planning, and in spite of the fact that there are no grounds for simplistic expectations either in the advance of justice in the world or in the churches as agents in relation to such advances, we need to spell out concretely and in far more details what a contemporary communitarian ethics should look like in respect to private and state production, maximum and minimum wages, equal employment of the various races and ethnic minorities, control of over-consumption, personal and collective participation in development aid, protection of the natural environment, irresponsable technological advance, progressive disarmament, social welfare, the role of labour unions, the use of public transportation, etc. etc. A valid model of society must relate all these issues and concerns to one another. In the recommendations of the Central Committee in 1984 the necessity of analyzing and evaluating the <u>whole</u> structure of society is not clearly recognized.

An ideological blueprint of society needs particularly to come to grips with the crucial problems as to how and to what extent today the individual needs to be educated, admonished and corrected by the community, and as to how and to what extent the community risks to dominate and to absorb the individual, and needs to be corrected in its over-emphases on the common well-being.

It is no longer stipulated in the ecumenical movement that the task of the churches and of individual Christians is to work for a 'Christian civilization', or a 'Christian social order' bearing the distinctive marks of the Christian understanding of humanity and society. But the thesis is still much defended that "the Christian faith alone gives the vision and power that are essential for the basic solution of the problems of this world." The ambiguity of this thesis is proved by the fact that the concepts of the responsible society and of the just, participatory and sustainable society were shared by Christians in isolation of people of other faiths and ideologies. An ideological blueprint of society needs to be hammered out by <u>all</u> citizens. Christians and churches have no special status or privilege to advance their model of society, if they develop a model at all.

The notion of people's participation in power politics moves in the direction of ideological programmes through which churches express their solidarity with the poor, the marginalized and the oppressed, because development in and humanization of society is not <u>for</u> them, but can be achieved <u>by</u> them and <u>with</u> them when they become full participants in the processes which lead to justice and liberation. This direction is only promising if indeed powerful and powerless, believers and unbelievers, liberal democrats, socio-democrats, socialists and others <u>together</u> spell out the attainment of more favourable political and socio-economic conditions of their society. It is as a demanding ecumenical enterprise as the first ecumenical task outlined. It truly concerns the entire World Council of Churches.

---

1.  The Churches Survey Their Task. Report of the Conference at Oxford, July 1937, on Church, Community and State. London: Allen & Unwin, 1937.

2.  The World Mission of the Church. Tambaram, Madras, Dec. 12-29, 1938. London: International Missionary Council, 1939. p. 22.

3.  Pius XI. Divini Redemptoris. New York: Paulist Press, 1937. p. 4 and 26.

4.  The First Assembly of the World Council of Churches at Amsterdam, August 22 - September 4, 1948. Ed. by W.A. Visser 't Hooft. London: SCM Press, 1949. p. 50.

5.  World Conference on Church and Society, Geneva, July 12-26, 1966. Geneva: WCC, 1967. p. 202.

6.  From Here to Where. Technology, Faith and the Future of Man. Ed. by D.M. Gill. Geneva: WCC, 1970. p. 76.

7.  Three Reports from Church and Society. Prepared by the Working Committee on Church and Society, meeting at Nemi, Italy, June 17-26, 1971, for the Ecumenical Inquiry on The Future of Man and Society in a World of Science-based Technology. In: Study Encounter, vol. VII, no. 3, 1971, p. 24.

8.  World Conference on Church and Society, Geneva, July 12-26, 1966. p. 206.

9.  Minutes of the Twenty-Seventh Meeting of the Central Committee, Berlin (West), August 11-18, 1974. Geneva: WCC, 1974. p. 31-32.

10. Study Encounter, vol. XI, no. 4, 1975. p. 1-2.

11. Breaking Barriers. Nairobi 1975. Ed. by David M. Paton. London: SPCK; Grand Rapids: Eerdmans, 1976. pp. 80-82.

12. Uniting in Hope. Reports and Documents from the Meeting of the Faith and Order Commission, Accra, 23 July - 5 August, 1974. Geneva: WCC, 1975 (Faith and Order Paper, no. 72). pp. 40-41.

13. Central Committee of the WCC. Minutes of the Twenty-Ninth Meeting, Geneva, 10-18 August 1975. Geneva: WCC, 1976. p.29.

14. Faith in the Midst of Faiths.Reflections on Dialogue in Community. Ed. by S.J. Samartha. Geneva: WCC, 1977. pp. 166-169, and 103-107.

15. Churches Among Ideologies. Report of a Consultation and Recommendations to Fellow Christians, Grand-Saconnex, Switzerland, 15-22 December, 1981. Geneva: WCC, 1982. pp. 3 and 47.

16. Central Committee of the WCC. Minutes of the Thirty-Fourth Meeting, Geneva, 19-28 July, 1982. Geneva: WCC, 1982. p. 59.

17. Perspectives on Political Ethics. An Ecumenical Inquiry. Ed. by Koson Srisang. Geneva: WCC, 1983.

# IX.
## Worship, Prayer and Spirituality

Worship and prayer have been major concerns in the ecumenical movement and in the World Council of Churches from the beginning. The concern for spirituality has become even more evident since the early seventies. This survey does not include references to the Prayer for Christian Unity.

### I.

The First Assembly of the WCC in Amsterdam 1948 was concerned that differences should be overcome with regard to "the relation between the Godward vocation of the Church in worship and her manward vocation in witness and service." It stressed that "a worshiping group of individuals is not necessarily a community. It is essential that each group becomes a real fellowship, through acceptance by all of full Christian responsibility for mutual service, and by breaking down the barriers of race and class. It is intolerable that anyone should be excluded, because of his race or colour, from any Christian place of worship."[1]

At the meeting of the Central Committee in Chicester in 1949, the report of the committee on worship was accepted. Concerning the creation of an ecumenical mode of worship, the report stated that "the liturgical creation is not a self-conscious act, but is the gift of the Holy Spirit to Christians who have already been given some degree of common belief and desire, which liturgy grows to express." A book should be envisaged which contains "(a) a selection of the great common inheritances, e.g. Psalms and other selections from the scriptures, some of the ancient canticles, the Lord's Prayer, etc.; (b) a section containing examples of some of the most distinctive treasures of our various traditions; (c) a section containing suggestions about how the elements to be found under (a) and (b) might be combined in the composition of special services." A warning was issued against the danger of 'Western provincialism', and a recommendation was made "to draw upon the hymnology and devotion of the Eastern church tradition."[2]

In preparation for the Third World Conference on Faith and Order at Lund, 1952, a whole volume on "Ways of Worship" was published in 1951. An international theological commission had started work on such a book as early as 1939. The volume is divided into three parts: the elements of liturgy; the inner meanings of word and sacrament; liturgy and devotion (all three parts deal with Roman Catholic, Orthodox, Anglican, Reformed and other traditions).[3] The report of the Lund conference struggled with several unsolved problems in the area: (1) differences of opinion as to the relation of word and sacrament; (2) the blessing of the eucharistic elements; (3) the difficulty of defining precisely 'liturgical' and 'non-liturgical' forms of worship; (4) worship led by any member of the congregation or by the ordained minister; (5) the sacrificial aspect of the eucharist; (6) the distinction between 'saints' and 'blessed saints'.

The report also concentrated on the intimate relation between faith and cultural tradition, and on non-theological, that is social and psychological, factors which prevent "the development of liturgical forms suitable to the age in which we live." Among several recommendations it was suggested that "a more detailed exploration, theological, metaphysical and psychological, of mystery in relation to worship" should be undertaken.[4]

## II.

The Second Assembly of the WCC at Evanston in 1954 expressed itself on worship and sacraments as follows: "The Church lives in this world by the proclamation of the Gospel, by worship and sacraments, and by its fellowship in the Holy Spirit...In worship and sacraments it participates in the life of the heavenly fatherland. In the fellowship of the Spirit it receives divine powers of growth, renewal, and enlightenment to which we cannot place a limit. The Church thus becomes, in the first place, witness and evidence of that which God has done, and the sign of that which He is doing and will yet do. By this alone the world is apprised of the historical Event and its more-than-historical significance and issues."[5]

An International Ecumenical Study Conference on Rapid Social Change also dealt with worship. It stated: "The Word and the Sacraments ought to be administered in such a way as to demonstrate clearly God's will and action, so that believers might return to their tasks in society filled with God's love for mankind. The churches must seriously ask why, in so many countries, people do not avail themselves of the means of grace which can speak to them in their need. In some countries, it may be a matter of outworn, or imported, forms of worship which are irrelevant to their needs. In others, it may be that the time and style of services do not take into account changes in the patterns of people's lives and thinking. Everywhere there is need for a renewed understanding of the meaning and significance of worship for man's life in the world."[6]

## III.

The official report of the Inaugural Assembly of the East Asia Christian Conference, held at Kuala Lumpur in 1959, contained the following paragraph: "In seeking to fulfill the mission of the Church the local congregations should bear the characteristic marks of the Church Universal, namely worship,

fellowship, witness and service. Worship shows forth the Body
of Christ gathered to the Head and must meet the need of the
members to acknowledge and proclaim the 'worship' of God, to
receive His cleansing and forgiveness, to hear His Word read
and expounded, to make fresh dedication of what they have and
are in response to the Gospel offered in the Word and the
Sacraments and to be commissioned afresh and sent forth in the
world in which lay members will have the task of being severally
and together the suffering servant."[7]

The Assembly of the East Asia Christian Conference at Bangkok in 1964 issued a warning that asceticism and puritanism
should not become ends in themselves, and emphasized that the
idea that matter is evil in contrast with spirit should be re-
pudiated. It affirmed the following: "The continuing call to
holy living comes from worship where takes place the true
meeting between the sacred and the secular. Here the call is
heard, maintained and renewed. In worship, the whole community,
which is the Church, receives the promise and the demand, 'I will
be your God and you shall be my people', and finds itself entrusted with the Holy Name to which by word and deed it must
witness. Man's response to this action of God is to say, 'Father
in heaven, hallowed be Thy name, Thy rule begin'. In this response the affirmation is made that unless God acts man can do
nothing, and that where God acts man can say with confidence,
'Send me'. The result is a life of work and worship in which
work is done as an offering of worship and worship becomes part
of the work to be performed... The call to holy living, then,
is both a promise and a demand; it is a consequence of God's
apartness in holiness as well as His involvement in love."[8]

The First Assembly of the All Africa Conference of Churches
at Kampala in 1963 struggled with the selfhood of the church in
Africa. It was critical of the fact that, during the missionary
period, foreign liturgies, hymns and rites had been imported to
Africa, thus stifling indigenous spirituality. Prefabricated
and imported liturgies reflect particular cultural traditions.
"Therefore they are unsuitable to the African climate. There
are certain emotional depths in the African which these liturgies can never reach. And their unsuitability is due prin-
cipally to the fact that they did not grow out of the life of
a living church in Africa. They are not a result of the yearning
of the Church's soul for the living God, not a natural means of
communion between Christ and His Church. Any liturgy which has
this defect is bound to be a frustration to the worshipping soul.
And we must not be deceived by the fact that the African Church
has put up with these foreign liturgies for a long time..."[9]

IV.

The Third Assembly of the WCC at New Delhi in 1961 reiterated
the importance of the intimate relationship between worship and
work. The worship of God is an end in itself and at the same
time serves to strengthen us for witness and service. In worship
we offer to God the work, the concerns and the people of his world,

and then return again as his servants into everyday life. In worship we confess our sins and receive forgiveness and courage for the old and new daily tasks. Worship helps us regain our perspective and gives us a certain freedom from the pressures of this world. The report wondered whether ordained ministers and lay people are really aware of the vital link between worship and work. It said, on the theme of 'joining in common prayer': "God is to be praised in every tongue and in the setting of every culture and age in an inexhaustible diversity of expression. Yet there are certain common factors in Christian worship such as adoration, penitence, intercession, petition and thanksgiving which are grounded inevitably in the unique acts of God in Christ, discernible still in our divided traditions. As we learn more of each other, we shall more clearly discern this common heritage and express it more fully."[10]

In Section IV "Worship and the Oneness of Christ's Church" of the Fourth World Conference on Faith and Order in Montreal in 1963 the subjects dealt with were: the nature of Christian worship; baptism and holy communion; Christian worship in the world today; worship, mission and indigenization; communion services at ecumenical gatherings. The growth of the liturgical movement in virtually all Christian traditions, a growing consensus in regard to the two great acts of sacramental worship, the quest for liturgical language, images and symbols adequately intelligible for the modern mind, the finding of ways of expression in worship rooted in the culture of people, the distinction between 'full communion', 'open communion' and 'intercommunion', and the fact that 'table fellowship' is demanded by 'Christian fellowship' were among the topics examined.

In Section I "The Church in the Purpose of God" of the Montreal conference, it was asserted: "We agree that the criteria of distinguishing a Christian community from a church (in the full sense of the word) are not to be found simply in formal adherence to a creed or confession, submission to a particular hierarchical authority, or possession of a particular ministerial order, but in the nature of its faith and worship and its resultant witness. Therefore it is most important that the aim of all conversation about Faith and Order should be mutual understanding not only in the sphere of doctrine, but also in that of devotion and spirituality, for it is in these fields that there probably lie unrecognized areas both of disagreement and of profound agreement. Such an understanding cannot be reached by any merely superficial comparison of externals, but rather by focusing attention upon the way in which the spirituality of each tradition is related to our common Christological and soteriological affirmations."[11]

V.

A consultation on "Eastern and Western Spirituality" took place at Bossey, near Geneva, 20-25 August 1962. The group discussions focused on: the biblical understanding of spirituality; spirituality and holiness; spirituality and daily life. Summing up some conclusions in The Ecumenical Review, Nikos A. Nissiotis wrote: "Unity is realized when church people study their spiritual life in Christ, regarding this study and discussion as a calling of the Spirit towards a new engagement in the Church everywhere, transcending geographical, ethnic and political boundaries."[12]

"The Worship of God in a Secular Age" was the theme of two consultations, the first at Taizé, 2-6 September 1966, and the second at Delemont, Switzerland, 14-18 July 1967. These two consultations were called by the Division of Ecumenical Action, in preparation for Section V of the Uppsala Assembly.[13]

The Uppsala Assembly emphasized continuity and change in worship. "We are bound to ask the church, whether there should not be changes in language, music, vestments, ceremonies, to make worship more intelligible; whether fresh categories of people (industrial workers, students, scientists, journalists, etc. ) should not find a place in the churches' prayers; whether lay people should not be encouraged to take a greater share in public worship; whether our forms of worship should not avoid unnecessary repetition, and leave room for silence; whether biblical and liturgical texts should not be so chosen that people are helped to worship with understanding; whether meetings of Christians for prayer in the Eucharist (Holy Communion, the Lord's Supper) should be confined to church buildings or to traditional hours. In the same way in personal prayer should we not learn to 'Pray our lives' in a realistic way ?"

Commenting on the work of the section on worship at the Uppsala Assembly, David L. Edwards noted that the original title given to the section "The Worship of God in a Secular Age" was replaced by the one word "Worship". During the discussions protest was voiced against too much emphasis by Western theologians on secular theology. Representatives from countries dominated by Buddhism, Hinduism, Islam and tribal religions felt that the chief problem was how to relate Christian worship to the religious traditions of other cultures. No agreement was "reached between the secularizing radicals and the heavenly conservatives... By taking worship as one of its themes, the Fourth Assembly showed that the problem is not to be left in the respectable obscurity of Faith and Order. Nor is it to be submerged in enthusiasm for the social Gospel." In Appendix XI of the Uppsala report, "The Church and the Media of Mass Communication", four recommendations were made to the churches "to give special attention to the question of broadcasting liturgical celebrations."[14]

VI.

A year later, a consultation on "Worship in a Secular Age" which met in Geneva, 8-13 September 1969, sponsored by the Commission on Faith and Order, included a wider variety of positions and views than had been presented at the Fourth Assembly. Papers were presented by Paul M. van Buren (The Tendency of Our Age and the Reconception of Worship); Charles Davis (Ghetto or Desert: Liturgy in a Cultural Dilemma); Raymundo Panikkar (Secularization

and Worship); Vilmos Vajta (Worship in a Secularized Age); Karl
Ferdinand Müller (Living Worship); Will Adam (Outdated and Modern
Forms of Worship); Metropolitan Anthony (Worship in a Secular
Society). In a preface to Studia Liturgica, which contains these
papers, Lukas Vischer wrote: "True there is need for imaginative
creativity. Stubborn adherence to traditional forms would prove
fatal to the future of Christian worship. But there was general
agreement that difficulties could not be finally solved by adap-
tations. The core of the problem lies in the understanding of
the Gospel itself..."[15]

The report of the Structure Committee, submitted to the Central Committee in 1971, dealt with "The Churches' Spiritual Life".
It made two points: "First, the issue is wider than that of the
spiritual style of life of the World Council of Churches as an
organization or an office with a staff. It affects also the
life of Christians in the member churches. Secondly, the diversity of spiritual styles in the churches and the ramifications
of this issue in all aspects of the Church's life and mission
make the subject difficult to deal with structurally."

The Structure Committee recommended that the WCC "initiate
a programme to assist the churches to face the crisis (of worship) through informed study with a view to help renew congregational worship, fellowship, study and action... and that
adequate staff assignment be made to engage the urgent attention
of all the programme units and sub-units of the WCC in the task
of envisaging and implementing programmes and activities to
deepen the spiritual life of Christians..."[16]


VII.


A study report on "Worship Today", presented to the meeting
of the Commission on Faith and Order at Louvain in 1971, was
divided into seven parts: 'worship' in a 'secular' age; how can
we describe 'today' in relation to worship; is it possible in
the present situation to worship meaningfully; where is the
starting point for renewal of worship; reforms are needed; the
crisis of worship cannot be solved by reforms; conclusions for
the ecumenical movement. A member of the gathering spoke of
three groups appearing in the discussion on worship: "those who
presuppose God, the Gospel, the Church as given certainties and
live their faith on this basis; those who set their faces against
every security in order to be able to be really open and questioning; and those who consider uncertainty as the genuine expression of faith and are determined to experience that uncertainty to the full."

The report stated: "New groupings are appearing and the
conflicts which potentially divide them from one another are so
great that they can only be held together by the passionate
expectation of the New which God wills to do and will indeed do."
The conference at Louvain recommended that "the Faith and Order
Secretariat should collect from many churches and areas examples

of forms and styles of worship which are proving especially
creative and enriching in relation to the life and activity of
the Church in the contemporary world."[17]

The appendix to the report of the Commission on Faith and
Order meeting at Accra in 1974, entitled "Affirmations of Hope",
contained a variety of material helpful for churches in account-
ing for their hopes.[18]

The Central Committee meeting at Berlin in 1974 "welcomed
the decision of the Commission on Faith and Order to give more
attention to problems of worship and spirituality than before.
Problems of the Christian's spiritual life go far beyond
matters of worship.  Worship and spirituality cannot and should
not be seen as matters exclusively related to Faith and Order
and will require the cooperation of several departments of the
WCC."[19]

Dealing with Dialogue with People of Living Faiths and
Ideologies, the Uppsala to Nairobi report stated: "A new emphasis, controversial but challenging, is the place of 'spirituality' - in particular, of devotion, prayer and meditation -
in dialogue.  This issue was either avoided entirely in previous
years or touched upon in the most superficial manner. The symbols
and signs of prayer, meditation and silence have deep meaning
for life in communities of faith.  Moreover, 'the spirituality
of the secular' in its thrust for self-transcendence is also
part of man's quest for meaning.  In every recent dialogue this
matter has been present, raising disturbing but searching questions not only for Christians but for people of other faiths as
well.  The question is not so much one of definitions or fear
or 'syncretism'.  Rather, how do we express the dimensions of
our spiritual life (a) in an age of science and technology when
quite a few people, including much of the world's youth, are
rejecting traditional forms of worship, and (b) at a time when
many people, including young people in the West, seem to be
turning to forms of Eastern spirituality, such as Yoga, Zen,
Hare Krishna movements, and the like.  In the context of inter-
religious dialogue the question also involves trying to understand the religious life of our partners not only through doctrines and academic concepts but in addition through religious
symbols, music, art and meditation."[20]


                        VIII.

A workshop on spirituality was held at Windsor Castle, England, 8-17 May 1975.  This workshop traced the discussion on
worship from the Uppsala Assembly to a consultation on "Worship
in a Secular Age" in Geneva in 1969, and the Louvain Faith and
Order Conference in August 1971.  Involved in experimental worship at St George's Chapel in Windsor Castle, the participants
were faced with a difficult question: what opportunities were
there for youth to bring the real struggles and problems of
daily life into worship ?  It was noted that as some 500,000
people move through St George's Chapel each year, it was in this

respect not unlike Notre Dame in Paris or the Holy Places in Jerusalem which are also tourist attractions.

Rex Davies, the organizer of the workshop, wrote the following sober words: "For many, Windsor was a painful experience. It high-lighted how different expectations can be, especially those of people who dream of a more brilliant worship which might free people for greater things, and those of people whose tradition gives a sense of stability, continuity and hope. The ambiguity of the chapel became a matter of pain: the eloquence of its architecture, which spoke to some of God's glory, told others of a history of torture and colonial oppression. There were too many tablets commemorating those who had fallen in the 'Indian Mutiny' for Jyoti Sahi to feel at ease. And the maleness of many of our accepted norms in worship precipitated a deep crisis for all. It was no longer possible to slide blindly past the pain women feel at the unthinking exclusion so carelessly imposed on them by men."[21]


IX.

The report of the Nairobi Assembly included several references to worship, intercession and spirituality. The Assembly was particularly concerned about a plurality of modes of worship. "Our experience in an ecumenical gathering like this Assembly, with its diversity of cultures, values, styles, practices, and languages, proves to us how limiting has been our education, how difficult it is to be patient and listen carefully to what is strange or new, and how closed our cultural and educational conditioning has made us to the rich potential of engagement and interchange in the name of Christ." In the preamble of the report of the workshop on spirituality it was stressed that "... it is clear that the WCC needs no specific 'department of spirituality', but that the whole ecumenical community, including the WCC staff, must live freed and united in Christ and thereby be able to assist individuals, congregations, and communities to organize and discipline their life in such a way that they become open to the movements of the Holy Spirit, and for the sake of Christ become more ready to give up their own ways of life for the sake of the freedom and the unity of all."[22]

Seventy persons of various confessions participated in a consultation on "Spirituality and Ecumenism", held at Bossey, 17 June - 1 July 1976. Papers were read by K. Raiser, P.R.Cren, J. Castermane, C. Argenti, J. de Bacchiochi, W.E.J. Hollenweger, M. Legaut and J.L. Cunchillos. The texts of the report and the papers are mainly in French.[23]

The Sub-unit on Dialogue with People of Living Faiths and Ideologies met at Chiang Mai in 1977 and reflected on the theme "Dialogue in Community". Concerning worship, the statement said: "As we sought again to enter into the thought-world of the Old and New Testaments, we all felt, from whatever culture we came, both the strangeness of the gospel and the wonder of God's self-involvement with His world. In worship we knew again that the

Christian community is one that shares in holy things given by
God and is both privileged and obliged to bear witness in a
positive way to these undeserved and often unexpected gifts of
God.  This newness and given-ness of the Christian message and
of the way that God has opened up for us, cut across the custom-
ary thought and behaviour of all our cultures.  To enter again
into the mystery of Christian worship, of access to God in His
transcendence through our Lord Jesus Christ who came among us,
was also a stimulus to take seriously the worship and meditation
of others as exemplified in both the ritual and the contemplative
life of the Buddhist monks who so helpfully received us as visitors of the Wats of Chiang Mai and its area."

Another significant paragraph in the statement reads: "We
were also aware of problems concerning the authority of the
Bible remaining unsolved amongst us and of the need for a much
closer attention than we had time to give to the problem of
relating Christian worship and the meditative use (rather than
simply the intellectual study) of the holy books of other faiths.
In one of our acts of Christian worship we were invited by the
leader in the course of the service to use responsively a passage
of the Bhagavadgita: this immediately made plain the rejection
or deep hesitation by some towards any such experience while we
discovered in conversation afterwards how meaningful some others
find such meditative acts.  We recognize the need for further
study of the issues thus raised."[24]


X.


In Bangalore in 1978, the Commission on Faith and Order commended the Ecumenical Prayer Cycle in the following words: "The
theme of "Growing Together into Unity" has its own integrity.
That integrity is nowhere more evident than when thoughts are
turned into prayers.  During the Bangalore meeting, the new
Ecumenical Prayer Cycle was used in daily intercessions.  This
use showed clearly that the Cycle is not simply a calendar of
names of churches, a useful instrument and nothing more. Rather,
it offers the opportunity to keep the relations between the
churches, their growing together into unity, firmly and clearly
on the spiritual level, deeply rooted in the life of prayer to
the Father in the name of the Son through the Holy Spirit. Intercession is a form of prayer which arises from the work of Christ
on our behalf, that perpetual intercession which He ever lives
to make for us (Heb. 7:25)."[25]

The Working Group of the Sub-unit on Renewal and Congre-
gational Life met at Stony Point, USA, 29 August - 5 September
1978, to discuss the theme "Spirituality and the Charismatic
Renewal".  A 'consultative group' met in December 1978 at Schloss
Schwanberg, Bavaria.  Its discussions were summarized in a paper
entitled "Towards a Church Renewed and United in the Spirit".
Another consultation on "The Significance of the Charismatic
Renewal for the Churches" took place at Bossey, 8-13 March 1980.
The papers and reports of these three consultations are contained
in The Church is Charismatic.[26]

Two other consultations were organized at Bossey, on "Christ, Liturgy and Culture", 16-22 June 1979, and on "Local and Ecumenical Dimensions of Worship", 25-31 March 1982. The first was a meeting of African and Asian theologians. The second was in preparation for the Vancouver Assembly. It considered three basic dimensions of worship: the confessional dimension; the cultural dimension; the contextual dimension.[27]

In Section III "The Church Witnesses to the Kingdom", the World Conference on Mission and Evangelism at Melbourne, 1980, was concerned with the search for a living community at the local level, or living the future now. "As Christians, we recognize the discrepancy between the reality of the kingdom of God and the actual condition of our empirical local congregations ... Under the influence of liturgical and sacramental renewal, charismatic movements and parish weekend retreats, local congregations were attempting to realize the fullness of Christian fellowship. House churches and other small prayer and study groups are providing greater opportunities for more honest and caring personal relationships than can be achieved in larger groups. Such small groups very often become ecumenical. A particularly vital form of congregational life is known as Base Christian Communities. The communities, arising among the poor and disenfranchised and committed to the struggle for their liberation, express common concerns for identity and a new dignity. They are a gift of God, offering renewal to the church and calling it to a new presence among the poor and the disfranchised."

With regard to a new understanding of the eucharist, the Melbourne Assembly said: "Where a people is being harshly oppressed, the Eucharist speaks of the exodus or redeliverance from bondage. Where Christians are rejected or imprisoned for their faith, the bread and wine become the life of the Lord who was rejected by men but has become 'the chief stone of the corner'. Where the church sees a diminishing membership and its budgets are depressing, the Eucharist declares that there are no limits to God's giving and no end to hope in him. Where discrimination by race, sex or class is a danger for the community, the Eucharist enables people of all sorts to partake of the one food and to be made one people. Where people are affluent and at ease with life, the Eucharist says, "As Christ shares his life, share what you have with the hungry." Where a congregation is isolated by politics or war or geography, the Eucharist unites us with all God's people in all places and all ages. Where a sister or a brother is near death, the Eucharist becomes a doorway into the kingdom of our loving Father."[28]


XI.

The report of the world conference on "The Community of Women and Men in the Church", at Sheffield in 1981 contained a section on "Ministry and Worship in New Community". It expressed its concern about the use of meaningful symbols. "In order to help create meaningful worship many things need to be taken into account. In addition to the function of the ordained minister,

there is the experience of the whole congregation and its particular context.  Some religious symbols appear to be universal,
connoting almost the same meaning in all cultures: for example
water, light, fire. They can be used in a Christian context. The
cross is a traditional Christian symbol  universally accepted
and understood.

Other religious symbols, such as colours, project quite
different meanings within different contexts.  A Sudanese man
explained that even the colour of clerical dress could make a
vast difference.  In his country, black (a colour symbolic of
clergy in Western culture) gave the impression of mourning for
the sins of the world, instead of aid or service.  Some symbols,
meaningful in one culture, may have the opposite connotation in
another.  Further, symbols from the past tradition may be elusive,
even misleading to the modern mind.  A Canadian woman, discussing
clerical dress, stated that this particular symbol - once signi-
fying service and celebration - is now often connected with male
authority and domination... The churches must be cautious in
using and proposing new symbols; the people in different contexts
should be free to create and use meaningful symbols that reflect
their experiences."[29]

A consultation on "Spirituality for Combat" was held in Sri
Lanka in September 1982, sponsored by the Urban Rural Mission
Department of the Christian Conference of Asia.  The phrase had
been used during the WCC Nairobi Assembly in 1975.  There were
four group reports: elements of people's spirituality and forms
in which it expresses itself; what are the elements of religious
and cultural history and how have these been combined with
scientific and modern secular insights to determine our perspective and vision; analyze the use and misuse of spirituality
and need for a continuing renewal in the face of a dominant
state ideology; symbols and rituals which give meaning to the
structures, and characteristics of groups which can sustain
spirituality in combat.[30]

An earlier workshop on the Worship of the Congregation had
taken place at the Orthodox Academy, Gonia/Chania, Crete, 8-15
April 1978, sponsored by the Sub-unit on Renewal and Congregational Life.  The report of the workshop was "a collation of
insights that emerged, disagreements that remained, and suggestions that are directed to the churches and the WCC for taking
the exploration further."  Such exploration, it was noted,
"demands of us all an openness to Christians of other confessions,
times, cultures and ideologies, as well as a willingness to
contribute to the quest of other Christians as they for their
part engage in the same pilgrimage of faith."

The workshop at Crete dealt with: worship: what it is, what
it is not; faithfulness and creativity; worship and culture;
worship and social engagement.  It recommended "that the WCC
initiate a three-year project of regional worship workshops,
possibly concluding with a worldwide evaluation meeting prior
to the next WCC Assembly."[31]

## XII

There is no doubt that the Sixth WCC Assembly at Vancouver
in 1983 was more deeply engaged in meaningful worship, prayer,
intercession and meditation than any previous assembly. Gwen
Cashmore, director of the Sub-unit on Renewal and Congregational
Life, described the many impressions and experiences in an
article, entitled "The Worship of the Sixth Assembly".[32]   This
article deals extensively with the preparations since 1981, the
sessions of the worship committee for the Assembly, the worship
tent, the acts of daily worship, and the special services, including the opening worship, the service of penitence and preparation for holy communion, the eucharistic service according
to the Lima liturgy, the vigil for peace and justice, the Orthodox liturgy and eucharist, and the closing worship.  The article
said: "Although most of the highlights of worship were in the
tent, yet worship penetrated the whole Assembly.  As we moved
from the tent to the plenary we were already a community of
faith and in many of the presentations on theme and sub-themes
we picked up and underlined again our faith commitment - through
personal testimonies, through the beautiful and simple Orthodox
rite of breaking bread, through a prayerful act of repentance or
a joyful hymn.  We found our roots and we found our context. We
are the Church, a world assembly of those who confess Jesus as
Lord and Life of the World, gathered together and marvelling in
our unity and diversity.
    We learned a new way of participating, less clerically
dominated, with women and children and disabled in visible roles,
and we saw with respect the humility of many renowned church
leaders ready to be simply part of the whole.

    David Gill, the editor of the Vancouver report, asked what
the secret of the quality of the liturgical life of the assembly
was.  "Partly it was the use of symbols, both traditional and
contemporary, that cut through barriers of language, culture and
denomination.  Partly it was the skilled combination of carefully
sculpted form and charismatic freedom."

    But he mentioned also three other factors that had deep
significance: "First, planners this time around managed to avoid
an instrumental view of worship, which is one of Protestantism's
besetting sins and has warped the liturgical life of many recent
ecumenical gatherings.  Prayers were offered to the divine Mystery - not efforts to moralize at the congregation about the
condition of the world and what we should all be doing to fix it
... Second, Vancouver revealed that the focus on Baptism, Eucharist and Ministry (BEM) is producing something far more important
than a cerebral theological encounter...  Third, an Assembly
always echoes what is happening, often unarticulated, in the
member churches.  Why people kept flocking to that tent merits
careful reflection, in terms of what it says about the spiritual
ethos of the churches in the Year of Grace 1983.  One thing it
says, perhaps, is that many Christians are recovering confidence
in worship - a confidence that took quite a battering, in some
churches, during the stormy sixties and seventies..."[33]

The statements of the Assembly on worship are contained in the Issue reports. Issue I, "Witnessing in a Divided World", contained the following sentences: "Worship is the central act of the life and mission, witness and service of the Church. It is a way in which women and men, rich and poor, able and disabled, share in God's grace and seek forgiveness. It is a liturgical, sacramental and public realization of the unique act of Jesus Christ for the life of the world. The evangelistic, redeeming power of worship lies in the very fact of the "announcement of the death of the Lord until he comes" (I Cor. 11:26)... for the sake of the witnessing vocation of the Church we need to find a true rhythm of Christian involvement in the world. The Church is gathered for worship and scattered for everyday life. Whilst in some situations in the witnessing dimension of worship there must be a 'liturgy after the liturgy', service to the world as praise to God, in other contexts it must be stressed that there is no Christian service to the world unless it is rooted in the service of worship."

Issue VII, "Learning in Community", was concerned with liturgical education: "It is through liturgy that the worshipping community expresses itself. Liturgy carrying in itself the dimension of learning includes the following elements: the experience of God's presence within the worshipping community; the revelation of Christ as a living reality transmitted through the proclamation of God's word and received in the sacraments; and our response to God in repentance, offering, thanksgiving, praise and remembrance.
All of this is fulfilled in communion with God and expressed in a specific order and language. Such language is not merely verbal, but includes non-verbal expressions - signs, symbols, drama, rites and gestures..."[34]

## Observations and Comments

1. As we have noticed, the First Assembly at Amsterdam in 1948 was already concerned with overcoming the division between Christian worship and Christian witness and service to the world. There have been many developments since in the understanding and the practice of worship, prayer and spirituality.

There is perhaps a need for further reflection on the dialectical and dynamic relation between penitence, adoration and political action. We have seen that from 1975 onwards the slogan 'spirituality for combat' has caught ecumenical attention. In Orthodox circles the expression 'the liturgy after the liturgy' is popular. These expressions can be misleading. Churches and their faithful do not neatly start with worship and spirituality, and then become involved in national and international politics. It is the full immersion in the chaos of humanity, a 'holy worldliness', which enables them to speak to humankind at large in a prophetic role. Our desperate struggles against classism, racism and sexism become a part of our spirituality and liturgy. Jesus withdrew often to a lonely place to commune directly with his Father after he had exposed himself to the wickedness of the

human race.  So the risky doing of God's will in the darkness of
our age - the WCC grant made in 1978 to the Patriotic Front in
Rhodesia is an example - is accompanied by the cry, 'And God
have mercy upon us'.

2.  Joan Puls, a Franciscan sister who read this survey
article, communicated in a memorandum the following: "There
seems to be a tendency on the part of the WCC, perhaps Protestants in general, in certain traditions at least, to think of
spirituality primarily in terms of worship.  Worship is perhaps
taken in a broad sense of prayer, devotion, eucharist, celebration, community-at-prayer.  The word worship is not used as
frequently in my Roman Catholic tradition, but we would in any
case not equate it with spirituality.  Before Vatican II we
probably spoke more of the spiritual life than of spirituality.
And spiritual life did tend to focus more on spiritual exercises,
devotions, prayer life, personal or communal.  After Vatican II,
however, we spoke more readily of spirituality, meaning the
whole of our life as it was shot through with faith...
Spirituality embraces one's ministry and service, one's
relationships, one's personal and communal prayer life, one's
approach to the political and social environment, in short,
one's life-style... Spirituality then is incarnational, daily,
integrated.  To be authentic it  must have dimensions of combat,
of search and retreat, of renewal, of discernment, of personal
growth, of ecumenicity, etc..."

These observations are of vital importance and help us, as
Sister Joan stated, "to continue to clarify and sharpen our
understanding of spirituality, in all its contexts and with all
its ingredients."

3.  Following its Sixth Assembly in Vancouver, the WCC chose
the concern for spirituality as one of its major emphases. There
is no doubt that this whole concern for a contemporary spirituality is widely shared by Roman Catholic, Orthodox and Protestant
churches.  In order to pursue this concern, a small consultation
was convened at Annecy, France, in December 1984, with participants from Protestant, Orthodox, Roman Catholic and Pentecostal
Churches.  Their task was to "undertake a common search for the
direction in which the church is being led in this time" and
"to discern the call of our time to enflesh the gospel and to
cooperate with the Spirit in the building up of the body of
Christ."

The report "A Spirituality for Our Times", written by Joan
Puls, has been widely appreciated, and translated for use as a
discussion document for groups.[35]  It is now available in French,
English, German, Spanish, Malagache and Malayalam. The Annecy
consultation is to be followed in April 1986 by a further consultation on monastic spirituality; it will give special attention to Orthodox contributions in the field.  In 1987 a further
consultation will be held on the "Fruits of the Spirit in Dialogue with People  of Living Faiths."

In 1985 Joan Puls's book "Every Bush is Burning" was published in the Risk Book Series. Under the heads life, search,
formation, conflict, obedience, freedom, and exchange she describes in this book a spirituality that is ordinary and everyday.

4. This survey may be concluded with an extract from the
Annecy report, which indicates where we are today in our search
for spirituality: "We believe the churches are called to a costly spirituality that is Christ-centred and enables us to more
effectively witness in the world. This inevitably demands constant conversion and ongoing formation and discipleship, is
rooted in a life of prayer and of solidarity with the poor and
oppressed, and leads to suffering. Encouraged and challenged
by a community that is nourished by word and sacrament, this
life is one of joy and hope in the risen Lord."

---

1. The First Assembly of the World Council of Churches, held
   at Amsterdam, August 22 - September 4, 1948.
   Ed. by W.A. Visser 't Hooft. London: SCM, 1949. pp.54, 67.

2. Minutes and Reports of the Second Meeting of the Central
   Committee held at Chichester, England, July 9-15, 1949.
   Geneva: WCC, 1949. pp. 48-49.

3. Ways of Worship. The Report of a Theological·Commission of
   Faith and Order. London: SCM Press, 1951.

4. The Third World Conference on Faith and Order, held at
   Lund, August 15-28, 1952. Ed. by Oliver S. Tomkins.
   London: SCM Press, 1953, pp. 40-47.

5. The Ecumenical Review, vol. VI, no. 4, July 1954. pp. 440-441.

6. Dilemmas and Opportunities. Christian Action in Rapid Social
   Change. Report of an International Ecumenical Study Con-
   ference, Thessalonica, Greece, July 25 - August 2, 1959.
   Geneva: WCC, 1959. pp. 34-35.

7. Witnesses Together. Being the official report of the
   Inaugural Assembly of the East Asia Christian Conference,
   held at Kuala Lumpur, Malaya, May 14-24, 1959.
   Ed. by U Kyaw Than. Rangoon: EACC, 1959. pp. 108-109.

8. The Christian Community within the Human Community.
   Containing Statements from the Bangkok Assembly of the EACC,
   Feb.-March 1964. Bangalore: CLS, 1964. p. 47.

9. Drumbeats from Kampala. Report of the First Assembly of
   the All Africa Conference of Churches, held at Kampala,
   April 20-30, 1963. London: Lutterworth, 1963. pp. 35-36.

10. The New Delhi Report.
    London: SCM Press, 1962. pp. 204 and 120-121.

11. The Fourth World Conference on Faith and Order, Montreal
    1963. Ed. by P.C. Rodger and L. Vischer.
    London: SCM Press, 1964 (Faith and Order Paper, No. 42).
    pp. 69-80, 47.

12. The Ecumenical Review, vol. XV, no. 3, April 1963.
    pp. 245-319.

13. In the Archives of the Division of Ecumenical Action.

14. The Uppsala Report 1968. Ed. by Norman Goodall.
    Geneva: WCC, 1968. pp. 81, 83-85, 401.

15. Studia Liturgica, vol. 7, nos. 2-3, 1970.

16. Central Committee of the WCC. Minutes and Report of the
    Twenty-Fourth Meeting, Addis Ababa, Jan. 10-21, 1971.
    Geneva: WCC, 1971. pp. 144-145.

17. Faith and Order. Louvain 1971. Study Reports and Documents.
    Geneva: WCC, 1971 (Faith and Order Paper, No. 59).
    pp. 102-116, 219.

18. Uniting in Hope. Reports and Documents from the meeting
    of the Faith and Order Commission at the University of
    Ghana, Legon, 23 July - 5 August, 1974. Geneva: WCC,
    1975 (Faith and Order Paper, No. 72). pp. 48-80.

19. Central Committee of the WCC. Minutes of the Twenty-Seventh
    Meeting, Berlin (West), August 11-18, 1974.
    Geneva: WCC, 1974. p. 28.

20. Uppsala to Nairobi 1968-1975. Ed. by David E. Johnson.
    New York: Friendship Press; London: SPCK, 1975.
    pp. 104-105.

21. Risk, vol. 12, no. 2, 1976. p. 25.

22. Breaking Barriers. Nairobi 1975. Ed. by David M. Paton.
    London: SPCK; Grand Rapids: Wm. B. Eerdmans, 1976.
    pp. 91, 311-312.

23. Spirituality and Ecumenism - Spiritualité et oecuménisme.
    Céligny: Ecumenical Institute, 1976.

24. Faith in the Midst of Faiths. Reflections on Dialogue in
    Community. Ed. by S.J. Samartha.
    Geneva: WCC, 1977. pp. 134-135, 142.

25. Sharing in One Hope. Reports and Documents from the Meeting
    of the Faith and Order Commission, 15-30 August, 1978,
    Bangalore, India. Geneva: WCC, 1978 (Faith and Order
    Paper, No. 92). p. 261.

26. The Church is Charismatic. Ed. by Arnold Bittlinger.
    Geneva: WCC, 1981.

27. Mimeographed reports in the archives of the Bossey Library.

28. Your Kingdom Come. Report on the World Conference on
    Mission and Evangelism, Melbourne, 12-25 May, 1980.
    Geneva: WCC, 1980.  pp. 197, 206.

29. The Community of Women and Men in the Church. A Report of
    the WCC's Conference, Sheffield, England, 1981.
    Ed. by Constance Parvey.  Geneva: WCC, 1983.  pp. 130-131.

30. Spirituality for Combat.  Hong Kong: Christian Conference
    of Asia, Urban Rural Mission, 1983
    (URM Discussion Series 1983).  pp. 49-57.

31. Report of a Workshop on the Worship of the Congregation,
    1978.  In the archives of the Sub-unit on Renewal and
    Congregational Life.

32. Cashmore, Gwen.  The Worship of the Sixth Assembly.
    In: Midstream, vol. XXIII, no. 1, Jan. 1984.  pp. 74-89.

33. Gathered for Life. Official Report of the VI Assembly of
    the WCC, Vancouver, Canada, 24 July - 10 August, 1983.
    Ed. by David Gill.  Geneva: WCC;  Grand Rapids: Eerdmans,
    1983.  pp. 12-13.

34. Ibid., pp. 34-35, 95-96.

35. Puls, Joan.  A Spirituality for Our Times.
    Geneva: WCC, 1985.

# X.
## The Role of Women
## in the Ecumenical Movement

### I.

The concern for the life and work of women in the church
and in the ecumenical movement has been voiced ever since the
World Council of Churches was created in 1948.  At its First
Assembly a Report on "The Life and Work of Women in the Church"
was received and commended to the churches for their serious
consideration and appropriate action.  The report stressed that
"organizations of women within the churches afford rich opportunities for service and self-expression, and a valuable
training-ground in Christian leadership."

Concerning the ordination of women the report stated:
"...Some churches for theological reasons are not prepared to
consider the question of such ordination; some find no objection
in principle but see administrative or social difficulties; some
permit partial but not full participation in the work of the
ministry; in others women are eligible for all offices of the
Church.  Even in the last group, social custom and public opinion
still create obstacles.  In some countries a shortage of clergy
raises urgent practical and spiritual problems.  Those who
desire the admission of women to the full ministry believe that
until this is achieved the Church will not come to full health
and power.  We are agreed that this whole subject requires
further careful and objective study."

Sarah Chakko who presented the Report felt that the question
of the ordination of women was only a minor part of the whole
problem.  Among the several recommendations were: "that an adequate supply of information about women's activities be provided through the Ecumenical Press Service and other channels;
that a great number of women be chosen to serve on the Commissions, the major Committees and the Secretariat of the World
Council of Churches."[1]

### II.

The Report of the Committee on the Division of Ecumenical
Action, presented to the Second Assembly at Evanston in 1954,
included the following statement: "The Department on the Cooperation of Men and Women in Church and Society, formerly the
Commission of Men and Women in Church and Society, is concerned
with certain quite special problems of dislocation and unbalance
in the life of the Church, now seen as urgent in many areas, but
which we dare hope may prove to be transitional.  Its task is
to promote among men and women the study of questions affecting
the co-operation and the common service of men and women in the
churches and in society."  The Report further emphasized that

"the member churches should be asked to recognize <u>the serious-ness of the problem of the co-operation of men and women</u> in various areas of church life, and to seek ways in which this problem can be solved so that both men and women can give their full contribution to the life of the Church. It should be recognized that these are not questions for women only, but for men and women to consider together."[2]

The Central Committee, meeting in 1955, agreed to commend the following statement on "<u>Cooperation of Men and Women in Church and Society</u>" to the member churches for their study and comment: "The basic concern of this Department, as of the entire World Council of Churches, is the wholeness of the Church. This wholeness can be achieved only when every part of the membership of the Church is enabled to participate fully in its life. Effective participation includes working together with others who have different gifts... It is inherent in our faith that men and women are called and sent together to do God's will in the Church and in Society. God created men and women and put them together under His blessing and His order. Christ came to save men and women and called them together to His discipleship. The Holy Spirit was given to men and women as members of the new community to witness together for the sake of Christ in the world."

It was added: "If the implications of the cooperation of men and women in all doctrinal and practical issues of the Church were generally recognized by the member churches and the departments of the World Council of Churches, there would be no further need for this Department. For the good of the Church and the effectiveness of its witness in the world, it is necessary, for the present, to continue to emphasize this special concern. The Department is trying to put the whole discussion on this issue on a new level and on the basis of theological thinking and sociological observations, to stimulate the churches to rediscover the full meaning of cooperation between men and women in Church and society."[3]

In the realm of rapid social change studies, the Department on Church and Society issued a second statement, which included the following paragraph: "Industrialization and trading sometimes bring employment to rural areas for girls and women. Economic independence then comes within their reach for the first time; the age of marriage and the traditions of dowry and bride-wealth are affected. The total result is a social dislocation that will make heavy demands upon Christians who must share the responsibility of leadership in trying to find new patterns of family life and new relations between men and women."[4]

The same subject was discussed at an International Ecumenical Study Conference held at Thessalonica in 1959. Under the heading "<u>Costs and Achievements in Rapid Social Change</u>" it was asserted: "... Rapid social change affects women perhaps more than men, changing relations between the sexes, as well as bringing material improvements in living which ease the drudgery of the daily round; and releasing women for education and training so that they can serve more fully both their families and communities in the changing pattern of urban and rural life. But men and women who are flung from the country into cities and industry have to make adjustments, not only to new physical situations and social structures, but also to ways of life and ideas and goals which demand fundamental changes in outlook and personality."[5]


## III.

The Report of the All Africa Church Conference at Ibadan, in 1958, contained a short section on "The New Status of Women", in which it was stated: "... Need was felt for winning the mothers for the Church, because of their influence on the family. The group was agreed that the place of women in the ministry of the Church required urgent examination. False ideas should be eradicated, among them that women must work to support their families. Their primary function in the Christian home is to create a good Christian family, working in partnership with the father, sharing all things and praying together. Training is needed in Christian family relationships, including sex training."[6]

The Inaugural Assembly of the East Asia Christian Conference at Kuala Lumpur, in 1959, resolved that "the East Asia Home and Family Life Committee be replaced by the Committee on the Co-operation of Men and Women in Home, Church and Society." The scope and the function of the Committee included: "... Helping men and women's organizations to improve their programmes so as to help them to participate more fully in the general life of the Church; helping the men and women to discover the points where they can enter the ministry of the work of the Church, e.g. chaplains in hospitals, hostels, orphanages, schools, etc.; and providing scholarships for training men and women for more responsible service in church and society."[7]


## IV.

Several consultations were held in the early period from 1948 to 1961. We mention the following. "Men and Women in Industry" was the subject of a conference held in Bièvres, France, June 14-19, 1951. Essays were prepared by a Dutch group (The Responsibility of the Employer. Its Field and Its Limitations); a French group (The Responsibility of the Manager Regarding Wages and Specialized Workers); a Swedish group (Selection, Promotion and Dismissal); a British group (The Christian Manager's Responsibility Towards His Subordinates, with Respect to Discipline and Efficiency). S.Dalziel presented a paper on "The Implications of Matthew 7:12 for the Christian Manager.[8]

Two consultations were held on "The Service of Women in the Church" at Ibadan, Nigeria, January 4-10, 1958 and at Mkongsamba, Cameroon, February 2-23, 1958. At the first consultation recommendations were made on sex education, female circumcision, 'bride-price', polygamy, marriage failures, prostitution and venereal diseases, birth control, married women and professional

life. Individual contributions were made by M. Barot, I. Igho-
daro, Th. Ekollo, W.A. Visser 't Hooft, Ph. Potter, A. Adegbola.
The second consultation was all African and attended by 100
participants.  Urgent questions on alcoholism, prostitution,
juvenile delinquency, sex relations before marriage, the situation of widows, the bride-price, polygamy and illiteracy were
raised. The recommendations sent to the churches were on: bride-
price, polygamy and biblical teaching on marriage.[9]

The consultation on "The Christian Approach to Women's
Questions- Freedom of Marriage - Freedom of Work" at the John
Knox House in Geneva, March 27-30, 1958, was sponsored by the
Department on the Cooperation of Men and Women and the World
Young Women's Christian Association.  M.H. Lefaucheux and D.
Kitagawa contributed to the theme: "Freedom of Marriage and Its
Relation to Family Patterns."  A. Rössel and Mrs. Dirkse-Bres-
ters reported on: "Freedom of Work, with Reference to Working
Women with Family Responsibilities."  A. Arnold gave a summary
of the Twelfth Session of the U.N. Commission on the Status of
Women.[10]

At Odense, Denmark, August 8-12, 1958, the theme was:
"Obstacles to the Cooperation of Men and Women".  Contributions
were made by M. Barot (The History and Raison d'Etre of the Work
of the Department); L. Anderson and H. Thimme (Obstacles Arising
From Economic Factors); B. Rohde and R. Mukerji (Obstacles
Arising From Family Responsibilities); A.D. Kelley and Miss
Skovgaard-Petersen (Obstacles Arising From Psychological Factors);
M. Batten (Obstacles Arising From Traditional Attitudes of the
Community); Sh. Johnson and A.J. Rasker (Obstacles Arising From
Biblical Assumptions).  C.Wedel (Conclusions).[11]

"Towards Responsible Cooperation Between Men and Women, Our
Christian Responsibility" was the subject of discussion of a
consultation   at Uplands, High Wycome, England, July 27 - August
2, 1960.  L. Nold, M. Cremer, V.T. Istavridis, G. Johnston,
M.E.Thrall made a contribution to "Cooperation - Its Nature and
Meaning."  M. Bührig and M. Barot contributed to "Proposals for
Special Study."  "Reflections on the Past Ten Years" were made
by M.A. Wyker.  M. Sahlin reported on the ministry of women in
Sweden;  A. Arnold reported on the Role of a Christian Women's
Movement among International Non-Governmental Organizations.[12]

A first consultation in Asia, initiated by the Department
on Cooperation of Men and Women in Church and Society, took
place at Madras, November 13-17, 1961.  The theme was "Changing
Patterns of Men - Women Relationships in Asia".  The East Asia
Christian Conference had already taken the lead in considering
the changing relationships of men and women.  Papers were presented by A.L. Mudaliar, K. Takeda Cho, T. Frantz, J.P. Am-
brosio, M.G. Wyllie, E. Ibiam, H.G. Cox, M. Bührig, D.T. Niles,
V.K. Alexander, H. Morton, E. Shipstone, T. Cherian, L. Nold,
M. Barot.[13]

At the Third WCC Assembly in New Delhi in 1961 an extensive Report of the Committee on the Department on Cooperation of Men and Women in Church, Family and Society was presented, amended and received. It dealt with the Church, the Family and Society in three sections. Various recommendations were made with regard to a greater participation of women in churchwork, lay-offices and policy-making boards, education, scholarships, further detailed studies on various subjects such as sex education, preparation for marriage, mixed marriages, responsible parenthood, part-time work, and "the enlistment of the EACC, the AACC and other groups, to ensure a world-wide viewpoint in the production of findings and material that may be sent to the churches for their information."[14] In the discussion of the Report the opinion was expressed that, because of divergent views on the ordination of women, the Department should continue to remain unaligned with a particular point of view.

VI.

At the First Assembly of the All Africa Conference of Churches in Kampala in 1963, a section was devoted to "Freedom and Unity in the Family" which contained insights and recommendations concerning women in the church, the African understanding of family and family life, polygamy, marriage, prostitution, divorce, church discipline, succession and inheritance. With regard to polygamy it was stated: "It is our opinion that monogamy, that is one man and one wife, is the mind of Christ. This is the standard to be placed before the people. The question of excluding polygamists from Holy Communion should be given further consideration by a group of men and women studying together." In view of rapid social changes, it was recommended that "Christian women should be encouraged to become active members of secular movements involved in social and political advance, and in maintaining good standards of private and public life, for instance in national councils of women, marriage guidance councils, and so forth."[15]

The Assembly was preceded by a consultation at Kampala, April 11-19, 1963, on "The Responsibility of Christian Women in Africa Today". The report of the consultation, held at Makerere University, included: (1) The spiritual life of the consultation; (2) The lectures; a) The women between traditional and modern ways; b) The woman as educator of the future; c) The woman as member of the Church; d) The woman, her civic rights and responsibilities; (3) A great variety of activities; (4) The seminars. There was an epilogue on (1) Women share responsibility in the assembly; (2) What happened with the report of the consultation; and recommendations to the All Africa Conference of Churches.[16]

The Minutes and Reports of the Central Committee, meeting
at Rochester, USA, in 1963, contain the Report of the Division
of Ecumenical Action and a Statement on Some Basic Considerations
concerning the Work of the Department on the Cooperation of Men
and Women in Church, Family and Society. It was stated: "Behind
all the varied activities of the department lies a concern with
basic Christian principle. The relations of men and women in all
aspects of life are only in certain isolated parts of the world
still organized on the all-inclusive pattern of paternalism. As
stable patterns break up it becomes more and more important that
partnership takes the form of a shared responsibility of men and
women before God. This partnership is not the result of social
change; it is a secret of the being of humanity, given in
creation."[17]

At the World Conference on Church and Society in Geneva in
1966 a sub-section on "Men and Women in Changing Communities"
of Section IV "Men and Community in Changing Societies" dealt
with: Men and Women Today: Personal Relationships; Cooperation
of Men and Women in Church and Society; Family and Society;
Responsible Parenthood: The Number and Spacing of Children.
It was noted that "two members of the sub-section were women
and that the proportion of women to men in the Conference as a
whole was even lower, in spite of the fact that the membership
and activity of women in the churches is far greater than that
of men." There were nine recommendations of the World Conference with regard to the relations of men and women in church,
family and society, including women's equal right to work,
status and pay, education for responsible parenthood, increasing
research on contraceptive technology, a common approach among
Protestant, Orthodox and Roman Catholic churches to these
questions.[18]

In the Report of the Committee on Cooperation of Men and
Women in Church, Family and Society, presented to the Uppsala
Assembly in 1968, it was noted: "We welcome the integration at
divisional committee level of this Department with the work of
the other four secretariats of the Division. We hope that concern about the cooperation between men and women might become
an integral part of all departments. We recognize that we still
need to make certain emphases in the three areas of church,
family and society." Section VI "Towards New Styles of Living"
contained a few paragraphs on "Creative Partnership". The last
paragraph stated: "Family patterns change in different social
settings, and Christian marriage can find its expression in a
variety of ways. We would like materials elaborating the problems of polygamy, marriage and celibacy, birth control, divorce,
abortion, and also of homosexuality, to be made available for
responsible study and action."[19]

## VIII.

The Conference on World Cooperation for Development at Beirut, in 1968, sponsored by the Exploratory Committee on Society, Development and Peace, stressed that "the development of education for women can make an indispensable contribution to new patterns of family life", and that "mothers and all teachers of others need the kind of education that makes them promoters of the modernizing process."[20]

The Consultation on Christian Concern for Peace at Baden, Austria, in 1970, sponsored by the Committee on Society, Development and Peace stated that with regard to the churches' instruments for peace making "family adjustments will have to be made as increasing opportunities arise for women to contribute to society in new economic and civic roles. On the problem of equal rights for women, it expressed itself as follows: "The idea of peace presupposes that all human beings, men and women, have equal rights. A woman is fully entitled as a man to the complete development of her talents and her personality. Within a family the husband and the wife complement each other, and many women find their most satisfying fulfilment in the duties and love of home and family; but many also seek to enter public life or to find work in industry. Yet in most of the countries of the world, developed as well as developing, women are under-privileged: legislative assemblies are overwhelmingly male in composition, and even when women do go out to work they often receive less pay than men who are doing identical work. This is clearly a grave social injustice, based mainly on male prejudice but partly also on outdated local customs. Such discrimination also prevails in the Churches."[21]

## IX.

The Assembly of the Commission on World Mission and Evangelism at Bangkok in 1973 was very outspoken on obstacles to the roles of women in the church and in the world: "Men and women are both made in the image of God, and it is in their complementary nature and in their co-operation together that God's purposes for the salvation of mankind can be fulfilled. This co-operation is not possible where women's destiny is determined exclusively by their biology where they are thus denied the possibility of full personhood.

"The roles that are assigned to women are all in terms of sex, of motherhood, of housekeeper or of helpmeet to the husband. They are all roles which add to the dominance of the male, and emphasize the subservience of the female. In any other vocation, which may be in addition to, or instead of, that of wife and mother, women are not given full and easy access to opportunities for development. They gain acceptance only if they accomodate to the styles and expectations of the male world. One effect of this is that God has been heard to speak predominantly with a 'masculine voice'. God's 'feminine voice' will only be heard as women are enabled to make their own particular contribution to theological thinking and in the whole life of the Church.

"In practical terms, this means that a deliberate attempt has to be made to bring women into positions of responsibility and decision-making. The structures, the style of working and the form of conferences and meetings all need radical change to ensure that women may make their full contribution, and that all may be liberated from the evil of power, domination and manipulation."[22]

"Sexism in the 1970s - Discrimination Against Women" was the title of the Report of a WCC Consultation at West Berlin in 1974. This report contains, besides several addresses and a concluding article, working group reports on: Women in the Church; Partnership; Women in Politics; Women in Economic Structures; Education; The Fifth WCC Assembly.[23] This world consultation reflected deeply the joy and despair, the excitement and disillusionment, the rewards and frustrations experienced by all its participants. They learned that the struggle for liberation of women is a universal struggle, in spite of differences in their cultural, racial, economic, and political perspectives, in spite of differences of opinion on what women's emancipation means and how it is to be achieved. It was the beginning of a new kind of community and a renewed commitment to work for change in order to end all those things which deny their humanity, and above all the creative purposes of God, for an end not only to sex discrimination but to all forms of oppression.[23]

In response to the West Berlin Consultation, the Central Committee, meeting in August 1974, agreed that
- public support should be given to the United Nations International Women's Year;
- adequate representation of women from member churches on all boards and communities of the Council be assured;
- a fund be set up for the political, social and cultural development of women, in both urban and rural areas, especially those living on the subsistence level;
- a Task Force on Sexism and Language be appointed;
- the WCC should  a) provide guidelines to all its speakers, writers and translators, to help eliminate sexist language, concepts and imagery from all speeches and documents...;
b) eliminate the sexist language from the study booklet, litanies, and the special hymn in the preparatory materials for the Fifth Assembly.[24]

X.

Several other consultations were organized and sponsored by the Department on Cooperation of Men and Women in Church, Family and Society, and from 1971 onwards by the Sub-unit on Women in Church and Society, during the period between the New Delhi Assembly and the Nairobi Assembly.

"Relationships of Men and Women at Work" was the subject of a consultation held at Founex, Switzerland, June 29 - July 4, 1964. The report of the consultation includes: I. The Scene is Set; II. Interdependence of Family and Work; III. New Kinds of Personal Relationships of Men and Women at Work; IV. The Involvement of the Church - The Way Ahead. The appendices contain lectures by E. Hymer, H. Ringeling, P. Heyde, M.Bührig, M. Nerling, and a Recommendation Concerning the Employment of Women with Family Responsibilities (adopted by the ILO-Assembly, June 1965).[25]

A Consultation on "Sexual Ethics Today" examined reports received from various groups in Europe which were classified in three categories: pre-marital problems (youth), problems of married people, problems of people free of marriage bond (single, widowed, divorced). Individual contributions were made by M. Bührig, A. Dumas, W.G. Cole, J. de la Croix Kaelin, H. Thimme. The report includes also Considerations for Further Study and German Interpretation of Considerations for Further Study.[26]

At Rome, October 1965 a consultation took place on "Women's Service in and Through the Churches". This interconfessional meeting, the first of its kind, in which thirty Orthodox, Roman Catholic, Anglican and Protestant women participated, was organized jointly by the WCC and the Vatican Secretariat for the Promotion of Christian Unity, with the assistance of the RC Permanent Committee for International Congresses of the Lay Apostolate. Participants were members of religious orders, deaconnesses, women engaged in church administration and lay-women working in secular organizations. Areas of common concern were explored including the role of women in the world and in the church. Recommendations were submitted to the Joint Working Group of the Roman Catholic Church and the WCC.[27]

"Marriage and the Division Among the Churches" was the theme of a consultation at Crêt-Bérard, June 20-24, 1966, sponsored by the Secretariat of Faith and Order and the Department on Co-operation of Men and Women in Church, Family and Society. It produced a World Council study document, which focused on (A) Five Theological Problems: (1) Marriage as a universal institution and marriage between Christians; (2) Marriage as a sacrament; (3) Marriage and the Church; (4) Uniqueness of marriage: divorce and remarriage; (5) Civil marriage. (B) Mixed marriages: Church relations. (C) Pastoral Considerations.[28]

At the "John Knox House Consultation" in Geneva, July 27-30, 1966, regional reports were given by A. Ebertova (Czechoslovakia); R.M Fagley and W.H. Genné (USA); J.K. Lawton (Great Britain); S. Nomenyo (Togo); G. Ademola (Nigeria); L.H. Mariam (Ethiopia); L.E. Fernando (Ceylon); R. Mukerji-Somasekhar (India). Mrs.Nold and A. Dumas made a presentation on the Christian teaching with regard to marriage. The future strategy of the Department was discussed.[29]

The Conference on "The Christian Women Co-artisan in a Changing Society" at Taizé, France, June 19-24, 1967, was organized by the Conference of Catholic International Organizations and the WCC Department on Cooperation of Men and Women in collaboration with the World Young Women's Christian Association. The report includes: Before Taizé (M. Barot); Questionnaire Sent to Women's Organizations; Synthesis of Replies to the Questionnaire; Ecumenical Dialogue (Report of Study Groups); Papers by J. Brothers, L. Simons, A. Dumas; Reports from Workshops; Recommendations of the Conference; After Taizé: Toward the Future (M. del Pilar Bellosillo).[30]

"Developing Relations of Men, Women and Children and Their Meaning for the Mission of the Church in Our Changing Society" was the subject of discussion of a consultation held at Österkär, Sweden, June 28 - July 2, 1968. Special reference was made to the developments in the Scandinavian societies. Three panel discussions were led by Dr. Holter, R. Virkkunen and M. Boethins. Individual contributions were made by D. Sysiharju, B. Kinnér M. Paloheimo, R. Holte, A. Dumas, D. Mace.[31]

The National Council of Churches in the Philippines, Caritas Internationalis, The Catholic International Union for Social Service and the Diakonia Desk of the WCC sponsored a consultation on "New Strategies for Social Welfare's Participation in Social Development." Theme speakers were: M. Barot, S. de Nave, G. Rocheau, B.T.Molander. The three sub-themes were: Familial values in a developing country; Education for new attitudes and leadership in rural areas; New values to promote development.[32]

Roman Catholics, Orthodox and Protestants participated in a consultation on "What is Ordination Coming To ?" at Geneva, September 21-26, 1970. During the preparation of this consultation a survey was sent to ordained women in order to obtain their reactions and experiences. They are included in the report. Presentations were made by Ian M. Fraser, S. Syvänne, T. Govaart-Halkes, J.L. Spangenberg, Ph. Guthardt. The three groups reports were on: I. The discussion on the ordination of women to the ministry in a new context; II. Psychological and sociological factors in the ordination of women; III. Initiatives for change.[33]

The Report of a Consultation on "Pastoral Care of Those Confronted With Abortion", held at Monbachtal, FRG, October 6-11, 1974, includes: Points of Agreement, Process of Ecumenical Learning, the Scope of Pastoral Care and Counselling, Perspectives for the Future, Letter to the Churches.[34]


XI.

Concerning the inequality of women, a Consultation on "Human Rights and Christian Responsibility" at St. Pölten, Austria, 21-26 October, 1974, organized by the WCC Commission of the Churches on International Affairs expressed itself as follows: "Even where equality between men and women is legally assured - this is far from being implemented - concrete social discrimination between the sexes is frequently found in practice. One illustration of this discrimination is the comparatively few women who occupy key positions in either church or state. Even in socialist countries which are known for their progressive legislation in this matter, women are not always able to make their full contribution to society due to the inherited concepts of the role of women in family and society. Historically, men have dominated women and this tradition remains and is perpetuated in the church today. The reluctance of some women to use their rights and assume their new roles also contribute to discrimination."35

The Faith and Order Commission, meeting at Accra in 1974, expressed the following on "From Within the Community of Men and Women": "Whenever women are seen primarily as a means of sexual behaviour, they are dehumanized. Within the Church, the convential use of male and female language and images in speaking about God and the Church stands in the way of a Christian community in which all can participate fully. Despite the prophetic vision in the Bible, the Church has made it difficult for women to become whole persons.

"Women are asking: Why can we participate so little in our church councils and other decision-making bodies ? Why, in so many churches, is the ministry open only to men ? Why is it that throughout the centuries only men were ordained to the priesthood ? And where the ministry is open to women, why do women so often meet hostility ? ... How can they come to a new self-awareness of the contribution they can make in the struggle for humanity in both Church and society ? What new ways can be found of appreciating and responding to Mary of Nazareth, mother of Jesus and woman of joyful hope ? There is a sign of hope in our attempt to understand each other and to reach out for the fruits of reconciled and reconciling life.

"All Christian education and upbringing which conditions men and women to these limited roles, which have been transcended in Christ, are not true to this vision... We look for language and images which will more fully reveal the truth of God to us. Called as men and women together to become signs of the promised kingdom, we hope for a true and complete community in Christ."36


VII.

At the Fifth Assembly of the WCC in Nairobi in 1975, a plenary session was devoted to "Women in a Changing World". Mrs. Takeda Cho presided. Speakers were Sylvia Talbot, Dorothy McMahon, Feny Simonian, Julia Okiambo. There was a panel in which three women participated: Prakai Nontawassee, Annie R. Jiagge and Una Kroll.

Section II "What Unity Requires" contained the following paragraph on "The Community of Women and Men and the Wholeness of the Body of Christ": "The Church's unity includes women and men in a true mutuality. As a result of rapid cultural, economic, and social change, women (and many men) reject the passive or restrictive roles formerly assigned to women, and search for fuller participation in the life of the Church and in society at large. The relations of women and men must be shaped by reciprocity and not by subordination. The unity of the Church requires that women be free to live out the gifts which God has given to them and to respond to their calling to share fully in the life and witness of the Church. This raises fundamental dogmatic issues on which we are not agreed, but which are further pursued in the study, "The Community of Women and Men in the Church", which will include the significance of the Virgin Mary in the Church and the question of the ordination of women..."

Section V "Structures of Injustice and Struggles for Liberation" contained a long list of recommendations with regard to theological studies of sexuality, the elimination of sexist terminology, the full participation of women in all ecclesiastical decision-making bodies, the ordination of women, the full participation in political, economic and social structures of society, the support of women by facilitating and funding specific projects, such as securing safe water supplies, etc., the affirmation of a partnership in mutual interdependence by the member churches and their support of women's concerns through special funds earmarked for the WCC Women's Desk.

In the Summary Report of Hearing 4 on Unit III, Education and Renewal, it was recommended that "the Sub-unit on Women should collaborate with the Commission on Faith and Order to ensure active continuation of the study "The Community of Women and Men in the Church and Society" over a period of three years (1976-78) in preparation for an ecumenical consultation under the auspices of the WCC in 1979-80."[37]

Besides endorsing the recommendation of the Review Committee of the Nairobi Assembly "that The study on the Community of Women and Men in the Church should proceede", the Central Committee in 1976 agreed "that the programme on Women in Rural Development should have high priority. An emphasis of this programme should be participation, education and leadership development." It was further agreed "to accept the offer of CCPD to contribute to the funding of this programme. It should be carried out in close cooperation with CCPD, CICARWS and CWME."[38]

At its next meeting in 1977, the Central Committee noted with approval that the Working Group of the Sub-unit on Women's attention had been drawn to instances of violations of human rights, particularly involving women: (a) migrant women; (b) 'indentured labour' (women being exploited through working arrangements in which they have no recourse to protection or to normal benefits or securities); (c) domestic workers; (d) refugees (the hardships of women separated from their families; (e) the politically oppressed (women are at a particular disadvantage in the situation of lengthy imprisonment).[39]

"The Role of Orthodox Women in the Church and in Society"
was the theme of a consultation at Agapia, Roumania, September
11-17, 1976. Individual contributions were made by E. Braniste,
C. Tarasar, E. Behr-Sigel, Metropolitan Emilianos, E. Theodorou.
The reports, edited by Constance J. Tarasar and Irina Kirillova,
included also: Our Concerns: Family, Monasticism, Society, Education, Church Service, Witness and Ecumenism.40

Eighty participants came from 40 different countries and
from all continents, the majority carrying responsibility for
work with Christian women, either within their own denomination
or at the level of councils of churches, to participate in a
consultation on "Church Women Executives" at Glion, Switzerland,
January 17-22, 1977. The consultation focused on the Lives
Women Lead in the Churches, in Rural Areas, under Conditions of
Stress, and on Agents of Change through the Churches, Other
Agencies, the WCC, New Life Styles and a New Economic Order.41

A "Consultation of European Christian Women" took place at
Brussels, January 29 - February 4, 1978. Various concerns were
expressed: the need for total disarmament; the fact that racism
and torture touch every region of the world; recognition that
inadequate education leads to powerlessness; the need for women
to affirm the dignity of their minds and bodies; the hope that
a new look at 'feminist' theology and the ministry of women
will encourage women seeking leadership in the churches. Lectures were given by E. Moltmann-Wendel, C. Halkes, B. Vischer,
R. Auvinen.42

The World Association for Christian Communication, the World
YWCA and the WCC sponsored a consultation on "Women in the Media"
at Beirut, February 19-24, 1978. Special concern was expressed
that the content of the mass media programmes should reflect
human realities, not distort them; include women's viewpoints
and values; endeavour to build an awareness of all exploitation,
especially of women; be free of sex stereotyping and encourage
real dialogue.43

Over 35 women from six Middle Eastern countries gathered for
a consultation on "Women in Church and Society" at Cairo, March
1-5, 1978, jointly organized by the Middle East Council of Churches and the Sub-unit on Women in Church and Society. Discussions
concerned three issues: A. The role of women in the church from
the perspectives of the Bible, history and Canon law; B. Women
in laws, both civil and religious; C. Women in Rural and Urban
Development. The Report of a Consultation on "Ministry, Mariology and Biblical Hermeneutics", held at Geneva, June 26-29,
1978 included: (1) Thesis from Discussion on Hermeneutics; (2)
Notes on Ministry (Community, Personhood, Ordination of Women,
Issues Regarding Church Unity); (3) Mariology (Working Points,
Mariology in the Churches as a Central Teaching).44

"Women Theological Students" was the subject of debate of a consultation held at Cartigny, Switzerland, July 24-30, 1978. Fifty-three women studying theology and women theologians participated. The table of contents of the Report is: Women who will become deacons, pastors, theologians; Address by C.S. Song; Women in Ministry (Africa, Asia, Europe, Latin America, North America); Vocation; Women and Emerging Theologies; Spirituality; Ministry; Regional Reports; Summary of Recommendations.[45]

A consultation on "Women, Human Rights and Mission" was organized by the Sub-unit on Women in Church and Society at Venice, June 24-30, 1979. The Report includes: I. What is Our Mission (1) Human rights and mission - Ruth Sovik; (2) The struggle for equality, development and peace - Lucille Mair); II. Identification of Issues (1) Women do not live in isolation; (2) Power relationships with the family; (3) Political prisoners); III. Where Should We Go From Here ? - Working Groups (1) Socio-economic-political structures which oppress women; (2) Employment; (3) Culture and conditioning; (4) Women political prisoners; (5) Women and their bodies - Sexual exploitation of women; (6) Racism and racial justice).[46]

"Choose Life - Work for Peace" was the subject of an international workshop at Nassau, Bahamas, November 27 - December 7, 1981. The table of contents of the Report: A Step Towards the Assembly; Letter from Participants; We Give Testimonies; Peace in Danger; Food for People; What We Learnt Together; Rooting Our Struggle; Water of Life. Through these themes elements for peace education were developed and a network of building of solidarity groups and many women-for-peace groups shared.[47]

XIV.

Several regional consultations were organized on "The Community of Women and Men in the Church", in preparation for the international conference on this study theme at Sheffield in 1981. They took place at: Bangalore, India, August 11-15, 1978; at Beirut, Lebanon, January 22-26, 1980; at Bad Segeberg, Hamburg, June 20-23, 1980; at Ibadan, Nigeria, September 15-19, 1980; at San Jose, Costa Rica, March 15-18, 1981; and at Stony Point, USA, March 25, 1981. Still three other consultations were organized by the WCC Community of Women and Men in the Church Study in preparation for the Sheffield Conference.

"Ordination of Women in Ecumenical Perspective" was the theme of a consultation held at Klingenthal, France, August-September 1979. There were Protestant, Orthodox, Anglican, Old Catholic and Roman Catholic participants. The Report is in two parts: Part One: Exploring the Context (1) The Partners in Discussion; (2) The Continuing Need for Dialogue; (3) For Those Engaged in the Debate: the Pro and Contra). Part Two: New Starting Points (1) Balancing the Theological Past: Male and Female Imagery; (2) Women and Men as Living Images of God: New Initiatives of Women in Ministry; (3) Dialogue: A Starting Point for Partnership in the Church). A paper by R.R. Ruether on "The Preacher and the Priest: Two Typologies of Ministry and the Ordination of Women" is added in an appendix.[48]

The theme of the consultation at Niederaltaich, FRG, September 1-6, 1980, was "Theological Anthropology: Towards a Theology of Human Wholeness". The Report is in five sections: I. Theological Anthropology: Exploring the Issues; II. The Consultation Speaks; III. The Imago Dei: Two Historical Contexts; IV. Existential Interpretation: Two Cultures; V. Recommendations for Future Work.[49]

"The Authority of Scripture in Light of New Experiences of Women" was the subject of discussion of the consultation at Amsterdam, December 1980. The table of contents of the Report is: I. Introduction; II. Women Speak: The Interaction of Scripture and Experience; III. Biblical Authority Reconsidered; IV. Recommendations: a) Regarding the Search for a New Understanding of Biblical Authority; b) Regarding Worship and the Preparation of Liturgical Materials; c) Regarding Christian Education; d) Regarding Ministerial Formation and Theological Education; e) Regarding Biblical Translation; f) Regarding Ecclesiastical Structures. Recommendations to the Faith and Order Commission and the entire WCC.[50]

As indicated before, the World Conference on "The Community of Women and Men in the Church" at Sheffield, England, July 10-19, 1981, marked the culmination of a process of study using extensive resources and the insights of various regional consultations. Individual contributions to the conference were made by Archbishop R. Runcie, Ph. Potter, E. and J. Moltmann, T. Balasuriya, J.B. Miller, E. Behr-Sigel, R. Zoé-Obianga, P. Webb, M. Oduyoye, J. Mayland. The wide scope of the conference is reflected in its section reports: Identity and Relationships in New Community; Marriage, Family, and Life Style in New Community; Scripture in New Community; Ministry and Worship in New Community; Authority and Church Structures in New Community; Tradition and Traditions - A Change for Renewal ?; Justice and Freedom in New Community. Constance F. Parvey, who directed the study programme from 1978-1982, edited the report and wrote a concluding chapter: "The Community of Women and Men in the Ecumenical Movement - Held Together in Hope and Sustained by God's Promise." A valuable bibliography for further reading is attached to the report.[51]

The Central Committee, meeting at Dresden in 1981, responded to the various Sheffield recommendations. It endorsed a follow-up of the study and recommended that it be adequately dealt with in all WCC units. It recommended to the Faith and Order Commission that
    a) the CWMC study process be incorporated especially into the ongoing study programme on the "Unity of the Church and the Renewal of Human Community";
    b) a number of theological issues, highlighted at Sheffield, find a place in the future work of the Commission...;
    c) issues dealing with 'tradition' be carefully examined as part of the Commissions's ongoing study "Towards the Common Expression of the Apostolic Faith Today"...;
    d) the Commission initiate programmes dealing with one or more of the following issues after the WCC's Sixth Assembly (power, authority, the structures of the Church, etc...);

e) a woman be appointed to the Faith and Order secretariat;
   f) the Commission make fuller use of liberation theologians, women and men, in its work... [52]

## XV.

At the Sixth Assembly of the WCC in Vancouver in 1983, 30.46 per cent of the delegates were women (at Nairobi 22 per cent; at Uppsala 9 per cent). A four-day women's pre-assembly took place in which about 300, including some men, participated. In Issue I "Witnessing in a Divided World" it was noted that in the realm of interfaith dialogue "it is important to involve women and young people. Their self-understanding of their role in the faith community will deepen and widen the theological quest."

Issue III "Moving Towards Participation" stated the following: "Women constitute the largest part of congregations around the world but the structures of power within and outside the churches inhibit their growth and full participation. Their own lack of confidence and their general aversion to manipulate power tactics sometimes mean that women miss opportunities to participate. Tradition, cultural patterns, the domination of imported theologies, and traditional male interpretations of the Bible make the situation even more difficult for women. Jesus Christ gave important roles to women, and they were the first witnesses of his resurrection. But the Church he founded, through the centuries marginalized women. Networks of women's organizations inside and outside the Church are however a hopeful sign in our day."

Issue III made the following recommendations on women:
1. Churches must evolve clear criteria to ensure that the structure provides a working mechanism for the participation of women.
2. In times of budget cuts, women and youth programmes must not suffer; they should be given financial priority.
3. In future team visits 50 % of the participants should be women.
4. Member churches should, through skills training especially in relation to advocacy roles, provide greater opportunities for women to participate. They should encourage women to participate in vital justice and peace issues and keep contact and maintain cooperation with these groups.
5. The Orthodox churches should take the initiative to provide simple study material and information on the Orthodox Church and the role of women, for the benefit of non-Orthodox women and men. This information would greatly strengthen the understanding and sisterhood between women of different confessions. The WCC should assist in this exercise.
6. While the position of Orthodox women needs to be respected, the ordination of women must still be kept actively on the ecumenical agenda."

Issue VI "Struggling for Justice and Human Dignity" was particularly concerned with various aspects of sexism. "Just as any attitude, action or structure, that treats people as inferior because of race is racism, so any domination or exclusion based on sex is sexism. Behind many of the diverse manifestations of

sexism are economic factors leading to exploitation and manipulation. Despite considerable change in traditional labour between men and women, women still have a long way to go in their
struggle for equality. The growing phenomenon of sex tourism
organized by international tourist agencies - affecting primarily
but not exclusively women and girls in some third world countries
- is an alarming development...

"The WCC study on the Community of Women and Men in the
Church... contributed to identifying the root causes of the
oppression of women, and furthered the understanding of power
as empowerment. In this view, power is not a finite quantity,
diminished for one group if acquired by another. Rather, empowerment can be limitless. It is not conceived of as a power
over someone, or over against another. It allows those who are
oppressed to stand for themselves and to be full partners in
the struggle for justice and dignity, towards the creation of
a true community.

"It is a sad reality that the churches often support or
tolerate oppression and domination. In too many instances
church life merely reflects its social environment while
society's weakest members - the poor, the racially oppressed,
women - have no part in leadership roles and the decision-
making processes."53

"Women under Racism" is the title of one of the recent PCR
Information. Reports and Background Papers.54 It includes
three articles: The Search for Survival - Labour Migrancy and
South African Women, by Anna Lawrence; A Burning Fever: The
Isolation of Asian Women in Britain, by Amrit Wilson; IAF-
Germany, by Heidemarie Pandey; Excerpts from a Seminar on
"Racial Discrimination and its Effects on the Economic Rights
of US Women"; Excerpts from the UN Document "Resolutions and
Decisions adopted by the World Conference of the UN Decade for
Women"; ANC Year of the Women of South Africa - A Report;
Migrant Women in France - A Report.


## Observations and Comments


1. The real break-through on many issues concerning the
role of women in church and society in the seventies was only
possible through the numerous studies, activites, consultations
and conferences in the previous decades. Progressively the
impact of the international work of the Department on Cooperation of Men and Women was felt. Concerns of equality in employment, education, illiteracy, prostitution, polygamy,
marriage, family life, birth control, divorce, abortion, the
development of women's talents and personlity, a greater share
in decision-making processes were clearly stated in the various
contexts of church and society. There were even early voices
which expressed the conviction that the partnership of women
and men concerns the whole church in its inner being and self-
understanding.

2.  From the early seventies onwards it was increasingly recognized that the liberating forces of the Gospel pertain as much to women as men.  God's reconciliation breaks down the sinful barriers between the sexes.  Discrimination between male and female vocations in the church is not yet healed by the admission of women to the ordained ministry.  As women are created, like men, in the image of God (Genesis 1:27), and face the new life, offered by the resurrected Christ (Galatians 3:28), not only their predicament of subordination needs to be changed, but their full participation in the life of the Christian communion and in the building up of a more just, human and peaceful society is required.  When women and men join together, women's demands are no longer felt to be embarrassing and traditional Christian theology is seen to be the real problem.  Only both partners of the human race can share together in God's intention for unity.  The new community of women and men in Christ is called to render a true Christian witness.  It releases a new dynamic for the human society, torn apart by discriminatory practices.

3.  Since questions of feminist theology cannot be settled by superficial concessions and friendly accomodations, because the credibility of the church's witness is at stake, and since the question remains whether Christianity does not in fact render a false witness, the problem of procedure is still open and difficult.  Many church leaders, theologians and lay people (male and female) continue to resist a thorough re-examination of Christian anthropology and ecclesiology, contaminated by an age-old system of patriarchal and paternalistic values, and the structures of a so-called Christian society.  How can a 'Copernican turn' in the ecumenical movement be communicated and shared ?  Bärbel von Wartenberg, Director of the WCC Sub-unit on Women in Church and Society, who coined the term, speaks of the vision of a world-wide sisterhood which has a price and a promise.  The price is the risk of the enterprise, the promise the inner and outer renewal of the women's movement and the church.

4.  The question of the vital role of women in church and society became particularly urgent and ineluctable when the study of the Community of Women and Men in the Church was lodged within Faith and Order.  Only in this theological context did the study gain its full weight and its inclusive focus.  Since women discovered the power of their own thinking and action, however, the churches and their hierarchies are suffering from ignorance, uncertainty, fear, embarrassment and defensiveness.  As much as new theological and biblical insights have been gained, as much psychological, sociological and cultural barriers to the understanding and acceptance of women's full contribution to the church and society remain.

The problem of the ordination of women threatens, more than ever before, the very unity and wholeness the churches are seeking.  How can the dialogue in love continue ?  How can men sustain the movements of women without becoming one-sided and sectarian ?  The working together toward a new community of men and women is not enhanced when young women deliberately take up position at the periphery of the church to manifest their op-

position and to state their criticism.  On the other hand,
Bärbel von Wartenberg is right to assert that we should not too
hastily speak of new community, partnership, cooperation and
equality of women and men.  The separate and joint struggles
must continue - and will continue for years to come - as part
of the preparation of the kingdom which will transcend them into
everlasting and full communion with God.  It is the foretaste of
the new humanity which prevents women and men to become weary,
exasperating and disillusioned.  The joy that John 17:21 has a
fundamentally ethical dimension and that Galathians 3:28 has a
fundamentally ecclesiological dimension renders them truly human.

---

1.  The First Assembly of the World Council of Churches held
    at Amsterdam, August 22 - September 4, 1948.
    Ed. by W.A. Visser 't Hooft.  London: SCM Press, 1949.
    pp. 146-148.

2.  The Evanston Report. The Second Assembly of the World
    Council of Churches, 1954.  New York: Harper, 1955.
    pp. 227 and 229.

3.  Minutes and Reports of the Eighth Meeting of the Central
    Committee of the WCC, Davos, Switzerland, August 2-8, 1955.
    Geneva: WCC, 1955.  pp. 47-48.

4.  The Common Christian Responsibility Toward Areas of Rapid
    Social Change. Second Statement.  Geneva: WCC, 1956. p. 17.

5.  Dilemmas and Opportunities. Christian Action in Rapid
    Social Change. Report of an International Ecumenical Study
    Conference, Thessalonica, Greece, July 25 - August 2, 1959.
    Geneva: WCC, 1959.  p. 8.

6.  The Church in Changing Africa. Report of the All Africa
    Church Conference, held at Ibadan, Nigeria, January 10-19,
    1958.  New York: International Missionary Council, 1958.
    pp. 29-30.

7.  Witnesses Together. Being the official report of the
    Inaugural Assembly of the East Asia Christian Conference,
    held at Kuala Lumpur, Malaya, May 14-24, 1959.
    Ed. by U Kyaw Than.  Rangoon: EACC, 1959.  p. 137.

8.  Report of the Third Conference on Men and Women in Industry.
    Bossey, 1951 (mimeographed).

9.  Report on two Consultations in Africa by Madeleine Barot,
    1958. (mimeographed).

10. Report of the Consultation on the Christian Approach to
    Women's Questions.  1958. (mimeographed).

11. Report of the Consultation on Obstacles to the Cooperation
    of Men and Women.  1958. (mimeographed).

12. Report of the Consultation on Towards Responsible Cooper-
    ation Between Men and Women, Our Christian Responsibility.
    1960. (mimeographed).

13. Report of the Consultation held at Women's Christian
    College, Madras on Changing Patters of Men-Women Relation-
    ships in Asia. 1962. (mimeographed).

14. The New Delhi Report.
    London: SCM Press, 1962. pp. 207-217.

15. Drumbeats from Kampala. Report of the First Assembly of
    the All Africa Conference of Churches, held at Kampala,
    April 20-30, 1963. London: Lutterworth, 1963. pp. 22-30.

16. Christian Women of Africa Share in Responsibility.
    Geneva: WCC, 1963.

17. Minutes and Reports of the Seventh Meeting of the Central
    Committee of the WCC. Rochester, New York, August 26 -
    September 2, 1963. Geneva: WCC, 1963. pp. 102-105.

18. World Conference on Church and Society, Geneva, July 12-26,
    1966. Geneva: WCC, 1967. pp. 162-170, 177-178.

19. The Uppsala Report 1968. Ed. by Norman Goodall.
    Geneva: WCC, 1968. pp. 92-93, 250-251.

20. The Conference on World Cooperation for Development.
    Beirut, Lebanon, April 21-27, 1968. Geneva: Exploratory
    Committee on Society, Development and Peace, 1968.
    pp. 31, 33.

21. The Consultation on Christian Concern for Peace.
    Baden, Austria, April 3-9, 1970. Geneva: Committee on
    Society, Development and Peace, 1970. pp. 45, 65.

22. Minutes and Reports of the Assembly of the Commission on
    World Mission and Evangelism, held at Bangkok, December 31,
    1972 and January 9-12, 1973. Geneva: WCC, 1973. p. 75.

23. Sexism in the 1970s - Discrimination Against Women.
    A Report of the World Council of Churches Consultation,
    West Berlin 1974. Geneva: WCC, 1975.

24. Central Committee of the World Council of Churches.
    Minutes of the Twenty-Seventh Meeting, Berlin (West),
    August 11-18, 1974. Geneva: WCC, 1974. pp. 45-47.

25. Consultation on Relationships of Men and Women at Work.
    1964. (mimeographed).

26. Report of the Consultation held at the Collège Protestant
    Romand at Founex. 1964. (mimeographed).

27. Ecumenical Press Service, no. 38, 28 October, 1965.

28. Study Encounter, vol. III, no. 1, 1967, pp. 21-35.

29. Documents of the John Knox House Consultation. 1966. (mimeographed).

30. Report of the Women's International Ecumenical Conference. The Christian Woman Co-artisan in a Changing Society, 19-24 June, 1967. Taizé, France.

31. Consultation on Developing Relations of Men, Women and Children and Their Meaning for the Mission of the Church in Our Changing Society. 1968. (mimeographed).

32. Report on the Study Session in Connection with the XV International Conference on Social Welfare, 1970.

33. What is Ordination Coming To ? Report of a Consultation. Ed. by Brigalia Bam. Geneva: WCC, 1971.

34. Report on the Consultation on Pastoral Care of Those Confronted With Abortion. Geneva: WCC, 1975.

35. Human Rights and Christian Responsibility. Report of the consultation St. Pölten, Austria, 21-26 October 1974. p. 41.

36. Uniting in Hope. Reports and Documents from the Meeting of the Faith and Order Commission, University of Ghana, Legon, 23 July - 5 August, 1974. Geneva: WCC, 1975 (Faith and Order Paper, No. 72). pp. 36-37.

37. Breaking Barriers. Nairobi 1975. Ed. by David M. Paton. London: SPCK; Grand Rapids: Wm. B. Eerdmans, 1976. pp. 19-21, 62, 113-115, 309-310.

38. Central Committee of the World Council of Churches. Minutes of the Twenty-Ninth Meeting. Geneva, 10-18 August, 1976. Geneva: WCC, 1976. pp. 52-53.

39. Central Committee of the World Council of Churches. Minutes of the Thirtieth Meeting. Geneva, 28 July - 6 August, 1977. Geneva: WCC, 1977. pp. 51-52.

40. Orthodox Women - Their Role and Participation in the Orthodox Church. Geneva: Sub-unit on Women in Church and Society, 1977.

41. Half the World's People - A Report of the Consultation of Church Women Executives. Geneva: WCC, 1978.

42. Consultation of European Christian Women. Geneva: Sub-unit on Women in Church and Society, 1978.

43. Ecumenical Press Service, no. 7. 2 March, 1978.

44. Report on Ministry, Mariology and Biblical Hermeneutics, 1978. Faith and Order Archives.

45. We Listened Long Before We Spoke.
    Geneva: Sub-unit on Women in Church and Society, 1979.

46. Report of a Conference on Women, Human Rights and Mission.
    Geneva: Sub-unit on Women in Church and Society, 1979.

47. Choose Life - Work for Peace. Report of an International
    Workshop.  Geneva: Sub-unit on Women in Church and
    Society, 1982.

48. Ordination of Women in Ecumenical Perspective. Workbook
    for the Church's Future. Ed. by Constance F. Parvey.
    Geneva: Community of Women and Men in Church and Society
    Study, 1980. (Faith and Order Paper, No. 105).

49. Theological Anthropology: Towards a Theology of Human
    Wholeness.  1980. (mimeographed).

50. The Authority of Scripture in Light of New Experiences of
    Women. 1981.  (mimeographed).

51. The Community of Women and Men in the Church. A Report
    of the World Council of Churches' Conference, Sheffield,
    England, 1981. Ed. by Constance F. Parvey.
    Philadelphia: Fortress Press;  Geneva: WCC, 1983.

52. Central Committee of the World Council of Churches.
    Minutes of the Thirty-Third Meeting, Dresden, GDR, 16-26
    August, 1981.  Geneva: WCC, 1981.  pp. 16-19.

53. Gathered for Life. Official Report, VI Assembly World
    Council of Churches, Vancouver, Canada, 24 July - 10 August,
    1983. Ed. by David Gill.  Geneva: WCC;  Grand Rapids: Wm. B.
    Eerdmans, 1983.  pp. 7, 41, 55, 58, 87-88.

54. Women under Racism. PCR Information. Reports and
    Background Papers, 1984.  No. 19.

# XI.
## Inter-Church Aid, Refugee
## and World Service

From the beginning the Church has been, or has tried to be, obedient to the command of Jesus to succour those in distress. An early instance of this is cited in Acts 11:29-30: "... The disciples agreed to make a contribution, each according to his means, for the relief of their fellow Christians in Judea. This they did, and sent it off to the elders, in the charge of Barnabas and Saul." This illustration could be multiplied endlessly. The outcome has been a ministry of service that has spread throughout the world.

Within the Life and Work movement the European Central Bureau for Inter-Church Aid was established in 1922 with offices in New York and Geneva and with Professor Adolf Keller as its Director. A pioneer venture in ecumenical relief, it began its work under the patronage of the Federal Council of the Churches of Christ in America and the Federation of Swiss Protestant Churches, later joined by other European churches. In 1944 the Central Bureau for Inter-Church Aid was merged into the new World Council Department of Reconstruction and Inter-Church Aid.

The change in the Department's function was signalized at the Central Committee meeting in Chichester, England, in 1949 by a change of the name of the Department. The new title was the Department of Inter-Church Aid and Service to Refugees. The title was changed again to the Division of Inter-Church Aid, Refugee and World Service in 1961 at New Delhi. In 1971 it became the Commission on Inter-Church Aid, Refugee and World Service.

In a memorandum, drawn up by W.A. Visser 't Hooft and approved by the Provisional Committee of the World Council of Churches in 1943, the following was stated on the mandate of the Department: "The paramount principle is that which is implied in the very existence of the World Council, namely that the task of reconstruction is to be conceived as an ecumenical task in which all the Churches participate to the limit of their ability, and that the common objective is to rebuild the life of the whole fellowship of Churches which finds expression in the World Council. If this ecumenical principle is taken seriously, this will mean that the Churches will agree to co-ordinate their policies and activities in order to make certain that all needy Churches receive adequate help, that the Churches will not confine their help exclusively to the Churches belonging to the same denomination or confession, and that the autonomy and desires of the receiving Churches are taken in full consideration."[1]

The Report of Committee IV on Concerns of the Churches, 4. <u>Christian Reconstruction and Inter-Church Aid</u>, presented to the first WCC Assembly at Amsterdam in 1948, expressed itself on: Reconstruction and Inter-Church Aid, Prisoners of War, Refugees and Uprooted Peoples. It was agreed that "while the need for material aid still continues, the emphasis of the future work of the Department should more and more take into account the basic and continuing necessity of inter-church aid... that, with the release and repatriation of P.O.W.s, the decision of the Commission to wind up its activities be approved..." The view was expressed "that Christian consideration of the refugee problems should not be confined to Europe and the Middle East... that the desperate plight of millions of uprooted peoples in the Far East should also be acknowledged as the concern and in the giving of the churches."[2]

Passing a series of important resolutions about the life and activities of the Department, the following observation was made by the Central Committee meeting at Chichester in 1949: "The Central Committee <u>decided</u> to remind the member Churches that Inter-Church Aid is a permanent obligation of a World Council of Churches which seeks to be true to its name; that many of the Churches in Europe are in dire need of assistance as they take part in the great spiritual struggle of our day; that the millions of refugees in Europe have an urgent and incontrovertible claim upon the help of the Churches; and therefore that a fresh approach must be made, by the Churches which are in a position to help, to their members for renewed and generous giving on behalf of their fellow-Christians in Europe."[3]

The Central Committee meeting at Toronto in 1950 commended "to all Churches the support of an active programme of Inter-Church Aid in Europe in 1950", and called "their attention to three commanding aspects of the work, namely, the areas where basic reconstruction of Church life has not been completed or scarcely been started; the experiments in evangelism and lay witness everywhere before the Churches; and the heavy load of responsibility for Displaced Persons and Refugees which must be carried, not only by the Churches, in whose countries they are to be found, but by the whole Christian community."[4]

The Central Committee meeting at Lucknow in 1953 adopted a report which reads as follows: "The Reference Sub-Committee has studied the proposed plan for cooperation between the International Missionary Council and the World Council of Churches for emergency inter-church aid and relief in countries outside Europe. It welcomes the suggestion that the Department of Inter-Church Aid and Service to Refugees should be entrusted with this responsibility...

"At the same time, the Reference Sub-Committee realizes that this plan will only become a reality in sofar as member Churches, mission boards and Christian relief agencies enter into the fullest ecumenical cooperation; it would therefore ask the members of the Central Committee to do everything in their power to ensure that this new approach to the pressing emergency needs of the Churches in countries outside Europe may receive the cordial support of all who are in a position to make it effective."[5]


## II.


The Second WCC Assembly at Evanston in 1954 recognized the Division's ever widening horizons and authorized it to be world-wide in its scope. It spelled the Basis of the Division out as follows: "Inter-Church Aid is based on the teaching of Scripture and the practice of the apostolic church. The Christian Church, which is the Body of Christ in the world, in obedience to her Lord seeks to "do good unto all men, especially unto them who are of the household of faith (Gal. 6:10), being reminded that "the body is one, and hath many members... and if one member suffer, all the members suffer with it" (Cor. 12:12,26).

The Division shall provide for:
a) consultation with world confessional associations on giving within the same church family and continual emphasis on the need for inter-confessional giving;
b) an increased service of information and publicity;
c) a system of identifying gifts and interpreting the meaning of Inter-Church Aid;
d) visitation and personnel exchanges;
e) attention to the need of minority churches;
f) aid to churches through loans as well as gifts;
g) health services;
h) a theological scholarship programme;
i) a theological literature programme;
j) experimental and pilot projects."

The Report includes an extract of a letter from the High Commissoner for Refugees: "It seems to me to be one of the greatest achievements of the Christian churches in recent times that they have started increasingly to translate their faith and their hope into terms of practical programmes and projects in fields where they bear responsibility. I do not think that I have any right to compare, but I would be surprised if there were any field in which the Christians have achieved so much as they have in the field of the refugee problem..."[6]

An account of discussions on "The Needs of Churches and Peoples in Areas of Rapid Social Change" was presented to the Central Committee, meeting at Davos in 1955. A definition of concern reads as follows: "Both the Division of Inter-Church Aid and the Division of Studies are concerned with the social and economic problems of areas of rapid social change. This is

a new interest which has been developed in cooperation with the
International Missionary Council, and through the Joint Committee.
The emphasis of the Division of Studies is on "responsibility
towards  areas of rapid social change"; that of the Division of
Inter-Church Aid is on "unmet" needs which are beyond  the
strength of regular church or mission support.  "These are both
provisional definitions... The two Divisions... must endeavour
to build up a pattern of relationships which will depend upon
the local churches and national councils and missions already
in operation in the field, without putting undue strain upon
them, and will take account of the needs and problems both of
the churches themselves and the whole community."

With regard to Rebuilding the Life of the Community it was
stated:"All relief action of the churches must have in view the
rebuilding or strengthening of the life of the Christian community and the total programmes.  Existing church and mission
institutions require assistance in developing their training so
that they can play a still larger and more effective part in
such programmes.  Pilot projects of econominc improvement
carried out by ecumenical teams under the auspices of the churches but in relation to national plans might be considered in
this connection.  Such pilot projects, and indeed all developments, of this kind, must be build on the experience and practice
of Church and mission.  It is in this area that the tasks of the
two Divisions should be most closely related."7

III.

At the annual consultation of the Division of Interchurch
Aid and Service to Refugees at Les Rasses, Switzerland, in 1956,
W.A. Visser 't Hooft said the following: "When we turn to the
New Testament it is at any rate clear that APOSTOLATE, that is
the mission of the Church, has three aspects of manifestations:
1) KERYGMA - this is the proclamation, the heralding of the
Good News.  It involves the spoken word, the announcement, the
preaching of the message of the Incarnation, the Cross, the
Resurrection and Ascension of Jesus Christ.
2) KOINONIA - this is the fellowship in the Gospel, created by
the preaching.  Koinonia does not simply mean "togetherness",
it means participation in the act of God in Christ.
3) DIAKONIA - this means the ministry, the expression of faith
in Christian love and compassion and in the service of the
needs of men.

"... The fact is they do not stand, as we sometimes mis-
takingly think, in an hierarchical order.  If, for example, we
look at the way in which DIAKONIA is used in the Bible, we find
that it is sometimes used of the total ministry of the Church.
Indeed all three words are at times used to express the total
ministry of the Church.  All of them declare the continuation
of the acts of God... All three functions, too, have an eschatological reference.  They are all related to the Kingdom - they
are related to the bringing of "SHALOM", the divine action to be

fulfilled and consummated at the last day, but entering into the world here and now."[8]

As the Division of Inter-Church Aid had to work out with the International Missionary Council a clear line of distinction between the projects for which the Division should seek support and those which were the concern of the IMC, criteria were established at Les Rasses and at Herrenalb, Germany, which became known as the "Herrenalb categories". Under the Herren-alb agreement, it was laid down that projects from Asia, Africa and Latin America, submitted through the Division, should be confined to:

1) Needs arising from situations which were strictly of an emergency character created by natural disasters, economic crises, political and social upheavals, and the like.

2) The needs of refugees and displaced persons.

3) The needs of churches not in regular relation with any missionary society and therefore not normally receiving help from this source.

4) Urgent inter-Church and ecumenical projects, whether designed to strengthen the churches or the service of the community, in so far as such projects could not be adequately supported either from local sources or through mission boards.

5) Social service or relief projects clearly demanded by the local situation but beyond the resources of local churches or the missionary societies co-operating with them.

6) Experiments aimed at ensuring the self-support of the Church or Christian community where these experiments had been adequately examined and duly commended.[9]

IV.

At the Inaugural Assembly of the East Asia Christian Conference at Kuala Lumpur, in 1959 the functions of the Committee on Inter-Church Aid for Mission and Service were discussed. Significant statements in the conclusion of the Report were: "The Churches in Asia have all suffered from isolation, from one another and from the universal fellowship of the Churches, because their relationships have so often been confined to one direct line with their parent Church. The WCC and the EACC bring the Asian Churches into new and wider relationships, and Inter-Church Aid is the practical and two-way traffic through which something of the universal Church is understood.

"The Asian Churches themselves, however poor they may be in material and personnel, must be given opportunities to learn the facts about the needs of other Churches and areas, and invited to share in the privilege of meeting those needs by making some direct contribution to them.

"We strongly urge that matter of giving and receiving be rethought. If Inter-Church Aid is conceived as a giving of funds by wealthy Churches for the bolstering up of the organisation and material welfare of weaker Churches, it is just as capable of creating self-righteousness on the one hand and dependence on the other, as any other paternalistic programme. Ecumenical Inter-Church Aid must _not_ be thought of merely as a giving by one group of Churches and a receiving by others. We need to recognise that for every need, both physical and spiritual, every Christian has an obligation to share. Our programmes must be so devised as to help us to understand that in the planning of projects those near at hand and those at a distance are _interdependent_ in their ministry to human need. In this way we enter into a new understanding of the meaning of giving and receiving."10

V.

Section III of the Third WCC Assembly at New Delhi, in 1961, dealt with The Service of the Church in a Divided World. It focused on: In a Changing and Dynamic Society; Individual Responsibility and Involvement; Corporate Christian Service; The Ecumenical Service of the Churches. In the Report of the Committee on DICARWS the new organizational structure of the Division and proposals for an extended service were outlined and recommendations made on: Relationships between the DWME and DICARWS. Refugees; Migration; Areas of Acute Human Need; Scholarships; ECLOF; Finance.

The aim of DICARWS was spelled out anew: "The aim of the division shall be to express the ecumenical solidarity of the churches through mutual aid in order to strengthen them in their life and mission and especially in their service to the world around them (_diakonia_), and to provide facilities by which the churches may serve men and women in acute human need everywhere, especially orphaned peoples, including refugees of all categories."

To this was added: "The basic approach of the division to the churches and peoples will be on the basis of areas. The area secretaries will have primary responsibility for the relations of the division with churches and councils in their areas and for relationships with such ecumenical regional organizations as are or may be established..."11

In a Statement from the first Meeting of the Divisional Committee of DWME, presented to the Central Committee, meeting at Paris, in 1962, the following was stated: "The missionary movement shows too little sign of moving. The causes of this immobility are no doubt varied and complex. Among them are:
1) the fact that we have inherited a structure based upon the recent period of human history in which Christian missions were conducted exclusively by the peoples of the "western" world. That period has ended, but many of our structures have remained unchanged.
2) the fact that we have not yet learned to see the missionary task as one common task for the whole people of God, in which the need of every part is to be the concern of all. Consequently resources have not been available swiftly enough at the point where they are needed.

3) the fact that too many Christians regard the Church as
a source of privilege for themselves rather than as a place of
responsibility for the neighbour, in whose service Christ is to
be served.  Consequently congregations have become self-centred
and have even made it plain that converts were not welcome."

Suggestions were made for the building up of a programme
of "Joint Action for Mission".  The Committee on Specialized
Assistance for Social Projects was established.[12]

The role of DICARWS, ways in which the Division seeks to
fulfil this role, new factors in the world situation, what joint
action for service calls for in these circumstances, and relationships between DICARWS and DWME, were again outlined in the
report of DICARWS to the Central Committee, meeting in Rochester,
USA, in 1963.[13]

VI.

The Herrenalb categories were replaced in 1966 by a new
agreement by which DWME, the successor to IMC, became responsible for long-term programmes and the Division of Inter-Church
Aid for projects usually expected to become self-supporting
within five years.  This agreement opened the way for missionary projects to be included in the DICARWS' project list. The
1967 project list was published by the Division in collaboration
with DWME - an innovation.  The project list has been widened
to include refugee projects and those world youth projects which
are compiled jointly by the WCC's Youth Department and the World
Council of Christian Education.[14]

The Digest of the World Consultation of DICARWS at Swanwick
in 1966, included several addresses by L.E. Cooke, S.L. Parmar,
Joseph Gremillion, Metropolitan Emilianos, R.S. Bilheimer,
E. Borges Costa; situation sessions on Africa, Asia, Australia,
New Zealand, Europe, Orthodox countries and the Middle East,
Latin America, USA and Canada, and ECLOF.  The section reports
were:  I. Development Aid;  II. Uprooted People;  III. The Role
of ICA in the Use and Training of the Churches' Manpower;
IV. The post-Herrenalb Situation.

Leslie E. Cooke, the Director of DICARWS, said  the following in his closing address: "... There will be many who have
been generous in their giving for relief who will become hesitant,
if not resistant, when they realize that our aim is to change
the status quo.  They will think that the Church has gone leftist, or socialist, or communist... There will be those among
the rising generation, and in the churches of the developing
countries, who are radical, who will say: "At last the churches
are with us - they have espoused our cause, they have joined
the revolution"...

"... That we are now caught up to go beyond aid to challenge
the structures of churches society, even by aid we give and the
purposes to which we give it, is beyond doubt.  The only two

uncertainties are what the cost will be and whether we are
prepared to pay it... We have to press on beyond co-operation
to community... The overwhelming compulsion to move from cooperation to community derives from the fact that it is clear
that many of the problems which face mankind can be solved only
by the building of a world community.  Perhaps the most significant contribution the churches can make is in manifesting that
they are a world community, that they in fact share a common
life in the body of Christ."[15]

In a WCC pamphlet The Role of the Diakonia of the Church in
Contemporary Society it was commented: "In a sense, the challenge
of the contemporary revolution to the churches' diakonia today
is to develop new policies, new concepts, new forms of action
which will, on the one hand, continue to meet individual, family
and wider social needs, and, on the other, to promote social
justice on a community or national and ecumenical world basis
rather than on a strictly personal one."[16]


                              VII.


Within Thy Gates was the title of a Report of a Conference
on Migrant Workers in Western Europe in 1963, organized by the
WCC Secretariat for Migration.  In the introduction to the Conference Statement and Recommendations it was stated: "The love
of Christ is the most powerful force in our relations as Christians with the migrant workers.  The parable of the Good Samaritan teaches us to love the foreigner.  Such love is comprehensive; it applies to all the strangers who come into our lives.
The arrival of migrant workers in our midst is not a burden but
a blessing for the Church."  The service to them "opens the way
to co-operation and communion between the different confessions
and gives opportunity for new forms of Christian unity."

Among the recommendations to be followed up were: recruiting
and placement, legislation, trade unions, teaching the language,
unmarried mothers, organization, economic aid to emigration
countries. An evening prayer held on the first evening of the
conference by a team of factory workers in West Germany included
the words: "God calls all of us, who stand outside, to His
Banquet, irrespective of person or nationality.  The host who
invites this mixed group of guests has no illusions about them;
He accepts them as they are, good and bad, the blind and the
lame, Spaniards and Italians, Greeks and Germans.  How ridicu-
lous it would be to imagine that God would consider national
prejudices at His Supper!  How atheistic it is that these prejudices exist in our Church, just as they do in our society!"[17]

In the Report of the Committee on DICARWS, presented to the
Fourth WCC Assembly at Uppsala, in 1968, it was outlined that in
dealing with people in need, the Division's actions "include
refugee service, relief work, the meeting of emergencies oc-
casioned by natural, political or social disasters, and aid in
finding a lasting solution to problems of poverty, disease,
hunger, under-employment, and unemployment." The project method
adopted by the Division was judged on the whole as satisfactory,
but it was suggested that a number of matters be further studied:

"a) The possibility of getting help faster, especially for
small projects, by shortening and simplifying the processes
involved;

b) The coordination in some measure of project listings by
the WCC and the various confessions;

c) The value for ecumenical relationships of some kind of
direct contact between churches participating in a project;

d) The method of finding support for certain international
projects;

e) The question of a relationship of strictly church-centred
projects and those aimed at service to the wider  community;

f) The question of how to inform the member churches
specifically about the scope and limitations of the projects
which the Division presents for support."

With regard to development it was resolved "that the Assembly
endorse the recommendation of the Committee that the Division
give the needs of development high priority in its total programme..." Concerning refugees and migrants, a deep sense of
concern was noted "that uprootedness and homelessness, whether
resulting from violence, war and revolution or other causes,
such as voluntary exile for reasons of conscience, continues to
afflict people in every continent. With regard to the Diakonia
Desk it was agreed "that it will endeavour to interpret the
ecumenical movement to the diaconal constituency of the churches
and help this constituency to discover the ecumenical dimension
of diakonia."[18] The Desk was established in July 1967 at the
urging of the International Federation of Inner-Mission and
Christian Social Work and the International Federation of
Deaconess Associations for an experimental period of three years.
Its mandate was prolonged until the end of 1971 by the Central
Committee meeting at Canterbury in 1969.

During the next few years the decentralization and consequent
regionalization of the project system was intensively discussed.
The Central Committee meeting at Addis Ababa in 1971 welcomed
"the Division's proposals to make major modifications in the
administration of the Project List in the direction of giving
greater decision-making power to the churches locally and
regionally." It was also noted that "the Division had been very
much involved in the discussions on new WCC structures."[19]

On Questions Concerning CWME's Relationship to Inter-Church Aid and Development during the meeting of the Commission on World Mission and Evangelism at Bangkok, in 1973, it was recommended to the CWME:

"1) To urge the churches and their agencies to consider seriously the joint Project List of CICARWS/CWME as an instrument of ecumenical sharing;

2) To urge the churches and their agencies to support projects to NCCs, to mission and evangelisation projects, to training of the ministry, laity and strengthening of the churches' spiritual and pastoral life."

With regard to Development it was recommended:

"1) To promote and support self-tax of individuals and churches everywhere as an expression of transfer of power from the powerful to the powerless. This should be linked to the WCC's 2% appeal which was adopted in Uppsala and reaffirmed in Utrecht;

2) To expose the negative influence of the 'donor mentality' manifested in development aid ('help-syndrome') thus perpetuating existing economic and political systems. In this connection CWME should draw on the CCPD study on effects of aid on social justice and self-reliance and publicize the conclusions of this study within its constituency;

3) To urge churches and missionary agencies to study together the effect of production and trade practices on the economy of their respective countries and the harmful restrictive business practices of multi-national corporations in terms of economic exploitation...

4) To promote new patterns of investment relations which serve the political and social liberation of the poor and the oppressed."[20]


IX.


In the Report of an Ecumenical Consultation on Ecumenical Assistance to Development Projects at Montreux, in 1970, the following was expressed on ways of work: "DICARWS and other units of the WCC are already engaged in development projects in continuing this work raising funds for their support. As the Commission develops its understanding of development strategy DICARWS and other units of the WCC will be influenced by the Commission's thinking.

"Within the framework of its basic policy, the Commission shall seek to delegate to relevant bodies different aspects of its work. This would mean in addition to its own direct activities that by agreement with the WCC units and the agencies concerned, it would seek:

1) To arrange for the carrying out of programmes and projects by DICARWS of other units of the WCC or other agencies;

2) To arrange for the possibility of loans and investments by ECLOF, or other agencies;

3) To arrange for technical services by ACTS or other agencies as may be needed; and

4) To arrange for aspects of its study, education and information work to be done with or by SODEPAX."[21]

In the Report Uppsala to Nairobi the specific issues involving Inter-Church Aid were summarized as follows:
"The future of the project system understood in the sense of
how the churches manifest their fellowship and solidarity and
share their resources - financial, spiritual and human - with
one another;
The appropriate style for emergency response which safeguards
the concern for the suffering as well as the integrity of the
local churches in such a way that immediate needs and long-term
plans can be met.
Under these issues are questions such as:
How can the "rich" churches and their counterparts in the
poor countries avoid being corrupted by their money and the
power that this brings ?
How can the "poor" churches be enabled to live out creatively
the mission of the Church as they understand it ?

All of these concerns feed in ultimately to the whole
question of the Programme Unit on Justice and Service. Up to now,
the separate sub-units have continued to retain their individual
identities to a substantial degree. This has obviously been,
and will continue to be, important, but to what degree should
they lose a part at least of their identities in the Unit structure ? What would this mean for CICARWS ?... The future is open.
Only one thing is absolutely clear. The churches cannot escape
from their obligation to render service and to be with the
oppressed in their struggle for justice. In that sense there
must always be something like a CICARWS within a Programme Unit
on Justice and Service..."[22]


X.


In the Summary Report of Hearing 3 on Unit II: Justice and
Service of the Nairobi Assembly in 1975, the following was
stated on the Ecumenical Sharing of Resources: "... We must
reach the state of true sharing of resources among equal partners. An emphasis should be given to non-material resources...
To accomplish this, the WCC should offer a wide variety of
instruments:
    a) the Project System, renewed and improved constantly in
the direction of "country programmes";
    b) ecumenical sharing of personnel, made operational
through increased resources;
    c) interchange of experiences, opportunities, and concerns;
    d) ecumenical scrutiny of partnerships between churches, to
coordinate and provide objectivity. The WCC should give a
special emphasis to enable smaller churches to become active
partners in the ecumenical sharing process."

With regard to <u>Service to Human Need</u>, Hearing 3 of the Nairobi Assembly stated:

"I. Because of widespread bilaterialism and lack of co-ordination among member churches, there is all the more need for ecumenical activity through WCC. Therefore

   1. The Project System is affirmed as an essential instrument:
     a) with expanded service to the larger community;
     b) with more help to the churches to recognize their own limitations and to perceive the felt needs of the larger community.
   2. WCC should continue action on behalf of and with churches in emergencies, disasters, and chronically needy areas.
   3. WCC should lead in developing new styles of service with churches and/or with governments, including community health care, rural development, appropriate technoloy, etc.
   4. WCC should develop consortia in which both giving and receiving churches share perspectives, goals and decisions on resource allocation.

II. In all ministries to uprooted persons WCC should stress:

   1. Pathological and psychological effects of displacement and the spiritual lostness which results, assisting churches in their efforts to deal with these.
   2. The special urgency of the churches' enlistment as advocates of migrant workers, political refugees, stranded students - all persons who are refugees by any definition...

III. Service to human needs requires changes in life styles both by personal resolve for Christian living and by corporate decisions for political action as a means of change.

   1. WCC can assist churches in giving witness by self-discipline.
   2. WCC can assist churches to be self-critical in the lifestyles they propose in their projects so they are neither elitist, a betrayal of their own culture's goals, nor thwarting of justice."[23]

During the meeting of the Central Committee at Geneva in 1977, the Unit Committee received and gave general approval to the report on CICARWS programmes. It noted particularly:

"1. Developments in regional activities and planning;
   2. Ecumenical sharing of personnel and efforts to influence personnel exchanges to become more multi-directional and more ecumenical;
   3. The churches' contemporary responsibilities to refugees; the Unit Committee approved the following directions for the Refugee Service:
     a) to identify and fight the root causes, including the injustices, which compel people to leave their homes and countries;
     b) to help promote effective legal protection;
     c) to provide basic, updated, action-provoking information on refugee situations;
     d) to facilitate and support training of refugee workers;
     e) to encourage and support self-help efforts of refugees;
     f) to work for the broadening of restrictive definitions."[24]

The CICARWS Commission meeting at Strasbourg, France in 1978 issued a Statement on Service and Unity. "It is in the Eucharistic act where we find the imperative for service in the world. The Lord whom we meet in bread and wine is the same Lord whom we meet in the poor, the oppressed and the needy. Our servanthood is our obedience to the Gospel and our response to Him who humbled Himself in obedience as servant of all. Our Lord sends us out to join Him in bringing good news to the poor and the oppressed.

"Unity is the work of the Holy Spirit and not the result of our own efforts, however ecumenical these may be. Service in obedience to the Gospel will not unite nor divide more than Christ Himself. The quality of our service can be enriched by the depth or our unity or limited by our divisions. Unity is expressed in service, deepened by service, and tested by service. Our growth in unity is challenged and renewed by the tensions we experience as we seek the wholeness of the church and the wholeness of humankind...

"The multiplicity of secular organizations and governments engaged in development and other service programs, many of whom call upon us to work cooperatively with them, impels us to clarify the distinctiveness of Christian service. This distinctiveness is found in our motivation and our unity of purpose: to share with each other, as good stewards, the gifts entrusted to us by the Lord of all creation, for the sake of the restoration of the wholeness of all humankind... The value of our programs should not be judged by size or scope. A limited local project which overcomes divisive relationships can have worldwide significance if the experience is shared. This is yet another expression of the unity experienced through interchurch aid."[25]


XI.


The Report of the Faith and Order Commission meeting at Bangalore in 1978 includes a report on Growing Together in Unity with a sub-section on The Unity of the Church and Interchurch Aid. Issues of the structures of aid, the politics of aid and the unity of the human community were outlined. Recommendations were made on World Council of Churches projects, the role of the WCC in Inter-Church aid, and suggestions to the Faith and Order Commission.[26]

Unit Committee II of the Central Committee meeting at Kingston, Jamaica in 1979, received the Statement on Service and Unity and the report on The Unity of the Church and Interchurch Aid, welcomed the joint effort of the two commissions to explore the relationship of service to unity and urged that it be pursued, and "stressed the importance of reflection on such problems as:
 - the one-way exchange between the churches of different regions of the world; the tendency of some diaconal agencies to isolate themselves from their churches;
 - the increase of bilateral relations compared to multilateral relations, the overburdening of small churches by

development projects; also broader issues such as the direct and indirect political consequences of aid and the relation between service and unity should be discussed."[27]

CICARWS and the Orthodox Task Force of the WCC convened a consultation on Church and Service: An Orthodox Approach to Diaconia in Chania, Crete, in 1978. Participants represented the various Oriental and Eastern Orthodox churches. On the theological background of service the following was stated in the report: "Christian diaconia... flows from the divine liturgy in which our offerings are sanctified by Christ's offering and requires our active cooperation (synergeia) with God in the exercise of our freewill which is rooted in our common agreement (symphonia)(Mt. 18:19). Diaconia is therefore an expression of the unity of the church as the Body of Christ. Each local celebration of the Eucharist is complete and universal, involving the whole creation, and is offered for the material and spiritual needs of the whole world.

"Christian diaconia is not an optional action, duty or moral stance in relation to the needy, additional to our community in Christ, but an indispensable expression of that community, which has its source in the eucharistic and liturgical life of the Church. It is a "liturgy after the Liturgy" and it is in this sense that diaconia is described as a judgment upon our history (Mt. 25:31-46). The main emphasis in this eucharistic and loving diaconia is not on quantity, money or material aid, but on quality and intention. The widow's "tiny coins" (Lk.21:2-3) are worth more than offerings from "More than enough"...

"The ultimate goal of diaconia is the salvation of man. But poverty, oppression and material penury often constitute an obstacle jeopardizing man's salvation, as the teaching of the apostles and the church fathers points out. Diaconia therefore embraces the need to liberate humankind from everything which oppresses, enslaves and distorts the image of God, and by doing so to open the way to salvation. In this sense, diaconia is liberation for salvation."[28]


# XII.


Do We Project Ourselves in Projects ? was written by Willem J. Schot. It is an examination of the project system in relation to service, mission and development. The contents of the pamphlet is: Overall purpose of projects: "Thy kingdom come"; History of the "project" in biblical times; Is there a Church history of the project?; The challenge of CCPD to CICARWS; The challenge of aid from PCR; The challenge of the call for a moratorium; Inter-Church Aid today; Quo Vadis Projects?; Objections to projects; Can something good be said about projects?[29]

The pamphlet The Churches and the World Refugee Crisis was published in 1981. It includes a public issue statement adopted by the Central Committee meeting in 1981; major issues and concerns (definitions: who is a refugee, asylum, "non-refoulement", mass exodus, refugee rights, solutions, understanding why); and guidelines for the churches.[30]

In 1976, the Review Committee of the Central Committee recommended a study on the ecumenical sharing of resources. In 1978 a joint evaluation of the Project List was undertaken by CICARWS and CWME which resulted in the report "Towards a New Process for Mission and Service" in 1979 (The Newby report). A joint CWME/CICARWS meeting took place at Cartigny, Switzerland, to review this report and take the study to the next stage. The 1980 Central Committee received with appreciation the final report on the study "Ecumenical Sharing of Resources", adopted a message to the churches and recommended the wide circulation of the study "Empty Hands".

The 1981 Central Committee received a progress report on consultations held and urged implementation of a joint funding instrument by 1983-1984. A consultation held at Glion, Switzerland, in February 1982 addressed the question of a new system for the sharing of resources. The proposal "A Resource Sharing System" was the result of this process. The Unit Committee in 1982 "recommended that the Central Committee receive its report and approve the proposed new resource sharing system and set in motion a process to ensure that all WCC funding instruments be coordinated into the new system with a view to progressive combination as appropriate... and to request the General Secretary to appoint the Resource Sharing Task Force to monitor the process leading to a new system according to the terms of reference and timetable..."[31]

The Central Committee meeting in 1984 affirmed "the action of the Executive Committee endorsing the direction taken towards developing an ecumenical commitment for resource sharing, and affirming the consultation process in preparation for a world conference to be held in the first half of 1986."[32]

Towards an Ecumenical Commitment for Resource Sharing was published in 1984. Its headings are: 1. Sharing Within the One Body; 2. Holistic Mission; 3. Comprehensive Sharing; 4. People's Participation in Planning and Programming; 5. Interdependent Relationships; 6. Community Decision Making; 7. Effective Communication; 8. Functional Structures and Systems; 9. Mutual Accountability.[33]


## Observations and Comments

1. A theology of inter-church aid and of the service of the church to the world has not been fully developed and spelled out. This also pertains to the service to refugees. The insights of the Bible are accepted that the Apostolate of the Church includes Kerygma, Koinonia and Diakonia. All belong together and

condition on another.  The aim of all charity and aid is to change the status quo in view of the kingdom of God breaking into this world.  All service is participation in the redeeming ministry of Jesus Christ.

2.  The history of inter-church aid, refugee and world service has often been difficult and complicated due to intricate denominational church structures.  It took a long time to combine the concerns of the Department of Inter-Church Aid and Service to Refugees, the International Missionary Council and the Division of Studies, the concerns of CICARWS, CWME, CCPD, etc. Yet CICARWS, the largest sub-unit of the WCC, has rendered continuous service throughout the years throughout the world. In many church circles the WCC is first of all known through the activities of CICARWS.

3.  From the sixties onwards the relation between giving and receiving churches has been increasingly questioned. Already in 1959 the East Asia Christian Conference was critical of the giving of ecumenical aid by rich churches to poor churches. In spite of the misgivings it has been extremely difficult to change the structures of one-sided support and monological communication. The project system remained for years largely under the control of the donor agencies.  Bilateralism continued to flourish. Since 1971 it took several years to clarify the overall mandate of Unit II: Justice and Service.  The discussion and the intention to implement the sharing of ecumenical resources is now almost a decade old.  The commitment of the churches to the new international system needs still to be tested.

4.  There has been an increasing awareness also of the complexity of the churches' involvement in their service to refugees. To deal with the effects of various refugee situations is not enough.  Refugees are victims of unjust social, economic and political structures of societies, of the consistent violation of human rights, and of merciless armed conflicts.  They need peace, justice and recognition of their human dignity. Refugee assistance is only valid when it makes a contribution towards meeting overall community needs.  Despite the difficulties of establishing human order in a disordered world, and of bringing new hope to refugees in despair, Christianity must express its determination to help ease and finally to bring the world refugee crisis to an end.

5.  In the Memoirs[34] of W.A. Visser 't Hooft the challenge of post-war reconstruction and reconciliation takes up a very central place.  The chapters dealing with this gigantic task are probably the heart of the auto-biography.  Unity and mission remain undoubtedly priorities in the ecumenical movement, but the strengthening of human relations between churches and their faithful and all others in need, the expression of tangible love and generous care is the quintessence of world Christianity. Matthew 25:31-46 is a truly ecumenical text for all churches and Christians.

---

1.  The Ten Formative Years, 1938-1948. Report on the Activities of the World Council of Churches During Its Period of Formation. Geneva: WCC, 1948. p. 33.

2.  The First Assembly of the World Council of Churches held at Amsterdam, August 22 - September 4, 1948. Ed. by W.A. Visser 't Hooft. London: SCM Press, 1949. pp. 167-171.

3.  The First Six Years, 1948-1954. A Report of the Central Committee on the Activities of the Departments and Secretariats of the Council. Geneva: WCC, 1954. p. 63.

4.  Minutes and Reports of the Third Meeting of the Central Committee of the WCC, Toronto, Canada, July 9-15, 1950. Geneva: WCC, 1950. pp. 35-36.

5.  Minutes and Reports of the Fifth Meeting of the Central Committee of the WCC, Lucknow (India), December 31, 1952 - January 8, 1953. Geneva: WCC, 1953. p. 54.

6.  The Evanston Report. The Second Assembly of the WCC 1954. New York: Harper, 1955. pp. 233, 235, 237.

7.  Minutes and Reports of the Eighth Meeting of the Central Committee of the WCC, Davos, Switzerland, August 2-8, 1955. Geneva: WCC, 1955. pp. 84-85.

8.  Addresses and Reports to the Annual Consultation of the Division of Inter-Church Aid and Service to Refugees, Les Rasses, Switzerland, May 28 - June 2, 1956. p. 85.

9.  Minutes of the Assembly of the International Missionary Council at Ghana, December 28, 1957 to January 8, 1958. London: IMC, 1958. p. 63.

10. "Witnesses Together". Being the Official Report of the Inaugural Assembly of the East Asia Christian Conference, held at Kuala Lumpur, Malaya, May 14-24, 1959. Ed. by U Kyaw Than. Rangoon: EACC, 1959. pp. 102-103.

11. The New Delhi Report. The Third Assembly of the WCC 1961. London: SCM Press, 1962. pp. 108-114, 230-248.

12. Minutes and Reports of the Sixteenth Meeting of the Central Committee of the WCC at Paris, August 7-16, 1962. Geneva: WCC, 1962. pp. 86, 88-89.

13. Minutes and Reports of the Seventeenth Meeting of the Central Committee of the WCC, at Rochester, USA, August 26-September 2, 1963. Geneva: WCC, 1963. pp. 76-83.

14. Central Committee of the WCC. Minutes and Reports of the Nineteenth Meeting at Geneva, February 8-17, 1966. Geneva: WCC, 1966. pp. 108-123.

15. Digest of the 1966 World Consultation on Inter-Church Aid at Swanwick, Great Britain. Geneva: WCC, 1966. pp. 127-130.

16. The Role of the Diakonia of the Church in Contemporary Society. Geneva: WCC, 1966. p. 34.

17. Within Thy Gates. A Report of the Conference on Migrant Workers in Western Europe, held at Arnoldshain, June 10-15, 1963. Geneva: WCC, 1964. pp. 73, 75-77, 85.

18. The Uppsala Report 1968. Ed. by Norman Goodall. Geneva: WCC, 1968. pp. 255-258, 260, 363.

19. Central Committee of the WCC. Minutes and Reports of the Twenty-Fourth Meeting at Addis Ababa, Ethiopia, January 10-21, 1971. Geneva: WCC, 1971. pp. 60-61, 248.

20. Minutes and Reports of the Assembly of the Commission on World Mission and Evangelism, December 31, 1972 and January 9-12, 1973. Geneva: WCC, 1973. pp. 14-15.

21. Fetters of Injustice. Report of an Ecumenical Consultation on Ecumenical Assistance to Development Projects, 26-31 January, 1970, Montreux, Switzerland. Ed. by Pamela H. Gruber. Geneva: WCC, 1970. p. 116.

22. Uppsala to Nairobi, 1968-1975. Ed. by David E. Johnson. New York: Friendship Press; London: SPCK, 1975. p. 177.

23. Breaking Barriers. Nairobi 1975. Ed. by David M. Paton. London: SPCK; Grand Rapids: Wm.B.Eerdmans, 1976. pp. 307-308.

24. Central Committee of the WCC. Minutes of the Thirtieth Meeting at Geneva, 28 July - 6 August, 1977. Geneva: WCC, 1977. p. 29.

25. Mid-Stream, vol. XVIII, no. 2, April 1979. pp. 174-175.

26. Sharing in One Hope. Reports and Documents from the Meeting of the Faith and Order Commission, 15-30 August, 1978, Bangalore, India. Geneva: WCC, 1978 (Faith and Order Paper, No. 92). pp. 274-278.

27. Central Committee of the WCC. Minutes of the Thirty-First Meeting at Kingston, Jamaica, 1-11 January 1979. Geneva: WCC, 1979. p. 62.

28. An Orthodox Approach to Diaconia. Consultation on Church and Service. Geneva: WCC, 1980. See also: Mid-Stream, vol. XVIII, no. 2, April 1979. pp. 175-179.

29. Schot, Willem J. Do We Project Ourselves in Projects ? An Examination of the Project System in Relation to Service, Mission and Development. Geneva: WCC, 1980.

30. The Churches and the World Refugee Crisis.
    Geneva: WCC, 1981.

31. Central Committee of the WCC. Minutes of the Thirty-Fourth
    Meeting at Geneva, 19-28 July, 1982.
    Geneva: WCC, 1982.  pp. 68-69.

32. Central Committee of the WCC. Minutes of the Thirty-Sixth
    Meeting at Geneva, 9-18 July, 1984.
    Geneva: WCC, 1984.  p. 28.

33. Towards and Ecumenical Commitment for Resource Sharing.
    Geneva: WCC, 1984.

34. Visser 't Hooft, Willem Adolf.  Memoirs.
    London: SCM Press, 1973.  pp. 173-203.

# XII.
## Ministry to the Poor
## and Ministry of the Poor

In the history of the World Council of Churches and its
various ecumenical constituencies there are very few official
references to poverty, even less to the ministry to the poor,
until 1968. One single sentence in the Report of the Assembly
at Amsterdam in 1948 stated: "Christians who are beneficiaries
of capitalism should try to see the world as it appears to many
who know themselves excluded from its privileges and who see in
Communism a means of deliverance from poverty and insecurity."[1]
The New Delhi Assembly in 1961 produced one rather awkward sentence on poverty: "The Christian is not afraid of change, for
he knows how heavy are the burdens of poverty and privation
carried today by the majority of mankind."[2] A conference of
Church and Society on rapid social change at Thessalonica in
1959 concluded that modern technology makes possible the eradication of poverty and that the right use of world resources and
partnership in world development is imperative.[3] The earlier
assemblies of the East Asia Christian Conference and the All
Africa Conference of Churches mentioned once poverty only in an
insignificant framework.

### I.

Surprisingly the Third World Conference on Church and Society,
held at Geneva in 1966, and being much concerned about the technical and social revolutions of our era and economic development
in a world perspective, bypassed the problem of poverty. Four
years later, however, at an Ecumenical Consultation on Ecumenical
Assistance to Development Projects at Montreux, sponsored by the
Commission on the Churches' Participation in Development, three
main speakers, Edward K. Hamilton, Samuel L. Parmar, and Helder
B. Camara referred to the injustice and cruelty of poverty.[4] The
desperately poor hundreds of millions were also not absent at a
first large conference of SODEPAX in Beirut in April 1968 which
discussed world development as a challenge to the churches.[5]

Great attention to the crucial problem of poverty was given
at the Uppsala Assembly in 1968. President Kaunda of Zambia and
Lady Jackson (Barbara Ward) presented memorable addresses on the
topic "The Rich and the Poor Nations". It was noted that development through cooperation had suffered a serious set-back and there
was a growing tendency towards neo-isolationism. Mass media both
aggrevate the fate of the poor and can make them aware of their
predicament.[6] The Nairobi Assembly in 1975 urged again member
churches "to plan their participation in development to be primarily in support of the poorest of the poor", to be aware of the
fact that "the struggle against oppression and injustice inevitably necessitates confrontations with powers and handling of

power", to create an international disaster relief fund, and to
consider a quality of life which includes "the obligation of the
affluent both to provide basic necessities for all the people of
planet Earth, and to modify their own consumption patterns..."[7]
At the Vancouver Assembly in 1983, Jan Pronk spoke of the dim
prospect that at least one billion people will be living below
any decent level of existence at the turn of the century.
In Issue VI "Struggling for Justice and Human Dignity" the joy
was expressed that "the poor, the oppressed and the discriminated
peoples are awakening everywhere to resist unjust powers and to
forge their own destiny. This is a sign of life." I will refer
later to a sub-section in Issue I "Witnessing in a Divided World"
which dealt specifically with "witnessing among the poor".[8]

At the meeting at Lima in 1971, where the union of the World
Council of Churches and World Council of Christian Education was
consummated, the opening address by Federico J. Pagura was entitled: "Through the Cry of the Poor", based on two biblical
texts: Psalm 12:5 and James 5:4, which both deal with the Lord's
safety for which the poor long.[9] Noting that "average income
among a majority of the urban population are so low that they
are unable to afford even minimal housing and essential services
and, more often than not, food, medicine and clothing," a Conference on Science and Technology for Human Development at Bucharest in 1974 analyzed "the failure of research and development
systems in developing countries... the gap between modern and
traditional technology... and the need for new patterns of production and consumption."[10]


## II.

Patterns of Poverty in the Third World [11], by Charles Elliott,
a staff member of SODEPAX, detailed the prospects for the poorest
fourth of the world's population - eight Third World countries,
plus Ireland and Sweden in the developed world. It was commissioned by and published in cooperation with the WCC in preparation of its Fifth Assembly. The Poverty Makers [12], by David
Millwood, is a short and popular version of Charles Elliott's
volume, helping a non-specialist readership to understand the
causes of poverty and injustice, systems and mechanisms that
perpetuate them and what could be done to challenge and to
change them.

Richard D.N. Dickinson wrote several books on aspects of
people's development. Line and Plummet [13] was a document produced
by him in 1968 for the WCC's Committee for Specialized Assistance
for Social Projects (SASP), the predecessor of the Commission of
the Churches' Participation in Development (CCPD). As an adviser
to CCPD, he wrote in 1975 To Set at Liberty the Oppressed [14] which
deals with a deeper understanding of Christian responsibilities
of development and liberation. Besides bringing Third World
cultures into a new perspective, noting a growing commitment to
social justice, and stressing the solidarity with people of other
faiths, he outlines some new theological emphases.

It is not adequate to speak of a 'theology of development', even less of a 'theology for development'. Theological reflection today must be characterized by engagement and reflection on engagement. Liberation _for_ or _towards_ something is as important as liberation _from_ oppression. Liberation is not only _from_ the Egyptians (and also _from_ the Israelites' own preference for the security of slavery), but _for_ a positive witness of co-partnership in continuing creation. A rediscovery of eschatology is, moreover, much needed in view of "the confrontation with ecological population and resource limits; high expectations for the improvement of the common lot sobered by the realities of sin, inhumanity and greed in social life; intercultural discussions of the nature of progress and development which revealed the shallowness of this-worldly preoccupation." Finally, as hundreds of thousands are dying of avoidable starvation, as power in the hands of few increases and oppressors remain intransigent maintaining the status quo, the whole question of violence and non-violence needs to be re-debated.

In another book by Richard Dickinson, _Poor, Yet Making Many Rich_, the emphasis in the sub-title is laid on The Poor As Agents of Creative Justice. The role of the churches has become threefold: to join in the struggle of the poor against domination and oppression rather than try to direct it along predetermined paths. Their second task is to incarnate in their own life their theological affirmation of the central role of the poor in history – God's special 'option for the poor', as the Medellin conference of 1968 so eloquently claimed. "The strength of the people themselves is transformed as that struggle (the victory of the justice of God over evil in history) is revealed to be the dynamic of the messianic Kingdom. People discover themselves as the subject of the Kingdom, moving through their actions towards justice, _koinonia_ and _shalom_ for all humanity." The third role is to interpret "the reality of the gospel through the experiences of the poor in their struggle for justice and wholeness, and to amplify those experiences so that others can hear."[15]

### III.

The trilogy _Good News to the Poor_[16], by Julio de Santa Ana, _Separation Without Hope ?_[17], and _Towards a Church of the Poor_ [18], both edited by Julio de Santa Ana, is a result of several years of activities by the WCC Commission on the Churches' Participation in Development. The first volume focuses on the challenge of the poor to the church, as felt by Christian communities during the first four centuries A.D. and again during the Middle Ages. The second volume concentrates on relations between churches and the poor working classes during the period of the industrial revolution and colonial expansion in the West. The last volume centres on the present challenge of the poor to the churches. Their participation in development must be understood as a sharing, in solidarity, of the expectations, pains and hopes of the poor and of their struggles for a better society. This implies that churches must continue to give major attention to the programmes through which they express their solidarity with the poor and the oppressed, because development is not _for_ the poor, but

can be achieved by them and with them when they become full
participants in the processes which lead to justice and
liberation.

In his book Rich Man, Poor Man - and the Bible, Conrad
Boerma combs the biblical text from Genesis to Revelation and
finds a consistency in its approach to poverty that must be
taken seriously.  The Bible always challenges poverty, which it
sees clearly linked to social structures.  God identifies himself with the poor, most clearly in Jesus of Nazareth, who was
not so much opposed to possessions as indifferent to them,
renouncing his comfortable middle-class upbringing.  Boerma
strikes right at the heart of every local church by revealing
how far short of the New Testament ideal the contemporary church
falls.  Instead of providing the secular world with the proto-
type sharing, loving, compassionate community of men and women
equal in the sight of God, he says "congregations often consist
of a number of closed social classes and detached individuals"[19]
He criticizes Albert Gélin, who in Les pauvres Dieu aime [20] describes the biblical exegesis in the period 1882-1965, for not
entirely avoiding the temptation to praise poverty as a specific
form of holiness.


IV.


Perspectives on Political Ethics. An Ecumenical Enquiry contains the report of a Consultation in Cyprus which was held in
October 1981.  "An ecumenical political ethic", it was stated,
"has to do with the evaluation of the understanding and exercise
of power, in faithfulness to the gospel, for the sake of social
justice, human dignity and authentic community."  The term
'people' as a new category was introduced consciously into the
discussion in order to point to a new political reality: the
awakening of the people who have hitherto only been the silent
objects or victims of political power.  The term people, it was
noted, is not free from ambiguity.  The people are not simply
all citizens of a given political community.  Sometimes the
people are considered identical with the deprived, oppressed
and poor in society.  "Ecumenical solidarity can take the form
of an 'incarnational' participation in the suffering of the
people as they seek to transform their political predicament.
The suffering of the people constitutes in itself a witness
against the illegitimacy of power, crying out not only for its
rectification but for a fundamental transformation."  People's
participation in politics "aims at people's power to act in
order to liberate themselves from all forms of bondage and oppression on the one hand and to create a new community of justice
and dignity, self-reliance and identity, freedom and compassion,
friendship and celebration on the other."  The Cyprus consultation
urged the churches "to be more faithful to their mission to the
world, sharing the sufferings and aspirations of the people,
even where the people may play no active role in the life of
the churches... The churches must transcend their confessional
and national boundaries and be in dialogue with people of other
religions and ideologies for mutual challenge, sharing and
learning."[21]

## V

At the World Conference on Mission and Evangelism in Melbourne, May 1980, Section I was devoted to the theme "Good News to the Poor". A distinction was made between poverty in the necessities of life, poverty amid material wealth and voluntary poverty. The Conference recommended to the churches to become in solidarity with the struggles of the poor, to join the struggle against the powers of exploitation and impoverishment, to establish a new relationship with the poor inside the churches, and to pray and work for the kingdom of God. It also noted that in some places "a new era of evangelization is dawning, where the poor are proclaiming the Good News." Stories of the poor show at the same time that there are "possibilities for a witness with and on behalf of the poor."[22]

This insight was taken a step further in Issue I "Witnessing in a Divided World" of the Vancouver Assembly. In "Witnessing Among the Poor" the joy was expressed "that the churches are growing today among the poor of the earth and that new insights and perspectives on the gospel are coming to the whole church from communities of the poor... The richness and freshness of their experience is an inspiration, blessing and challenge to the established churches." Children, the disabled and women are often among those who suffer most seriously the cruelty and despair of poverty. "God is working through the poor of the earth to awaken the consciousness of humanity to his call for repentance, for justice, for love."[23]

### Observations and Comments

1. It is only from 1968 onwards that the world-wide phenomenon of poverty and its possible eradication has become a major concern in the ecumenical movement. Before Uppsala the slogan 'The rich are becoming richer and the poor are becoming poorer' could not have been coined and would have fallen on too many deaf ears. The whole debate on development of the last fifteen years must be seen in the light, or rather in the darkness, of the church's endorsement of colonialism and neo-colonialism, and its divorce from the working classes, which go hand in hand. The churches did not draw the consequences from their estrangement of the masses of the poor and the exploited for several centuries. Christianity clearly did not succeed in taking adequate account of the demands made on it by the unexpected development of new economic and social conditions and to adjust its mission and ministry accordingly.

Throughout the period of Western industrial revolution, the structures of the church institutions, with minor adjustments, continued to be those of the pre-industrial world. Instead of listening to the plea of the new underprivileged classes the

churches stood aside and remained isolated from the radical
aspects of what was happening. The gulf between the growing
marginal population and the Christian institutions constantly
widened. The loss of memory leads the church too easily and
too quickly to believe that it has caught up with its questionable past and now behaves as a kind of an avant-garde. It remains
a striking fact that in spite of many WCC documents the Central
Committee never engaged in a thorough discussion of poverty.
Only after 28 meetings in 1976 did it adopt a Report of the
Review Committee in which the word poverty among the words injustice, waste and deprivation was mentioned.[24] Bossey never
sponsored a consultation on world poverty and its consequences.[25]

2. The terminology of the proposals to the churches in
Towards a Church of the Poor, for instance, need careful scrutiny.
It was proposed that the churches
   a) align with the poor by sharing at appropriate levels, but
mainly in direct ways, their struggles for justice
   b) develop and support action-study of the Bible among those
who share the struggles of the poor for justice
   c) search out groups of the poor from whose struggles new
theological formulations may be arising
   d) commit resources of community organizers and action educators
to the task of developing ways of analyzing the structures and
contexts within which the struggles for liberation occur
   e) seek active partnership with those movements for liberation which revindicate the rights of the poor
   f) activate their various networks of support for the
struggle of the poor
   g) reconsider their organized structures to permit maximum
deployment of their resources to the struggle for a just, participatory, liberated and sustainable society.

A number of questions come forcibly to the fore: Do the verbs
align, develop, support, commit and activate still not connote
a paternalistic and condescending attitude ? Are not other
institutions than the churches better equipped to practice a
solidarity with the struggles of the poor ? How did unjust
structures of society come into being ? Who contributed to them
and prolongs them ? Are the churches without blame ? Do the
poor need the alignment of the churches with their fate ? Can
they have confidence in the effectiveness of the churches' networks ? Are liberation movements of poor and exploited people
not manipulated or streatened by powerful leftist or rightist
regimes with which churches tacitly identify ? These and other
questions show that it is very difficult to speak of relations
and interactions between the institutional churches and groups
of poor people wherever they are to be found. They are in fact
often unrelated to one another and seldom truly serve each other
in spite of the rediscovery of the liberating force of the Bible.

3. The precarious language of 'the church in solidarity
with the poor' and 'the church of the poor' has never been
tested in the ecumenical dialogue with people of other living
faiths and ideologies. No bi-lateral or multi-lateral dialogue,
sponsored by the WCC, has made poverty and the fate of the poor
a subject of inter-religious discussion. No attempt has been

made to discuss with Marxists their key concept of the 'dictatorship of the proletariat', the necessary length of that dicator-
ship for the growth of justice in society, and the ecumenical
rediscovery of the ministry of the poor. The absence of the
poor in inter-religious and secular encounters indicates that
the ecumenical movement is not ready yet to draw some fundamental
theological consequences from its present predicament.

It is more within a world community of communities than within the Christian community alone that ecumenical bodies should
express that in and through the world God is present to human
beings and crucified by them. The incarnation of Christ was a
'secular' event, particularly in view of the perilous plight of
the poor, and his coming again will be a 'secular' event, because
the poor will be with us until the end of the world. How will
other world religions react to this statement ? When we confuse
'alienation from the Church' with 'separation from God', we deny
both the reality and the efficacy of Christ's cross and resurrection. God in Christ has once and for all laid claim to the world
and shown the extent of his love for it, especially for those
who are in dire need. Nothing can be placed beyond the range of
his redemption, neither by the greed and lust for power of human
beings nor by the indifference of Christians.

Ministry to the poor and ministry of the poor are simply
abstractions unless they become real in the very local situations
in which we live. The disillusionment with the structures of
the church and the redeeming value of those who are suffering
and agonizing are to be experienced in our own neighbourhood, in
particular where the vast majority of the poor adhere to another
faith then the Christian faith. The theological assertion that
in God's plan of salvation my poor fellow human beings are playing a role in my redemption becomes most daring if it is lived
out in my own environment of disobedience and failure.

4. A vital and natural link between <u>Baptism, Eucharist and
Ministry</u> and the whole concept of the 'Church of the poor' needs
still to be established. It has become increasingly clear that
the sacraments of baptism and the eucharist are effective anti-
dotes against all status distinctions and against the separation
of the communities of the powerful and the powerless in the
church and in the world. Baptism makes living and dignified
human beings out of poor and dying people. Their baptism in the
dying and risen Christ takes place in order that their righteousness may be revealed. Baptism is the prerequisite for freely
joining liberation movements in order that more justice be ob-
tained and genuine personhood and authentic humanity in Christ
become visible.

The eucharist is the sacrament through which all sins are
forgiven, all human weaknesses healed and all frustrations of
poverty overcome. Eating Christ's body and drinking his blood
puts an end to the indulgence in the life to come of the rich
and kindles a spirituality of creation of the poor. At the
Lord's table it becomes clear that the unity of the church is
only cheap grace when rich and poor come together remaining
affluent and destitute. The Lord's supper rules out all un-

restrained profit-centred economy. It is the banquet of both the spiritually and materially poor. "The eucharist celebration demands reconciliation and sharing among all those regarded as brothers and sisters in the one family of God and is a constant challenge in the search for appropriate relationships in social, economic and political life."[26]

As much as these insights have enriched the life of the church and contributed to an inclusive ecclesiology, as much the 'inner-directed' ordained ministry with the church has not been linked to the 'outer-directed' ministry of the church in the world. The ministry of pastors and priests stops at dispensing the sacraments, preaching the gospel, teaching the faith, caring for the flock and coordinating the gifts of all the members for the edification of the body in love. No specific features of the ordained ministry are adapted to the varying socio-political and cultural contexts of a society in which the church finds itself. The apostolic nature of the church is still over-emphasized at the cost of its apostolate.

Consequently, all lay ministries, even those to the marginalized and the helpless, are still considered of another order and of less importance. Woman ministries are accepted as necessary and meaningful, except the ordained women ministry. If only priests represent in their activities the immanence of the divine presence in creation, a metaphysical clericalism, which places them on a higher level of being than the rest of the faithful, will continue to bar the way to many reforms at the present time. The host of baptized believers, rich and poor, are sacramental instruments to allow the broken human race to be transformed into God's blessing. The most ordinary, this-worldly ministries and especially the ministry to the poor and of the poor are truly sacramental, because they are a part of Christ's ministry.

Needless to say that the four points I raised with regard to the ministry of the poor have their bearing on a radical overhaul of theological education in all its aspects if ecclesiology and diakonia are to become the two sides of the same coin. The ecumenical movement is still on its way to manifest the unity and the mission of the one church in one faith and in one life, in order that the sacred (other-worldly) and the romantic (this-worldly) notions of the people of God become biblically-eschatologically transparent. We are continuously on the long road of becoming that indefinable people of the Sermon on the Mount.

---

1.  The First Assembly of the World Council of Churches, held at Amsterdam 1948. Ed. by W.A. Visser't Hooft. London: SCM Press, 1949. p. 78.

2.  The New Delhi Report. London: SCM Press, 1962. p. 94.

3.  Dilemmas and Opportunities. Christian Action in Rapid Social Change. Report of an International Ecumenical Study Conference at Thessalonica, Greece, July 25 - August 2, 1959. Geneva: WCC, 1959. pp. 18-19, 72-75.

4. Fetters of Injustice. Ed. by Pamela H. Gruber.
   Geneva: WCC, 1970. pp. 27-28, 64-66.

5. World Development: Challenge to the Churches.
   Ed. by Denys Munby.
   Washington: Corpus Books, 1969. pp. 15-16, 43.

6. The Uppsala Report 1968. Ed. by Norman Goodall.
   Geneva: WCC, 1968. pp. 41, 127-129, 391-392.

7. Breaking Barriers. Nairobi 1975. Ed. by David M. Paton.
   London: SPCK, 1976. pp. 136-137, 140.

8. Gathered for Life. Official Report of the VI WCC Assembly
   at Vancouver. Ed. by David Gill.
   Geneva: WCC, 1983. pp. 26, 83.

9. Encuentro. New Perspectives for Christian Education.
   In: World Christian Education, vol. 26, 1971, no. 3-4.
   pp. 260-262.

10. Science and Technology for Human Development.
    Bucharest, June 24 - July 2, 1974. Findings of a conference
    concluding the five-year WCC study programme on the future
    of man and society in a world of science-based technology.
    In: Anticipation, 19. pp. 14, 20, 26.

11. Elliott, Charles. Patterns of Poverty in the Third World.
    A Study of Social and Economic Stratification.
    New York: Praerger, 1975.

12. Millwood, David. The Poverty Makers.
    Geneva: WCC, 1977.

13. Dickinson, Richard D.N. Line and Plumment.
    The Churches and Development.
    Geneva: WCC, 1968.

14. Dickinson, Richard D.N. To Set at Liberty the Oppressed.
    Towards an Understanding of Christian Responsibilities
    of Development/Liberation. Geneva: WCC, 1975.

15. Dickinson, Richard D.N. Poor, Yet Making Many Rich.
    The Poor as Agents of Creative Justice.
    Geneva: WCC, 1983. pp. 159-160.

16. Santa Ana, Julio de. Good News to the Poor.
    Geneva: WCC, 1977.

17. Separation Without Hope ? Ed. by Julio de Santa Ana.
    Geneva: WCC, 1978.

18. Towards a Church of the Poor. The Work of an Ecumenical
    Group on the Church and the Poor. Ed. by Julio de
    Santa Ana. Geneva: WCC, 1979.

19. Boerma, Conrad.  Rich Man, Poor Man - and the Bible.
    London: SCM Press, 1979.

20. Gélin, Albert.  Les pauvres que Dieu aime.
    Paris: Cerf, 1967.

21. Perspectives on Political Ethics. An Ecumenical Enquiry.
    Ed. by Koson Srisang.
    Geneva: WCC, 1983.  pp. 16, 25, 27, 35, 37.

22. Your Kingdom Come. Report on the World Conference on
    Mission and Evangelism, Melbourne, Australia, 12-25 May,
    1980.   Geneva: WCC, 1980.  p. 176.

23. Gathered for Life. Official Report of the VI WCC Assembly
    at Vancouver.  Ed. by David Gill.
    Geneva: WCC, 1983.  pp. 37-39.

24. Central Committee of the World Council of Churches.
    Minutes of the Twenty-Ninth Meeting, Geneva, 10-18 August,
    1976.   Geneva: WCC, 1976.  p. 96.

25. Bent, Ans J. van der.  Six Hundred Ecumenical Con-
    sultations 1948-1982.
    Geneva: WCC, 1983.

26. Baptism, Eucharist and Ministry.
    Geneva: WCC, 1982 (Faith and Order Paper, No. 111).
    p. 14.

# XIII.
# Human Rights


The Universal Declaration of Human Rights, together with
the later adopted International Covenants on Economic, Social
and Cultural Rights, and on Civil and Political Rights, are
international instruments, which, if they are fully implemented,
constitute a solid platform from which human rights can be
advocated, everywhere in the world. The WCC Commission of the
Churches on International Affairs played an important role in
the preparatory work on the Declaration as it was chosen
several times as a mouthpiece for those non-governmental
organizations who were active in that stage of the work of
the United Nations.

                                I

The First Assembly of the WCC at Amsterdam in 1948 called
"upon its constituent members to press for the adoption of an
International Bill of Human Rights making provision for the
recognition, and national and international enforcement, of
all the essential freedoms of man, whether personal, political
or social." It also adopted a Declaration of Religious Liberty
which emphasized that: "1.Every person has the right to determine his own faith and creed; 2.Every person has the right to
express his religious beliefs in worship, teaching and practice,
and to proclaim the implications of his beliefs for relationships in a social or political community; 3.Every person has
the right to associate with others and to organise with them
for religious purposes; 4.Every religious organisation,
formed or maintained by action in accordance with the rights
of individual persons, has the right to determine its policies
and practices for the accomplishment of its chosen purposes."[1]

The scope of this analytical and bibliographical survey
of human rights does not allow for a similar extensive treatment of religious liberty, although it has been an important
concern of the WCC throughout its years of activities and many
statements on religious freedom have been issued.

After discussing the racial question the Central Committee
in 1949 re-affirmed the findings of Section IV of the Amsterdam Assembly and stated: "... We are profoundly concerned by
evidence from many parts in the world of flagrant violations
of human rights. Both individuals and groups are subjected to
persecution and discrimination on grounds of race, colour,
religion, culture or political conviction. Against such
actions, whether of governments, officials, or the general
public, the Churches must take a firm and vigorous stand,
through local action, in co-operation with Churches in other

lands, and through international institutions of legal order. They must work for an ever wider and deeper understanding of what are the essential human rights if men are to be free to do the will of God."[2]

At its next meeting in Toronto in 1950, the Central Committee devised "A Comprehensive Programme of Action" with regard to the Universal Declaration of Human Rights and a draft of the Covenant on Human Rights, with particular reference to the violations of religious liberty. It resolved: "1) To declare its opposition to all practices by which governments, Churches, or other agencies curb the exercise of religious freedom; to call upon the Churches to disseminate information and to take individual and collective action for promoting in their own countries conditions under which religious freedom may be fully practiced; and further, to make representation regarding infringements to the religious authorites which have jurisdiction in the countries concerned; 2) To encourage the development of a comprehensive and coordinated programme of action, national and international, and thereby to pursue affirmative, preventive, and remedial measures for promoting the observance of religious freedom for all men."[3]

In the Report of Section IV, "International Affairs: Christians in the Struggle for World Community", of the Evanston Assembly in 1954, a section was devoted to the "Protection of Human Rights." The following was stated: "A call for the protection of human rights is all the more insistent in this age when, in various parts of the world, totalitarianism - based on ideologies sometimes atheistic and sometimes under the guise of religion - oppresses the freedom of men and of institutions and denies those God-given rights which are His will for all men. A system of justice which defends the rights and dignity of the human person is fundamental... The struggle for the essential freedoms of man as defined in the Universal Declaration of Human Rights is the struggle for peace. The World Council of Churches' current study and support of the right of conscientious objection, as authorized by the Central Committee in 1951, is a necessary step in the direction of national and international action for its protection.

"... The importance of attempts to secure international legal safeguards for human rights is not diminished by the obstacles. The fundamental concern of the churches, however, is to promote mutually recognized rights in the ethos and practices of society. International covenants offer a valuable means to this end, but there are limits to what can be achieved through such means. International law is more often the fruit than the source of community. To build a strong defence of human rights requires vigorous, broad and persistent educational efforts. Christian education can make an important contribution here.

"The love of God for man lays upon the Christian conscience a special measure of responsibility for the care of those who are the victims of world disorder. By governmental action and by international co-operation, as well as by the direct effort of the churches, measures should be taken for the relief of refugees, migrants, still un-repatriated prisoners, civil and military, and similar groups of suffering and oppressed men and women, whatever their origin, race or religion. More important still than their relief is a just and permanent solution of their problem."[4]

In the Report of the Committee on the Commission of the Churches on International Affairs of the New Delhi Assembly in 1961 the following was stated: "The protection of human rights by international instrument has grown in more recent development to be a fundamental concern of international law and order. It has been the constant endeavour of the CCIA to urge governments to implement the standards proclaimed in the Declaration of Human Rights of the United Nations and to assist in the work, yet to be completed, of elaborating covenants by which all states will undertake to assure civil and political as well as economic, social and cultural rights. International efforts to advance the status of women are also followed with care...

"The position of man in society, as defined by declarations and conventions on human rights in international law, can be more effectively secured by the creation of international safeguards for the observance of those rights. This will open for individuals direct access to international institutions against infringements upon these liberties by their own governments. The European Convention on Human Rights and Fundamental Freedoms has created such institutions and these are working well. The CCIA could profitably explore similar developments in other regions, always provided that such international standards as have been recognized shall not be lowered.

"... Christians living together in the common brotherhood of the family of God must oppose racial discrimination in all its forms as contrary to Christian doctrine. They must work as individuals and as communities for the abolition of racial privileges and injustice, and thereby bear witness to the Christian faith."[5]


II

At the Inaugural Assembly of the East Asia Christian Conference in 1959 the following was stated on the functions of the state in contemporary Asia: "In response to the changing social situation in East Asia today the state has a dynamic role. It is called to function not merely as a guardian of peace and order but as the chief organiser of human welfare and promoter of the growing sense of national self-hood. In connection with these three functions of the state in Asia - to promote national community, economic revolution and human rights - we are often faced with the question of priorities. Many Asians, especially intellectuals and workers, are fascinated and challenged by the quicker space of economic development in China under communism. They would like to put economic progress as the first priority even when they are aware of the disregard of human rights involved. Others would give national independence or individual freedom the first place.

"This is no doubt a real problem of practical politics. However, as Christians, our concern is not to set precise priorities but to insist that all three purposes of the state must be preserved in the best possible balance. The pursuit of any one of them at the expense of the other will result ultimately in the denial of all."[6]

Discussing in Section III "The Asian Churches and International Affairs" the Second Assembly of the East Asia Conference of Churches in 1964 stated in the sub-section on "Human Rights, International Law and World Structures": "The Universal Declaration of Human Rights has exerted considerable influence in countries where such rights were denied to a large section of people. Many of the East Asian countries have written into their constitutions these basic rights which express the liberation of the human spirit. In others, the demand for it goes on. The growing demand for human rights and the widening scope of the concept itself are indeed matters of joy to Christians everywhere. The post-war world has been constantly made aware that denial of rights to people in any nation constitutes a threat to world peace and a matter of concern to the international organs and agencies working for peace. There is a special responsibility for Christians everywhere, who believe that human rights are the gift of God to all his creatures, not only for the use of the rights bestowed on them but also for the attainment of their neighbours rights."[7]

In the Report of Group III, "Statements on the Church and Citizenship", the All Africa Church Conference in 1958 addressed itself to governments as follows: "On the basis of Christian conviction that all men are called to share in the common responsibility for the just ordering of the life of their nation and society, we give thanks to God for the statesmanlike policy of those governments which have allowed dependent territories in Africa to move towards self-determination and self-government. The Conference commends this policy to all the governments of the continent provided that rights such as those set out in the Universal Declaration of Human Rights are written into any new Constitution for existing and emerging States; and in particular those rights of citizenship which belong to man as created in the image of God, and those privileges, responsibilities and duties pertaining thereto, such as franchise rights, rights of participation in the government of the country, freedom of worship, freedom to propagate the faith, freedom of speech, freedom of assembly, freedom of association, freedom of movement, freedom of organization into trade unions, and the right to protection against violence.

The Conference endorses the statement of the Second Assembly of the World Council of Churches in 1954 that "any form of segregation based on race, color, or ethnic origin is contrary

to the Gospel and is incompatible with the Christian doctrine
of man and with the nature of the Church of Christ." The Conference further calls for vigilence wherever self-government
is achieved lest any of these rights be impaired, including
the right of constitutional opposition within and without the
Legislature."[8]


## III

In the Report of Section III, "Structures of International
Cooperation: Living Together in Peace in a Pluralistic World
Society", the World Conference on Church and Society at Geneva
in 1966 called "upon Christians 'in each place' to urge their
governments to ratify and enforce the various UN Covenants on
Human Rights, not only as ends in themselves, but also as a
stimulus to the evolution of an international moral ethos.

"The church as an institution has itself too frequently
been a segregated body - it must increase its zeal in the
reversal of this history, and strive to be faithful to its
spiritual heritage and teaching... The pulpit shares with the
classroom the important task of giving instruction in the
Gospel and its meaning for full brotherhood without discrimination. It must press for adoption of educational curricula
that stress the oneness of humanity instead of its differences,
and inculcate appreciation and respect for the culture of other
peoples. It must take positive initiatives to ensure such
teaching especially within the church itself.

"... The churches should call upon their governments to
ratify at the earliest possible moment, and to enforce, the
UN Covenant on the Elimination of All Forms of Racial Discrimination, adopted by the 20th General Assembly; and to
support the creation of an Office of UN High Commissioner on
Human Rights to oversee the implementation of the Covenant."[9]

In the Report of Section IV, "Towards Justice and Peace
in International Affairs", the Uppsala Assembly in 1968 expressed itself as follows on the "Protection of Individuals
and Groups in the Political World": "The application of social
justice to all human relations demands a common understanding
between nations for the recognition and protection of the inherent dignity of man, and of full human equality between men
of all races and nations, and respect for the adherents of all
religions and ideologies.

"... Human rights cannot be safeguarded in a world of
glaring inequalities and social conflict. Even slavery has
not yet been totally abolished in every country. A deep change
in human attitude is now required. Christians and Christian
churches should in their own relations set an example of respect for human dignity, equality and the free expression of
thought even in print. The active engagement of people of all
ages in development, reconciliation and social work is to be

encouraged and supported as an expression of world-wide solidarity. The churches must assist in channeling this engagement.
The Governments should recognize and support such services as
ranking at least as national service.

"... Violations of human rights in one place may be quickly
communicated to all, spreading an evil and destructive influence abroad. Nations should recognize that the protection of
fundamental human rights and freedoms has now become a common
concern of the whole international community, and should therefore not regard international concern for the implementation of
these rights as an unwarranted interference.

"... "All peoples have the right to self-determination".
This is a basic essential of human dignity and of a genuine
family of nations. But nations are seldom altogether one
homogeneous people. Most nations have ethnic, cultural or
religious minorities. ... The churches must defend minorities
when they are oppressed or threatened. They must at times urge
restraint upon minorities in the pursuit of their ambitions.
But also they must help majorities to respond creatively to the
impatience of minorities in their struggle for justice."[10]

The Central Committee meeting at Addis Ababa in 1971 issued
a Memorandum on Human Rights and called upon "the member churches of the WCC to impress upon their governments the urgent
need to establish or to strengthen national channels through
which complaints about the violation of human rights can be
handled impartially and through which the protection of such
rights or remedies in case of their violation can be assured
speedily for all." It also adopted a statement on "Unity and
Human Rights in Africa Today."[11]

At its next meeting in Utrecht in 1972, the Central Committee issued a "Report and Further Recommendations on Human
Rights."[12] At the following meeting of the Central Committee
in Geneva in 1973, CCIA presented proposals for a consultation
on "Human Rights and Christian Responsibility". The Central
Committee adopted a draft programme for a consultation.[13]


IV

The international consultation on "Human Rights and Christian Responsibility" at St. Pölten, Austria, October 21-26,
1974, moved from information-giving and -sharing to the development of action strategies for the churches. There were two
different kinds of working groups. The first were on a) the
right to live and to work; b) the right to equality; c) the
right to national sovereignty, to self-determination and to
international community; the proliferation of political prisoners and political refugees. The second series of working
groups concentrated on 1) equipping the local and national
churches to identify human rights violations and to protect

the victims;   2) equipping regional ecumenical bodies and the
WCC for more effective defense and promotion of human rights;
3) promoting greater international ecumenical understanding
and cooperation for the defense and implementation of human
rights.  Various preparatory documents were issued.

The St. Pölten Consultation made the following theological
statement: "The emphasis of the Gospel is on the value of all
human beings in the sight of God, on the atoning and redeeming
work of Christ that has given to man his true dignity, on love
as the motive for action, and on love for one's neighbour as
the practical expression of an active faith in Christ.  We are
members of one another, and when one suffers, all are hurt.
This is a Christian interpretation of 'human solidarity'."[14]

A month before a consultation took place at the Ecumenical
Institute in Bossey, August 29 - September 2 on "The Struggle
for Fundamental Human Rights".  The main areas of discussion
were:  a) Problems and tasks of juridical machinery in dealing
with human rights issues;  b) Problems and tasks of extra-
juridical machinery in dealing with human rights issues;
c) The need for action and strategy in the struggle for fundamental human rights.  Papers were given by D. Jenkins,
A Kiapi, P. Kraemer, D. Morrison, C.D. Watyoka.[15]

The consultation on "The Churches on Human Rights" in
Africa, at Khartoum, Sudan, February 16-22, 1975 was jointly
sponsored by the All Africa Conference of Churches and the
CCIA.  The objective of this consultation was to bring together
human rights specialists, church leaders - both lay and clergy
- and people who have occupied central positions in the political life of their respective African countries to meet for
intensive discussions of violations of human rights in the
interdependent African nations.  The report contains, besides
the findings and the statement, addresses by President Nimeiry
of the Sudan, J. Rudolph Grimes, Burgess Carr and Louis Mba
Neto.[16]

A consultation at Montreux, July 12-15, 1977 on "The Churches' Role in the Application of the Final Act of the Conference on Security and Cooperation in Europe" brought together
official representatives of the member churches in the signatory
states of the Helsinki Final Act, and of the Conference of
European Churches, the National Council of Churches in the USA,
and the Canadian Council of Churches.  It was convened on
behalf of a planning group drawn from Eastern and Western
Europe and North America by the CCIA.  The consultation re-
affirmed the conviction of the St.Pölten consultation that
"the emphasis of the Gospel is on the value of all human beings
in the sight of God..."[17]

## V

A consultation on "Christian Concern for Peace", at Baden, Austria, April 3-9, 1970, sponsored by the Committee on Society, Development and Peace (SODEPAX), discussed extensively in Section IV the subject of "Human Rights and World Peace". The section opened with the following statement: "There is a fundamental relationship between peace and human rights which is grounded in justice. Structures which deprive persons of their human rights and dignity prevent justice from being realized and force men to resort to violence and war. In our societies these structures are so entrenched that the possibility for radical change is becoming increasingly remote. No progress can be made towards the achievement of any lasting peace while there remain such fundamental injustices which deny basic human rights."

The report of Section IV has the following headings: Flagrant Violation of Human Rights, Minorities, Tortures and Inhuman Treatment, Special Sodepax Machinery, Nuclear, Chemical and Bacteriological Weapons, Rights of Conscientious Objectors, Right to Resist Oppression, Further Important Aspects of Human Rights, Freedom of Information, Cultural Injustice, Socioeconomic Problems, Human Environment, Equal Rights for Women, Rights of Youth, Implementation of Human Rights, Teaching of Human Rights, Ratification of Human Rights Conventions, Implementation Machinery, Historical and Dynamic Dimension, Conclusion.[18]

A world consultation on "Sexism in the 1970s" at West Berlin in 1974 made the following recommendation on human rights: "Realizing that the liberation of women cannot be separated from liberation from other forms of discrimination and oppression and is linked with the liberation of all humanity; recognizing the fact that the liberation of women is not an end in itself but a means of achieving the liberation of all human beings under any form of oppression; affirming human dignity and the fundamental rights of all without discrimination of race, or sex, or religion, or social origin, we recommend that the WCC call on all men and women of good will to work together for the elimination of all forms of oppression, including racism, apartheid, colonialism and neo-colonialism, and for an end to discrimination on the grounds of sex, religion, and political affiliation."[19]

VI

In Section V, "Structures of Injustice and Struggles for Liberation", the Nairobi Assembly in 1975 concentrated particularly on human rights. In the introduction it was stated: "Our concerns for human rights are based on our conviction that

God wills a society in which all can exercise full human rights. All human beings are created in God's image, to be equal, infinitely precious in God's sight and ours. Jesus Christ has bound us to one another by his life, death and resurrection, so that what concerns one of us concerns us all." The section dealt with: The Right to Basic Guarantees for Life; The Rights to Self-Determination and to Cultural Identity, and the Right of Minorities; The Right to Participate in Decision-Making within the Community; The Right to Dissent; The Right to Personal Dignity; The Right to Religious Freedom; Human Rights and Christian Responsibility. The section further outlined: Education and Conscientization on Human Rights; Legal Machinery for the Protection of Human Rights; Action at Local, National, and Regional Levels; Responsibility of the WCC. The Report of Policy Reference Committee III of the Nairobi Assembly dealt with human rights in Latin America.[20]

In 1975, the CCIA published How to File Complaints of Human Rights Violations by Glenda da Fonseca. It introduces the UN Commission on Human Rights, the International Labour Organization, Other Special Procedures of the UN, Regional Procedures (I. European Commission on Human Rights; II. Inter-American Commission on Human Rights), and Where to obtain documents.[21]

The minutes of the Central Committee meeting at Geneva in 1976 contain a discussion of a Report on Religious Liberty and Human Rights which the WCC General Secretary submitted to the Colloquium held at Montreux, July 24-28, 1976.[22] At the meeting of the Central Committee at Geneva in 1977 an Advisory Group on Human Rights, to deal with the global concerns of the WCC in this field, was proposed. Its various functions were spelled out.[23] The Advisory Group on Human Rights should meet annually, prior to the meeting of the CCIA Commission.

The CCIA presented a Progress Report on Human Rights to the Central Committee, meeting at Kingston, Jamaica in 1979. The Central Committee requested the CCIA "through the Human Rights Advisory Group to continue to give special attention to the incidence of torture; and to aid the churches in their efforts to eradicate torture by sharing amongst them information on other churches' initiatives, and by continuing to provide information regarding the establishment and application of improved international machinery to eliminate torture and other cruel, inhuman or degrading treatment or punishment."[24]


VII

A consultation was held on "Women, Human Rights and Mission" at Venice, Italy, June 24-30, 1979. The report of the consultation includes: I. What is Our Mission (1.Human Rights and Mission - Ruth Sovik; 2. The Struggle for Equality, Develop-

ment and Peace - Lucille Mair);  II. Identification of Issues
(1. Women do not Live in Isolation;  2. Power Relationships
within the Family;  3. Political Prisoners);  III. Where Should
We Go From Here ? - Working Groups (1. Socio-Economic-Political
Structures Which Oppress Women;  2. Employment;  3. Culture and
Conditioning;  4. Women Political Prisoners;  5. Women and
Their Bodies - Sexual Exploitation of Women;  6. Racism and
Racial Justice).25

The CCIA sponsored a consultation on "The Relationship
Between Militarism and Human Rights" at Glion, Switzerland,
November 10-14, 1981.  The consultation was held in order to
study more in detail the precise relationship between militarism and human rights and also to bring together prominent
experts in the field with a view to examining studies which
have already been undertaken, as well as to outline areas which
need more intensified attention in the future.  Papers were
presented on Militarism and Human Rights: Their Interrelation-
ship; Militarism, Technology and Human Rights: The International Repression Trade and Superpower Intervention in the
Third World; National Security Doctrines and Their Impact on
Militarism and Human Rights; Human Rights, Militarization and
Underdevelopment in the Philippines; Militarism and Human
Rights in Puerto Rico.26


                              VII

In Issue 6, "Struggling for Justice and Human Dignity",
the Vancouver Assembly in 1983 expressed itself as follows on
"The Rights of the People":  "The dominant and oppressive
powers collaborate in various forms, and violate people's
rights in manifold ways, including their religious rights and
the rights of the disabled.  The rise of authoritarian and
dictatorial powers, the perversion of the doctrine of national
security, militarization, and the misuse of systems of science
and technology, are integral elements in the oppressive process
that denies the civic, political and cultural rights of the
people in many countries.

"Gross and systematic violations of human rights occur in
most societies.  People suffer arbitrary arrests, torture,
summary executions and disappearance - almost always in extrajudicial forms - and on an unprecedented scale in our time.
Economic domination and unjust social structures suppress the
socio-economic rights of people, such as the basic needs of
families, communities, and the right of workers.  Racial domination denies land rights to indigenous, ethnic and aboriginal
peoples, often leading to the unlawful imprisonment of entire
groups of the population.  Churches are called to be in solidarity with the people, especially those who struggle among
and alongside them in defending their rights, including those
among the churches and Christian communities whose witness -
even to martyrdom - has galvanized the worldwide ecumenical
fellowship."

The Vancouver Assembly also issued a <u>Statement on Human Rights</u>. Turning to <u>lessons from the past</u>, the following was asserted: "Drawing on the International Bill of Human Rights (The Universal Declaration of Human Rights, the United Nations International Covenant on Economic, Social and Cultural Rights, and the United Nations International Covenant on Civil and Political Rights together with its Optional Protocol) and after extensive consultations among the churches, the Nairobi Assembly affirmed its commitment to the promotion of human rights under the following categories: the right to basic guarantees of life; the rights to self-determination, to cultural identity and the rights of minorities; the right to participate in decision-making within the community; the right to dissent; the right to personal dignity; and the right to religious freedom. Following Nairobi, the churches have seen the need to broaden their understanding of human rights to include the right to peace, the right to protection of the environment, the right to development and the right to know one's rights and to struggle for them. We have also come to appreciate more clearly the complexity and inter-relatedness of human rights. In this regard we recognize the need to set individual rights and their violation in the context of society and its social structures.

"We are increasingly aware of the fact that human rights cannot be dealt with in isolation from the larger issues of peace, justice, militarism, disarmament and development. The fuller the rights that every person enjoys in society, the more stable that society is likely to be; the fuller the implementation of human rights globally, the more stable international relations are likely to be. Injustice in a society, including the corruption of public officials, may contribute to domestic, economic and political disorder, which in turn may lead to the deterioration in relations among nations. We have moved beyond mere reflection to concrete engagement in human rights struggles. In doing so, however, we have discovered how difficult and painful it is to cope with human rights and their violations. We have found that in promoting the rights of women, youth, children and disabled persons, for example, the churches need to examine and often alter their own structures and methods of operation. In struggling for justice many Christians are experiencing the way of the cross."

Discussing <u>the future agenda</u> the Vancouver Assembly noted the increasingly sophisticated forms of physical and psychological torture, the practice of "disappearances" and extrajudicial executions, the plight of indigenous people, the employment of a doctrine of national security to justify the denial of basic human rights, the growing climate of religious fanaticism and the rise of political fundamentalism, the right of workers to establish and join trade unions which genuinely represent their interests, the predicament of refugees throughout the world and of migrant workers who face the prevailing problems of unemployment and deprivation of civil liberties in their own countries or in the countries of their adoption.

With regard to <u>implementation</u> the <u>Statement on Human Rights</u> urged "the World Council of Churches and its member churches to continue their practice of a pastoral approach, which combines prayer, preaching and practical efforts in action. We appeal to the churches to dedicate themselves with renewed vigour to raising the consciousness of the people concerning their profound responsibility for the implementation of human rights and for the demonstration of their biblical foundation. The churches and the ecumenical movement should strengthen their work of monitoring, advocacy and study in which they are already engaged.

"... Considerable thought needs to be given to the development of new initiatives in order to improve the churches' record of implementation. Among the possible initiatives that might be undertaken are the announcement of an international day of prayer for human rights, the creation of a world action week for the education of church members and the promotion of human rights, and the establishment of a series of regional and global review conferences to evaluate the work done by the churches in the field of human rights."[27]

The Central Committee meeting at Geneva in 1984 made the following recommendations on human rights:

"1. Regional instruments for human rights should be strengthened in collaboration with regional conferences of churches.
2. Within the framework of the ecumenical consensus on human rights, the diversity of situations in which the churches live and the limitations of many churches have to be taken into account, making necessary a variety of strategies in the advocacy of human rights both in the WCC and in the churches.
3. The right to work also should be given emphasis.
4. The proposal to form a Human Rights Advisory Group is welcomed, and after the composition and functions are determined by the Commission, financial arrangements should be made to ensure regular meetings of the Advisory Group."[28]


VIII


In the Section "<u>Justice and Service</u>" the Sixth Assembly of the Christian Conference of Asia also concentrated on "<u>Human Rights and International Affairs</u>". It stated the following: "Human rights begin with the right to live, which is systematically denied to vast numbers of Asia's people, especially peasants, outcaste and minority peoples, the unemployed and workers in the factories and fields. Hunger, disease and cultural deprivation are the result. Further, those who assert their human dignity against the forces that deprive them are subjected to political deprivation, detention without trial and often to cruel and degrading torture. Labour mouvements are

suppressed. Legal systems are manipulated. Political parties
are made mockeries of the democratic process.

"In all sectors of our societies, women suffer the greatest
denials. They are cast in inferior roles, exploited as cheap
and vulnerable labour sources, enjoyed and degraded as sex
objects, and subjected, when they rise up in protest, to un-
speakably inhuman treatment at the hands of their torturers...

"Why this cruel denial of rights, which appears to be
growing worse ? To traditional inhuman treatment of women and
men sanctified by ancient Asian custom and religion are added
pressures caused by the weakness and dependence of Asian
nations and economies within an international setting controlled by the actions and conflicts of the super-powers. Some
Asian political regimes have made critical choices in the name
of "Revolution", "Development" or "National Security" which
have led to the establishment of authoritarian political control unanswerable to the people. In responding to pressures
from the major economic and political centres, governments have
often impaired or destroyed their own capacity to respond to
the people who suffer most. While economic growth and military
strength make great stirdes, the people are neither developed
nor secure."

The Sixth Assembly of the Christian Conference of Asia made
several recommendations concerning theological understanding
and reflection on human rights, public awareness raising, effective channels of communication and close collaboration with the
World Council of Churches and other bodies concerned about
human rights.[29]

At its Seventh Assembly the Christian Conference of Asia
re-affirmed the findings of the previous assembly and continued
to state: "... Most living religions and religious movements,
and political ideologies prevailing in Asia subscribe to upholding human dignity and working towards a society which will
allow people to live and enjoy a fuller human life. But in
practice what we see is that in most cases the religious and
political structures in Asia have become instruments of dehumanizing large sections of people for the benefit of a small minority. The institutionalized churches in various parts of
Asia tend to support the powers like the state bureaucracy,
the military, police force, feudalism or powerful trading
monopolies, which dominate people and rob them of their rights.

"However, in the Asian scene we also see individuals and
groups who have raised their voices against the violation of
human rights. We see individuals and groups within the church,
other religious communities and secular groups who interpret
their faith or principles to bring out the liberating message
hidden in them, and so provide people with new understanding
of their faith and destiny. They question the rituals,
ceremonies and traditions which have become anti-people and
strive for new rituals, symbols and art forms which will bring
out the message of liberation and human dignity to all.

"We request CCA to give priority in all its programmes to human rights issues in the next quadrennium." The Assembly also made a number of recommendations, in particular that CCA undertake a theological study of violence and non-violence with their implications for the human rights struggle in the Asian context.[30]

In September 1985 a report was published summing up a five years' experiment on the part of the Churches' Human Rights Programme for the Implementation of the Helsinki Final Act, sponsored by the Canadian Council of Churches, the National Council of the Churches of Christ in the USA and the Conference of European Churches. The report describes various developments from 1980 onwards, the delibarations of several consultations and draws a number of conclusions.[31]

## Observations and Comments

1. Ever since 1948 the ecumenical movement has been concerned with violations of human rights, including religious liberty, and with justice which defends the freedom and dignity of human beings. Not only has the list of human rights been gradually extended; the interrelation between human rights and evil structures of society has been more and more stressed. Particularly in the Third World political structures have become instruments of dehumanizing large sectors of the population. In many nations, also in the First and Second World, the violation of human rights has increased to such an extent that the struggle to improve the fate of many people is ever more desparate. The strategies in the advocacy of human rights are so numerous and their limitations so obvious that the problems of network - and confidence building, of communication, education and effective action in the ecumenical movement need continuous new experience, new insight and new commitment. This survey on human rights amply demonstrates the gap between lofty pronouncements and the obedient suiting of actions to words in concrete situations.

2. Creation and redemption play a crucial role in the theological thinking on human rights. God has made the world and humankind to reflect his love and glory. Jesus Christ has reconciled God and the world. The Holy Spirit makes possible human community with a purpose - to grow towards the coming kingdom in which all things are to be fulfilled. The entire function of the church as a reconciling community is under challenge to be reviewed and renewed by the Christian commitment to human rights.

3. Ecclesiastical structures often do not permit participation and action on the levels of decision-making and power politics. Endorsing the status-quo situation of society, churches tacitly favour many forms of discrimination and inequality,

in particular those of women, children, minorities and coloured people. As the compromise with forces of oppression is a historical heritage and a total vision of the gospel is absent, Christian communities often tend to lock themselves up in a sectarian realm of ignorance, innocence and well-being and remain unaware of the fact that hardly any society is exempt from grave human rights problems. The Vancouver Assembly did not hesitate to state that "the churches need to examine and often alter their own structures and methods of operation." The ecumenical notion of the participation of the people is meaningless if church institutions are not conducive to self-examination, confrontation, mobilization and involvement.

4. In many parts of the world there are hopeful signs that oppressed, intimidated and silent people apprehend the reality of their political, socio-economic and personal predicament as they discover and live the liberating forces of the gospel. The relation between true faith and genuine life becomes evident and leads to the courage of systematically denouncing the many violations of human rights in spite of new threats of aggression and humiliation. In some nations Christian communities are one of the voices of protest, if not the only one, against the insidious repression of human rights. Aware of their authentic hopes and aspirations they have begun to organize themselves to guarantee their determined participation in the process of communicating their convictions, of claiming their fundamental individual and collective rights and of supporting new popular and institutional structures which appear as the only valid alternatives.

5. At the meeting of the WCC Central Committee in Buenos Aires in 1985 the presentation of the Argentinian churches on human rights was the most dramatic and challenging event. It has been argued that in comparison to this convincing presentation the discussion of the official theme "God's Justice - Promise and Challenge" was redundant and artificial. It is undoubtedly one of the primary tasks of the World Council of Churches and its constituency to draw attention to people's struggles against the violation of human rights in their daily confrontation with oppressive ruling powers. The complexity, fierceness, anxiety and endurance of these struggles reveal the demonic interconnection between industrial and military interests, the exploitation of natural resources and cheap labour, the inability to face unemployment and underemployment, the arms race and the export of weapons, the monopoly and the manipulation of multinationals, the myth of national security, the economic control of food production, the idolizing of revolutionary change. The rigidity and the radicalization of traditional socio-political models of society must be demythologized "from the bottom up".

The work of Christians for human rights is not for abstractions called "justice" or "liberty" or "equality". Human beings cannot be nourished on ideals alone. Christians work for human rights in order that they and their fellow-human beings might enjoy human rights. Christians work not only to survive, but to fulfill the potential which God has placed in each of them.

The work, therefore, must go on in local communities. People in smaller groupings can sift among choices more easily and learn more quickly what works and what does not work.

Governments (and other structures), on the other hand, which are not accessible to people should be challenged. They can be redesigned in more accountable ways. In this respect the World Council of Churches can serve the churches as an instrument of juridical interpretation of the tension between human rights as international consensus or international law and the claims of the nation-state. The timidity of the churches' witness in the face of human rights violations in their own country needs to be corrected. The creation of a true communication network between parish communities, church councils and groups, and national councils of churches is a first urgency. Improving human rights is an important aid to confidence building and will eventually lead to justice, peace and "undisturbed security" (Isaiah 32). Even though it may take decades the spiritual pilgrimage of the churches can become a distinctive contribution to the world-wide human rights debate.

---

1. The First Assembly of the World Council of Churches held at Amsterdam, August 22 to September 4, 1948. Ed. by W.A. Visser 't Hooft. London: SCM, 1949. pp. 96-99.

2. Minutes and Reports of the Second Meeting of the Central Committee of the World Council of Churches held at Chichester (England), July 9-15, 1949. Geneva: WCC, 1949. p. 21.

3. Minutes and Reports of the Third Meeting of the Central Committee of the World Council of Churches held at Toronto (Canada), July 9-15, 1950. Geneva: WCC, 1950. pp. 72-84.

4. The Evanston Report. The Second Assembly of the World Council of Churches 1954. London: SCM, 1955. pp. 140-141.

5. The New Delhi Report. The Third Assembly of the World Council of Churches 1961. London: SCM, 1962. pp. 276-277.

6. "Witnesses Together", Being the Official Report of the Inaugural Assembly of the East Asia Christian Conference, held at Kuala Lumpur, Malaya, May 14-24, 1959. Ed. by U Kyaw Than. Rangoon, 1959. p. 62.

7. The Christian Community within the Human Community. Containing Statements from the Bangkok Assembly of the EACC, February-March 1964. Madras: Christian Literature Society, 1964. pp. 37-38.

8. The Church in Changing Africa. Report of the All-Africa Church Conference, held at Ibadan, Nigeria, January 10-19, 1958. New York: International Missionary Council, 1958. pp. 56-57.

9. Christians in the Technical and Social Revolutions of Our Time. World Conference on Church and Society, Geneva, July 12-26, 1966. The Official Report. Geneva: WCC, 1967. pp. 136-137.

10. The Uppsala Report 1968. Official Report of the Fourth Assembly of the WCC, Uppsala, July 4-20, 1968. Ed. by Norman Goodall. Geneva: WCC, 1968. pp. 64-65.

11. Central Committee of the World Council of Churches. Minutes and Reports of the Twenty-Fourth Meeting at Addis Ababa, January 10-21, 1971. Geneva: WCC, 1971. pp. 66-71.

12. Central Committee of the World Council of Churches. Minutes and Reports of the Twenty-Fifth Meeting at Utrecht, August 13-23, 1972. Geneva: WCC, 1972. pp. 147-149.

13. Central Committee of the World Council of Churches. Minutes and Reports of the Twenty-Sixth Meeting at Geneva, August 22-29, 1973. Geneva: WCC, 1973. pp. 206-214.

14. Human Rights and Christian Responsibility. Report of the Consultation, St. Pölten, Austria, 21-26 October, 1974. Geneva: WCC, CCIA, 1975.

15. The Struggle for Fundamental Human Rights. Bossey, 1974 (mimeographed).

16. CCIA Background Information, no. 2, 1975.

17. The Churches in International Affairs, Reports 1974-1978. Geneva: CCIA, 1979. pp. 175-183. See also: Ecumenical Review, vol. XXX, no. 1, January 1978.

18. Peace - The Desperate Imperative. The Consultation on Christian Concern for Peace. Baden, Austria, April 3-9, 1970. Geneva: SODEPAX, 1970. pp. 51-72.

19. Sexism in the 1970s. Discrimination Against Women. A Report of a World Council of Churches Consultation, West Berlin 1974. Geneva: WCC, 1975. p. 111.

20. Breaking Barriers. Nairobi 1975. Ed. by David M. Paton. London: SPCK; Grand Rapids: Wm. B. Eerdmans, 1976. pp. 102-107, 115-118, 177-179.

21. Fonseca, Glenda Da. How to File Complaints of Human Rights Violations. A Practical Guide to Inter-Governmental Procedures. Geneva: WCC, CCIA, 1975.

22. Central Committee of the World Council of Churches. Minutes of the Twenty-Ninth Meeting. Geneva, 10-18 August, 1976. Geneva: WCC, 1976. pp. 10-15. The full text of the General Secretary's Report appeared in The Ecumenical Review, vol. XXVIII, no. 4, October 1976.

23. Central Committee of the World Council of Churches. Minutes of the Thirtieth Meeting. Geneva, 28 July - 6 August 1977. Geneva: WCC, 1977.  pp. 106-109.

24. Central Committee of the World Council of Churches. Minutes of the Thirty-First Meeting. Kingston, Jamaica, 1-11 Jan., 1979.  Geneva: WCC, 1979.  pp. 64-66.

25. Report of Conference on Women, Human Rights and Mission. Geneva: WCC, Sub-unit on Women in Church and Society, 1979.

26. CCIA Background Information, 1982/3.

27. Gathered for Life. Official Report of the VI Assembly of the World Council of Churches, Vancouver, Canada, 24 July - 10 August, 1983.  Ed. by David Gill.  Geneva: WCC; Grand Rapids: Wm. B. Eerdmans, 1983.  pp. 88-89, 139-143.

28. Central Committee of the World Council of Churches. Minutes of the Thirty-Sixth Meeting at Geneva, 9-18 July, 1984. Geneva: WCC, 1984.  p. 52.

29. Christian Conference of Asia. Sixth Assembly at Penang, 31 May - 9 June 1977.  pp. 115-117.

30. Christian Conference of Asia. Seventh Assembly at Bangalore, May 18-28, 1981.  pp. 85-86.

31. Tschuy, Theo.  An Ecumenical Experiment in Human Rights. A Publication of the Churches' Human Rights Programme for the Implementation of the Helsinki Final Act.  1985.

# XIV.
# Development

   This survey includes  major statements of assemblies and
conferences and records of a number of consultations on development, developed nations and developing nations.  It deals only
partly with the concern for development education by reason of
limited space.  The subjects and concerns of the just, participatory and sustainable society, world hunger, new life styles,
the church of the poor, transnational corporations, the activities of Specialized Assistance to Social Projects (SASP), the
Ecumenical Church Loan Fund (ECLOF), Ecumenical Assistance to
Development Projects, the Ecumenical Development Fund, and the
project systems of CICARWS and CCPD are not covered in this
survey.

   Development has become a major ecumenical theme since the
Uppsala Assembly in 1968 which did more than make declarations
to the world at large.  It made specific recommendations to the
churches everywhere, in rich countries and poor ones.  It spoke
of the educational and prophetic tasks, as well as the service
functions of the churches.  To determine how the WCC could carry
out its mandate a World Consultation on Ecumenical Assistance
to Development Projects was held at Montreux in 1970 which
recommended the establishment of a new WCC Commission on the
Churches' Participation in Development (CCPD).  This commission
and its constituency has engaged in reflection and action of
world-wide development ever since.


                              I.


   In the Report of Section III, "The Church and the Disorder
of Society", the Amsterdam Assembly in 1948 stated: "... Technical developments have relieved men and women of much drudgery
and poverty, and are still capable of doing more.  There is a
limit to what they can do in this direction.  Large parts of
the world, however, are far from that limit.  Justice demands
that the inhabitants of Asia and Africa, for instance, should
have benefits of more machine production.  They may learn to
avoid the mechanisation of life and the other dangers of an
unbalanced economy which impair the social health of the older
industrial peoples.  Technical progress also provides channels
of communication and interdependence which can be aids to
fellowship, though closer contact may also produce friction."[1]

   Section III, "Social Questions: The Responsible Society in
a World Perspective", of the Evanston Assembly in 1954 contained a sub-section on "The Problems in the Economically
Underdeveloped Regions".  It stated: "Society in Asia, Africa,

and some parts of Latin America today is characterized by the urge to national self-determination in political and economic matters... The peoples of these countries have awakened to a new sense of fundamental human rights and justice and they are in revolt against enslaving political, economic, religious and social conditions. There is also the pressure to achieve changes rapidly. All of the processes of social development - increasing productivity, raising standards of living, democrat- ization and the rest - which have taken centuries in the West, demand in these areas to be completed together and within decades. The temptation is to use irresponsible methods of collectivism, whether of the right or the left, in the desire for rapid results. In such circumstances the Church has the duty to point the way to responsible society and herself to follow it."

The sub-section agreed with "a number of specific points which can be faced and tackled only as world problems and should be the concern of all the churches", outlined by an Ecumenical Study Conference at Lucknow, India, in December 1952: "a) Devel- opment of political institutions; b) Land reform and rural development; c) Industrial development; d) Population; e) Independence and the responsibilities of interdependence."

The conclusion was that "in all these fields, the real dangers are complacency, lack of imagination, and the dull sense of hopelessness that settles upon those of little faith. World economic and social interdependence involves a new di- mension in the task of creating a responsible society, which men will have to face realizing that statistics are only in- adequate indications of desperate human need. Upon Christians rests a special responsibility to see the challenge, to press the governments to take the issue seriously and themselves to act sacrificially..."[2]

In the Report of the Section on "Service" of the New Delhi Assembly in 1961 the following was stated: "... The new nations and their existing political order depend upon their success in achieving rapid economic progress to match the expectations of their peoples. Therefore, they must seek aid where they can and avoid alignments which would limit the sources of assistance. The powerful nations must respect these proper pre-occupations, and should welcome the contributions which non-aligned countries can make in world affairs. The reality of political independence is threatened by economic dependence either upon other countries or upon international industries. Aid from outside is sometimes suspect even when wanted, and is confused by the number of agencies and missions seeking to give it. There is need for more effective use of international agencies to ensure a correlation and simplification of aid programmes and their adjustment to real needs, and also res- ponsible administration by the receiving countries of the proffered resources. But above all the churches must not cease to champion the cause of making the riches of the developed countries available to those poor in resources."

In the Report of the Committee of CCIA to the Assembly a
section was devoted to <u>Problems of New and Developing Countries</u>.
It was stated: "... The urgency of the situation in less developed countries and the rising expectations of their people
call not only for a quantitative increase in assistance but for
a qualitative planning, so that the best results may be secured
within a reasonable span of time. Frustrated expectations may
lead people to destructive revolt rather than along the path
of peaceful revolution... In the long run trade, not aid, is
the most effective instrument in furthering development. International co-operation to secure effective markets for the developing countries is necessary. Safeguards against the impact on
the economics of these countries of changes in international
monetary policies and of fluctuations in prices, both of primary
commodities and of machinery for productive purposes, have to
be developed.

"... Aid can never be and should not be a one-way affair.
Out of their rich cultural heritage, the developing nations
have much to contribute to the enrichment of the life of the
people of the world as a whole. Nations should contribute to
each other from the wealth of their wisdom, experience and
other resources that the life of each may be the richer for
it."[3]

II.

In the Report on "<u>Reshaping the Pattern of Missionary
Activity</u>" of the IMC Assembly at Willingen in 1952 a section
was devoted to <u>Technical Assistance and Welfare Services</u>. The
following was stated: "... Believing that the extreme inequalities of wealth between different areas constitute a
challenge to the Christian conscience, we consider that it is
the duty of Christians everywhere to encourage and assist the
governments concerned in programmes for raising the standard
of living of the hungry and under-privileged areas of the world.

"... We therefore urge governments and other agencies
offering technical assistance: 1) To recognize the fundamental
rights and the cultural heritage of the peoples served. 2) To
give attention, in selecting technical experts, not only to
professional qualifications but also to the moral and spiritual
requirements of the work they do. 3) To co-operate with
nationals already engaged in working for technical and welfare
services, and to foster their training and development. 4) To
concentrate effort upon those fundamental improvements which
will enable the people to help themselves. 5) To include in
the capital estimates for any given project an item for the
provision of needed welfare services. 6) To avoid any confusion of long-range technical aid with mutual obligations
for defence."[4]

In a Report on "<u>Christian Concerns in Economic and Social
Development</u>", received by the Central Committee in 1958,
attention was drawn "to the following vital points:

1. Social and economic progress require balanced programmes of social and economic development, including agriculture, industry, basic services, education and health programmes. Christians should be aware of the inter-relationship of such programmes as well as sensitive to the effects on people of these vast changes.

2. Economic assistance takes many forms. This variety has many advantages, but requires better correlation, preferably under United Nations auspices, so that assistance can be more rationally planned, with safeguards against misuse, and can gain more dynamic public support. Regional development schemes may favour the kind of joint planning required for effective collaboration and mutual respect.

3. Far more grants and generous loans are essential. Contributing countries need to work out long-term policies for their assistance. If at least one per cent of the national income of countries were devoted to these purposes, the picture would become much more hopeful. So that people can recognize their responsibilities and failures, we need both at the international and at the governmental level a clear statement of what is being done and how it is being done.

4. In pressing for further assistance we are aware that this raises a number of economic difficulties for contributing countries. It may require an increase in private savings from foreign investment and an increase in taxation where aid comes from public funds. Such assistance may also make it possible for a country to utilise to a greater extent its own productive capacity. As Christians, we call on nations to make the necessary adjustments in their economic policies.

5. Trade and monetary policies of the more developed countries often have a quite disproportionate effect on the ability of the less developed countries to carry out their development programmes. The former need to take fully into account the international effect of their policies. This particularly concerns their attitude to schemes for stabilizing commodity prices, whose instability is often crippling to underdeveloped countries.

6. International private investment has an important role to play, and both receiving and contributing countries have to follow constructive policies so that such investment can be stimulated to share responsibility in the common task.

7. Economic aid will be most effective only when there is honorable trusteeship in the administration of such developmental plans. Governments and their leaders should be scrupulously responsible in their relations to each other and realize the need of public confidence."[5]


III.


Church and Society engaged in the fifties in an ecumenical study on "The Common Christian Responsibility Toward Areas of Rapid Social Change". A Second Statement on this subject in 1956 included chapters on: Impact of the West and International Co-operation; Social Change in Rural Communities; Industrialization and Urbanization; Responsible Citizenship.

In the Conclusion it was stated: "... A common obstacle to Christian action in society is the bewilderment of Christians who confront for the first time the multiplicity and the complexity of the problems of rapid social change. Sometimes this spiritual bewilderment leads Christians to a negative attitude toward all change. Sometimes it results in an apocalyptic dramatisation of hopes and fears. Christians can guard against such bewilderment by a deepening of their faith. As followers of the One Who said, 'Behold I will make all things new', we must demonstrate in our thought and action that new life in men and their societies is a part of God's purpose for the world and that our task of social witness, service and redemptive action is never finished but will continue 'until He come'."[6]

The Report of an International Ecumenical Study Conference at Thessalonica, in 1959 on "Christian Action in Rapid Social Change" included a third part on Christian Responsibility for Economic Development, and was subdivided as follows: I. Economic Change - Its Dynamic Nature and the Opportunities it Provides for Men; II. The Christian Attitude Towards the Development of the World's Resources; III. The Fundamental Conditions of Efficient and Responsible Economic Change; IV. Choices, Cost and Values in Economic Development.

Regarding spiritual dangers in economic development it was stated: "Support of economic development in Africa, Asia and Latin America is, in our view, a responsibility of Christians toward God and their fellowmen. It does not, however, carry within itself any guarantee against new spiritual and moral dangers nor the assurance of an ultimate solution to man's deepest problems. This is an illusion from which the Christian view of man should free us and against which we should contend as we work with others to further economic development. These dangers are latent in man's ignorance and in his pride and disobedience. They are revealed in all aspects of life, including the economic. We suggest a few of these dangers which appears at various levels of economic development: 1. Men do not necessarily know how to consume responsibly; 2. Men become absorbed in the means and techniques that make for an affluent society; 3. When men get richer they worship riches and forget God; 4. Society may become marked by new forms of social stratification, conspicuous consumption, and status seeking, as people look for marks and symbols of personal prestige and success; 5. Men may become slaves of the production machine and victims of the vast and elaborate apparatus upon which they have come to depend for material abundance."

Concerning perfection impossible the following was expressed: "It is impossible to foresee an ideal pattern of economic development without difficult problems. Some costs in human hardship and misery are inevitable. It will often be necessary to work out proximate goals and least-harmful measures. Christians must accept the hard facts of economic life and be ready to take the necessary choices and to run the unavoidable risks."[7]

The East Asia Christian Conference at Kuala Lumpur in 1959 stated the following on Recommendations for Study on Economic and Social Development: "Some necessary projects for the churches and national councils in Asia are as follows:

1) Study groups involving laymen, such as economists and trade union leaders and businessmen, are needed in many countries to keep the church informed of important developments in economic life and to provide a Christian interpretation of the basic problems of economic growth.

2) Special consultations on specific issues are also needed: the meaning of the responsible society in rural areas undergoing chance; the social problems of the new industrial urban areas; the effects of shifting population from rural to town, impact of city on family and individual; the problem of trade unions and other mass movements; the Christian understanding of work and vocation in newly industrialized societies; working conditions in industry; the task of the church in witnessing to new industrial workers."8

IV.

The Report of Section I, "Economic Development in a World Perspective" of the World Conference on Church and Society at Geneva in 1966 was made up of the following parts: I. Introduction; II. The Changing Economic and Social Pattern of the Advanced Countries (Three Types of Economic Policy, Assessment of Different Economic Systems, Challenges to the Various Systems, Ethical Problems of Consumption, Income, Wages and Prices, Ethical Problems of Work with Changing Technology, Men in Affluent Societies); III. Issues of Special Importance to Developing Countries (Motivations for Growth, Physical Resources Needed for Development, The Development of Human Resources, The Population Question, Problems of Labour Migration, Food and Agricultural Productivity, International Transfer of Capital and Skills, The Institutional Basis of Development, Pattern of Development); IV. World Economic Relations (The Present Structures of World Economic Relations, Towards an International Development Standard, The Role of the Churches: The Pastoral Ministry in the Context of World Economic Relations, The Educational Task of the Church, The Challenge to the Churches); V. Conclusions and Recommendations.

On the problem of development in advanced countries the following was stated: "In the next twenty years, barring major political or military disasters, the economies of the developed world will continue to grow... All richer countries have to work out a balance of policies relating to full employment and the distribution of income among individuals, among regions, and among rich and poor countries. There are many objectives of economic policy other than growth: price stability, balance of payments equilibrium, the balance between private and public enterprise, freedom of personal choice, increase of leisure, the progress of knowledge, and improvement in the quality of all aspects of life, as well as keeping within bearable limits the insecurity and violence to which rapid evolution necessarily exposes every man. There are legitimate differences of judgement about the relative importance of these objectives; the balance between them is the source of most political controversy both within and between countries."

On issues of special importance to developing countries the following was outlined: "... Economic development depends upon three basic factors: motivations, resources, and institutions. These differ from country to country, and what is perhaps more significant, their inevitable interactions also differ in nature and magnitude. The basic problem of economic development is to determine how these forces operate, how they can be modified in order that the objectives of the society may be achieved, and what new interactions of these forces occur as economic development takes place. Not all of these interactions may be conducive to sustained economic growth.

"In some countries economic development may demand a profound revolutionary change in structure of property, income, investment, expenditure, education, and political and administrative organization, as well as in the present patterns of international relations. However, there can be no universal prescription for economic development. In an age in which international economic development has become a social and political creed, the special problems of development within each country or region must be understood in terms of both the internal and external forces at play, and must be tackled in their own context and within that of the community of nations. Economic development is a common objective, but it is vain to search for simple formulae to understand it, and a uniform pattern to achieve it."

The following was stated on world economic relations: "Technological progress gives mankind the possibility of eradicating want and misery from the face of the earth. If it is to do this, growth of power must be matched by growth of responsibility. Increasingly national economic policies have been geared to growth with social justice. The challenge of our times is to extend this understanding to the world community. All our fine phrases about 'human solidarity', 'one world', etc. sound hollow in the face of increasing international inequalities. If contemporary economic and social policies are failing to arrest this tendency, they must be radically altered. It is not enough to say that the world cannot continue to live half developed and half underdeveloped: this situation must not be allowed to continue. Therefore, all nations, particularly those endowed with great economic power, must move beyond limited self-interest and see their responsibility in a world perspective. The Church must say clearly and unequivocally that there is a moral imperative behind international economic cooperation. (The conference recognized that these are highly complex questions on which further detailed study is needed)."[9]

## V

It is difficult to summarize the most important insights of the Report of Section III, "World Economic and Social Development" of the Uppsala Assembly in 1968. This assembly will be long remembered for its strong emphasis on development and remains still today the charter of a main task of all the churches and of the ecumenical movement itself.

The major points were:

1) Christians in the latter part of the twentieth century must learn the moral issues in the economic life of the world as they came to see those issues at the end of the nineteenth and the beginning of the twentieth century in the life of individual nations.

2) Neo-isolationism is gaining ground in both developed and developing nations because they earlier supposed that world development could be accomplished without "radical changes in institutions and structures at three levels: within developing countries, within developed countries, and in the international economy." These changes will not come without a new instillation of a morality which includes total human solidarity and world-wide justice. "If our false security in the old and our fear of revolutionary change tempt us to defend the status quo or to patch it up with half-hearted measures, we may all perish."

3) "... Since mankind is politically organized in nation-states, these instruments have to be related to the politics of sovereign nations." In a world which is becoming unified technically at an amazing pace, the political instrumentalities to cope with that new fact must be developed, and churches must be concerned even politically (in this sense) or they will be irrelevant to the real solutions of the development problems. "No structures - ecclesiastical, industrial, governmental or international - lie outside the scope of the churches' task..."

4) Public opinion must be persuaded to support changes in both developed and developing nations. Not only must the churches work at this programme of education, but "students and the intelligentsia can play a crucial role in the shaping of public opinion... Powerful political lobbies are essential to create the necessary conditions of commitment to development."

5) "The central issue in development is the criteria of the human. We reject a definition of development which makes man the object of the operation of mechanical forces..." The humanization of modern technological life must be a chief concern of the churches in both developed and developing nations. It must not be taken for granted that modernization, as such, is good for human beings. A variety of cultures, a distribution of power, non-discrimination with respect to race, class or sex, must be included in the churches' concerns.

6) The production and distribution of food in the coming years must be a technical preoccupation of all who are interested in development. The population explosion lays heavy burdens upon nations which are attempting to develop technologically. Means of population control must be sought and implemented even though Christians are divided on the question of what are the moral means for family planning.

It was recommended that the churches should appeal to governments of developed nations "as a first step, to increase annually the percentage of GNP (Gross National Product) officially transferred as financial resources to developing countries with a minimum net amount of 1 per cent to be reached by 1971."

Regarding the individual task the following was outlined: "The individual Christian is called:
1) to know the facts about areas of poverty and Christian responsibility for economic justice;
2) to pray for the needs of men everywhere and to seek wisdom and courage to meet them;
3) to engage in constant dialogue with others and to join with them informing groups pledged to launch a constructive effort of education and commitment;
4) to urge educational authorities to include information about development in their curricula;
5) to become involved in projects of community development;
6) to make the issue of development a major factor in his electoral choice and in other political commitments;
7) in developed countries, to make available for development aid, by means of a voluntary self-tax procedure, a percentage of his income related to the difference between what his government spends in development  aid and what it should spend for this purpose;
8) to consider the challenge of world development in deciding on one's vocation and career;
9) to make a personal commitment of his resources, personal and material, to the struggle for human dignity, freedom and justice."[10]


## VI.

The social encyclical of Paul VI Populorum Progressio ("On the Development of Peoples") in 1967 was undoubtedly one of the most significant statements of modern times. The document contains two parts: For Man's Complete Development and, The Development of the Human Race in the Spirit of Solidarity. It stated unequivocally the Church's support for the revolutionary hopes of the world's poor and oppressed peoples and made explicit recommendations for radical social and economic reforms to help realize these hopes. The Church must follow the example of the Incarnate Word; it cannot be disincarnate without betraying its mission. This theme is prominent in the encyclical (cf. pars. 12,14,15-16,21,28,32,74,80-81). The practical application of the supreme Christian virtue of love must become manifest in economic and social fruits among human beings.

The Christian vision of man does not deny but rather absolutely demands a true humanism which will be open to the transcendent action of Christ (par. 16). It is a direct response to Marxist humanism, which is closed to a higher synthesis of the human and divine orders. To work for more humane conditions among men is, in reality, to work for the extension of the spirit

of Christ, the extension of the Gospel into the world of men
(par. 32). Those who turn to the poor and the weak are turning
to the very person of Christ, who is identified with these
(par. 74). Thus a universal fraternity is born from these
efforts to secure social justice among men; the resulting peace
and harmony is premonition of the perfect peace and justice to
be established when Christ comes to inaugurate the final kingdom (par. 80).11


## VII.


In a Letter to Member Churches, the Central Committee,
meeting at Canterbury in 1969, expressed the following:
"... Clearly what moved people most at Uppsala was a vivid
awareness of human solidarity in Christ 'the new man'. The
widening gap between rich and poor was therefore seen as a
direct challenge to Christian conscience and it brought many
of our churches to action. Within a few months of Uppsala,
a number of churches began to consider how they could set apart
some of their resources for development. Self-tax movements
sprang up in a number of countries. Conferences made issues
of world-wide social and racial justice and development the
major themes of their study. Churches saw the need to educate
their own membership and influence public opinion towards a
new awareness of these problems. Youth especially took them
seriously and carried our Assembly recommendations to the heart
of their church's life. We are also grateful that in these as
in many other areas, we can increasingly work together with
our Roman Catholic brothers. In many places these issues gave
new impetus to ecumenical action both locally and internationally. We learned more about the unity of mankind and
the unity of the church."

The Report of the Central Committee contained also in
Appendix XI a report of the Staff Working Party on Development,
"World Council of Churches' Concern for Development". It was
composed of the following parts: I. The challenge of Uppsala
and the response of the churches; II. Plans of WCC units in
the field of development; III. Three Areas of common concern:
a) A fuller Christian understanding of development; b) Development education; c) Assistance to development projects; IV. Urgent
Issues Demanding Our Attention (e.g. relationships with mission
bodies of the churches, with the Roman Catholic Church, and with
international development agencies like UNDP, FAO and UNESCO).12

The Central Committee meeting at Utrecht in 1972 recommended
1) "that the 2 per cent for development appeal to member churches of the World Council be renewed; 2) that in renewing the
appeal stress be laid on: the call to sacrifice and to the
commitment of the whole life of the Church with the 2 per cent
figure being no more than indicative..."

It further encouraged the churches to:
"a) Reflect on the process of development and the root causes of underdevelopment and to examine their own structures as well as those of their own national society, with a view to assessment as to whether those are help or hindrance to the development concept.
b) Help Christians and others to understand the development process and to motivate them for effective participation in that process...
c) Offer active support for efforts which are aimed at such change of structures which will guarantee the poor majority a fair share in the economic, social and cultural resources of their country and responsible participation in shaping their destiny...
d) To bring such pressure to bear that the national resources are mobilized for use in strategic areas for the benefit of the poor majority in the total community and to examine and take appropriate action for the mobilization and redeployment of the churches' own resources, including investment capital, landed property and human resources for development purposes."[13]

The Report of a World Consultation on Ecumenical Assistance to Development Projects, held at Montreux in 1970, contained, besides several individual addresses, the reports of five Working Groups:  I. The Debate about Development;  II. Policy and Procedures for Church Support to Development Projects; III.Structure and Organisation of Ecumenical Assistance to Development Projects;  IV. Technical Assistance for Church Sponsored Development;  V. The Mobilization of Funds.

The following recommendations were made:
1) We propose all churches accept now as an objective for their giving in 1971 a minimum of two per cent of their regular income from all sources...
2) We recommend that part of such and other resources for development be made available for a World Development Fund... In order to initiate such a fund, we propose at least 10 million dollars for 1970.
3) ... Not only a redeployment of the annual income of all church bodies (contributions of individuals to churches, capital income and other income) should be taken into consideration, but also a redeployment of the church capital which is invested in land, buildings, investment portfolios, etc... The discussion should lead to decisions on long-term commitments whereby the two per cent should be considered as nothing more than a minimum for 1972 and the following years."[14]


VIII.


The Report of the Conference of Society, Development and Peace (SODEPAX) at Beirut in 1968 on "World Cooperation for Development" stated in the introduction the following: "... We live in a new world of exciting prospects.  For the first time in history men can see the unity of mankind as a reality.  For

the first time in history we know that all men could enjoy the
prosperity that has hitherto been enjoyed by a few.  The new
technological possibilities turn what were dreams into realities.
The adventure of cooperation with all men for the development of
the earth for all men is open for all of us, and youth at least
is aware of its pull.  As of today we have the means, so we are
without the excuse of ignorance about the condition of men
throughout the earth.  It is one world and the gross inequalities
among the peoples of different nations and different continents
are as inexcusable as the gross inequalities within nations."

At the end of the Report it was stated: "... Joint action
for development will serve basic Christian aims.  To work for
development is to express in practical measures the aspiration
for brotherhood and human dignity of every individual...
Development can gradually reduce the gross imbalances that
promote instability; working together can encourage a wider
sense of community among mankind...  Thus, in supporting the
development effort, the churches will be true to one of the
most basic commands of the Christian faith: 'to love thy neigh-
bor as thyself'.  And they will also be playing their proper
part in the long, arduous task of building a more stable international order of well-being and peace for the whole human
family."15

A conference of SODEPAX at Montreal, 1969, on "The Challenge
of Development" was a sequel to the Beirut Conference in 1968.
This conference re-defined the concept of development, examined
structures, patterns and objectives of aid, and concentrated on
specific issues (agriculture and nutrition, industrialization,
environmental pollution, urbanization and employment, population
pressures and responsible parenthood, terms of trade, tariffs,
preference and access to markets, distribution of economic power,
technology, education).  The conference was critical of the use
of such words as 'aid', 'technical assistance', and 'free trans-
fers' as they are symptomatic of the continuous paternalistic
tendency of the developed countries to limit or even remove the
possibilities of self-determination in the underdeveloped coun-
tries.16

A Consultation on "Christian Concern for Peace" at Baden,
Austria in 1970, sponsored by SODEPAX, stated the following:
"... What is our response to the need for development ? ... The
radical meaning of peace as wholeness of life coincides with
the biblical conception of justice, the loving purpose of God
for all mankind.  Christ is socially present in the poor and
oppressed of the world.  He speaks to us from their conditions
and circumstances and demands a response from those who profess
to be his followers.  It is in this sense that development, the
struggle of the poorer nations for a better life, is the new
name for peace."17

## IX

In the Report of an Exploratory Conference on "Technology, Faith and the Future of Man", held at Geneva in 1970, the following paragraphs were of significance: "... Bearing in mind that every year millions of people in the Third World die of hunger and disease creeping in under the shadow of famine and that the working capacity of the living is severely hampered by hunger and disease, and bearing in mind that the industrial countries are almost exclusively responsible for this situation, we can see how close we really are already to the silent violence of the B weapons. The aid we fail to give is in many quarters seen as a war-like offensive against the underdeveloped countries.

"... How can the highly industrialized countries be saved from their own industry, and what can the developing countries do to advance the quality of life for their people without repeating the mistakes of the West ? This calls for drastic new thinking on all sides. Perhaps the 'have' nations must cease dreaming of endlessly rising standards of living and start working instead for what will constitute, in the light of the dual imperatives of world-scale economic justice and ecological sanity, a reasonable standard of living. It may even, some suggest, entail 'de-development' by the affluent nations to a lower level of resource consumption."

"... It speaks volumes for the provincialism of the rich nations that people can speak so glibly of an end to man's desperate struggle for survival - as if the poor nations did not exist or were no concern of theirs. The West certainly does need a new set of goals, but paramount among these must be commitment to global economic justice which will include the more effective transfer of technology and its benefits to industrially backward areas."[18]

The Report of a World Conference on "Science and Technology for Human Development", held at Bucharest in 1974, was composed of the following sections: I. The Significance for the Future of Pressures of Technology and Population on Environment, and of Natural Limits to Growth; II. Self-Reliance and the Technological Options of Developing Countries; III. Quality of Life and the Human Implications of Further Technological Change; IV. Human Settlements as a Challenge to the Churches; V. World Social Justice in a Technological Age; VI. The Theological Understanding of Humanity and Nature in a Technological Era. Within these five sections subjects of importance to the concern of development were: A New Ethic of Resource Use; A Long-Term Concept of a Sustainable and Just Society; Technology, Power and Justice: Perspectives for Developing Countries; Third World People in Affluent Society; Economic Structures for International Justice.

In the introduction of the Report it was stated on "Justice and Interdependence": "... Humanity faces the urgent task of devising social mechanisms and political structures that encourage genuine interdependence, and will replace mechanisms and structures that maintain domination and subservience. Contemporary societies, highly organized around intricate technologies, coordinate the activities of immense numbers of people. Vast aggregates of power - economic and political and social - inevitably arise... It becomes increasingly important to distinguish between policies that require centralized decisions, for the sake of the safety and the quality of life of many people, and policies that can be determined locally by smaller communities. It likewise becomes important to distinguish between those areas where individual gain must yield to social need and those where personal conscience is inviolable and personal spontaneity desirable. New institutional devices are required to enable people to participate in the decisions that affect them."

With regard to Economic Structures for International Social Justice the Bucharest Conference stated: "... A qualitative change has to take place in the rich nations, involving an examination of their previous assumptions about world development and their predominant role in it. In addition the development of a new political will is of the utmost importance. Without this a new strategy and the new institutions will never be realized. At the moment, the educated élite, the owners of capital and the governments of affluent nations are not prepared to accept such a strategy and to convince their people of its necessity. What is required is a process that will demonstrate to all social strata that the world is one, that all peoples have a common interest and that humanity will only be able to survive if it lives according to the responsibilities deriving from this interdependence. A new political will is of utmost importance."19

The Director's Report to the Assembly of the Commission on World Mission and Evangelism, meeting at Bangkok in 1973, stated the following: The early tradition of Christian mission, having been concerned with justice and welfare of people, "has been wonderfully carried forward in the past two hundred years or so by the modern missionary movement from Europe and North America to the rest of the world, through the preaching and teaching of the Gospel, through education, medical care, agricultural and social work. And yet, the facts of the past decade show the continuing appalling exploitation by the rich nations of the poor nations, even in the name of development. Development has been seen purely in economic terms and that means on the basis of the structures, values and dynamics of societies which adhere to the doctrine of the survival of the fittest. A closer look at the situation shows clearly that the rich nations are spiritually and morally underdeveloped, functioning on the philosophy of aggressive individual and corporate egoism. Development, like mission, must be seen to involve all six continents."20

A multilateral dialogue of Buddhists, Christians, Hindus,
Jews and Muslims, who met at Colombo, Sri Lanka in 1974, stated
the following on A Provisional Approach to "World Community":
"... If physical realities of economics and politics constitute
evidence, then world community can already be observed in embryo.
In view of this some of us are already anxious as to how existing or potential deformities may be avoided or overcome. We may
also be challenged by a vision of how such a community could
mature, in many forms and styles.  Such a vision should not be
a new and alternative social or spiritual absolute, but could
give a spirit of unity in diversity, could challenge false
absolutes, and could sustain those who choose or are forced
into disengagement from existing structures which they see as
unjust or blasphemous.

"The fundamental assumptions behind science and technology
as world-objectifying approaches to reality need to be examined.
Some feel that the normal evolutionary development of the forces
now operative in the world is more likely to lead to global
catastrophe than to world community.  According to them only a
radically new approach to reality going beyond our present type
of science and technology can hope to achieve a new pattern of
human existence in which authentic and just world community
could be achieved.  It was thus recognized that any notion of
world community would always be provisional.  It must remain
a transcendent ideal whose functional importance is proportional
to its usefulness as a criterion for evaluation and as an
orientation point for all human social achievements."[21]

In its Report on Giving Account of the Hope That is Within
Us, the Faith and Order Commission, meeting at Accra in 1974,
expressed the following: "... There have now appeared in many
Asian societies such growing problems as the widening gap
between the rich and the poor, the exploitation of the majority
by international economic and technological expansion, and the
increasing suppression of basic freedom and people's participation in nation-building in the name of law and order...
Because the traditional cultural, spiritual, and moral values
which held sway in the pre-secular societies have been under-
mined by the acids of modern civilization, there is now a quest
for a new spirituality, a new set of moral values and a new
authority.

"... In these situations, Christians in Asia are hard pressed
for a re-examination of their understanding of the nature of the
Church, its mission and unity.  They are facing the task of
articulating in words and deeds what it means to have one hope
in Jesus Christ in specific Asian situations.  The answer may
be found in the Christian's concrete participation in the task
of nation-building, in their  discriminating discernment of his
redeeming and renewing work in the nations, and in their identification with and alertness to the sufferings and aspirations
of their fellowmen.  Between now and the coming of Christ,
Christians in Asia are called to be the clear signs of his
promise that He is making all things new."[22]

## X

A number of consultations on development took place between
1968 and 1975. "The Problem of Development in the Light of
Christian Social Ethics and Business Experience" was the subject
of a consultation at Rotterdam, June 6-7, 1968. It was sponsored
by the Department on Church and Society and UNIAPAC, and had by
its nature an outspoken Western character. Six basic questions
on development were discussed. It was recommended that officials
of international business organizations be deeper involved in
the concerns of the ecumenical movement.[23]

At a consultation on "World Development" at Rome, March 1969,
chaired by J.R. Nelson, the churches' responsibility to assist
in the development of Third World nations was stressed. There
were 90 participants. The Food and Agriculture Organization,
the Pontifical Commission Justice and Peace, the World Food
Programme, the Freedom of Hunger Campaign and the Commodities
Division for the UN Commission on Trade and Development were
represented.[24]

Twenty-eight theologians from various denominations and all
continents participated in a consultation at Cartigny, Switzerland, November 1969 on the theme "In Search of a Theology of
Development", sponsored by SODEPAX. Preparatory papers were
prepared by P. Löffler, R.A. Alves, J. Moltmann, A. Sigmond,
V. Cosmao, G. Gutierrez, Ph. Land, T. Rentdorff. Papers were
read by J.C. Bennett, Ch. Elliott, P. Löffler, B. Lambert,
D. Jenkins, Ph. Land, V. Cosmao.[25]

"The Interests of the Developing Countries and International
Monetary Reform" was the subject of discussion at a consultation
in Geneva, February 1970, organized by SODEPAX. The report and
the background documents of the consultation were offered to
the churches as a help to the senzitization of a wider public
to the issues raised. Papers were presented by C.M. Elliott,
A.N. McLeod, J. Márquez, E. Kemenes, J.B. Zulu.[26]

A consultation on "Church - Communication - Development",
at Driebergen, Holland, March 12-16, 1970, sponsored by SODEPAX ,
brought together 55 specialists in the mass media communications
of the various churches from 20 countries. The Report contains
in Section I  20 preparatory notes, prepared by various experts,
and in Section II the papers of the consultation, the final
document and the report of the newly formed SODEPAX Communications Working Group for Africa.[27]

A conference on "Liberation, Justice, Development" at Tokyo,
July 14-22, 1970 was jointly sponsored by the EACC and SODEPAX.
Among the 180 participants were also representatives of the
major religions from Asia, consultants of the UN, the WCC, the
Vatican, and fraternal delegates from Africa, the Pacific,
Europe and North America. The main work of the conference
centred around seven working groups:  A) Rural and Agricultural

Development;  B) The Role of the Church in Urban and Industrial
Development;  C) Education and Communication for Cultural Trans-
formation;  D) The Role of the Church in World Co-operation for
Development and Self-Reliance;  E) Influencing Structural and
Institutional Change;  F) Health Development and Population
Growth;  G) Theological Perspectives.  The Report concluded with
a Statement on Organizational Follow-Up at National and Regional
Levels.[28]

"The Churches in Development Planning and Action" was the
theme of a consultation at Limuru, Kenya, January, 1971,
organized by SODEPAX.  Church leaders and individual Christians
from Botswana, Kenya, Lesotho, Malawi, Tanzania, Uganda and
Zambia participated, discussed the ecumenical involvement in
development work, and issued a call for the transfer of greater
powers of decision making from the donors to the recipients so
that the relation between them could become more genuinely one
of partnership.  The report was addressed to the churches for
their consideration and appropriate action.[29]

A consultation on the theme "Called To Be", at Chaguaramas,
Trinidad, November 15-21, 1971, was organized by a Planning
Committee which included Archbp. S. Carter, J. Montalvo, E.
Desueza, D. Chaplin, I. Hamid, J. Grace, R. Cuthbert.  Papers
were presented by R. Neehall (Justice, Liberation and the Christian Gospel);  G.S. Ramphal (The Search for Caribbean Identity);
Bp. R. Adames (Conscientization).  Eight study papers (booklets)
were issued in preparation of the consultation, all published
by the Caribbean Ecumenical Consultation for Development. A further consultation took place in Port-of-Spain, Trinidad, November 22-24, 1971.[30]

A first conference in Africa of Christian communicators,
both Catholic and Protestant, on "Communications in Development",
took place at Lusaka, Zambia, December 1971.  Five delegates,
specialists in either the electronic media or in the print media,
came from Kenya, Malawi, Tanzania, Uganda and Zambia.  The conference concentrated on basic principles for effective communication in development and issued a number of resolutions and
recommendations for action.  Ecumenical communications reports
for the five African countries were given.  The Report of the
conference was issued on behalf of SODEPAX and the Communications Departments of the National Christian Councils and the
Catholic Episcopal Conference of East and West Africa.[31]

A consultation at Codrington College, Barbados, January
3-8, 1972 on "Church - Communications - Development" received
and studied the findings of the consultation which was held at
Chaguaramas, Trinidad, in November 1971.  Major addresses were
given by A. Clarke, D. Mitchell, H. Cholmondeley, A. van Dulst.
The report includes also a message to the churches, reports of
the workshops and a section on interpretation and priorities.
The consultation was sponsored jointly by the Caribbean Christian Communications Network (CCCN), Christian Action for
Development in the Caribbean (CADEC) and SODEPAX.[32]

Some 70 theologians, political scientists, educators, economists and sociologists participated in a consultation on "Power and Development" at Aguas Buenas, Puerto Rico, February 25 - March 4, 1973. The meeting, sponsored by CCPD, searched for ways and means of political action, especially church action in North America and Western Europe. In addition to working groups there were three public sessions: 1) An analysis of a giant multinational corporation by R. Philipps; 2) A speech and a film on the work of the United Farm Worker's Union by J. Govea; 3) A presentation of the case for Puerto Rican independece and freedom from economic and cultural dominance and exploitation by the United States.[33]

XI.

Section VI, "Human Development: Ambiguities of Power, Technology and Quality of Life", of the Nairobi Assembly in 1975 stressed the following: "... More than ever before, we find it difficult to articulate our understanding of the development concept and consequently to decide on the patterns of participation in the development process. In the past few years there have been many conscious efforts to give human development a conceptual clarity that it lacked, but the relation between concept and reality seems to become more diffused and more evasive. The uncertainties and ambiguities resulting from this situation are made more pronounced because of the few certainties that cannot be evaded: that after two decades of efforts to remove poverty and reduce inequality there are today more people in the grips of dire poverty and the gap between the rich and the poor has widened; that in a world with tremendous technological possibilities, there is the persisting threat of famine; that in the spaceship earth the expenditure on armaments is steadily mounting; that in numbers mankind is continuing to grow at an unprecedented rate. In the quest for development, thus, we fund ourselves caught in a pensive mood, raising many questions and finding few answers.

"... In recent years the development concept has been seriously challenged by the 'limits to growth' debate. While controversies still remain about the immediacy of the depletion of physical resources, the debate has brought to the light the excessive utilization of the resources of the world by a small affluent minority. It has also been shown that 'growth' in an economic order based on the so-called 'free market' system has a built-in exploitative tendency where resources are unevenly distributed. In this context Christians are called upon to examine carefully the patterns of utilization, control, and ownership of resources."

Many subtle forms of neo-colonialism, particularly visible in trans-national corporations, "play an important role in shaping the world economy not only in countries based on the principle of private ownership of means of production, but also in relation to trade with the socialist world. These corporations claim to bring capital and technology to countries where they operate and thereby to create employment and income. But essentially, their aim is to take advantage of the cheap labour that is available in the host countries and to draw out profits from them, making use of the immense control they exercise over world trade and prices. It must be mentioned that their operations in the poorer countries are with the approval of national governments and often in active collaboration with local private business enterprises. But the type of goods they produce is meant invariably to satisfy the needs of an elite class, the technology they use is ill-suited for the needs of these countries, and the employment they create and the incomes they generate are only to the advantage of the higher income groups in the host countries."[34]

The Central Committee in 1976 stressed that, regarding studies by CCPD, top priority should be given to the New International Economic Order and transnational corporations. In 1979, it recommended that "CCPD should give high priority to the study of the concepts of collective self-reliance and economic 'de-linking' between developing and developed countries", and should explore "the relationship between the study on the Church and the poor and the analysis of economic theory and systems." In 1980, the Central Committee approved of the CCPD study document "Towards a Church in Solidarity with the Poor" and asked the churches "responding to the WCC appeal (made at the Uppsala Assembly, and later reiterated at the Nairobi Assembly and the Central Committee meeting in Kingston, Jamaica) to contribute 2 per cent of their annual budgets to support actions of the poor aiming at justice and development."[35]

In 1982, the Central Committee received the report "JPSS Follow-up: Focus on Political Ethics" and commended the Programme Report on "Transnational Corporations" to member churches and ecumenical bodies for study and action. In 1984, the Central Committee called "on churches, councils of churches, local parishes and other church-related groups, to commit themselves to the support of actions for justice and development in their own situation as well as in other parts of the world through
a) transferring part of their income, by a deliberate budgetary decision, to organizations which express the struggle of the poor and oppressed and to programmes which help to build awareness of the need to challenge the structures of injustice;
b) making use towards the same goal a part of their worship, their educational programmes, their building and land, their investment funds and most importantly their influence in society;
c) calling their members to commit in the same way part of their financial resources, their time, their professional skills, their personal contacts and political activity."[36]

## XII.

Section II, "The Kingdom of God and Human Struggles" of the World Conference on Mission and Evangelism at Melbourne in 1980 stated the following on unjust economic structures: "The kingdom of God brings in shalom - peace with justice. Any socio-

economic system that denies the citizens of a society their
basic needs is unjust and in opposition to the kingdom of God.
The churches have to exercise the prophetic gift of assessing
the effectiveness of the various socio-economic systems in the
world and speak in favour of exploratory models of a new international economic order in the light of the thrust of the Gospel.
The churches are called upon to take sides with Third World
peoples who suffer from repressive systems in order to maintain
the standard of living of affluent countries, and with those
who are forced into foreign economic patters."[37]

At a Public Hearing on Nuclear Weapons and Disarmament at
Amsterdam in 1981, the following was stated on economic interests - the military-industrial complex: "In many situations
economic groups pursuing profit (through private or public
corporations engaged in arms research, development and production) have a big stake in the continuation of the arms race.
They inevitably develop close ties with the military, and
together they operate powerful lobbies which often deflect
political and social judgements based on wider considerations.
This is especially so in times of economic recession and unemployment when a government can argue that the arms industry
produces economic advantages for its country. However, recent
studies have shown that investment in non-military activity can
produce more jobs than military related industry. It is clear
that it will take a vigilant and informed public to overcome
this kind of influence and to chart alternative courses based
on the long term interests of the world community."[38]

In the Report of an International Consultation on
"Ecumenical Perspectives on Political Ethics" on Cyprus in 1981
the following was stated on political processes and international economic structures: "The present international monetary
system came into being at the end of World War II in order to
preserve economic stability in the Western world. Today this
system has become a major obstacle in the way of human development, especially in the Southern hemisphere. Its maintenance
absorbs vast political energies. It progressively eliminates
the autonomy of political life by making political processes
and decisions exclusively dependent upon economic logic and
calculus.

Under the present pattern of international political economy,
industrialized countries are facing growing and chronic unemployment, inflation, environmental problems, unsustainability
of systems of public welfare and resulting internal political
pressures. The same world economic process reduces political
life in the developing countries to an endless struggle for
economic survival. As a consequence of this situation, it is
being realized by a growing number of politicians and economists
that a new understanding of the world economy has to be developed
and that political life has to be liberated from economic deter-
minism by reordering the relationship between economic means and
political goals... There is thus a necessity for economics once
again to become political economy, with primary emphasis on the
overall direction of society. Basic changes in human values are
a prerequisite for such a transformation."[39]

280

In a Working Group Report on Culture of the Faith and Order
Commission, meeting at Lima in 1982, the following was stated
concerning modern science and technology as pipelines of culture: "... Reliance on science and technology has tended to
replace faith in God, thereby producing a new idolatry. We need
to continue investigating the theological implications of modern
science and technology as producers and transmitters of a universal culture which is materially satisfying but spiritually
empty.  We need even to raise the question whether this universal technological 'civilization' is not primarily the promotion
of Western cultural interests."[40]


XIII.


In Issue 5, "Confronting Threats to Peace and Survival", of
the Vancouver Assembly in 1983, the following was stated on
militarism in relation to economic justice: "We believe that
the present military build-up and arms race are integrally
related to the practices of an unjust world economic order.
The worldwide trend towards militarization is not a mere confrontation and tension between the major powers, but also an
expression of the desire to repress those emerging forces which
seek a more just world order.  It is this latter which poses a
fundamental threat to peace.  Whereas people's aspirations for
and expectations of a more just order have been supported as
legitimate, the big powers still use military might to buttress
the unjust order in order to protect their own interests. The
defence of these interests can often be disguised as appeals
for national security, the upholding of law and order, the
defence of democracy, the protection of the 'free world', the
need to maintain spheres of influence and sometimes even the
cause of peace."

In Issue 7, "Learning in Community", it was suggested that
"the churches as well as the WCC... may wish to consider a change
of name from 'development education' to 'education for justice
and peace'."[41]

"The Church and the Poor" was the overall theme of a consultation at Ayia Napa, Cyprus, September 1978, organized by
CCPD.  At the level of theological reflection on the Church and
the Poor between 1975 and 1977 a first study was published by
the WCC in Good News to the Poor.  A second stage followed in
which a study was made on relations between the poor and the
church in the crucial period of Western colonial expansion and
the industrial revolution.  The title of the second volume was
Separation Without Hope ?  To fulfill the CCPD mandate a third
stage was initiated which resulted in a third volume Towards a
Church of the Poor.  A number of consultations on development
education and transnational corporations from 1975 onwards are
not listed here.

## XIV

In the Report of Section I, "Living in Christ with People: Confronting the Structures of Power", of the Seventh Assembly of the Christian Conference of Asia in 1981, the following was stated: "... We believe that there is no dichotomy between national security, development and human dignity. What we question are the concepts of national security and development propagated in Asia which keep people in bondage. We believe that true national security should ensure security to all its people and true development should mean development of all the people in a given society in all aspects of their lives. We also see national governments who claim to be democratic become oppressive once they get the majority in election. The very people who elected them are not allowed to challenge their actions.

"... We suggest that the churches be required to fulfil their Christian involvement in the fate of all people as Jesus had initiated by words and deeds. We think that the churches should take the same stand as Jesus took in his time, which he would take if he comes now to our world. We should help churches know the facts by adopting an effective programme of information, so that churches would have no excuses nor fail by default." 42

## Observations and Conclusions

1. Hardly any theme and concern has been so inadequately handled in official ecumenical statements during the period 1948-1965 than that of economic and integral development. A naïve and romantic conviction prevailed that once poor peoples in the Third World obtain a minimum of technology and are profiting from "the benefits of more machine-production", the process of development will move in the right direction and the living standards of a large part of the population will be raised. The ecumenical concept of the "responsible society" was indiscriminately applied to developed and underdeveloped nations. The capability and the willingness of the affluent West to send generous aid to the rest of the world and the harmful effects of that aid were not questioned. There was an undue optimism that the Christian churches can play an important role in assisting disrupted peoples in technical and welfare services and thus will enable them to help themselves.

As interdependence was viewed as being instrumental to fellowship, there was little or no awareness that interdependence between partners of power and of no power leads to dominance and dependency, instead of mutually beneficial relations. The issue of power was hardly addressed and it was assumed that the interests of the poor and the rich could be gradually reconciled.

The "rapid social change" studies, to be sure, draw attention to a new rising nationalism in many Third World countries and their awakening to a sense of human dignity and their struggle to discover and express their corporate selfhood. There was no insight, however, that the development of the concern for social change required new theological-ethical categories. As the Western churches still placed great confidence in the validity of traditional structures of world political and economic relations, they were unable to note that Christian communities in the South started to challenge the assumption of "international law and order", developed by the Western powers and imposed on the rest of the world. Even the New Delhi Assembly was unprepared to cope with the new situation and to engage in a radical re-examination of social and political change in a world perspective. Only the CCIA report to the assembly pointed for the first time to elements of political economy, including international monetary policies and fluctuations in the prices of commodities.

2. Only in 1966 did the Geneva World Conference on Church and Society make a serious attempt on the part of the WCC to understand the revolutionary realities which shape the modern world. It made the issue of world economic development a major concern of the churches and stressed that large contributions from the rich nations are needed and deep changes in world economic and political structures are required if global economic growth is to be achieved.

The Uppsala Assembly was even more conscious of the bankruptcy of the <u>status quo</u> and eager to support concrete programmes proposed in the area of world development and to approve their theoretical and theological foundations. "The death of the old may cause pain to some, but failure to build up a new world community may bring death to all", it stated. Still today it remains a mystery how in such a short period of time so much expertise on world development was gathered together and communicated.

The reports of the conferences which SODEPAX sponsored from 1968 to 1971 remain of penetrating insight and great quality. Yet they were too optimistic that the prosperity so far enjoyed by a minority would eventually be shared by the majority of the human race. Only in the eighties was it realized that "reliance on science and technology has tended to replace faith in God, thereby producing a new idolatry." Similar optimism was expressed with regard to the constructive policies of transnational corporations. Only the Nairobi Assembly recognized that transnationals do not create genuine growth in the poor countries. Even the Uppsala Assembly stated that "the production and distribution of food in the coming years must be a technical preoccupation of all who are interested in development... means of population control must be sought...", while finally the Vancouver Assembly pointed to the political dimension of the food problem.

3. CCPD started its work with the growing conviction, that justice should be the focus of the churches participation in development. The most frustrating aspect in the development process during the past decades has been the lack of political will to bring about distributive justice within and among nations to enable the poor majorities of the people to have a fair share of the benefits of development and better participation in directing the process. CCPD has stressed from the beginning that programmes of development, supported and carried out by the churches, must promote social justice and self-reliance.

From 1976 onwards the WCC has attempted through CCPD to make contributions to the search for a just, participatory and sustainable society, to the concern for people's participation as a social phenomenon in history which poses challenges to social structures as well as to the church, to people's technologies which fit in with their values and cultures, to a deeper analysis of the crushing economic power of the trans-national corporations, to various aspects of development education, and to "new life-styles" in the churches. CCPD also developed a theological concept of the "church of the poor" on which the Central Committee in 1980 commented: "... Theology done in the context of the struggles for liberation and justice of the poor may be expected to widen its application, further its intention to be self-corrective, and submit a broader spectrum of traditional Christian symbols to theological reflection."

Yet during the last ten years a mood of impotence, resignation and even despair has often prevailed. In the secular realm international organizations like UNCTAD, UNESCO, FAO and others have experienced the crippling assumptions of prestiguous development blueprints. In the religious realm the idea of the church of the poor has not re-inforced the tremendous thrust and commitment of the Uppsala Assembly. Few consequences have been drawn by the churches from their new insight in God's preferential love for the poor and the exploited. The 2 per cent appeal for development aid as an action model has been accepted and practiced by few Christian communities. Only the governments of Norway, the Netherlands and Sweden spend between 1.2 and 0.8 per cent from their GNP on development aid.

Foreign assistance itself remains a controversial issue. Its critics believe that it is either often badly administered, severely reducing its ability to promote development and tackle poverty, or that it is harmful in principle. Following centuries of colonialism and neo-colonialism the era of aid prolongs dependency, poverty and underdevelopment.

4. The ecumenical movement and the WCC need to promote the following issues and concerns:
a) This survey has shown that there has not been sufficient reflection on how the concept of development evolved. Economic justice, social justice, wide participation, human development, cultural integrity and spiritual well-being have to be related to one meaningful whole. A theology of development which deals

with the humanization of modern technolological life from all
angles still needs to be spelled out.

b) The whole development process is intimately related to
concerted political action. Established powers, however, are
not favourably disposed to development programmes which in-
troduce the element of liberation and benefit mainly the poor
and the oppressed. Many churches likewise are so entangled in
enslaving economic structures that their professed solidarity
with the poor is hardly credible. Consequently their action at
the level of the centres of decision-making goes unnoticed
and is ineffective. It is only through the building up of
public opinion and powerful political lobbies that the necessary national and international conditions of commitment to
development can be created. Political parties which do not
make development an integral part of their strategy should be
exposed.

c) Unless there is a much deeper awareness among the churches about the world disparities and the reasons for their
existence, the opportunities they have to change the structures
of their own existence and to contribute to the establishment
of a new international economic order will remain unused. Engagement in development education at the grass roots is surely
necessary. But the whole church, in particular its hierarchy,
needs to become aware, that it lives in a world which is
totally different from the world fifty years ago. The fact
that God in Christ divested himself of all power, taking the
nature of a slave, accepting, suffering unto death on a cross,
takes up a new meaning. Denouncing injustice and exploitation
and announcing liberation in Christ through corporate words,
deeds and life-styles is necessary and possible. Christian
ignorance and complacency can be turned into daring consciousness and contagious commitment.

d) CCPD should beware of engaging itself in too many tasks
at the same time. Its primary focus should remain to relate
the qualities of the unity and the mission of the church to the
vision of the one human family. Concepts of and concerns for
development should deeply penetrate the outlook and hope of
the whole ecumenical movement which raison d'être in the socio-
political realm is an ever deeper appreciation of the fundamental unity of humankind and the mutual responsibility of the
family of nations.

e) In this context CCPD can build on its past and continue
to define development as an inter-related process of social
justice, self-reliance and economic growth, based - and this is
most important - on the exercise of people's participation, that
is continuous struggle from the bottom up. At a meeting in Crete,
March 24-30, 1980, the Commission gave high priority to the
strengthening of the network of groups committed to the comprehensive struggle of the poor and oppressed. It is particularly
in this way that churches and Christians can be part of world-
wide social, cultural and economic development.[43]

In Asia this challenge was taken up by an Asia Forum on
Justice and Development at Singapore, November 26-30, 1984,
assessing 15 years of churches' involvement in the development
of the poorest continent in the world.[44] The Forum participants

agreed on the urgent need to set up alternative communication
networks to share the truth and make it available to all people,
and to link people and movements throughout Asia and the world
for fuller exchange of information, insights and experiences.
In this process churches are liberated from their historical
captivity to power and start placing themselves firmly on the
side of destitute and revolting people. And in this new predicament Christian communities can leave it to God to transform
their involvement into the healing of the human race.

---

1. The First Assembly of the World Council of Churches held
   at Amsterdam, August 22 to September 4, 1948. Ed. by W.A.
   Visser 't Hooft. New York: Harper, 1949. p. 75.

2. The Evanston Report. The Second Assembly of the World
   Council of Churches 1954. London: SCM Press, 1955.
   pp. 123-126.

3. The New Delhi Report. The Third Assembly of the World
   Council of Churches 1961. London: SCM Press, 1962.
   pp. 106-107, 275-276.

4. Minutes of the Enlarged Meeting of the Committee of the
   International Missionary Council, Willingen, Germany,
   July 5-21, 1952. London: IMC, 1952. pp. 83-84.

5. Minutes and Reports of the Eleventh Meeting of the Central
   Committee of the World Council of Churches, Nyborg Strand,
   Denmark, August 21-29, 1958. Geneva: WCC, 1958.
   pp. 124-125.

6. The Common Christian Responsibility Toward Areas of Rapid
   Social Change. Second Statement. Geneva: WCC, 1956.
   pp. 3-39.

7. Dilemmas and Opportunities. Christian Action in Rapid
   Social Change. Report of an International Ecumenical Study
   Conference, Thessalonica, Greece, July 25 - August 2, 1959.
   Geneva: WCC, 1959. pp. 67-89.

8. "Witnesses Together" being the Official Report of the Inaugural Assembly of the East Asia Christian Conference,
   held at Kuala Lumpur, Malaya, May 14-24, 1959. Ed. by
   U Kyaw Than. Rangoon: EACC, 1959. p. 77.

9. Christians in the Technical and Social Revolutions of Our
   Time. World Conference on Church Society, Geneva, July
   12- 26, 1966. Geneva: WCC, 1967. pp. 55, 66, 80.

10. The Uppsala Report 1968. Ed. by Norman Goodall.
    Geneva: WCC, 1968. pp. 45-55.

11. Encyclical Letter of His Holiness Paul VI to the Bishops,
    Priests, Religious, the Faithful and to All Men of Good Will.
    On the Development of Peoples. Vatican Polyglot Press,1967.

12. Central Committee of the World Council of Churches. Minutes and Reports of the Twenty-Third Meeting. Canterbury, Great Britain, August 12-22, 1969. Geneva: WCC, 1969. pp. 20, 207-215.

13. Central Committee of the World Council of Churches. Minutes and Reports of the Twenty-Fifth Meeting. Utrecht, the Netherlands, 13-23 August, 1972. Geneva: WCC, 1972. pp. 26, 273.

14. Fetters of Injustice. Report of an Ecumenical Consultation on Ecumenical Assistance to Development Projects, 26-31 January, 1970, Montreux. Ed. by Pamela H. Gruber. Geneva: WCC, 1970. pp. 101-132.

15. World Development: Challenge to the Churches. The Official Report of the Conference on Society, Development, and Peace (SODEPAX) held at Beirut, Lebanon, April 21-27, 1968. Ed. by Denys Munby. Washington: Corpus Books, 1969. pp. 8, 37-38.

16. The Challenge of Development. The Montreal Conference, May 9-12, 1969. Geneva: SODEPAX, 1969. pp. 12-29.

17. Peace - The Desperate Imperative. The Consultation on Christian Concern for Peace. Baden, Austria, April 3-9, 1970. Geneva: SODEPAX, 1970. p. 37.

18. From Here to Where? Technology, Faith and the Future of Man. Report of an Exploratory Conference, Geneva, June 28 - July 4, 1970. Ed. by David M. Gill. Geneva: WCC, 1970. pp. 19, 27, 55.

19. Science and Technology for Human Development. The Ambiguous Future and the Christian Hope. Report of the 1974 World Conference in Bucharest, Romania. In: Anticipation, no. 19, November 1974.

20. Minutes and Report of the Assembly of the Commission on World Mission and Evangelism, December 31, 1972 and January 9-12, 1973. Geneva: WCC, 1973. p. 53.

21. Towards World Community. The Colombo Papers. Ed. by S.J. Samartha. Geneva: WCC, 1975. p. 118.

22. Uniting in Hope. Reports and Documents from the Meeting of the Faith and Order Commission. 23 July - 5 August, 1974, University of Ghana, Legon. Geneva: WCC, 1974 (Faith and Order Paper, No. 72). pp. 42-43.

23. Study Encounter, vol IV, no. 3, 1968. p. 148-153.

24. Ecumenical Press Service, no. 10, 13 March, 1969.

25. In Search of a Theology of Development. Geneva: SODEPAX, 1970.

26. Money in a Village World.  Geneva: SODEPAX, 1970.

27. Church - Communication - Development.
    Geneva: SODEPAX, 1970.

28. Liberation, Justice, Development. An Asian Ecumenical
    Conference for Development. Madras: Diocesan Press, 1970.

29. Picking Up the Pieces. A Report of a SODEPAX Conference
    on the Churches in Development Planning and Action.
    Geneva: SODEPAX, 1971.

30. Called To Be.  Bridgtown, Barbados: CADEC, 1972.

31. In African Accents.  Lusaka: Multimedia Zambia, 1972.

32. Consultation on Church - Communications - Development.
    Geneva: SODEPAX, 1972.

33. Ecumenical Press Service, no. 7, 8 March, 1973.

34. Breaking Barriers. Nairobi 1975. Ed. by David M. Paton.
    London: SPCK; Grand Rapids: Wm. B. Eerdmans, 1976.
    pp. 122, 123, 131.

35. Central Committee of the World Council of Churches. Minutes
    of the Twenty-Ninth Meeting, 1976, p. 34;  Minutes of the
    Thirty-First Meeting, 1979,  pp. 68-69;  Minutes of the
    Thirty-Second Meeting, 1980.  p. 54.

36. Central Committee of the World Council of Churches. Minutes
    of the Thirty-Fourth Meeting, 1982, pp. 64-66;  Minutes of
    the Thirty-Sixth Meeting, 1984, pp. 57-58.

37. Your Kingdom Come. Mission Perspectives. Report on the
    World Conference on Mission and Evangelism, Melbourne,
    Australia, 12-25 May, 1980.  Geneva: WCC, 1980.  p. 184.

38. Before It's Too Late. The Challenge of Nuclear Disarmament.
    Ed. by Paul Abrecht and Ninan Koshy.  Geneva: WCC, 1982.
    p. 14.

39. Perspectives on Political Ethics. An Ecumenical Enquiry.
    Ed. by Koson Srisang.  Geneva: WCC, 1983.  pp. 19 and 32.

40. Towards Visible Unity. Commission on Faith and Order,
    Lima 1952.  Volume II: Study Papers and Reports. Ed. by
    Michael Kinnamon.  Geneva: WCC, 1982 (Faith and Order
    Paper, No. 113).  p. 216.

41. Gathered for Life. Official Report. VI Assembly of the
    World Council of Churches, Vancouver, Canada, 24 July -
    10 August, 1983. Ed. by David Gill.  Geneva: WCC;
    Grand Rapids: Wm. B. Eerdmans, 1983.  pp. 74, 99.

42. Living in Christ with People. CCA Seventh Assembly,
    Bangalore, May 18-28, 1981.  Singapore: CCA, 1981.
    pp. 83-84, 88.

43. Building a Fellowship of Commitment. Report of the CCPD
    Network Meeting Crete, 1980. Ed. by Wolfgang Schmidt.
    Geneva: WCC, 1980.

44. Asia Forum on Justice and Development. Ed. by Yong-Bock Kim.
    CCA-WCC/CCPD, Singapore, November 26-30, 1984.
    A popular edition has also been published.

# XV.
## Health, Healing and Wholeness

This survey starts with the year 1964. Although the concern
for health and healing has been an integral part of the ecumenical missionary movement from the beginning, it was only from
the sixties onwards that special consultations and conferences
on the subject were organized. The WCC Christian Medical Commission (CMC) was created in 1967 to stimulate reflection on
church and health, to enable necessary re-orientation and to
coordinate church-related medical work in six continents. This
survey also includes literature and statements on the disabled,
who, besides in the CMC, became a particular concern in the
realm of Faith and Order.


I.


A consultation on The Healing Ministry in the Mission of the
Church, at Tübingen, FRG, May 1964, was sponsored by the Lutheran
World Federation and the Division of World Mission and Evangelism.
Preparatory papers were sent in by L. Newbigin, E. Kayser, M.
Scheel and J. Wilkinson. The report, includes, besides these
papers, the findings and next steps. The headings of the find-
ings were: I. The Christian Concept of the Healing Ministry;
II. The Role of the Congregation in the Ministry of Healing;
III. The Healing Ministry in Theological Training; IV. The
Training of Medical and Para-Medical Workers as a Task of the
Church; V. The Institutional Forms of a Healing Ministry;
VI. The Relationships of a Christian Healing Ministry to Govern-
ment; VII. Joint Planning and Use of Resources for the Healing
Ministry; VIII. A Continuing Programme of Study and Work.

In the preamble of the Findings the following was stated:
"The members of this Consultation are well aware of the fate of
most reports. In view of their unanimous adoption of these
findings, and because of their concern for a new look at the
Christian healing ministry, they would urge a deep and continuing
study of these findings by the Division of World Mission and
Evangelism of the World Council of Churches and the Commission
on World Mission of the Lutheran World Federation, which bodies
called them together. In addition, they would request that all
churches, young or old, church councils, mission boards and
societies as well as theological colleges and seminaries would
singly or in partnership examine and test them and where they
are found valid implement them, whether in pilot projects or
as ground work for the adoption of new policies."[1]

Health and Community was the theme of a consultation for psychiaters and theologians at Bossey, April 11-16, 1966. Preparatory papers were sent in by J.C. McGilvray, F. Hahn, W.L. Nutte, P. Verghese, G. Bally, O.H. Mowrer, W. Kütemeyer. V.V. Alexander reacted to a paper "Illness and Health in the Community of Mankind" by A. Siirala. H.-R. Weber presented a paper and a Bible study on "Christ's Victory over the Satanic Powers."[2]

Continuing the discussion of the Tübingen consultation in 1964, a consultation in the same city concentrated September 1-8, 1967 on the theme Health and Salvation. It re-examined the nature of the Church's ministry through medicine, particularly as it was exemplified in 'missionary' medicine in the developing nations. Individual contributions were made by H. Hellberg, M.H. Scharlemann, D.C. Moir, I.T. Ramsey, L. Jansen Schoonhoven, G. Hoffmann, Sister M. Luke, D.E. Jenkins, G.C. Harding, H.Florin, R.A. Lambourne, S. Hiltner, A.D. John, T.F. Davey, F. Norstad and A.H. van Soest.

The second meeting in Tübingen discussed in greater detail three specific insights concerning the Church's task in healing which the previous 1964 consultation had summarized as follows: "1. That the Christian understanding of health is unique; 2. That the Christian understanding of health and healing is intrinsically related to God's plan of Salvation; and 3. That the Christian ministry of healing belongs primarily to the congregation and only in this context to those who are professionally trained in the healing arts."[3]

Christian Medical Work in India was the theme of a consultation at Bangalore, January 12-17, 1969, sponsored by the CMC. It recommended that a co-ordinating Board for Christian Health Services in India be strengthened with a full-time secretary and a board of seven persons. The consultation further called for a memorandum on construction of new hospitals, the employment of an indigenous leadership in church and mission-related hospitals within five years, amalgamation of hospitals when funds are not available to continue independent operation, training programmes for hospital personnel.[4]

## II.

Dealing with the CMC during its first year, the Central Committee meeting at Canterbury in 1969, expressed itself on co-ordination as follows: "To promote a more effective use of the resources for church-related medical work the CMC has been involved in establishing structures for joint planning and action between the churches themselves and in relation to respective Governments. This has meant contacts with medical personnel in church-related institutions, national church leaders (Protestant, Orthodox and Roman Catholic) and representatives of local and national Governments. In addition this involves negotiation with supporting organizations like mission boards and donor agencies, again both Protestant and Roman Catholic."

With regard to programme the Central Committee said: "In
order to provide a more relevant service as part of the mission
of the Church our medical work needs a change of emphasis from
an almost exclusive involvement in disease-oriented hospital-
centred care towards a community oriented comprehensive health
programme... The need for a community oriented approach has also
been underlined in the advice to the various area secretaries of
DICARWS in relation to requests for support to medical projects
... For information and advice relationships have also been developed with WHO, International Hospital Federation, International
Council of Nurses, International Planned Parenthood Federation,
American Medical Association, etc."[5]

Addressing the ecumenical consultation on Ecumenical Assistance to Development Projects at Montreux, 26-31 January, 1970,
Samuel L. Parmar said: "... If we take a nation's long-term
interest, as we should in discussions of development, an improvement in the health of the people improves the quality and productivity of human resources. It also subscribes to the tenets
of social justice by providing facilities to a group which is
unable to do so for itself."[6]

Three consultations discussed the subject Coordinators for
Church-Related Health Work in Africa. They were held at Limuru,
Kenya, February 1970, Blantyre, Malawi, February 1972, and at
Mombasa, Kenya, February 1975. The first gathering, organized
by the CMC, was in conjunction with a conference on "The Healing
Ministry of the Church." Those delegates specifically related
to the coordinators conference included 18 representatives from
12 African countries. The second consultation took place with
the Private Hospital Association of Malawi and the Government
of Malawi through the Ministry of Health and Community Development. In the third consultation health workers and coordinators
from 15 African nations participated. The agenda included three
main topics: 1) The integration of all church-related health
care programmes in national health planning; 2) The potentials
within each country for development of primary health care projects as the highest priority; 3) The detailed implications of
localization of staff at the senior level in both coordinating
agencies and in the direction of programmes.[7]

A study group met at Hong Kong, July 1972, and concentrated
on the theme Health Care in China. It collected information
from Chinese medical publications, from interviews with people
who served in the Chinese medical services, and from unpublished
and oral evaluations by foreign specialists who had travelled
in China during the last three years. Three members of the group
had visited China and contributed their first-hand observations
to the study. The report includes chapters on The Relationship
of Health to National Development Goals, Health Care Organization,
Epidemic Disease Control, Population Policies, Traditional and
Western Medical Practices, Manpower for Health Care, and the
Prevention and Treatment of Mental Illness.[8]

## III

Meeting at Bangkok, Thailand in 1973, the Commission on World Mission and Evangelism agreed and adopted the following report on emphasis for the CMC:
"We support the appeal made by the CMC to both local churches and funding agencies to move beyond established institutions such as hospitals, to the development of community-based agencies involving all people, including church members, to meet health needs.
We also support the development of the team approach to the provision of health care which would include non-professional workers in close collaboration with professionals whose training is relevant to the current health needs of the locality in which the team is at work.
We express our deep concern over the brain drain and exploitation of trained technical personnel from developing nations, lured away to the service of the health institutions in developed countries."

The conference at Bangkok further drew attention to the work of the CMC and noted in particular that: "a) Every health care service must have clear objectives and be objective-orientated. The primary objective should be the provision of comprehensive health care and not the emulation of medical care and hospital services in other developed countries;  b) The participation of the community in a programme of health care is of vital importance;  c) The community must be educated to be aware of its own potential to identify its own problems and to seek and implement solutions;  d) Effective health care can be carried out in the simplest of rural clinics with a minimum of drugs by persons who though adequately instructed need not be doctors."[9]

The exploratory consultation on Primal World-Views was held in Ibadan, Nigeria in 1973, under the auspices of the Sub-unit on Dialogue with People of Living Faiths and Ideologies, the All Africa Conference of Churches and the Theological Education Fund.  The consultation dealt extensively with healing in the Bible and in primal world views and stated: "... While technological man comes to terms with nature by regarding it as neutral matter to be exploited at his will, primal man insists that he lives in mutual obligation with nature.  The healing process is concerned as much with the harmonious interaction of the whole cosmos, of which man is a part, as with interpersonal relationships and the physical symptoms of the patient.  A primal healer is thus concerned with misfortune in general and not simply with 'disease'.  He is not only, in contemporary terms, physician (and perhaps surgeon)  and psychologist, but social worker and ecologist.  He is concerned with the whole man in his total environment...

"...The basic issue is that, in the Platonian tradition, the affairs of the soul have been regarded as more important than those of the body.  Primal healers are concerned equally for both. A closely related issue is that of 'spirit' which some wish to add as a third substantive to man's wholeness, while others see it rather as the ultrahuman organizing principle which termines the perfection or the disruption of that wholeness. Here, again, any evaluation of the primal views can be made only after the evidence has been fully studied.

"...Many 'older' churches are in the grip of a faith crisis and need to re-discover a recognition that the Gospel is concerned with the body as well as with the soul. Is it possible to re-discover the whole church ? While being conscious of the dangers of some commercial and even deceitful 'faith-healing', Christians should avoid instinctive suspicion and disparagement, and should humbly claim a bolder attitude to implementing ministries of prayer, anointment and healing."[10]

IV.

Dealing with "Asia's Need for New Patterns of Production and Consumption", the World Conference on Science and Technology for Human Development at Bucharest in 1974 stated the following: "Resources should be applied to the production of essentials and withdrawn from less essential production. For instance, low cost housing rather than luxury apartments and five-star hotels; public and medium cloth rather than fine textiles, expensive silks, synthetic materials, etc.; small irrigation projects rather than huge multipurpose projects; training for basic rural health services more than for modern medical skills which lead to a concentration of medical facilities in urban areas. All these shifts in production can be introduced immediately."[11]

In the discussion of the theme of The Unity of the Church and the Unity of Mankind at the meeting of the Faith and Order Commission in Accra in 1974, John Deschner noted the following on the concern for the disabled: "...Our discussion of the handicapped – clearly the sub-theme most interesting to the Commission as a whole – posed a question not only about the wholeness of a congregation which segregates the weak, but quite specifically about our alertness to the ministry of the powerless in embodying the presence of the Crucified. As far as I am aware, our consensus work on the ministry has yet to reflect this discussion."[12]

Two workshops on health care programmes took place in Africa in 1975. Church and Mission Health Programmes in Sierra Leone was the theme of a consultation in Freetown, Sierra Leone, May 30-31. It was the culmination of an effort to foster communion in service in providing medical care to the people of Sierra Leone. A Christian Medical Group was set up to share information, services and representation to the government and to engage in a study of present activities in health care delivery.[13] The Future Role of the Church in Health Care Programmes in Ghana, was the subject of debate of a workshop in Greenhill, Ghana, August 17-23. The Christian Health Association of Ghana invited staff of the CMC to participate in this workshop. The serious financial situation of the 35 church-related hospitals, clinics and health posts in the country were examined.  Contributions were made by M.A. Baddoo, J.C. McGilvray, D. Belcher, M. Kromberg.  The report, compiled by Sister Mary Zosso, contains also a summary of the recommendations.[14]

V.

In Section II, What Unity Requires, of the Nairobi Assembly, the following was stated on The Handicapped and the Wholeness of the Family of God:"The Church's unity includes both the 'disabled' and the 'able'.  A Church which seeks to be truly united within itself and to move towards unity with others must be open to all; yet able-bodied church members, both by their attitudes and by their emphasis on activism, marginalize and often exclude those with mental or physical disabilities. The disabled are treated as the weak to be served, rather than as fully committed, integral members of the Body of Christ and the human family; the specific contribution which they have to give is ignored.

"This is the more serious because disability - a world-wide problem - is increasing.  Accidents and illness leave adults and children disabled; many more are emotionally handicapped by the pressures of social change and urban living; genetic disorders and famine leave millions of children physically and mentally impaired.  The Church cannot exemplify 'the full humanity revealed in Christ', bear witness to the interdependece of humankind, or achieve unity in diversity if it continues to acquiesce in the social isolation of disabled persons and to deny them full participation in its life.  The unity of the family of God is handicapped where these brothers and sisters are treated as objects of condescending charity.  It is broken where they are left out.  How can the love of Christ create in us the will to discern and to work forcefully against the causes which distort and cripple the lives of so many of our fellow human beings ? How can the Church be open to the witness which Christ extends through them ?"[15]

The Report of Group C on Christian Concern in Traditional Religions and Cultures of the consultation at Chiang Mai, Thailand, 1977, sponsored by the Sub-unit on Dialogue with People of Living Faiths and Ideologies stated the following: "In traditional culture disease and sickness are not only physical but affect the whole person.  Healing is therefore not only a response to the physical manifestation of sickness and disease but is related to the whole mental and spiritual outlook of the person. When a person falls ill, it is moreover not only the problem of the individual and his or her family, but it is a concern of the community.  It is the community which provides the active, dynamic context for healing to take place. The response to sickness in such communities points toward the hidden dimension upon which all inter-personal relations are founded, and both the above aspects help to sensitize the Christian community to the importance and relevance of the biblical understanding of sickness and healing for our own times."[16]

The report of the Commission on Faith and Order to the Central Committee meeting at Geneva in 1977 contained the following section on The Role of the Disabled in the Church: "In response to the discussion at its Louvain meeting, the Faith and Order Commission is engaged in preparing a volume on the "Role of the Disabled in the Church." Though welcoming this initiative, the Committee felt that the issue requires more sustained attention and recommended that ways be explored to give it more prominence in the WCC programme. This is of particular importance since the United Nations have declared 1981 as the "Year of the Disabled"; the churches should prepare their contribution for this year. Several sub-units are engaged in some activities in this field. The Committee suggests that the General Secretary appoint a staff task force and entrust it with the task to study the possibility of intensifying the efforts..."[17]

Partners in Life. The Handicapped and the Church was published in 1979. Its content is: I. Theological Basis; II. Practical Steps; III. The Present Situation; IV. Appendices. 1) Present Rehabilitation Services, their Deficiencies and New Directions for Disability Prevention; 2) The Life and Witness of the Handicapped in the Christian Community – the Bad Saarow Memorandum.[18]

VI.

It was in Bad Saarow, GDR, April 3-7, 1978, that a consultation was jointly organized by Faith and Order, CICARWS and CMC in close collaboration with the Interior Mission and Service Agency of the Protestant Churches in the GDR. Its theme was Life and Witness of Disabled Persons in a Christian Parish. Among the participants from 15 countries in Europe were disabled persons with their spouses, parents of disabled children, specialized doctors who work in homes and institutions, and people in charge of the diaconal work. The preoccupation of the meeting was seeking ways in which the disabled could be fully integrated in the Christian community and to discuss the role of specialized institutions in the life of the Church.[19]

Several other regional consultations took place from 1979 to 1981. Go and Tell was the theme of a consultation at Port of Spain, Trinidad, March 12-16, 1979. Contributions were made by W. Watty, A. Sovik, J. Steensma. The meeting was jointly chaired by S. Talbot and M. Scheel. It produced a consensus that "health and wholeness imply the ability to grow physically, mentally, socially and in our relationship to God; that social and economic injustices stand in the way of wholeness and that churches must recognize where they prevent wholeness as well as the opportunity they have to foster it within their communities."[20]

One Expression of Love in Society is Justice was the subject of discussion of a consultation at Omoa, Honduras, March 19-23, 1979. It was jointly moderated by G. Parajon and E. Castro. Keynote papers were presented by E. Castro, R. Kinsler and V. Vaca. The major subject areas identified for discussion in groups were:

The Gospel and Health; Discovery of Challenges; Resources and
Methodology of Health of the Total Person; The Prophetic Responsibility of the Church.[21]

At a consultation in Gaborone, Botswana, October 15-19, 1979,
participants concentrated on the subject Health, Healing and
Wholeness. This African regional meeting was chaired by N.
Barrow and E. Ram. The topics identified were similar to those
examined in the earlier meetings, and all were central themes
of the Study-Enquiry, e.g. Wholeness, The Congregation's Role
in Healing; Primary Health Care, Government-Church Relationships;
Financing of Health Care. The participants' approach to these
themes was, however, conditioned by the African social and cultural context from which they came. Two additional topics,
Traditional Healing and the Christian Concept of Healing in an
African Setting, were particularly relevant to, and for, the
region.[22]

A consultation at New Delhi, India, August 25-29, 1980, on
the theme The Christian Understanding of Health, Healing and
Wholeness, was the fourth in a series of consultations called
by the CMC in the last two years. The over-70 participants were
drawn from India, Sri Lanka, Nepal, Pakistan, and Bangladesh,
and represented a wide range of disciplines: pastors, doctors,
theologians, nurses, psychiatrists, social workers, health educators, development workers, hospital administrators, national
coordinators of church-related health service, community health
workers, lay church workers, charismatic healers, practitioners
of indigenous systems of medicine (Ayurveda, Unani, Yoga and
Homeopathy). The highlights of the group reports were: 1) Church
and Health; 2) Financing Community Health Programmes; 3) Development; 4) Human Values and Human Relations; 5) Charismatic
Healing.[23]

Forty four participants and four observers from Indonesia,
the Philippines, Malaysia, Thailand, Singapore and Burma, many
of them working in isolation, discussed the theme The Christian
Understanding of Health, Healing and Wholeness at a consultation
in Dhyana Pura, Bali, April 25 - May 1, 1981. As in previous
regional consultations, the participants split into a number of
interest groups to study themes they themselves had identified
and struggled with what health, healing and wholeness means in
their own environment.[24]

Some 55 participants came from 16 countries in the Pacific,
including Australia and New Zealand, to concentrate on the subject Health, Healing and Wholeness in the Pacific, at Madang,
Papua New Guinea, October 23-29, 1981. Two recurrent themes of
the meeting were: 1) The importance of traditional medicine in
Pacific culture and the questions raised by the beliefs and
practices for Christians involved in the healing ministry; 2)
Economic and social justice in the Pacific, its roots and effects
on the health and wholeness of Pacific people; the special problems of Australian Aboriginals and New Zealand Maoris, and how
the church should exercise its healing ministry in this context.[25]

Finally, a regional consultation took place at Quito, Ecuador, June 14-23, 1982. Its theme was <u>People-Orientated Health Care in the Struggle Against Social Injustice</u>. Some 70 participants came from Cuba, Puerto Rico and the Dominican Republic, 40 per cent being Roman Catholic, the rest representing Protestant and Evangelical traditions. There were also 'official' representatives from the Pontifical Council Cor Unum (the Vatican), the World Health Organization and the Latin American Council of Churches.[26]

## VII.

In the presentation on the CMC study on <u>Health, Healing and Wholeness</u> to the Central Committee meeting at Dresden, GDR, 16-26 August 1981, the following was stated: "...It is still too often true, as it was 14 years ago, that church-related medical work established to serve the poor is providing a service beyond the ability of the poor to pay for and utilize. Many hospital-based programmes also remain insensitive to the needs of the community and therefore are largely ineffective and inefficient. On the other hand, in its ever-widening search, the CMC has been able to discover a number of innovative and highly successful health care programmes, several of which have become international models for primary health care.

Over the past five years, the CMC study has grown and communication has been sustained by many means with groups and communities in all regions. Central to this process has been the series of regional meetings, with encounters already held in the Caribbean, Central America, Africa, Egypt, South Asia and South-East Asia. Others are being planned for the Pacific and South America. The objective of the regional meetings is to bring people of varying backgrounds out of their isolation to engage in a search shared by those of medical training as well as those of theological vocation, a search for their common role in contributing to health and wholeness in their communities.

Recurring themes in these broadly ecumenical meetings included: 1) Health and wholeness: "Health in a dynamic state of wellbeing of the individual - physical, mental, social and spiritual - of being in harmony with each other, with the natural environment and with God." 2) Traditional healing systems are being explored to maximize useful and effective practices and discourage harmful ones, and help these find their place in today's concern for healing. 3) Relationship of health to justice has emerged as a concern in many parts of the world. 4) Responsibility for health must be shared by all those who live together, enabling all to realize fully their human potential. 5) The Church has its role to play; renewal of the Church's mission and ministry can be helped with a new concern for healing, moving all towards "life in all its fullness".[27]

At the Central Committee meeting in Geneva, 19-28 July, 1982, the Unit Committee recommended "that the CMC study on <u>The Christian Understanding of Health, Healing and Wholeness</u> be commended to the churches for their continuing reflection and further study."

This was urged in the light of: "the clarifying emphasis which the study places on human <u>wholeness</u> and a <u>wholistic</u> approach to health care; the stress it places on community-based and congregation-based concerns for promoting health; the helpful model it provides for regional study of health and healing activities of the churches; its recognition of the contribution made by traditional healing systems to health; the focus it brings to questions of social justice and participation as they relate to health; and the call it makes for vigorous study of a number of aspects of the healing ministry of the church which require further clarification."[28]

## VIII.

Two other consultations need to be recorded. The CMC and the Ecumenical Institute sponsored a consultation at Bossey, June 25 - July 7, 1979, on <u>The Healing Ministry of the Church</u>. Papers were presented by A. Bittlinger, G. Westberg, A. Allen, J. Schwarz, S.J. Ingma, S. Kruyt, E. Proudfoot, C. Baroi, C.F. Midelfort, B. Opitz and M. Damiani. The Group Reports were on: 1) Theology and Bible; 2) Liturgy and Worship; 3) Ethics and Morality; 4) Community and Individual Health Care; 5) Diversity of: Health and Healing.[29]

The WCC Office of Family Education organized a consultation at San Bernardo, Sao Paulo, Brazil, November 23-30, 1981, on the theme <u>The Humanity and Wholeness of Persons with Disabilities</u>. The majority of the 52 participants came from 15 countries in Latin America, North America, the Caribbean, Europe, Asia, Africa and Australia, many of them disabled. Also attending were ministers, psychiatrists, educationists working with mentally retarded children, and relatives of disabled people. The Latin American Council of Churches and the 156-group Brazil Section of the Christian Fraternity of Sick and Disabled People were also involved in the consultation which focused in particular on the urgency of preventing and fighting the poverty and repression that cause many disabilities.

The report includes personal life stories by G.A. Kahn, H. Wilke, B.C. Buchanan, J. Howard, M. Howard, A.P. de Assef, M. Negin, A.R. Nava, L. and J. Taylor, M. de Lourdes, L. Vincentre, E. Gonçalves de Araujo, N. Del Vecchio, Peter O Mba. Basic papers were presented by Masamba ma Mpolo, J. Howard, H.H. Wilke, A. Darnbrough. The appendices include: I. Bibliography; II. Organizations Interested in the Disabled; III. United Nations Declaration on the Rights of Disabled Persons; IV. The Manila Statement; V. Movement for the Rights of Disabled Persons in Sao Paulo.[30]

## IX.

Issue 4 of the Sixth Assembly of the WCC at Vancouver, Canada in 1983, dealt with <u>Healing and Sharing Life in Community</u>. The following was stated on the healing ministry of the Church: <u>Love, justice and health</u>. "The Church exists in the midst of the world where brokenness and lack of harmony find their expression not only in sickness and conflicts but also in the marginalization and oppression that many people endure due to economic, racial, political and cultural reasons. This situation is a challenge to the Church to carry out its healing ministry in a holistic way, and in a praxis renewed by the power of Christ's love - which is the basis of the ministry.

"Many nations, with only limited resources, must order their national priorities accordingly; others, with adequate resources, have not justly managed their priorities. In all cases the question of justice in the distribution of these resources is of paramount importance. In so many countries only a privileged few have access to such health care. Where the doctrine of national security based on the force of arms prevails, the possibilities of meeting basic health care needs decrease. In such cases the urban and rural poor always lose out. While the emphasis on distributive justice is vital for developing countries, many industrialized and affluent states also have the problem of unjust distribution of resources. The urban poor living alongside health care institutions of high excellence still suffer from malnutrition and appalling health conditions. The Church expresses its concern over the growing hunger and malnutrition in <u>all</u> regions, and recognizes the need to tackle the complex questions surrounding the local and global supply of food.

"It was strongly affirmed that the churches have an important role to play to bring about change both locally and abroad, through their own health policies and programmes, as well as through their governments' national and international health policies. The role of transnational corporations needs to be carefully analyzed in the context of justice and health - both their operations in the developing countries and their impact on the societies of industrialized and affluent countries.

"<u>The churches' health care programmes</u>. The churches must continue to emphasize and explore primary health care as one of the ways to overcome the injustice of the present system of distribution of health resources. This emphasis does not rule out the need to maintain and use institutional services which, however, must be humanized. The study of traditional healing practices and of the contribution of traditional healers should be a part of this effort.

"The role of spiritual healing as well as the healing ministry of the congregation calls for further study. Pastoral counselling is an integral part of the holistic approach to healing. A congregation can only become a healing community when it provides the opportunity to its members to participate fully in every aspect of its life and healing mission.

"The key to the success of health care is <u>people</u> who are well trained and motivated. Therefore, the involvement of churches in health care must be pursued at several levels: <u>policy</u>-direction and objectives guided by the concern for outgoing love and justice; <u>planning</u>-identification of priorities, resources and technologies; <u>service</u>-functioning, management, motivation; <u>training</u>-recruitment, education, deployment, course content.  Such an approach to health care can provide a basis for church-government collaboration. The churches are called to play a major role in terms or reorienting the health policy of their governments, both at home and abroad, towards a more community-based and just health care programme.

"The selection of priority areas in response to local needs must begin with a broad concern for both rural and urban poor and the populations most at risk, children, and women in their childbearing years.  It must also include a concern for the role of women as providers of care, as food providers, and as those with special health needs.

"<u>Human values and ethical issues</u>. The churches must emphasize the humanization of health care in the participation and responsibility of every individual in the health care of the community as well as in his/her own.  This must be accompanied by a vigorous approach to some of the ethical issues which face society and the Church.

"Medical technological advances should be viewed in their proper perspective, as gifts of God, in order to avoid the dehumanizing idolatry of science.  Such idolatry can result in the loss of many human values and the Christian understanding of health, disease and death, and encourage the persisting belief that disease is a simple dysfunction of body organs or the result of unfortunate accidents which scientific medicine can prevent or cure.

"<u>Disability and ageing</u>. The all-inclusive nature of this topic is seen in this fact: 450 million people, 85 % of them in the Third World, are disabled; and <u>all</u> of us are ageing and, in a sense, are dying.  Disability may be caused by accidents, disease, hereditary and congenital disorders, torture, hunger and wars. Underlying many of these are the conditions of economic and social injustice and poverty with which so many must live. This presents to both society and Church a challenge that cannot be ignored, because disability cuts across every cultural, social and economic stratum.  That challenge begins to be answered with a preventive approach to both the root causes and the immediate causes of disability.

"In the past, persons with disabilities, as well as the elderly and the dying, were often cut off from meaningful participation in family life, denied opportunities for education or self-expression, or simply shut away in institutions.  They were obliged to exist with little or no emotional or spiritual support from either society or Church.  The consequences in dehumanization, loneliness, deprivation, fear, guilt and economic dislocation have been beyond description.

"It is not only those who are disabled, ageing and dying, who must face their mortality and come to terms with it; all of us must. By learning to accept ourselves, we will be able to accept others. By the grace of God we will be able to accept and love each other as Christ has loved us.  Generally the Church has been slow to take a leadership role in helping the disabled, ageing and dying. Only recently are we beginning to recognize this neglect and rejection."[31]

## X

In its report to the Central Committee meeting at Geneva in 1984, the Unit Committee "especially took note of the insights gained in the study of the Christian Understanding of Health, Healing and Wholeness thus far and affirmed plans to continue the theological exploration on this topic with special emphasis on biblical understanding of suffering, sickness and dying; and the role of reconciliation and hope in the healing task of the churches.

"It also reviewed and endorsed CMC's main thrust in the area of community based primary health care and the programme in making essential pharmaceutical supplies available to people in need, particularly in the developing countries. The relationship between CMC's concern for healing and other issues like peace, justice and the integrity of creation was noted, and the role of CMC in food and hunger issues reaffirmed.

"The churches are encouraged to ask their governments to support the efforts of the World Health Organization to combat alcoholism and drug abuse."[32]

## Observations and Comments

1. Although the Christian Medical Commission has been active for almost twenty years in stimulating reflection on church and health, in enabling necessary re-orientation, in coordinating health and healing programmes in many countries, in sponsoring numerous consultations and issuing a great number of publications in several languages, its activities and programmes are relatively little known, and deserve far more attention, in the constituency of the WCC and in the ecumenical movement at large. Comparing the Christian Medical Commission with the Programme to Combat Racism and the Churches' Participation in Development, for instance, which were also initiated in the late sixties, there is no doubt, that the whole new orientation in the realm of health, healing and wholeness has as many progressive, and even revolutionary, elements as the other programmes. Churches, mission boards and agencies, national and regional councils of churches, and theological schools throughout the world need to examine more carefully the considerable developments in health care systems during the last twenty years, to stimulate more intensively information and communication and to work more effectively in partnership.

2. The solid foundations of the CMC were laid at the very beginning. The two consultations at Tübingen in 1964 and 1967 were of primary importance. The book by John Bryant, Health and the Developing World[33] was an essential tool of study, analysis and evaluation. Based on research sponsored by the Rockefeller Foundation and carried out by a survey team and a distinguished advisory committee, the book analyzed health programmes and the

obstacles they must overcome, whenever possible using examples from countries observed firsthand. Dr. Bryant was for several years the chairman of the CMC. Also the book <u>Medical Care in Developing Countries</u>[34], edited by Maurice King and published with a grant from the Ford Foundation, paved the way for organizing appropriate medical care for masses of sick people in poor nations by synthesizing the African, mostly missionary, experiences in initiating rural health work. Both books influenced a new medical policy of the World Health Organization with regard to widespread poverty, disease and hunger in the Third World.

3. Health, healing and wholeness has been an outspoken ecumenical programme. The CMC has been assisted by several Roman Catholic staff members and its commission includes Roman Catholic members, as the Commission on Faith and Order. Protestants and Roman Catholics together continue to emphasize community health-care with the accent on people's involvement in the own care as part of total development, and as a way of meeting health needs and the requirements of justice of large sections of populations. Protestant and Roman Catholic church-related hospitals join forces with government agencies in these endeavours.

4. The CMC and its constituency have struggled hard and long to truly integrate the social justice dimension of health with personal wholistic considerations. Attempts to relate true people's participation and decision making to management and technological imperatives have often been frustrated. The main purpose of several consultations has been to face new contradictions and continuous ambiguities. Still today each group and each individual person need to discover and to re-discover the intimate relationship between health, healing and wholeness of poor, oppressed, marginalized and diseased peoples. The harvest of twenty years of worldwide activities and programmes is still to be reaped.

5. The CMC and its constituency need to do more work in the realms of spirituality and Christian health work, the use of symbols in a technological environment in order to convey a profounder meaning of healing, the practice of collective and personal repentance and the acceptance and offering of forgiveness in healing, the need to accept in faith that sickness, suffering and grief can be part of God's hidden plan of salvation.

1. The Healing Church. The Tübingen Consultation 1964.
   Geneva: WCC, 1965 (World Council Studies, No.3). p. 34.

2. <u>Study Encounter</u>, vol. II, no. 3, 1966. pp. 122-166.

3. Health. Medical-Theological Perspectives.
   Geneva: WCC, LWF, 1967.

4. <u>Ecumenical Press Service</u>, No. 5, 6 February, 1969.

5.  Central Committee of the WCC. Minutes and Reports of the
    Twenty-Third Meeting, held at Canterbury, Great Britain,
    August 12-22, 1969. Geneva: WCC, 1969. pp. 161-163.

6.  Fetters of Injustice. Report of an Ecumenical Consultation
    on Ecumenical Assistance to Development Projects,
    26-31 January, 1970, Montreux, Switzerland.
    Ed. by Pamela H. Gruber. Geneva: WCC, 1970. p. 47.

7.  The Third Conference for Coordinators of Church-Related
    Health Work in Africa, Mombasa, Kenya.
    Geneva: CMC, 1975. See also: Contact, no.26, April 1975.

8.  Health Care in China: An Introduction. The Report of a
    Study Group in Hong Kong. E.H. Paterson, Chairman;
    S.B. Rifkin, Secretary. Geneva: CMC, 1974.

9.  Minutes and Report of the Assembly of the Commission on
    World Mission and Evangelism of the WCC at Bangkok,
    December 31, 1972 and January 9-12, 1973.
    Geneva: WCC, 1973. pp. 35 and 95.

10. Primal World-Views. Christian Involvement in Dialogue with
    Traditional Thought Forms. Ed. by John B. Taylor.
    Ibadan: Daystar Press, 1976. pp. 35-41, 50-54, 123-124.

11. Science and Technology For Human Development.
    The Ambiguous Future and the Christian Hope. Report of
    the 1974 World Conference in Bucharest, Romania.
    In: Anticipation, no. 19, November 1974. p. 26.

12. Uniting in Hope. Reports and Documents from the Meeting of
    the Faith and Order Commission, 23 July - 5 August, 1974,
    at Accra, Ghana. Geneva: WCC, 1975 (Faith and Order Paper,
    No. 72). p. 86.

13. Survey of Church and Mission Health Programmes in Sierra
    Leone and Workshop. Ed. by Stuart J. Kingma.
    Geneva: CMC, 1975.

14. The Future Role of the Church in Health Care Programmes in
    Ghana. Proceedings of a Workshop. Geneva: CMC, 1975.

15. Breaking Barriers. Nairobi 1975. Ed. by David M. Paton.
    London: SPCK; Grand Rapids: Eerdmans, 1976. p. 61-62.

16. Faith in the Midst of Faiths. Reflections on Dialogue in
    Community. Ed. by S.J. Samartha.
    Geneva: WCC, 1977. pp. 164-165.

17. Central Committee of the WCC. Minutes of the Thirtieth
    Meeting, held at Geneva, 28 July - 6 August, 1977.
    Geneva: WCC, 1977. p. 23.

18. Partners in Life. The Handicapped and the Church.
    Ed. by Geiko Müller-Fahrenholz.
    Geneva: WCC, 1979 (Faith and Order Paper, No. 89).

19. _Ecumenical Press Service_, no. 11, 20 April, 1978.

20. _Contact_, no. 51, June 1979.

21. Ibid.

22. _Contact_, no. 54, December 1979.

23. _Contact_, no. 59, December 1980.

24. _Contact_, no. 63, August 1981.

25. _Contact_, no. 65, December 1981.

26. _Contact_, no. 69, August 1982.

27. Central Committee of the WCC. Minutes of the Thirty-Third
    Meeting at Dresden, GDR, 16-26 August, 1981.
    Geneva: WCC, 1981.  p. 31.

28. Central Committee of the WCC. Minutes of the Thirty-Fourth
    Meeting at Geneva, 19-28 July, 1982.
    Geneva: WCC, 1982.  p. 74.

29. Seminar on the Healing Ministry of the Church.
    Bossey, 1979.  Mimeographed.

30. Report of Consultation on Humanity and Wholeness of
    Persons with Disabilities.
    Geneva: WCC Office of Family Education, 1982.

31. Gathered for Life. Official Report of the VI Assembly
    of the World Council of Churches at Vancouver, Canada,
    24 July - 10 August, 1983.  Ed. by David Gill.
    Geneva: WCC; Grand Rapids: Eerdmans, 1983.  pp. 64-67.

32. Central Committee of the WCC. Minutes of the Thirty-Sixth
    Meeting at Geneva, 9-18 July, 1984.
    Geneva: WCC, 1984.  p. 51.

33. Bryant, John.  Health and the Developing World.
    Ithaca: Cornell University Press, 1969.

34. Medical Care in Developing Countries. A Primer on the
    Medicine of Poverty and a Symposium from Makerere.
    Based on a Conference assisted by WHO/UNICEF.
    Ed. by Maurice King.
    Nairobi: Oxford Univeristy Press, 1966.

# XVI.
# Education

This survey deals with general education, Christian
education, Sunday school education and theological and ecumenical education.  It should be kept in mind that the WCC
Division of Ecumenical Action was born at the Second Assembly
in Evanston in 1954.  This Division included the Laity Department, the Department of Cooperation between Men and Women in
Church, Family and Society, the Youth Department and the Ecumenical Institute.  At Uppsala in 1968 the Fourth Assembly
added the Office of Education.  After a process of restructing
the WCC Unit III, Education and Renewal, was created in 1971
which includes Education, Women in Church and Society, Renewal
and Congregational Life, Youth, Biblical Studies and Theological Education.

A decisive element in the process of change in the ecumenical movement was the World Council of Christian Education
(WCCE) which traced its history even further back in time than
the Mission and Evangelism, Faith and Order, and Life and Work
movements.  It began with Sunday school conventions in the
nineteenth century and was organized formally at Rome in 1907
as the World Sunday School Association.  Successive assemblies,
held every four years, met in all parts of the world: Toronto,
Tokyo, Belfast, Nairobi, Lima.  During the 1960s the WCCE moved
its headquarters to Geneva and increasingly shared in many activities with the WCC, chiefly in youth work and education.
In 1964 a WCC/WCCE Joint Study Commission on Education was
established which presented its report to the Uppsala Assembly
in 1968.  In that same year a joint negotiating committee went
to work and, in 1971, at its Assembly in Lima, Peru, the WCCE
voted to integrate with the WCC.

Mention should also be made of the Theological Education
Fund (TEF) which the International Missionary Council established in 1958.  It supported until 1977 theological schools in
Asia, Africa and Latin America and strengthened their libraries
through the provision of theological textbooks, commentaries
and Bible dictionaries in indigenous languages.  The example
of TEF was followed by the creation in 1964 of a similar Fund
for Christian Literature.

I

In Section II, "Evangelism: The Mission of the Church to
Those Outside Her Life", the Evanston Assembly stated in 1954
on Christian Education: "One of the most important areas of
evangelism is that of childhood and youth.  Every new generation requires the fresh presentation of the gospel.  Among the
most important methods of Christian nurture are Sunday schools,

306

youth programmes, Bible fellowships, discussion groups, and most
of all, Christian training in the home."[1]

In the Report of the Committee on the Division of Ecumenical Action to the New Delhi Assembly in 1961 the need was
expressed "to help the churches to relate ecumenical thinking
to Christian concern for education in all its aspects, and to
encourage experiments in new methods of ecumenical education."
The following explanation of this function of the Division was
added in the Report: "Everywhere in the churches and the world
there is a deepening interest in education, and the Committee
believes that this matter might become a major part of the
future work of the World Council. The Committee on the Division of Ecumenical Action thought it would be helpful to
start with an explanation of what is meant by 'the Christian
concern for education in all its aspects'. It distinguishes
between:

1) 'ecumenical education', i.e. information about the
history and present expressions of the ecumenical movement and
education for personal participation in ecumenical responsibilities of witness, service and unity;
2) 'Christian education', i.e. the total work of the churches and congregations in teaching and training adults as well
as children and youth to understand the Christian message and
its implications for living;
3) 'education in general' as concerned with the basic
question of how educational institutions and organizations may
help people to become mature persons and to be responsible
members of modern society." The Committee stressed the desir-
ability of closer and more general relationships of the WCC
with the WCCE and continuing cooperation with the World Alliance
of YMCAs, the World YWCA and the World Student Christian Federation.

The Section of the Reports of Committees of the New Delhi
Report also includes in an appendix a Memorandum for the
Central Committee on WCC-WCCESSA Relationships.[2]

Discussing problems and challenges of the family, an International Ecumenical Study Conference at Thessalonica in 1959
stated the following on education: "The Christian concept of
education stems from the belief that God wills the salvation
of every man and that human society is the context in which
this high destiny of man is developed. The task of Christians
in education, therefore, is to help people to grow into the
'full nature and stature of Christ'. To this end, education
should help them to develop their abilities and gifts to the
utmost and to use them in the service of their fellow men.
The problem today is to realize this within the context of
rapid social change. This means that all boys and girls have
a right to an education suited to their abilities and needs,
and that any form of discrimination in education on any grounds
such as race, religion, caste or social group is wrong. It also
means that education not rooted in religious belief lacks an
essential element, and that Christians have a special responsibility for the provision of religious education.

"Social change presents many dilemmas in the field of
education. In many areas of Africa, Asia and Latin America the
Church has led in this field, and has often had a virtual
monopoly. A consequence of change has frequently been the
displacement of the Church from this privileged position, as
governments and other secular authorities have increased their
activities... It is important that Christians cooperate with
the State at every possible level. No opportunity should be
lost to participate in boards, committees, advisory bodies,
school and college councils and other governing bodies where
Christian influence can affect policy and practice. The churches should see that they are represented by able men and women.
Here the laity has its contribution to make, but it requires
special training.

"... In areas of rapid social change, the clergy are far
too often insufficiently trained for the teaching ministry.
Great emphasis must be put on the training of clergy and laity,
improving standards of theological education and releasing the
clergy from administrative and secondary activities for their
proper function of preaching, teaching and pastoral counselling.
There is a special need for better training of pastors in Christian social ethics related to the real problems of social change
...

"... If Christians are to fulfill their prophetic calling,
they must devote time to studying the facts of the situation,
making use of disciplines such as sociology, psychology,
economics and political sciences. This is necessary because,
without knowing the trends in society, it is impossible to discern clearly and realistically the way in which God is at work.
True understanding also requires identification with those who
struggle and suffer with evil."[3]


II

Three consultations on Christian education were held at the
Ecumenical Institute in Bossey from 1949 to 1961. "The Christian in Education" was the theme of a consultation, August 10-
20, 1949. Eight questions arose on which members of the gath-
ering expressed different points of view: Secular or Christian
Schools; Natural Theology, Practice versus Theory; Teacher-
Pupil Relationship; Objectivity; Religious Teaching; Boarding
or Day Schools. The following papers were presented: A.D.Baly
on "The Boarding House as a Christian Community"; A. Krause on
"Geography as Taught by a Christian"; G. Landberg on "The
Christian History Teacher"; D.H.Horne on "Christianity in
Science Teaching"; D. Roberts on "Psychology and the Christian
Teachers"; A. Leenhardt on "The Christian in a Secular School".[4]

"The Churches' Responsibilites for Children and Young People
in Need of Care: Aims and Methods in Their Education" was the
theme of a consultation, January 3-8, 1951. The Report contains
a foreword by S. de Dietrich, and introduction by M. Veillard,

and papers by L. Bovet, D.Q.R. Mulock Houwer, K.O. Finkensieper, R.M.Braithwaite, and the findings (Use of psychological methods; Boarding-out in foster-homes; Institutional Care; Recruitment and Organization of Social Workers).[5]   At a consultation on "Christian Education", August 8-15, 1952  the speakers were: D.G.O. Ayerst, O. Hammelsbeck, W. Horton, F. Knapp, P.S. Minear, G.C. van Niftrik, W. Oakeshott, L. Pont, M.K. Powell, L. Rese, K. Witt.  Six groups concentrated on:  I. The Responsilbility of the Church in Education;  II. Presuppositions of the Church's Action;  III. Methods for the Church to Use, and issued a report.[6]

"The Function of the Gospel in School Education" was the subject of discussion of a consultation, July 17-22, 1958. The sub-themes were:  1) The place given to Christian education in the schools of different countries today;  2) The Gospel as a decisive dimension in school education;  3) The school as a human community in the light of the Gospel;  4) The Christian mission of the teacher in the human community of the school. Five study groups concentrated on:  a) Religious instruction in schools;  b) The socio-psychological background for the attitude of modern youth;  c) General world problems in education;  d) Problems of modern education;  e) The elaboration of new methods of Christian instruction in schools according to modern theological research.[7]

III

The Inaugural Assembly of the East Asia Christian Conference in 1959 was much engaged in a discussion on "Christian Schools in a Changing Society", and on "Theological Education". It stated the following: ... "It is sad to note that in many countries of East Asia education is in the hands of politicians rather than educationalists.  This interference of the politicians often has detrimental consequences which are far reaching. We urge that the State in its dealing with education, set up semi-autonomous organs consisting mainly of educationalists.  While granting the right of the State to plan education, the right of the Christian school to carry out its primary purpose in education must also be conceded by the State, i.e. education for life, recognizing that only under God has life meaning and purpose.

"In this context the right of parents to guide the education of their children under the total education plan must be granted. This includes choice of school, choice of medium of instruction and also of religious education.  The increasing State control of education has this to its credit that it would normally provide free primary, secondary, and university education for every child that can use this opportunity.  The temptation of the State to interfere with University education should be resisted."

The following recommendations were made to the Church to go into new educational fields:  a) strengthening the Sunday schools; b) responding to the needs of women's education;  c) adult edu-

cation, especially in civil rights and responsibilities;
d) youth training, youth camps, and exploration of the possibility of youth of different faiths 'living together'.  The
section on Theological Education contained the following heads:
1) Standards;  2) The Language of Theological Education;
3) Libraries;  4) Higher Theological Education;  5) Exchange
of Students;  6) Exchange of Faculty;  7) Theological Institutes;
8) Theological Training for Laymen and Women;  9) Curriculum ;
10) Refresher Courses for Clergy;  11) Cooperation in Theological Education.[8]

At its Assembly in 1964, the East Asia Christian Conference
in the section on "The Call to Renewal in the Churches of Asia"
suggested "... a change from church-oriented to a world-oriented
pattern of living with Bible study that is geared to action and
related to the cultural and social environment" ... and "a development of Christian education directed more specifically to
training the whole people of God for their ministry in the world,
and the laity in particular, for their encounters and decisions
in daily life."[9]

Dealing with the major theme, "The Church, Youth and the
Family", the All Africa Church Conference in 1958 noted that
"Sunday schools are still undeveloped in many places, but thought
and effort are being given to the provision of a comprehensive
curriculum for African Sunday Schools, and many are taking this
as an impetus to use the agency of the Sunday School to serve
the need which is being created by the taking over of day schools
by the governments...  More emphasis is being laid on the interrelation of agencies for Christian education, viz., the home,
the church and the school in one respect, and the Sunday School,
uniformed organizations, S.C.M., Y.M.C.A., Y.W.C.A., etc., in
another respect.  The growth of these organizations is noted,
and the value of seeing and comparing the syllabi and programmes of each with those of the others is recommended.

"Although teacher-training colleges are being taken over by
governments, nevertheless it is still possible in some places
to create extra-curricular courses in Christian education for
young students.  In any case, churches should make sure that
theological students and those being trained in the Bible
Schools have a thorough course in Christian education... It is
noted, on the whole, that the acceptance of responsibility is
one of the most important factors in the development of leadership."[10]

In the Section, "Freedom and Unity in Society", the First
Assembly of the All Africa Conference of Churches in 1963 noted
the following: "The Church has pioneered in education; in all
parts of Africa, in all walks of life, there are many who have
received their education under missionary auspices.  Though the
Christian population of Africa is put between 15 per cent and
20 per cent of the total population, the contribution the Church
has made to social progress through education is of far greater
significance than these statistical figures would indicate."

With regard to the Church and the Student World the Assembly stated: "The Churches should tackle more seriously the problem of evangelizing the student population in schools and universities. Hence there should be more concern for better training of the ministry to meet the present-day challenges. The young people today are asking questions which teachers, the clergy and, where possible, parents, should answer to the best of their ability; hence the need for trained leadership... Bearing in mind that the African community is becoming more educated and sophisticated, the leaders of the Church should be trained to meet the challenge of the new situation. It is necessary that these leaders should be persons who have undergone systematic intellectual discipline."[11]

IV

In an Appendix to Section II, "Scripture, Tradition and Traditions", the Fourth World Conference on Faith and Order in 1963 stated: "The document presented to the Section on 'The Revision of Catechisms in the Light of the Ecumenical Movement' contains a number of important proposals which are highly relevant to our work on Tradition and Traditions. Catechetical instruction or religious education is obviously one important way in which the traditionary process works, for the instruction of the young is a continual effort at indigenization in each new generation. There are many questions which the churches ought to address to themselves about the effectiveness and fidelity of their catechisms and other teaching materials as instruments of the traditionary process. We confine ourselves however to one main question: How far do the teaching materials which are used in our churches reflect their ecumenical commitments and intentions ? Negatively stated the question would be: How far do these teaching materials reflect prejudices and misunderstandings which we ought to have outgrown, and perhaps thought that we had outgrown ?"

Four questions were addressed to the churches:

"a) What statements of ecumenical intention has your church issued ? What are the ecumenical commitments which your church has undertaken ? How are these intentions and commitments reflected in your educational materials, e.g. catechisms which are teaching instruments, Sunday-school lessons and textbooks ?

b) How do your educational materials deal with the dilemma created by the fact that we acknowledge one Baptism into Christ and yet live as separated churches ?

c) How are the other Christian bodies described in your educational materials ? Is the description accurate and fair ? Would the other churches recognize themselves in the picture you draw of them ?

d) What proportion of time is spent on teaching our common faith and our common history as Christians, and what proportion on teaching that history and doctrine which distinguishes your church from other churches ?"[12]

In Section I, "Economic Development in a World Perspective", the World Conference on Church and Society in 1966 noted that "education is the key to long-term progress for the developing nations. In the past its scope and content have been limited, so people have not been equipped to make the contribution to society of which they are capable. Technical and business training are greatly needed, although the liberal arts are equally important... Educational patterns need not duplicate those of the more developed countries, though they may have much in common. Advancing technology opens up enormous possibilities for the conquest of illiteracy and for a rapid rise in educational achievement. Churches have concentrated on the provision of primary and liberal education and have not generally come to grips with the equally, if not more important need for technical and business training. While they will never be able to meet entirely the need, their most important task is to move from primary to technical, vocational, agricultural, and business education, supplementing existing opportunities in government institutions and universities..."

Concerning The Educational Task of the Church the Geneva Conference outlined four forms of education:

a) Theological education to show the relationship of Christian belief and ethics to economic problems.

b) Economic education to encourage an understanding of world economic relations and structures and, in developed countries, to show the urgent need to replace economic paternalism or domination by economic partnership among all nations; and, in developing countries, the necessity of national and regional planning and cooperation.

c) Political education: some are convinced that radical changes are necessary in both developed and developing countries; others would stress education for full and informed political participation in national and international affairs. The purpose of church participation in political education is to produce the political will for a world economic and social order compatible with Christian conscience.

d) Social education: one of the major tasks of the churches in this field is social education designed to help society understand and accept the costs of world economic development."

The Geneva Church and Society Conference also made the following additional recommendations: "... In recognition of the significance of theological education for the future work of the Church, we recommend that it be radically changed in such a way as to further the real confrontation of the Church with the realities of the changing modern world. Behavioural sciences can help normative theology, since in the Bible and in the Church's tradition theology is a concrete prophecy concerning human beings. The churches in their educational policy should move collectively to initiate new programmes for social change in the form of a new specialized ministry of clergy and laity, especially training for full-time active involvement in efforts to preserve and bring about social justice..."[13]

## V

The following consultations took place from 1962 to 1967.
The World Christian Youth Commission and the Ecumenical Insti-
tute at Bossey sponsored a consultation on "The Impact of
Secondary Education on Young People", March 28 - April 1, 1962.
Contributions were made by D.E. Woods, P. Wells, H. Makulu,
M. Gibbs, E. Adler, J.P. Mitchell, L.P. Fitzgerald, F.J. Glen-
denning, R. Stöver, J.P. van Praag.[14]  The Faith and Order
Secretariat, the Youth Department and the World Council of
Christian Education organized a consultation on "Christian
Education and Ecumenical Commitment" at Bossey, May 3-8, 1965.
The Report contains the findings, individual contributions by
J.K.S. Reid, L. Vischer, G. Downey, E.G. Rupp, D. van der Plas,
M.B. Handspicker, R. Henderlite, H. Archibald, a case study by
a sociological team of the Taizé community, and a postscript by
A.H. van den Heuvel.[15]

Three consultations were held on "Christian Education" at
Berlin, August 1-10, 1964,  Glion, Switzerland, April 19-22,
1965, and Sussex, England, August 24 - September 2, 1965. These
were consultations sponsored by the Joint Study Commission of
Education, which had its origin in the instruction of the New
Delhi Assembly to the Division of Ecumenical Action to "relate
ecumenical thinking to Christian concern for education in all
aspects" and in the Institute and the Seminar for theologians
conducted by the WCCE on "What is education and specifically
what do we mean when we talk of Christian education ?"[16]

Three consultations were also held on "Patterns of Ministry
and Theological Education" at Hong Kong, March 1965, Seoul,
November 1966, and Northwood, Middlesex, England, July 1967.
The consultation at the London College of Divinity was the final
meeting in a series of the WCC study on Patterns of Ministry and
Theological Education.  The recommendations of the Northwood
consultation concern:  I. General Policy;  II. Theological Curriculum;  III. Structures and Relationships;  IV. Theological
and Educational Standards;  V. Educational Methods;  VI. Learning in Community.  Individual contributions were made by J.
Smolik, P.R. Clifford, R. Rendtorff, V. Istavridis, K. Grayston,
J. Radha Krishan, K.C. Joseph, H. Servotte, G. Créspy, W.Blum.[17]

"Theological Education in North-East Asia" was the theme of
a consultation in Seoul, Korea, November 28 - December 2, 1966.
It was the second consultation on theological education on a
regional basis recommended by the Second Assembly of the EACC
in 1964.  The first was held in Hong Kong in March 1965 for the
South-East Asia region.  The consultation report had four sections:  I. Ministry and Ministries;  II. The Aim and Purpose of
Theological Education;  III. The Pattern and Curriculum of
Theological Education;  IV. Joint Action for Theological Education.[18]

A consultation on "The Teaching of Practical Theology" at Bossey, August 21-27, 1967 was attended by Orthodox, Roman Catholic and Protestant theologians and a few lay persons. H.-R. Weber was the convenor of the consultation. Papers were given by S. Bornkamm, J. Scharfenberg, and H.-R. Weber, who also submitted a plan for an ecumenical bibliography on pastoral theology. The final report reflected the work of four working groups.[19]

VI

In its Report to the Uppsala Assembly in 1968, the Committee on Education suggested that the following matters of study and action be placed high on the agenda of the new WCC Office of Education:

"1. The goals of general education, as they are pursued, consciously and unconsciously, in different cultural contexts, and as they are understood in various theological traditions. (This study should be undertaken on a six-continent basis).

2. The economic and social obstacles to making a full education accessible to all of every race, religion and class and of both sexes; the social and psychological process of education, in the light of the changing patterns of family life and the modern understanding of human development and learning.

3. The availability of the WCC Secretariat as a means by which the mission boards of the churches and the churches themselves can be brought together to carry out their educational task in a coordinated way in the political context in which they find themselves.

4. The distinctive nature and purpose of Christian education in family, church and school, its relation to general education, and its function of equipping Christians to live as creative members of society.

5. The provision of educational services and the development of curricula for the training of indigenous leadership, especially in the Third World by the strengthening of national and regional councils and in other ways.

6. (In conjunction with the other departments concerned). The aims and curricula for the training of theological students and lay people, both in seminaries and through in-service training, to take part in the pastoral and educational tasks of the churches."

In Section VI of the Uppsala Assembly, "Towards New Styles of Living", the following was stated on Christian Education: "A close link with the life of a Christian community and a study of the Scriptures are essential for nurture in faith. This will ensure that Christian education is not purely intellectual or doctrinal but related to the whole person in his individual and social setting, both in the world and in the Church. Education must play a constructive and at times radical part in the process of changing the world. This also holds true of ecumenical training. Experiments in sharing, serving and praying together are the best ways of deepening our ecumenical involvement. The ecumenical movement as well as the changing world challenge the churches to undertake thorough revision of their teaching material."

Appendix XI, The Church and the Media of Mass Communication, of the Uppsala Report, contains the following paragraphs on Special Ministries: "We call on the churches to free and train people for special ministries in the mass media and encourage their laymen to enter the field. Trainees should be used, either by the churches or in the secular field, after gaining experience, and the training itself should normally be undertaken in cooperation with the secular activity rather than as a separate church-centred operation.

"The proper use of the media requires special skill. The churches have traditionally concentrated on the parish ministry, but special attention needs to be given to those media by which it is possible to reach millions. Writing and broadcasting demand a high degree of professional skill and training... We plead for the creation of 'media chairs' in faculties and seminaries and the appointment of specialist professors who can probe and study the media and their relevance for Church and society. Where such expertise is already available, scholarships should be given to students who show aptitude for such training."[20]

Appendix VII of the Report of the Central Committee in 1969 contains a Proposal for the Establishment of an Education Renewal Fund, to be jointly sponsored by the WCC and the WCCE. It spells out the rationale, the aim and functions, the programme and the structures and operations of the Fund.[21] In the moderator's report to the Central Committee meeting in 1972 M.M. Thomas said on the philosophy of education of Paulo Freire: ... His "philosophy of education has three affirmations. First, since the Incarnate Word is 'transforming presence here and now', it is 'only in history that the Church fulfils her transcendent task'. Second, 'the educational task of the Church resides in her utopian proclamation' which gives hope of a liberated future to the oppressed; therein lies the 'prophetic presence of the Church in the world'. Third, 'education can never be neutral'; it is either for the 'liberation of man from oppression or for his domestication to it'."[22]

"The World Educational Crisis and the Church's Contribution" was the theme of a conference at Bergen, Holland, May 17-22, 1970, and the first attempt of the WCC Office of Education to understand the distinctive tasks and challenges facing education throughout the world and to envisage the particular contributions of Christians. The Report contains several excerpts of individual contributions, extracts from regional group reports and working hypotheses from the Office of Education (1. What is Education ?; 2. What is Education Good For ?; 3. Who Decides in Education ?; 4. How Do We Educate ?; 5. Who Gets Education?).[23]

The Memorandum of a <u>Multilateral Dialogue of People of Living Faiths</u> at Ajaltoun, Lebanon in 1970 contains the following section on education: "The implications of dialogue might also be considered in the educational field. The academic study of religions can contribute to preparation for dialogue and can itself be enriched by such experience.

a) Religious education syllabuses should provide facilities for sensitive teaching about different faiths.

b) Theological colleges and seminaries should develop provisions for the study of other faiths in the context of dialogue with adherents of other faiths (e.g. with visiting professors).

c) Educational institutions of one faith should provide pastoral care and religious instruction for students of other faiths in their own particular traditions.

d) Text books on religious education might be revised or written afresh, perhaps in collaboration with UNESCO in order to ensure a proper presentation of the place of religions in the modern world and to avoid any caricature of one religion by the adherents of another.[24]

A Consultation on <u>Primal World-Views</u> at Ibadan, Nigeria in 1973, said on the subject <u>Preparations for Dialogue</u>: "We welcome the many signs in university departments of religion and in theological seminaries of new courses on the primal religions of their region or continent, and we observe that the student response is usually very favourable. Yet many teachers feel the need for some basic training in more empirical methods, especially those of the history and the phenomenology of religion. This could be acquired under the right conditions in perhaps one year: from this new orientation they could then proceed to develop professional skills in the course of their own study and teaching. We regard this as one of the key points for a break-through towards an approach with real understanding for the primal religious world, and we draw the attention of the Theological Education Fund, the WCC's Scholarship Fund and similar bodies to this recommendation."[25]

Sub-section C, "<u>Salvation in Relation to National Planning</u>", of the Assembly of the Commission on World Mission and Evangelism at Bangkok in 1973 stated the following on <u>Education</u>: "Education is of crucial importance in any programme that is calculated to free people from enslaving structures, and dehumanizing value structures. The aim of education should be empowering the powerless, giving a voice to the voiceless, so that people may become aware of their own problems, resources and potentials, weigh possibilities that are open to them and choose their own course of action with regard to their duty to society. Education is for developing full human beings and integrated persons and must go on throughout the whole of life.

a) We recommend educational experiment and research in all six continents. Particular attention should be given to the fact that both individual rights and cultural identity demand the use of the mother tongue in education and the free access to modern languages and culture.

b. The whole village or community should be considered a community of learners and teachers in an imaginative system of education.

c. Christians should exert their influence to ensure that educational systems should exist, not just for evolving the few who will receive tertiary education, but to help all to give of their best to the community. Educational systems must be relevant both to the individual and the community.

d. When national goals are in conflict with cultural and social goals planning itself becomes oppressive. Any national education planning must be carried out in close consultation with the community.

e. Education must not be conditioned by the needs of society and the availability of jobs. However, the value structure and wage structure of society must be so ordered that well educated persons may find fulfilment in serving the needs of society rather than in obtaining prestigious employment.

f. We consider the role of Christian teachers to be very important in discovering new styles of education and experimenting with them. We strongly urge churches to re-emphasize teaching as a high Christian calling."

The Bangkok Assembly in 1973 also recommended that "CWME and the Office of Education of the WCC be requested to consider the convening of consultations on education in strategic parts of the world. These should bring together the Office of Education, churches mission boards, local authorities and, where possible, governments." The Assembly further endorsed the following concerns:

1) Re-appraisal of the Christian nurture of members in congregations (Sunday schools, catechetical classes, youth work, adult study, action-reflection groups) to relate Christian faith and commitment more incisively to mission, family life, social action, world perspective.

2) Next steps and directives in the growth of area, laity and study centres, and varied leadership training enterprises, with emplasis on redefinition of the church, mission, roles of clergy and laity, church and society witness.

3) The radically altered situation of the church schools at all levels amid soaring governmental provision for and control of general education, posing sharp new questions of goals, relations and strategies for churches and councils.

4. The incredible increase in general education, both formal and informal, causing churches to be critics (and/or supporters) of the goals, contents, methods and human impacts of general education."[26]

The Report of the Working Group on Women and the Church of a World Conference on Sexism at West Berlin in 1974 recommended "that the Church give serious thought to education for family life and interpersonal relationships, and that in its programmes of education and counseling, it take into account the following concerns:

1. life-long planning for a woman so that she will recognize that she has other roles than that of wife and mother;
2. educating society to recognize that a woman has a right to a creative life of her own;
3. setting value on the work of looking after a home and family;
4. educating people for a true sense of partnership;
5. creating awareness in both men and women that the making of a successful relationship is a long-term enterprise which two people must undertake together;
6. providing sex education to prepare people for this essential dimension of true partnership; it is recognized that the clergy need to be provided with adequate training to prepare them for education and counseling in this area."

The Working Group on Education of the West Berlin Conference in 1974 stated: "... In most churches, women are conditioned into dependence by exclusion from the priesthood, from the councils of the Church, and from decision making bodies. The whole Church suffers from a male-dominated theology. Women must be educated to participate with full and equal responsibility in all areas of life. When true education takes place, we women become aware of the ways in which we have been limited and exploited, and conditioned to accept our role of dependency ... When this awareness dawns, we experience a sense of liberation...

"We recommend that the WCC initiate an education programme through national churches to draw attention to the causes as well as the manifestations of the needs of people, especially women, throughout the world wherever they are economically, socially and culturally oppressed. This education programme should be particularly but not exclusively directed to women's organizations in the Church... We recommend that the member churches of the WCC set up training programmes for women to enable them to become aware of their own potential as persons, to overcome sexist attitudes in themselves and others, and to develop their potential as leaders in Church and society."[27]

Two conferences, sponsored by the Exploratory Committee on Society, Development and Peace, were also concerned with various problems of education. The Conference on World Cooperation for Development at Beirut, 1968 outlined the following: "... While the developing countries have given high priority to schools over the last twenty years, much of the schooling has been ill-suited to the needs of development. Some way, perhaps the national development plan, must be found to mesh educational output with the real social and economic requirements of the country. This means balanced school systems, instruction geared to producing modernizing attitudes and modern schools and updated vocational training... Institutions engaged in these activities must not ignore the fact that education should not limit itself to the acquisition of new technical skills and competences, but must develop the potentialities of individuals so as to prepare them to assume social responsibilities.

"The churches have played an important role in education
in many developing countries.  They could do even more, as by
helping to develop improved teaching methods, and by providing
scholarships for training.  They could play a much larger role
in providing all rural people and especially women with appropriate education for farm life, in educating to social leadership, in assisting in the work of extension education.  Adult
education, so vital to modernization and to satisfying human
development, ought to be a field the churches generously
contribute to.

    "... Guide-lines and model curricula are needed for
subsequent adaptation to local school systems.  These curricula
should show the place of development and social justice in the
various disciplines - religious instruction, history, sociology,
political science, economics, geography, applied science - and
encourage pupils' grasp on the facts of dynamic change. The
special needs of agricultural and technical training should be
included in these curricula.  Since UNESCO has done a good deal
of work in this field, its advice and cooperation should be
sought..."[28]

    At the Consultation on Christian Concern for Peace in
Baden, Austria, in 1970, SODEPAX engaged in an extensive discussion on Education for Peace, outlined the obstacles to education for peace, the church and instruments for peacemaking
and made several proposals and suggestions.  In the introduction
to this section it was stated: "... Education for peace means
not only a radical new understanding of the dynamic nature of
peace, but a radical reform of existing educational practices.
It also involves an active engagement of the people of every
Church in every land in the process of creation of a common
framework of standards as to how the earth's plenty should be
shared.  It involves harnessing the Christian commitment to the
pursuit of truth to a scientific search for understanding of
the conditions out of which conflicts emerge at every level of
human interaction from the family to the international system...

    "Much of the current educational activity of the Church is
tied to excessively formal Western teaching methods and tools.
It is rarely recognized that every individual is both a learner
and a teacher, and that the teaching-learning process is not a
one-way, but a reciprocal process.  Adults and youth ideally
each teach the other perceptions about the world we live in
which are not directly available to the other because each sees
the world through the lenses of his own life experience.
Similarly rural and urban people within a country have much to
teach each other.  Among nations, the industrializing have much
to teach the industrialized, as well as vice versa."[29]

## VII

Several consultations were held in the period from 1968 to
1975. "Dogmatic or Contextual Theology" was the subject of
a consultation at Bossey, August 26-31, 1971, organized jointly
by the Institute and the Director of the Humanum Studies. The
minutes of the consultation contain: I. Definition of the
Notion of 'Contextual'; II. Comments by Scientists; III. Contextual Theology in the Light of the Christian Doctrine of Man;
IV. The Place of Doctrine in Theology and Church Life; V. General Remarks on the Main Theme. Papers were given by A.O.
Dyson, R. Mouton, E. Schlink. There were three panel presentations. The first included: J. Coulson, L. Thunberg, N. Nissiotis; the second: H.H. Wolf, P. Verghese, D. Jenkins; the third:
C. van Peursen, F. Konrad, W.A. Whitehouse, Y. Kumazawa.[30]

The consultation on "Doctrine and Change", June 19-24, 1972,
continued the discussion of the previous consultation at Bossey.
The report is in six parts: I. Christology and the Doctrine of
Man. Ethical and Social Implications of Christology; II. Theo-
sis and Change; III. Place and Value of the Doctrine in the
Life of the Church; IV. Doctrine and Change; V. Hermeneutical
Bases for the Interpretation of Church Doctrine; VI. Panel
Presentation (R. McKinney, B. Cooke, E. Flesseman-van-Leer,
E. Schlink, D.E. Jenkins). Individual presentations were made
by: J.-L. Leuba, D.E. Jenkins, P. Verghese, G. Sauter, G. ter
Schegget, L. Wenzler.[31]

"New Perspectives for Christian Education" was the theme of
the conference at Huampani (Lima), Peru, July 8-21, 1971.
A total of 380 delegates from 77 countries to the World Council
of Christian Education met for the purpose of discovering new
perspectives in Christian education and voted to integrate the
WCCE in the WCC.[32] "Learning Community" was the subject of a
consultation at Glion, Switzerland, September 24-28, 1973.
Participants evaluated the Sunday school contribution to church
education in Europe. There were observers from Africa, the
Middle East, Australia, and North America.[33]


# VIII

Section IV, Education for Liberation and Community, of the
Nairobi Assembly in 1975 dealt with: The Context of Education,
Alienation from and Assimilation into Our Culture and History,
the Christian Community as a Sign of Liberation, Doing Theology
and a Creative Life Style for Community. It made various recommendations concerning priorities for educational activities.

With regard to alienation from and assimilation into a
specific culture Section IV stated: "We cannot be liberated if

we are divorced from the culture which bred us and which continues to shape and condition us. Many are taught to despise
their culture, many are not participants - except by omission -
in the shaping of it. Some educational programmes play a large
part in creating false images: prejudice, fear, hatred are
instilled into persons through selective and biased curricula
and teaching, and this situation is aggravated by the false
expectations which people derive from the influences of social
organizations. Education policies in many countries serve
development strategies that are harmful to their societies.
We are not romanticizing indigenous culture: it too can have
elements which enslave and degrade, but we advocate that people
be brought to a critical awareness of the strengths and weaknesses of their own culture for the development they desire for
themselves, rather than being disruptively separated from it to
serve the purposes of others.

"... The educational system and institutions are all too
often mirror images of society, reinforcing by their practices
the values which society holds. Though not plagued as severely
by the drop-out problem which blights the educational provision of some developing countries, the developed countries
share with them in the provision of an education which dis-
qualifies the large majority of 'success'. Content becomes
more theoretical and abstract, the practical is degraded, experience counts for little, the cognitive becomes increasingly
emphasized over other values and virtues, until in higher education it is the pre-eminent if not the only concern. We are
aware of a deep and pervasive sense of anxiety about systems
of formal education in many parts of the world. The formal
education system it itself in ferment. The naive utopianism
which equates technological development with progress is being
abandoned. This is paralleled in the education system which
serves that development, with the abandonment of the view that
more and more schooling is a good thing in itself."

Concerning theological education Section IV outlined:
"... The tradition of theological teaching will continue to be
an integral part of training for the ordained and other specialized ministries, but the diversified needs of the Church require
alternatives. Particularly restrictive has been reliance on
Western models of theology and the adoption in other places of
Western models of theological education. The new alternatives
in extension programmes, field work programmes for theological
students, lay institutes, and the provision of continuing
theological education are urgent priorities today. As many
societies become more multi-cultural, another urgent priority
is the need for a theological training which allows dialogue
to be opened at all levels with those of other faiths, no faith,
or faiths which are anti-Christian.

"... Theological education belongs to the whole people of
God in the equipping of them for ministry. The times are witnessing changes in the development and organization of the
ordained ministry, the development of more kinds of specialized
ministries, and ministries open to a greater variety of persons

in a greater variety of situations than ever before. The Church
needs to respond to this situation of divergence with other than
a single mode of theological education, if it is to respond
adequately... The aim of theological education is to contribute
to growth in Christ through community. Such growth takes place
through conscious intellectual reflection, the nurturing of
spriritual awareness, the proclaiming of the good news of human
redemption, and the involvement of the people in the total
liberation process."[34]

The Central Committee in 1976 received and endorsed the
Report of the Review Committee in which "Education and Renewal
in Search of True Community" was proposed as the fourth major
programme thrust of the WCC in the future. The Report stated:
"The task of equipping and enabling God's people for life in
Christ in worship, witness and service in the world is a continuing major concern. Moreover, we believe that the place
where this task is most effectively carried out is the local
and Christian community. But the means for equipping and enabling and the forms of congregational life are not always
conducive to the achievement of this task. They must therefore
be continually re-examined and renewed in the light of the
Gospel and its demands in a given situation in ways that will
indeed build up the Christian community in the spirit of unity
and common witness. This task has become more urgent because
of the spiritual crisis in today's world."[35]

Meeting at Bangalore in 1978, the Commission on Faith and
Order concentrated on "Growing Together into Unity". A Group
Report on "Towards Common Ways of Teaching and Decision-making"
stated: "... Before the Church performs acts of teaching, she
exists and lives. Her existence and her life are the work of
the triune God who calls her into being and sustains her as his
people, the Body of Christ, the fellowship of the faithful in
the Spirit. The authority of the Church has its ground in this
datum of her being. The whole Church teaches by what she is,
when she is living according to the Gospel. The Gospel we
proclaim is the Gospel of God's free grace. He calls us into
his grace and sets us free. Therefore, the authoritative
teaching of the Church assumes the form of a joyful witness to
God's liberating truth... All members of the Church are called
upon to manifest the truth of the Gospel in their own lives
and to share their faith with all people. Thus, authoritative
teaching is a responsibility of the whole Christian community."
The Group made also various recommendations with regard to the
implementation of the authoritative teaching of the Church.[36]

Section III, "Science and Education", of the World Council
of Churches' Conference on Faith, Science and the Future in
1979 contains the headings: 1. Science Education and Ethics;
2. Science Education and the Third World; 3. Science Education and Non-Scientists; 4. Science Education and Society;
5. Science Education and Research. Among the 12 recommendations the following two are selected: "7. Churches should take
the initiative to provide opportunities for scientists, theologians and ethicists to study and to discuss the relation of

science and faith and the insights theology and ethics bring to the decisions scientists must make. ...12. We recommend that the WCC give more attention to appropriate forms of adult education in relation to science and technology. We recommend in particular that its Programme on Theological Education give attention to the need to incorporate at least minimal requirements regarding scientific and technological knowledge in the curricula of all clergy and theologians."[37]

The World Conference on The Community of Women and Men in the Church in 1981 recommended to the WCC Sub-unit on Education that:
a. it request the member churches to monitor their own educational Sunday School and other materials to ensure that they are not reinforcing stereotypes through the languages, illustrations and concepts used;
b. in the light of insights emerging on new and changing patterns of family life and partnership relations, it incorporate, together with the Sub-unit on Women, women's experiences and perspectives into the study of all aspects of sexuality opened up by the Community Study;
c. it collect and share material from a women's perspective to facilitate education within and between churches on sexuality from theological, psychological, sociological, ethical, and legal perspectives, and that it encourage member churches also to produce materials;
d. it encourage churches to be aware of special needs of single women and men and lone parents, and of the handicapped in relation to both church and society;
e. in light of increasing violence in many societies, it continue its educational efforts to emphasize the responsibilities of women and men in the specific areas of violence in the home and in the community, including concerns with regard to prostitution, teen-age pregnancies and issues of family panning;
f. it produce understandable Bible Study materials and worship materials for use by small groups and local churches wanting to study the issues of community developed in the CWMC Study."[38]

In the Report of Life and Action of the Christian Conference of Asia in 1977 the following was stated on "Education for Full Humanity": "Our goal in education is the achievement of full humanity for all people. This will be achieved only in a community which affirms the equal human dignity, rights and freedoms of all its people, particularly children, women, the handicapped, the aged, and other marginalised groups of people. The true growth of persons will take place only through an education process which frees rather than limits. Seen in this light, Christian education will extend beyond church-based education and involve engagement in society which includes both action and spirituality."

The Report expressed itself on "Non-formal Education" as follows: "It is said 'the future of Asia is in its classrooms'. However, there is a shortage of classrooms and trained teachers

in many Asian countries.  Besides, the classrooms are often
educational instruments of oppressive forces.  In order to meet
the urgent need to education of people for justice, development,
freedom, human rights and dignity, non-formal education is often
more suitable and strategic in the Asian reality.  Therefore,
we recommend that the CCA collects the models of non-formal education in Asia and hold a consultation of educators in order to
promote various types of non-formal education which will meet
needs of change in Asian society.  This work needs to be done
at several levels - national, sub-regional and regional - and
in cooperation with other related organizations."[39]

The Seventh Assembly of the Christian Conference of Asia
in 1981 expressed itself in Section II, "Living in Christ with
People - A Call to Community" on Education as follows: "In order
to carry out Christ's ministry of reconciliation and the healing
of all brokenness, the church continues to equip people for his
service, and to teach what it means to make this real in every
aspect of personal and corporate life... The concern for those
who are deprived of the opportunity to live fully human lives
to share in the resources which exist in all countries, and to
participate in the decision making which affects their lives,
means that Christians need to be equipped to share in the ministry of freeing people from such bondage, and it involves
making the resources which the churches have at their disposal
available for this ministry.  The awareness of the need for
human development in Asia and the desire to discover a truly
Asian Christian response to this situation, can lead to the
development of new attitudes and values which are important,
not only for the church, but also for the societies in which
the  churches work and witness."  There were several recommendations to develop the church's education ministry. "... We
recommend, in regard to all the above programmes, the strengthening of ties and cooperation with the WCC and regional ecumenical councils, as well as the WSCF, ACWC."[40]


IX

The following consultations were held between 1976 and 1982.
"Ministry to the Poor" was the theme of a consultation held at
Alajuela (San Jose), Costa Rica, July 1976.  The Committee of
the Theological Education Fund faced the question as to whether
the poor have riches to offer to the understanding and practice
of ministry and ministerial training.  Papers were presented
by J. Pantelis, H. Assmann, J. Aagaard, R. Vidales, S. Amirtham,
M.J. Gaxiola, Bena Silu.[41]

The WCC Programme on Theological Education sponsored a consultation on "Orthodox Theological Education for the Life and
Witness of the Church" at Basel, Switzerland, July 4-8, 1978.
The consultation shared information and discussed some of the
problems involved in ministerial formation, as well as the
challenges raised by contemporary issues.  Reports of various

Orthodox theological schools were presented. Roman Catholic observers participated. Papers were given by J. Anchimink, S. Harakas, J. Zizioulas, N.A. Nissiotis.[42]

A consultation at Cartigny, Switzerland, July 24-30, 1978 on "Women Theological Students" was attended by 53 women studying theology and female theologians. The Report contains: Women who will be deacons, pastors, theologians; Address by C.S. Song; Women in Ministry (Africa, Asia, Europe, Latin America, North America); Vocation; Women and Emerging Theologies; Spirituality; Theological Education; Contextual Theology; Christ and Culture; Ministry; Regional Reports; Summary of Recommendations.[43]

Southern European Christians from Greece, Italy, Spain and Portugal met at Figueira da Foz, Portugal, November 1978, discussed the theme "Development Education", and challenged colleagues from the North to accept involvement in socio-political processes in their own societies as a vital part of any development education. The consultation, called by CCPD, reflected on the theological aspects of development education and the need to relate it to a wider constituency within the churches, particularly at the congregational level.[44]

Sixty people participated in a consultation on "Theological Education and Concern for the People of God" at Manila, Philippines, September 1979, sponsored by the Programme on Theological Education. Besides members of the PTE Commission, representatives of regional theological education bodies, consultants from the Philippines, representing various concerns of the church's mission, were invited. The consultation was planned to test and to deepen the notion of ministerial formation which had been adopted as the focus of the WCC programme.[45]

Christians from Orthodox, Anglican, Roman Catholic, Lutheran and Reformed traditions discussed "Marriage and Family Education in Theological Perspective" at Milan, Italy, November 2-7, 1979. The two main objectives of the consultation were: 1) to reflect on biblical, theological, socio-psychological and pastoral implications of selected areas of family living and relationships between women and men; 2) to make a priority list and recommendations to churches on issues of common concern in family education for study and ecumencical dialogue.[46]

"Theological Education for Ministerial Formation" was the theme of a consultation held at Herrnhut, GDR, October 8-14, 1980. The following sub-themes were also discussed: I. Theological Education in the European Contexts; II. Theological Education and the Scientific Approach; III. Theological Education and the Church; IV. Ministerial Formation; V. Ecumenical Dimensions of Theological Education.[47]

A follow-up of the Oaxtepec (Mexico) meeting at Alexandria, Epypt, November 10-16, 1980, on "The Multicultural Context of the Eighties" faced the following questions: 1) What are the

changes that have taken place in your community and how have
they been affecting family life and human relationships ?
2) What new family types have been emerging in your community
and what factors seem to be accountable for this phenomenon ?
3) What does family life mean to youth, women, single parents
at this time of social change ?  4) Are there any theological
pastoral and educational guidelines that could help our churches in their pastoral care for and with families ?[48]

A consultation on "Christians and Education in a Multi-
Faith World" at Salford, England, July 1981, was organized by
the WCC and the Centre for the Study of Religion and Education
in the Inner City in view of many large migrant communities in
Western Europe who are members of the world's different faiths.[49]
"Global Solidarity in Theological Education" was the theme of
a consultation at Toronto, July 12-15, 1981, sponsored by PTE
in North America.  The deliberations were shared by many individuals and organizations concerned with theological education in that continent.[50]

A consultation on "Education for Effective Ecumenism" at
Bossey, June 20-29, 1982, was organized by the Sub-unit on
Education and the Ecumenical Institute.  There were six regional
groups (Africa, Asia, Europe I and II, North and South America,
Caribbean, Pacific).  Papers were given by E. Bethge, A. Brash,
D. Brezger, H. Goedeking, J. Linz, G. Rüppell, G. Scheibe.[51]

Twenty-five theological educators, church leaders, and
church agency representatives from South Asia, North America
and Europe participated in a consultation on "Self-Reliance and
Contextualization of Theological Education in Southern Asia"
at Geneva, November 16-17, 1982.  Coordinated by PTE, the consultation proposed that a Fund be associated with the Board of
Theological Education of the Senate of Serampore College in
India.  Its goal should be "to enable theological education in
the region to be self-reliant and so able to set up its own
priorities and programmes and to assist the institutions to
venture into innovative programmes."[52]


X


Issue 7, "Learning in Community", of the Vancouver
Assembly in 1983 reflected on future goals of learning in
community: "to help each other to believe in Jesus Christ as
the source of life and to grow in faith as Christian persons;
to discover together that God has given us one world; to participate in the struggle for global justice and peace; to participate in communities of prophetic witness; to relate our
local struggles to global perspectives.

"This is the overarching vision we see for the future of
the ecumenical movement as a fellowship of learning.  It was
discussed and expressed in our Issue Group in six major sec-

tions: family education, liturgical education, congregational education, formal education, theological education and development education. In each and all of these areas the phrase 'learning in community' implies for Christians that it is both a personal and communal process, that both method and message are important, that full participation of all affected is crucial, that in various ways all participants are both teachers and learners, that an important goal of learning is the creation of a richer and more inclusive community, and that community of whatever size does not just happen but must be struggled for in the power of the Holy Spirit and according to the criteria of the Gospel image of the kingdom."

Issue 7 of the Vancouver Assembly made various recommendations to the churches regarding the six different forms of education.[53]

## Observations and Comments

1. The late nineteenth and early twentieth centuries saw the rise of a number of international Christian organizations, such as the YMCA, the YWCA, the World Student Christian Federation, and the World Sunday School Association, which were not only, in varying degrees, expressions of the ecumenical movement, but to a large extent concerned with Christian education, primarily with education of young people and students. There has been considerable interlocking between these organizations, especially in their leadership and sources of support, and with the formation of the WCC provision was made in the Council's constitution for the participation of fraternal delegates from these bodies. Right from the beginning in 1947 the World Council of Christian Education was not only concerned with nurture in the Christian faith but with the more fundamental question of what education is in the light of the Christian understanding of the meaning of life and the nature and destiny of human beings.

Although the New Delhi Assembly in 1961 distinguished between ecumenical education, Christian education and general education, it was only from the seventies onwards that the whole spectrum of education, conscientization and learning of all age groups and social classes was discovered and followed through. The progress in the various fields of education from Uppsala 1968 to Nairobi 1975 has been described as "one of widespread change, trial and error, yet always open to new ideas and insights." The basic orientation has been increasingly towards people - women, youth, children, families, students, congregations, oppressed and poor - in order that each and all of them may be prepared for active engagement in renewing the life of the churches and for intelligent participation in God's work in a changing world. Within these new emphases the task of Christian educators has been approached from a holistic perspective ("Seeing Education Whole"). It has also been based on theological reflection, keeping in mind the two elliptical poles of general education and Christian education, world and worship, liberation and community, education and renewal.

2. In spite of the fact that throughout its recent history the WCC Programme Unit III has tried to respond to the changing needs in ecumenical education it has attracted little attention from the churches. Not only has funding been hard to find but Christian denominations have often not been able to seek ways of translating new insights gained in ecumenical debate into their own life and calling. It will take a long time before the wealth of new ecumenical knowledge and experience will create and permeate inclusive Christian communities.

Also within the WCC itself Unit III has remained to a large extent a separate pursuit, blessed but left alone by the much older and experienced movements of Faith and Order, World Mission and Evangelism, Church and Society, Inter-Church Aid. They have felt competent to deal with the proclamation of the apostolic faith, the fostering of growth to fuller Christian unity and the facing of the brokenness of the human situation without being disturbed by the self-evidence of educational implications. As long as there is no deep inter-penetration of ecumenical learning and unity, witness, dialogue and service, Unit III will remain a sectarian enterprise.

The ecumenical concern for conscientization and sharing will not become relevant and conclusive when the very issue of the nature of the church is not at stake. The church is more than a democratic institution in which educated clergy and able administrators need also learning and practice in participation. If the principle of democracy is applied church leaders will not allow 'people' to share in church power and decision making process when the notion of people is absolutized. Education must leap with clergy and laity alike to the marvellous discovery that the parochial conscience of Christians can be liberated, enabling them to live in a global world. Questions concerning ecumenical learning and questions concerning the ecclesiological significance of the WCC are intimately related and need to be answered with equal theological profundity. To this effect the systematic practice of exchange, cooperation and solidarity between the three WCC Units is indispensable and vital. The same is true for regional and national ecumenical organizations.

3. Unit III needs also to struggle still more extensively with its own history of evolution, its educational assumptions and its theological methodology. It is not enough to state that learning and participation of the whole people of God are the primary foci. These emphases have often been part of a liberal, sentimental and simplistic Christianity. To become involved in calling the entire laity to their true responsibilities in changing patterns of life in church and society can mean falling prey to a secularized eschatology. The terms 'learning' and 'participation' are loaded with jargon. Who are after all the people ? Are they the particular networks Unit III relates to,

namely women and youth organizations, evangelical and lay academies, dialogue and retreat centres, basic communities ? Are
these not specially selected constituencies ? Does the WCC as
a whole relate only to institutional churches and not to communities of people ?

4. In trying to relate all forms of education - formal education, adult education, theological education, development
education, interfaith education, etc. - to one another and to
bring them into one meaningful whole, it is easily forgotten
that in the realm of pedagogy religion is a means, not an end.
Faith is the only end. Faith and not religion should be the
sole concern of Christian education. "When the Son of Man comes
will he find faith on earth ?" (Luke 18:8). Surely he will find
religion-creeds, textbooks, artifacts, and the like - but he may
not find faith.

The more the Christian faith diminishes, the more the
schooling-instructional paradigm has encouraged people to be
busy with teaching about the Christian religion and to advance
in organization, curriculum and teaching methods. The paradigm
works against the necessary primary concern for the faith of
persons. Faith cannot be taught by any method of instruction;
we can only teach religion. We are not saved by our refined
knowledge and statements of belief, but by the anguish and love
of God. A sound basis must be found again for human thought
which will lead to a new, vital experience of wholeness in Christ.
The young generation in particular can perceive the real meaning
of the gospel of salvation, even when it is distorted by false
notes and crooked interpretations. More than ever before exposed to the multireligious, indifferent and atheist world it does
not need to get its Christianity from catechisms and religious
curriculum material, Western style, nor even from a literary
reading of the Bible. True faith is transmitted by the Holy
Spirit from generation to generation in spite of all educational
motivation.

---

1.  The Evanston Report. The Second Assembly of the World Council
    of Churches 1954. London: SCM, 1955. p. 103.

2.  The New Delhi Report. The Third Assembly of the World Council
    of Churches 1961. London: SCM, 1962. pp. 198-200, 227-228.

3.  Dilemmas and Opportunities. Christian Action in Rapid Social
    Change. Report of an International Ecumenical Study Confer-
    ence, Thessalonica, Greece, July 25 - August 2, 1959.
    Geneva: WCC, 1959. pp. 23-25, 36-37.

4.  Report on the Third Education Conference. Bossey, 1949.
    (mimeographed).

5.  Report of the Study Conference on the Churches' Responsi-
    bilities for Children and Young People in Need of Care :
    Aims and Methods in Their Education. Bossey, 1951.
    (mimeographed).

6. Report of the Conference on Christian Education. Bossey, 1952. (mimeographed).

7. Conference for School Educators and Theologians. Bossey, 1958. (mimeographed).

8. "Witnesses Together". Being the Official Report of the Inaugural Assembly of the East Asia Christian Conference, held at Kuala Lumpur, Malaya, May 14-24, 1959. Ed. by U Kyaw Than. Rangoon, 1959. pp. 110-118.

9. The Christian Community within the Human Community. Containing Statements from the Bangkok Assembly of the EACC, February-March 1964. Bangalore: CLS, 1964. p. 57.

10. The Church in Changing Africa. Report of the All Africa Church Conference, held at Ibadan, Nigeria, January 10-19, 1958. New York: International Missionary Council, 1958. p. 31.

11. Drumbeats from Kampala. Report of the First Assembly of the All Africa Conference of Churches held at Kampala, April 20-30, 1963. London: Lutterworth Press, 1963. pp. 46, 48-49.

12. The Fourth World Conference on Faith and Order, Montreal, 1963. Ed. by P.C. Rodger and L. Vischer. London: SCM, 1964 (Faith and Order Paper, no. 42). pp. 60-61.

13. Christians in the Technical and Social Revolutions of Our Time. World Conference on Church and Society, Geneva, July 12-26, 1966. The Official Report. Geneva: WCC, 1967. pp. 70-71, 88-89, 184.

14. Consultation on the Impact of Secondary Education on Young People. Bossey, 1962 (mimeographed). See also: The Impact of Secondary Education on Young People and Its Implications for the Christian Youth Movements. Geneva: World Christian Youth Commission, 1962.

15. Risk, vol. II, no. 1, pp. 1-126.

16. Education and the Nature of Man. Geneva: WCC, 1967. See also: Study Encounter, vol. 2, no. 4, 1966.

17. Study Encounter, vol. 3, no. 4, 1967. see also: Mackie, Stephen. Patterns of Ministry - Theological Education in a Changing World. London: Collins, 1969.

18. Theological Education in North-East Asia. Geneva: Theological Education Fund and Study on Patterns of Ministry and Theological Education, 1967.

19. Consultation on the Teaching of Practical Theology. Bossey, 1967 (mimeographed).

20. The Uppsala Report 1968. Official Report of the Fourth
    Assembly of the World Council of Churches, July 4-20, 1968.
    Ed. by Norman Goodall.
    Geneva: WCC, 1968.  pp. 198-199, 93-94, 400-401.

21. Central Committee of the World Council of Churches. Minutes
    and Reports of the Twenty-Third Meeting at Canterbury,
    Great Britain, August 12-22, 1969.
    Geneva: WCC, 1969.  pp. 175-181.

22. Central Committee of the World Council of Churches. Minutes
    and Reports of the Twenty-Fifth Meeting at Utrecht, the
    Netherlands, 13-23 August, 1972.
    Geneva: WCC, 1972.  p. 127.

23. Seeing Education Whole.  Geneva: WCC, 1970.

24. Dialogue Between Men of Living Faiths. Papers presented at
    a Consultation held at Ajaltoun, Lebanon, March 1970.
    Ed. by S.J. Samartha.  Geneva: WCC, 1971.  p. 117.

25. Primal World-Views. Christian Involvement in Dialogue with
    Traditional Thought Forms.  Ed. by John B. Taylor.
    Ibadan: Daystar Press, 1976.  p. 13.

26. Bangkok Assembly 1973. Minutes and Reports of the Assembly
    of the Commission on World Mission and Evangelism, December
    31, 1972 and January 9-12, 1973.
    Geneva: WCC, 1973.  pp. 95-96, 11-12.

27. Sexism in the 1970s. Discrimination Against Women. A Report
    of a WCC Consultation, West Berlin 1974.
    Geneva: WCC, 1975.  pp. 107-108, 119-120.

28. World Development - The Challenge to the Churches. The Con-
    ference on World Cooperation for Development. Beirut, Leba-
    non, April 21-27, 1968.
    Geneva: SODEPAX, 1968.  pp. 32-33, 44.

29. Peace - The Desperate Imperative. The Consultation on
    Christian Concern for Peace, Baden, Austria, April 3-9, 1970.
    Geneva: SODEPAX, 1970.  pp. 42-50.

30. Report of the Consultation on Dogmatic or Contextual Theo-
    logy. Bossey, 1971 (mimeographed).
    The address of A.O. Dyson is printed in: Study Encounter,
    vol. 8, no. 3, 1972.

31. Report of the Consultation on Doctrine and Change.
    Bossey, 1972 (mimeographed).

32. Encuentro, vol. 26, nos. 3-4, 1971.

33. Learning Community.  Geneva: WCC Office of Education and
    the LWF Department of Studies, 1973.

34. Breaking Barriers. Nairobi, 1975.  Ed. by David M. Paton. London: SPCK; Grand Rapids: Wm. B. Eerdmans, 1976. pp. 86-97.

35. Central Committee of the World Council of Churches. Minutes of the Twenty-Ninth Meeting at Geneva, 10-18 August, 1976. Geneva: WCC, 1976.  pp. 95 and 97.

36. Sharing in One Hope. Reports and Documents from the Meeting of the Faith and Order Commission. Bangalore, 15-30 August, 1978.  Geneva: WCC, 1979 (Faith and Order Paper, no. 92). pp. 257-260.

37. Faith and Science in an Unjust World. Report of the World Council of Churches' Conference on Faith, Science and the Future. Massachusetts Institute of Technology, Cambridge, USA, 12-24 July, 1979.  Volume 2: Reports and Recommendations. Ed. by Paul Abrecht.  Geneva: WCC, 1980. pp. 39-48.

38. The Community of Women and Men in the Church. A Report of the World Council of Churches' Conference, Sheffield,England, 1981.  Ed. by Constance F. Parvey. Geneva: WCC, 1983.  p. 87.

39. Christian Conference of Asia. Sixth Assembly at Penang, Malaysia, 31 Mai - 9 June 1977. Singapore: CCA, 1977.  pp. 103 and 105.

40. Christian Conference of Asia. Seventh Assembly at Bangalore, May 18-28, 1981.  Singapore: CCA, 1981.  pp. 97-99.

41. International Review of Mission, LXVI, no. 261, January 1977.

42. Orthodox Theological Education for the Life and Witness of the Church.  Geneva: WCC, PTE, 1978.

43. "We Listened Long Before We Spoke". Geneva: WCC Sub-unit on Women in Church and Society, 1979.

44. Ecumenical Press Service, no. 30, 9 November, 1978.

45. Ecumenical Press Service, no. 25, 20 September, 1979.

46. Marriage and Family Education in Theological Perspective. Geneva: WCC, Office of Family Education, 1980.

47. Theological Education in Europe.  Geneva: PTE, 1981.

48. The Multicultural Context of Family Education Challenges of the Eighties.  Geneva: WCC, Office of Family Education, 1981.

49. Christians and Education in a Multi-Faith World. Considerations on Christian Participation in Education in a Multi-Faith Environment.  Geneva: WCC, 1982.

50. Global Solidarity in Theological Education. Geneva: WCC, PTE, 1981.

51. Education for Effective Ecumenism.  Bossey, 1972.
    (mimeographed).

52. Ecumenical Press Service, December 6-10, 1982.

53. Gathered for Life. Official Report. VI Assembly of the
    World Council of Churches at Vancouver, Canada, 24 July -
    10 August, 1983.  Ed. by David Gill.
    Geneva: WCC; Grand Rapids: Wm. B. Eerdmans, 1983.
    pp. 94-102.